CHILDREN'S ISSUES, LAWS AND PROGRAMS

PARENTS WITH SUBSTANCE USE DISORDERS AND CHILD PROTECTION ISSUES

CHILDREN'S ISSUES, LAWS AND PROGRAMS

Additional books in this series can be found on Nova's website under the Series tab.

Additional E-books in this series can be found on Nova's website under the E-book tab.

SOCIAL ISSUES, JUSTICE AND STATUS

Additional books in this series can be found on Nova's website under the Series tab.

Additional E-books in this series can be found on Nova's website under the E-book tab.

CHILDREN'S ISSUES, LAWS AND PROGRAMS

PARENTS WITH SUBSTANCE USE DISORDERS AND CHILD PROTECTION ISSUES

THOMAS P. BROUWER
EDITOR

Nova Science Publishers, Inc.
New York

Copyright © 2011 by Nova Science Publishers, Inc.

All rights reserved. No part of this book may be reproduced, stored in a retrieval system or transmitted in any form or by any means: electronic, electrostatic, magnetic, tape, mechanical photocopying, recording or otherwise without the written permission of the Publisher.

For permission to use material from this book please contact us:
Telephone 631-231-7269; Fax 631-231-8175
Web Site: http://www.novapublishers.com

NOTICE TO THE READER

The Publisher has taken reasonable care in the preparation of this book, but makes no expressed or implied warranty of any kind and assumes no responsibility for any errors or omissions. No liability is assumed for incidental or consequential damages in connection with or arising out of information contained in this book. The Publisher shall not be liable for any special, consequential, or exemplary damages resulting, in whole or in part, from the readers' use of, or reliance upon, this material. Any parts of this book based on government reports are so indicated and copyright is claimed for those parts to the extent applicable to compilations of such works.

Independent verification should be sought for any data, advice or recommendations contained in this book. In addition, no responsibility is assumed by the publisher for any injury and/or damage to persons or property arising from any methods, products, instructions, ideas or otherwise contained in this publication.

This publication is designed to provide accurate and authoritative information with regard to the subject matter covered herein. It is sold with the clear understanding that the Publisher is not engaged in rendering legal or any other professional services. If legal or any other expert assistance is required, the services of a competent person should be sought. FROM A DECLARATION OF PARTICIPANTS JOINTLY ADOPTED BY A COMMITTEE OF THE AMERICAN BAR ASSOCIATION AND A COMMITTEE OF PUBLISHERS.

Additional color graphics may be available in the e-book version of this book.

LIBRARY OF CONGRESS CATALOGING-IN-PUBLICATION DATA

Parents with substance use disorders and child protection issues / editor, Thomas P. Brouwer.
    p. cm.
 Includes index.
 ISBN 978-1-60692-400-6 (hbk.)
 1. Child welfare--United States. 2. Child abuse--United States. 3. Parents--Substance use--United States. 4. Children of drug abusers--United States--Social conditions. 5. Children of alcoholics--United States--Social conditions. I. Brouwer, Thomas P.
 HV741.P367 2011
 362.29'130973--dc22
                        2011003546

Published by Nova Science Publishers, Inc. ✦ *New York*

CONTENTS

Preface		vii
Chapter 1	Protecting Children in Families Affected by Substance Use Disorders *United States Department of Health and Human Services*	1
Chapter 2	Parental Substance Use and the Child Welfare System *United States Department of Health and Human Services*	101
Chapter 3	Drug Testing in Child Welfare: Practice and Policy Considerations *United States Department of Health and Human Services*	113
Chapter 4	Substance Abuse Specialists in Child Welfare Agencies and Dependency Courts: Considerations for Program Designers and Evaluators *United States Department of Health and Human Services*	151
Chapter 5	Substance-Exposed Infants: State Responses to the Problem *United States Department of Health and Human Services*	191
Chapter Sources		265
Index		267

PREFACE

Each day, the safety and well-being of children across the Nation are threatened by child abuse and neglect. Many of these children live in homes where substance use disorders create additional and compounding problems. The child welfare and alcohol and drug abuse treatment fields are working to find effective ways to serve families where this overlap occurs. Intervening effectively in the lives of these children and their families is not the responsibility of a single agency or professional group, but rather it is a shared community concern. This new book provides a basis for understanding parental substance abuse and its relationship to child maltreatment.

Chapter 1- The relationship between substance use disorders (SUDs) and child maltreatment is compelling and undeniable. More than eight million children in the United States live with at least one parent who abused or was dependent on alcohol or an illicit drug during the past year. These children face a heightened risk of maltreatment. One study, for example, showed that children of parents with SUDs are nearly three times more likely to be abused and more than four times more likely to be neglected than children of parents who do not abuse substances.

Chapter 2- Parental substance use continues to be a serious issue in the child welfare system. Maltreated children of parents with substance use disorders often remain in the child welfare system longer and experience poorer outcomes than other children (U.S. Department of Health and Human Services [HHS], 1999). Addressing the multiple needs of these children and families is challenging.

Chapter 3- Alcohol and other drug use can impair a parent's judgment and ability to provide the consistent care, supervision, and guidance that all children need. For child welfare workers who are charged with ensuring the safety of children, it is often difficult to determine what level of functional improvement will enable a parent with a substance use disorder to retain or resume his or her parental role without jeopardizing the child's well-being. Child welfare professionals are faced with the difficult task of collecting adequate information about families, making informed and insightful decisions based on this information, and taking timely and appropriate action to safeguard children.

Chapter 4- For more than a decade, studies have suggested that a sizable majority of the families involved in child welfare services are affected by parental substance use disorders. With the passage of the Federal Adoption and Safe Families Act (ASFA, Public Law 105-89, 1997), the complex issues of parents with a substance use disorder who are involved with the child welfare system have become the focus of increased attention. Under ASFA, parents have limited time to comply with reunification requirements, including attaining and demonstrating recovery from their addiction and safely care for their children, or face permanent termination of their parental rights. Given the historical low rates of reunification and extended duration of foster care placements for families with substance use disorders, these families are likely to compose most of the families affected by this legislation. In addition, since substance abuse treatment can be a lengthy process and the recovery process often takes longer than is allowed under the ASFA timelines, it is important that substance-abusing parents be engaged in treatment as soon as possible. As a result, finding effective ways to address concurrent substance use and child maltreatment problems in families has taken on renewed importance.

Chapter 5- In 2005–2006, the National Center on Substance Abuse and Child Welfare (NCSACW) undertook a review and analysis of States' policies regarding prenatal exposure to alcohol and other drugs, in order to help local, State, and Tribal governments.

Chapter 1

PROTECTING CHILDREN IN FAMILIES AFFECTED BY SUBSTANCE USE DISORDERS

United States Department of Health and Human Services

ACKNOWLEDGMENTS

Contributing Authors

Kathleen Feidler, M.S.W., a consultant with ICF International, has more than 15 years of experience in the evaluation of substance use disorder programs. She also has researched and written several articles and papers about the impact of substance use disorder in child welfare cases.

Karen Mooney, L.C.S.W., C.A.C. III, is the women's treatment coordinator for the Alcohol and Drug Abuse Division of the Colorado Department of Human Services. Formerly, she was a child protective services caseworker for 7 years, during which she specialized in screening, assessing, and engaging parents of children involved in the child welfare system in substance use disorder and addiction treatment. Since that time, she has served as a child protection and substance use disorder treatment consultant to several national organizations and universities.

Mary Nakashian, M.A., is a consultant specializing in public policy and management, training, and technical assistance with special expertise in the areas of welfare reform, child welfare, and substance use disorder. She has served as the Deputy Commissioner for Welfare in the State of Connecticut, as the Executive Deputy Commissioner for Welfare in New York City, and as vice president at the National Center on Addiction and Substance Abuse at Columbia University.

Jill Sanclimenti, M.B.A., a consultant with ICF International, has spent the last 16 years conducting research and writing publications on child maltreatment and other issues related to children, youth, and families. She previously served as manager of product development and program services for the National Clearinghouse on Child Abuse and Neglect Information (now Child Welfare Information Gateway).

Matthew Shuman, M.S.W., a consultant with ICF International, has more than 10 years experience in the human services field. He previously worked as an analyst in the Office of the Secretary of the Department of Health and Human Services on a variety of child welfare issues, including foster care, adoption, and child care. He also has written and edited various child welfare publications, including other manuals in the *User Manual Series*.

Carl Tacy, M.S.W., has more than 12 years of experience working in clinical, policy, and management positions primarily addressing substance use disorder, domestic violence, health, and child welfare issues. He has managed projects responsible for developing, marketing, and disseminating products, publications, and communications in those topic areas. Additionally, he has authored or co-authored several publications, including *The Underage Drinking Prevention Action Guide and Planner*, *The Tips for Teens Series*, and *The Role of Educators in Preventing and Responding to Child Abuse and Neglect* of the *Child Abuse and Neglect User Manual Series*.

Acknowledgment of Prior Edition

This manual is an update of the 1994 publication, *Protecting Children in Substance-Abusing Families*, by Vickie Kropenske and Judy Howard with Cheryl Breitenbach, Richard Dembo, Susan B. Edelstein, Kathy McTaggart, Annette Moore, Mary BethSorensen, and Virginia Weisz. The prior work informed and contributed to the content of this publication.

Reviewers

    Paul DiLorenzo, Independent Consultant
    Kathy Nardini, National Association of State Alcohol and Drug Abuse Directors
    Colleen O'Donnell, National Association of State Alcohol and Drug Abuse Directors
    Kathy Pinto, Howard County, Maryland, Department of Social Services
    Bob Scholle, Independent Consultant
    Sarah Webster, Texas Department of Protective and Regulatory Services (retired)

Technical Advisory Panel

The following were members of the January 2001 Technical Advisory Panel for the *User Manual Series* contract. The organizations identified reflect each member's affiliation at that time.

Carolyn Abdullah
FRIENDS National Resource Center
Washington, DC

Lien Bragg
American Public Human Services Association
Washington, DC

Sgt. Richard Cage
Montgomery County Police Department
Wheaton, MD

Diane DePanfilis, Ph.D.
University of Maryland at Baltimore
School of Social Work
Baltimore, MD

Pauline Grant
Florida Department of Children and Families
Jacksonville, FL

Jodi Hill
Connecticut Department of Children and Families
Hartford, CT

Robert Ortega, Ph.D.
University of Michigan School of Social Work
Ann Arbor, MI

Nancy Rawlings
Kentucky Cabinet for Families and Children
Frankfort, KY

Barry Salovitz
Child Welfare Institute/National Resource Center on Child Maltreatment
Glenmont, NY

Sarah Webster
Texas Department of Protective and Regulatory Services
Austin, TX

Ron Zuskin
University of Maryland at Baltimore
School of Social Work
Baltimore, MD

Additional Acknowledgments

The third edition of the *User Manual Series* was developed under the guidance and direction of Irene Bocella, Federal Task Order Officer, Office on Child Abuse and Neglect, and Catherine Nolan, Director, Office on Child Abuse and Neglect. Susan Orr, former Associate Commissioner, Children's Bureau, provided critical input that shaped both this manual and the series. Also providing input was Sharon K. Amatetti, Public Health Analyst, Center for Substance Abuse Treatment, Substance Abuse and Mental HealthServices Administration.

1. PURPOSE AND OVERVIEW

The relationship between substance use disorders (SUDs) and child maltreatment is compelling and undeniable. More than eight million children in the United States live with at least one parent who abused or was dependent on alcohol or an illicit drug during the past year.[1] These children face a heightened risk of maltreatment.[2] One study, for example, showed that children of parents with SUDs are nearly three times more likely to be abused and more than four times more likely to be neglected than children of parents who do not abuse substances.[3]

According to the National Child Abuse and Neglect Data System (NCANDS), in 2006, an estimated 3.3 million referrals were made to child protective services (CPS), representing 6 million children. From this population, approximately 905,000 children were found to be victims of child abuse or neglect. Of the maltreated children, 66.3 percent were neglected (including medical neglect), 16.0 percent physically abused, 8.8 percent sexually abused, and 6.6 percent psychologically maltreated. Additionally, 15.1 percent of victims were associated with "other" types of maltreatment, such as abandonment or congenital drug addiction. A child could be identified as a victim of more than one type of maltreatment.[4] Additionally, while estimates vary, most studies suggest that parental SUDs are a contributing factor for between one- and two-thirds of children involved with CPS.[5]

Overview of the Connection between Substance Use Disorder and Child Maltreatment

SUDs often affect the way people live, including how they function, interact with others, or parent their children. Studies suggest that SUDs, by impairing parents' judgment and priorities, can influence parental discipline choices and child-rearing styles and have negative effects on the consistency of care and supervision provided to children.[6] The time and money parents spend on seeking out or on using drugs or alcohol may limit the resources available in the household to meet their children's basic needs. In addition, families affected by SUDs often experience a number of other problems—including mental illness, domestic violence, poverty, and high levels of stress— which also are associated with child maltreatment.

Children of parents who have SUDs and who are also in the child welfare system are more likely to experience emotional, physical, intellectual, and social problems than children whose parents do not have SUDs. Additionally, abused and neglected children from families affected by substance abuse are more likely to be placed in foster care and to remain there longer than maltreated children from families not affected by substance abuse.[7]

> ### NOTE ON TERMINOLOGY
>
> Those working with individuals, families, and communities affected by the use and abuse of alcohol and drugs use a wide variety of terms to describe the same or similar concepts, especially the spectrum of substance use. While some readers may be more accustomed to using the term "substance abuse" to mean any dependence, addiction, or abuse of a substance, this manual uses the term "substance use disorder," which encompasses both abuse and dependence (addiction). (See Chapter 2, *The Nature of Substance Use Disorders*, for more details about the definitions of these terms.) The phrase "substance use disorder" has been adopted by the public health and alcohol and drug treatment fields as less stigmatizing and more reflective of the disease's characterization as a disorder with biological, psychological, and social origins. Some with in the child welfare field have also begun to use this term.
>
> Additionally, reliable, consistent, or generalizable data are limited concerning the relationship between substance abuse and the frequency of child maltreatment because researchers often define terms such as "substance abuse" or "child abuse" differently, they collect data from sources that have divergent perspectives, and neither State alcohol and drug abuse treatment nor State child welfare data systems consistently require staffto report information about this overlap. When presenting results of studies, this manual, where possible, uses the same terminology as used in the research description.
>
> For more information about terminology related to SUDs, please refer to the following:
>
> - *National Association of Social Work Standards for Social Work Practice with Clients with Substance Use Disorders* (**http://www.socialworkers.org/practice/standards/ NASWATODStatndards.pdf**)
> - *Substance Use Disorders: A Guide to the Use of Language* (**http://www.pacdaa. org/pacdaa/lib/ pacdaa/Substance_abuse_disorders.doc**), a publication of the Center for Substance Abuse Treatment, Substance Abuse and Mental Health Services Administration, U.S. Department of Healthand Human Services.

CPS caseworkers and SUD treatment providers also report conflicting pressures that arise from trying to meet concurrently:

- The timeframes required by the Adoption and Safe Families Act to promote permanency for abused and neglected children
- The time required to access open treatment slots
- The time necessary for successful treatment participation
- The developmental needs of children. [8]

These challenges underscore the need for quick and effective screening, assessment, and treatment, if necessary, of SUDs among families in the child welfare system. Further, they point to the need for partnerships between the CPS and SUD treatment systems to support parents in obtaining the services they need, while ensuring the safety and well-being of children.

Organization of the Manual

To assist families experiencing SUDs as well as child maltreatment, CPS caseworkers must recognize and address each problem and their interaction. This manual is structured first to provide CPS caseworkers and other readers with the groundwork for understanding SUDs and their dynamics, characteristics, and effects. The manual then places parental SUDs into the context of child protection and describes its impact on children, as well as its relationship to child maltreatment. Several chapters are devoted to helping CPS caseworkers understand how to recognize and to screen for SUDs in child maltreatment cases, to establish plans for families experiencing these problems, and to support treatment and recovery, as appropriate. The manual also addresses ways in which CPS and SUD treatment providers can coordinate their work, which is critical to improving outcomes for both parents with SUDs and their children.

Specifically, the manual addresses:

- The nature of SUDs
- The impact of parental SUDs on children
- In-home examination, screening, and assessment for SUDs
- Treatment of SUDs
- The role of the CPS caseworker when an SUD is identified
- Similarities and differences between CPS and SUD treatment providers
- "Putting it all together"—making the systems work for families.

Readers should note that no single publication can address all the intricate factors and interactions related to the connection between SUDs and child maltreatment, but this manual can contribute to an increased understanding of the issues and identify avenues for enhanced services to families. Professionals should supplement it with other information, training, and professional development activities.

2. THE NATURE OF SUBSTANCE USE DISORDERS

IN THIS SECTION
- The continuum of alcohol and drug use
- Appropriate and inappropriate uses of substances
- Characteristics of addiction
- Why some people become addicted
- Negative consequences of SUDs
- Co-occurring issues

Understanding the nature and dynamics of substance use disorders (SUDs) can help child protective services (CPS) caseworkers in screening for SUDs, making informed decisions, and developing appropriate case plans for families experiencing this problem.

The Continuum of Alcohol and Drug Use

Substance use, like many human behaviors, occurs along a broad continuum from no use to extremely heavy use. The likelihood of an individual experiencing problems stemming from substance use typically increases as the rate of use increases. The continuum for the use of substances includes substance use, substance abuse, and substance dependence or addiction.

Substance use is the consumption of low or infrequent doses of alcohol or drugs, such that damaging consequences are rare or minor. In reference to alcohol, this means drinking in a way that does not impair functioning or lead to negative consequences, such as violence. In reference to prescription drugs, use involves taking medications as prescribed by a physician. Regarding over-the-counter medications, use is defined as taking the substance as recommended for alleviating symptoms. Some people who choose to use substances may use them periodically, never use them to an extreme, or never experience life consequences because of their use.

Substance abuse is a pattern of substance use that leads to significant impairment or distress, refl ected by one or more of the following:

- Failure to fulfill major role obligations at work, school, or home (e.g., substance-related absences from work, suspension from school, neglect of a child's need for regular meals)
- Continued use in spite of physical hazards (e.g., driving under the influence)
- Trouble with the law (e.g., arrests for substance- related disorderly conduct)
- Interpersonal or social problems. [9]

Additionally, use of a medication in a manner diff erent from how it is prescribed or recommended and use of an intravenous drug that is not medically required are considered substance abuse.

Individuals may abuse one or more substances for a certain period of time and then modify their behaviors because of internal or external pressures. Abuse is characterized by periodic events of abusive use of substances, which may be accompanied by life consequences directly related to its use. With proper intervention, an individual with substance abuse problems can avert progression to addiction. At this level of progression, the abusers often are not aware, or if they are, they may not be honest with themselves that the negative consequences they experience are linked to their substance use. With proper intervention, these individuals are able to choose to limit or to cease substance use because of the recognition of the connection between use and consequences. Other people, however, may continue abusing substances until they become addicted.

Substance dependence or addiction is the progressive need for alcohol or drugs that results from the use of that substance. This need creates both psychological and physical changes that make it difficult for the users to control when they will use the substance or how much they will use. Psychological dependence occurs when a user needs the substance to feel normal or to engage in typical daily activities. Physical dependence occurs when the body adapts to the substance and needs increasing amounts to ward off the effects of with drawal and to maintain physiological functioning. Dependence can result in:

- **The continued use of a substance despite negative consequences**. The individual continues drug or alcohol use despite incidents, such as accidents, arrests, or a lack of money to pay for food because it was spent on drugs.
- **An increase in tolerance to the substance** . The individual requires more of the alcohol or drug to obtain the same effect.
- **Withdrawal symptoms** . The individual needs to consume the substance in order not to experience unpleasant with drawal effects, such as uncontrollable shaking and tremors or intense nausea.
- **Behavioral changes**. The individual who is dependent:
  - Uses more than intended
  - Spends a majority of the time either obtaining, using, or with drawing from the use of the substance
  - Cannot stop using until the substance is gone or the individual passes out.

Criteria for diagnosing substance dependence and substance abuse as an SUD have been defined in the *Diagnostic and Statistical Manual of Mental Disorders, 4ThEdition, Text Revision* (DSM-IV-TR), the American Psychiatric Association's classification index for mental disorders. (See Appendix D, *Diagnostic and Statistical Manual of Mental Disorders Criteria*, for more information on this topic.)

Appropriate and Inappropriate Uses of Substances

Certain substances, when used appropriately, have helpful and even lifesaving uses. Many individuals use various drugs to help overcome physical and psychological problems. Drugs can alleviate cold and flu symptoms, make it easier to sleep, reduce physical or emotional pain, and help overcome feelings of anxiety, panic, or depression. Some of these drugs require a prescription from a doctor to be obtained legally, while others are considered safe enough to be sold over the counter to the public. Although these drugs have many health benefits, many also can be used in a higher quantity or in combination with other substances to produce either a "high" or a numbing effect. Combining these drugs with alcohol or other drugs can intensify their effects and increase risks to the user and to those around the user. Individuals who abuse prescription medication sometimes resort to forging prescriptions, to visiting several doctors who will prescribe the same drug with out asking questions ("doctor shopping"), or to buying stolen drugs. Exhibit 2-1 provides key statistics for commonly abused substances.

> **EXHIBIT 2-1. SELECTED DRUG STATISTICS FROM THE NATIONAL SURVEY ON DRUG USE AND HEALTH(NSDUH)**[*]
>
> - An estimated 19.9 million Americans, or 8.0 percent of the population aged 12 or older, were current illicit drug users in 2007.[**] (This figure reflects use of the following drugs: marijuana, cocaine, heroin, hallucinogens, and inhalants and the nonmedical use of prescription-type pain relievers, tranquilizers, stimulants, and sedatives.)
> - The estimated number of Americans who were current users of the following drugs in 2007:
>   - Marijuana: 14,448,000
>   - Cocaine: 2,075,000 (including 610,000 users of crack)
>   - Hallucinogens: 996,000 (including 503,000 users of Ecstasy)
>   - Inhalants: 616,000
>   - Heroin: 338,000
> - In 2007, approximately 6.9 million people aged 12 or older (2.8 percent of the population) were current users of prescription-type psychotherapeutic drugs taken nonmedically, including pain relievers, tranquilizers, stimulants, and sedatives. This includes 529,000 individuals who were current users of methamphetamine, which can be manufactured illegally using existing prescription drugs.
> - An estimated 22.3 million Americans aged 12 or older in 2006 (9.0 percent of the population) were classified with substance abuse or dependence. Of these:
>   - 3.2 million abused or were dependent on both alcohol and illicit drugs;
>   - 3.7 million abused or were dependent on illicit drugs but not alcohol;
>   - 15.5 million abused or were dependent on alcohol but not illicit drugs.[10]
>
> [*]These statistics are drawn from the 2007 NSDUH, an annual survey of the civilian, noninstitutionalized population of the United States aged 12 or older. To see the full results of the most recent survey, visit the website of the U.S. Department of Health and Human Services, Substance Abuse and Mental Health Services Administration, Office of Applied Studies: http://www.oas.samhsa.gov/nsduhLatest.htm.
>
> [**] "Current users" reflect persons who used the specified drug during the month prior to the NSDUH interview.

Other substances may not have medicinal qualities but can affect users psychologically and physically or lower inhibitions and impair judgment if misused. For instance, some individuals drink alcohol at social gatherings to feel more comfortable talking and relating to others. Being of legal age and drinking alcohol is a commonly accepted practice in the United States. Of course, alcohol often can be misused and can negatively affect events ranging from traffic safety to the ability to care adequately for children.

> **QUICK FACTS ON ALCOHOL USE**
>
> - Slightly more than half of Americans aged 12 or older, or approximately 127 million people, reported being current drinkers of alcohol in the 2007 NSDUH. (Current drinkers were defined as having had at least one drink in the 30 days prior to the survey.)
> - An estimated 17 million people (6.9 percent of the population) were heavy drinkers. (Heavy drinking was defined as having five or more drinks on the same occasion on at least 5 different days in the past 30 days.)
> - Among pregnant women aged 15 to 44, an estimated 11.6 percent reported current alcohol use, and 3.7 percent reported binge drinking. (Binge drinking was defined as having five or more drinks on the same occasion on at least 1 day in the past 30 days.)
> - Excessive alcohol use is the third leading lifestyle cause of death in the United States and was determined to be a key factor in approximately 79,000 deaths annually from 2001–2005.
> - The U.S. Dietary Guidelines for Americans recommends no more than one drink per day for adult women and no more than two drinks per day for adult men. It also lists several types of individuals— including children, adolescents, and pregnant women— who should avoid alcohol completely.[11]

For more information on commonly abused substances, see Appendix E, *Commonly Abused Substances*.

With respect to child protection, substance use becomes problematic when it contributes to the harm of children. This can be difficult for CPS caseworkers to identify because the distinction between "normal" alcohol use and problematic use may be blurred and subject to interpretation. (See Chapter 4, *In-home Examination, Screening, and Assessment of Substance Use Disorders*, for more information about identifying SUDs.)

Characteristics of Addiction

Knowing the characteristics of addiction can help inform effective intervention and practice with individuals suffering from SUDs. Characteristics include:

- **Progressive Nature**. A central feature of addiction is a progressive use of a substance, whether alcohol, prescription medications, or illegal drugs. The physical, emotional, and social problems that arise from addiction typically continue to worsen unless the SUDs are treated successfully. If left untreated, addiction can cause premature death through overdose; through organic complications involving the brain, liver, heart, and many other organs; and by contributing to motor vehicle crashes, homicide, suicide, and other traumatic events.
- **Denial and Concealment**. Addiction can be difficult to identify, even for individuals experiencing it. People who are addicted to a substance often engage in elaborate strategies to conceal the amount being consumed and the degree to which

the substance is affecting their lives. Another dimension of addiction is that individuals who suffer from it often do not perceive that their pattern of drinking or drug use creates or contributes to their problems. Additionally, the use of substances may affect their memory or perception of events or of what they have said or done. This lack of recognition commonly is identified as denial.

- **Chronic Disease** . The National Institute on Drug Abuse has defined addiction as a chronic disease, like heart disease, hypertension, and diabetes. Studies have shown alcohol and drug abuse treatment is about as effective as treatments required for these other chronic diseases. Lifetime management of chronic diseases in all cases requires individuals to change their habits and activities and to take precautions that prevent them from relapsing or worsening their condition.
- **Lapses and Relapses** . Lapses and relapses are common features of addiction. A lapse is a period of substance use after the individual has been clean and sober for some length of time. A relapse is not only using the substance again, but also returning to the problem behaviors associated with it.[12]

Addiction is difficult to deal with ; many individuals lapse or relapse one or more times before being able to remain abstinent. If lapses or relapses occur, they do not necessarily mean that treatment has failed. They can point the way toward needed improvements in how those individuals are approaching recovery. Most individuals who have lapsed or relapsed can identify, prior to the lapse or relapse, certain situations, thoughts, or behaviors that contributed to the use of the substance.

Why Some People Become Addicted

Many theories and explanations have been proposed to describe the reasons why some individuals become addicted to substances and others do not. Research on the causes of addiction is not conclusive, and multiple factors may contribute to it. Early explanations for addiction included moral weakness, insanity, demonic possession, and character pathology.[13] These explanations, combined with the problematic behaviors that sometimes accompany addiction, have created a serious stigma. Recent research, however, indicates that substance addiction is a brain disease that changes its structure and functioning, which in turn affects an individual's behaviors. Although the initial use of a substance may be voluntary, a person's ability to control future use may be seriously impaired by changes in the brain caused by prior use.[14]

Some research, including adoption and twins studies, has demonstrated a biological and genetic predisposition to addiction, with scientists estimating that genetic factors account for 40–60 percent of an individual's risk of addiction.[15] These studies suggest that an individual's genes play a role in vulnerability to addiction. For example, one study found that children whose parents are addicted to drugs or alcohol are three times more likely to develop an SUD later in life than children whose parents are not addicted.[16] Other research emphasizes a social factor to explain that addictions appear to "run in the family." These studies suggest that children who grow up in families with SUDs may model their adult behavior on what they have seen and known in their familial experience.[17] Risk for addiction can also be affected by gender, ethnicity, developmental stage, and social environment.[18] In other words, both nature and nurture contribute to a person's vulnerability or resistance to substance abuse.

Many self-help groups, such as 12-step programs, consider addiction a progressive illness that is physical, spiritual, and emotional in nature. They believe that individuals who are addicted must admit that they are powerless over the substance; that is, they are unable to resolve the problem on their own and must seek help outside themselves.[19]

ADDICTION

People who are addicted to drugs are from all walks of life. Many suffer from poor mental or physical health, occupational, or social problems, which make their addictive disorders much more difficult to treat. Even if there are few associated problems, the severity of addiction itself ranges widely among people.

Isn't drug addiction a voluntary behavior? A person may start taking drugs voluntarily, but as times passes and drug use continues, something happens that makes a person go from being a voluntary drug user to a compulsive drug user. This happens because the continued use of addictive drugs changes the brain. These changes can be dramatic or subtle, but often, with out treatment, they result in compulsive or even uncontrollable drug use.

How is addiction similar to a disease? Drug addiction is a brain disease. Every type of drug abuse has its own mechanism for changing how the brain functions. Regardless of which drug a person is addicted to, many of the effects on the brain are similar. These may include modifications in the molecules and cells that make up the brain, changes in memory processes and thinking, transformation of moods, and sometimes changes in motor skills, such as walking and talking. These changes can have a significant

influence on all aspects of a person's behavior and can cause the individual to do almost anything to obtain the drug.

Why can't drug addicts quit on their own? In the beginning, almost all addicted individuals believe that they can stop using drugs on their own, and most try to stop with out treatment. However, most of these attempts fail to achieve long-term abstinence. Research has shown that long-term drug use results in significant changes in brain function that persist long after the individual has stopped using drugs. These drug-induced changes in brain function can have many behavioral consequences, including the compulsion to use drugs despite adverse consequences—one of the defining characteristics of addiction.

Understanding that addiction has such an important biological component may help explain the difficulty in achieving and maintaining abstinence with out treatment. Psychological stress from work or family problems, social cues (e.g., meeting individuals from one's drug-using past), or the environment (e.g., encountering streets, objects, or even smells associated with drug use) can interact with biological factors to hinder sustained abstinence and to make relapse more likely. Research studies indicate, however, that even the most severely addicted individuals can participate actively in treatment and that active participation is essential to good outcomes.[20]

Negative Consequences of Substance Use Disorders

Negative consequences from alcohol and drug use, abuse, and dependence generally fall into three categories: loss of behavioral control, psychophysical with drawal, and role maladaptation.

Loss of behavioral control happens when individuals do things they normally would not do because their inhibitions and reasoning abilities are impaired. Loss of behavioral control can include passing out, having a blackout (i.e., short-term memory loss), behaving violently, leaving children unsupervised or in a potentially unsafe situation, and neglecting children's basic needs.

Psychophysical with drawal occurs when individuals experience physical symptoms that result from with drawing from using a substance. Indicators of psychophysical with drawal include becoming nauseated or vomiting; feeling feverish, hot, sweaty, agitated, or nervous; and experiencing significant changes in eating or sleeping patterns. In advanced cases, with drawal may include experiencing, seeing, or hearing things that are not there, such as having the sensation of bugs crawling on the skin or having seizures or convulsions. Physical with drawal, particularly from alcohol and heroin, can be life threatening.

Role maladaptation occurs when individuals cannot conform to what are generally considered their expected roles (e.g., parent, breadwinner). For parents, this can mean difficulties in caring properly for their children (e.g., prioritizing a need for drugs over a child's needs for food and clothing). Other examples of role maladaptation due to SUDs include relationship problems, failure to keep a job, difficulties paying the bills, and criminal activity.

Problems in one area will not necessarily indicate or predict problems in other areas. Someone who experiences regular hangovers from drinking (defined as anxiety, agitation, nausea, and headaches) can experience these symptoms with out experiencing a significant loss of behavioral control or role maladaptation. Others struggling with addiction, however, may suffer from all three consequences.

Co-Occurring Issues

CPS caseworkers must place SUDs into context with the other problems that families may face. In general, these families have more numerous and complex issues to address than those who are not abusing or addicted to alcohol and drugs. Similarly, child abuse and neglect seldom occur in a vacuum; these families often are experiencing several layers of problems. For both SUDs and child maltreatment, common co- occurring issues include mental and physical illnesses, domestic violence and other trauma, economic difficulties or poverty, housing instability, or dangerous neighborhoods and crime.[21] All of these challenges can constitute barriers to successful participation in SUD treatment and, when addressed, can improve an individual's chances of attaining long-term abstinence. The following sections describe some of the most common co-occurring issues experienced by families affected by child maltreatment and SUDs. The goal is to increase caseworker awareness of the variety of symptoms and factors, particularly those most likely to affect assessment and decisions regarding services for families and children involved in CPS cases.

Mental Illness

SUDS have a strong association with mental illness. In 2007, an estimated 24.3 million adults aged 18 or older had a serious mental illness.[22] (Having a serious mental illness is defined as having a diagnosable mental, behavioral, or emotional disorder during the past year that met the DSM-IV criteria.) Adults with a serious mental illness are much more likely to have used illicit drugs with in the past year than those adults with out a serious mental illness (28.0 percent versus 12.2 percent).[23]

It is not clear why there is a high correlation between SUDs and mental illness. Three ways in which they may relate to one another are:

- The disorders may occur independently of each other.
- The mental health disorder may place an individual at greater risk for SUDs.
- Alcohol or drug intoxication or with drawal may result in temporary mental healthdisorders, such as paranoia or depression.[24]

It is common for either the SUD or the mental health issue to go undiagnosed. In addition, not all mental health problems affecting a parent necessarily will appear severe or profound. As a result, when one issue is identified, it is important to screen for the other. When both are identified, current accepted practice is to treat both disorders simultaneously, especially with individuals who have serious mental illnesses.

Physical Health Problems

SUDs can cause or worsen physical health problems. For example:

- Alcohol abuse can cause numerous physical problems related to the function of the liver, heart, digestive system, and nervous system.
- Marijuana use is associated with ailments ranging from a burning or stinging sensation in the mouth or throat, to respiratory problems, to an increased likelihood of cancer in the throat and lungs.
- Individuals who inject drugs, such as heroin or methamphetamine, put themselves at risk of contracting infectious diseases, such as HIV/ AIDS and hepatitis C, through the sharing of syringes and other injection paraphernalia.

Domestic Violence and Other Forms of Trauma

Trauma can take the form of a physical injury or a painful or disturbing experience that can have lasting effects. It can result from exposure to a variety of events ranging from natural disasters to violent crimes. The consequences of trauma can be significant, affecting the victim on biological, psychological, social, and spiritual levels.

Individuals who have experienced a traumatic event sometimes turn to drugs or alcohol in an effort to deal with the resulting emotional pain, anxiety, fear, or guilt. If the pattern becomes well established, it may indicate that the person has an SUD. SUDs, particularly if they are active over a period of time, increase the likelihood of further exposure to accidental and intentional acts that may result in additional trauma. In addition, individuals who have not experienced a traumatic event, but have an SUD, have an increased likelihood of exposure to events that may then result in trauma, such as being assaulted.

Studies have shown that a high percentage of women treated for SUDs also have significant histories of trauma.[25] Women who abuse substances are more likely to experience accidents and acts of violence, including assaults, automobile accidents, intimate partner violence, sexual abuse and assault, homicide, and suicide.[26]

Alcohol commonly is cited as a causal factor and precursor to adult domestic violence. Research studies indicate that approximately 25 to 50 percent of domestic violence incidents involve alcohol and that nearly one-half of all abusers entering batterer intervention programs abuse alcohol.[27] Despite the evidence that many batterers and victims abuse alcohol, there is no empirical evidence that substance use disorder directly causes domestic violence. However, SUDs increase the severity and frequency of the batterers' violence and interfere with domestic violence interventions.[28] They also contribute to the increased severity of injuries among victims.[29]

POST-TRAUMATIC STRESS DISORDER

Women who abuse substances sometimes cite continued substance use as a perceived aid in controlling symptoms of post-traumatic stress disorder (PTSD).[30] PTSD is a psychiatric disorder that can occur following the experience or the witnessing of life-affecting events, such as military combat, violent or sexual assaults, or natural disasters. People who suffer from PTSD often relive the experience through nightmares and flashbacks, have difficulty sleeping, and feel detached or estranged. PTSD also is associated with impairment of the ability to function in social or family life, including employment instability, marital problems and divorce, family discord, and difficulties in parenting. Research has indicated that women with PTSD are twice as likely to abuse or to be dependent on alcohol and are four times as likely to abuse or to be dependent on drugs.[31] When compared to other traumas, sexual abuse and physical abuse have been found to be associated with the highest rates of PTSD.[32]

Poverty

SUDs cross all socioeconomic lines, but studies show that there is a relationship between poverty and substance abuse.[33] People living in poverty sometimes turn to substances for relief from the anxiety and the stress associated with economic insecurity. Of course, spending money on alcohol or drugs often only contributes to economic problems. Dealing illegal drugs is viewed by some as a source of income and a means of escaping poverty. Unfortunately, some individuals suffering from economic hardship feel that they have little to lose if they get involved in drugs, no matter what the effects are on themselves or their families.

Parents who are distracted by their financial problems may have less energy and attention for parenting. In some homes, the psychological distress of poverty may be directed toward the children. Research has indicated a strong association between child maltreatment, particularly neglect, and poverty.[34] CPS case plans invariably need to address issues related to poverty and establish service plans for families.

Homelessness

In some cases, extreme poverty and other factors may lead to homelessness. Homeless people typically experience several overlapping challenges, including SUDs, mental illnesses, and a variety of physical health problems. Parents with children account for approximately 11 percent of the homeless population, and this number appears to be growing.[35]

Crime

Crime has a strong association with drug use. In the most recent study of its kind, more than three out of every four State, Federal, or local jail inmates previously were involved seriously with drugs or alcohol in some way (e.g., convicted of a drug- or alcohol-related crime, used illicit substances regularly, were under the influence of alcohol or drugs when they committed a crime).[36] Another study found that adults who were arrested for a serious offense were much more likely to have used an illicit drug in the prior year (60.1 percent) than those who were not arrested (13.6 percent).[37] In addition, many individuals in prisons and jails experience multiple, overlapping problems. For instance, research indicates that among inmates with a serious mental disorder, 72 percent have a co- occurring SUD.[38] It often is challenging for these individuals to obtain appropriate services either in prison or upon their release.

Because women are generally the primary caretakers of their children, the increase in the number of incarcerated women over the past decade is particularly relevant to CPS caseworkers. The Bureau of Justice Statistics reports that the female prison population increased from 44,000 in 1990 to more than 111,000 in 2006.[39] One-third of incarcerated women have been convicted of drug off enses, and approximately 65 percent of women in prison report having used drugs regularly.[40] Additionally, 75 percent of incarcerated women are mothers, and two-thirds have minor children, who often are placed outside the home while their mothers are incarcerated.[41]

In response to problems arising from low-level, nonviolent drug offenses, many States and localities have established alternative, less putative programs, such as drug courts, to rehabilitate offenders. (For more information on drug courts, see Chapter 8, *Putting It Together: Making the Systems Work for Families.*)

METHAMPHETAMINE USE AND ITS IMPACT ON CHILDREN

Methamphetamine is a powerfully addictive drug, and individuals who use it can experience serious health and psychiatric conditions, including memory loss, aggression, violence, psychotic behavior, and potential coronary and neurological damage.[42] Its use in the United States has become an issue of great concern to professionals working with children and families. In 2007, there were an estimated 529,000 current users of methamphetamine aged 12 or older. Approximately, 5.3 percent of the population reported using this drug at least once in their lifetime.[43] Methamphetamine is also known by ever-changing street names, such as speed, ice, crystal, crank, tweak, glass, bikers' coffee, poor man's cocaine, chicken feed, shabu, and yaba.[44]

As with any children of parents with an SUD, children whose parents use methamphetamine are at a particularly high risk for abuse and neglect. What compounds the problem for children of methamphetamine users is that the drug is relatively easy to make, and therefore, many of these children are exposed to the additional risks of living in or near a methamphetamine lab. During 2005, an estimated 1,660 children were injured, killed at, or affected by methamphetamine labs. In each of the prior 3 years, the number of affected children was over 3,000.[45] The manufacture of methamphetamine involves the use of highly flammable, corrosive, and poisonous materials that create serious health and safety hazards. Children affected by methamphetamine labs may exhibit symptoms such as chronic cough, skin rashes, red or itchy eyes, agitation, inconsolable crying, irritability, and vomiting.[46]

Many communities have Drug Endangered Children (DEC) programs that assist CPS caseworkers, law enforcement, and medical services to coordinate services for children found living in environments where drugs are made. For more information on DEC programs, visit **http://www.whitehousedrugpolicy.gov/ enforce/dr_endangered_ child. html**.

CPS agencies have witnessed the effects of methamphetamine use on the child welfare population. In a 2005 survey by the National Association of Counties, 40 percent of CPS officials reported that the number of out-of-home placements due to methamphetamine use had increased in the previous year. In addition, 59 percent of the CPS officials reported that methamphetamine use had increased the difficulty of family reunification.[47]

Because of the dramatic escalation of methamphetamine use and the severity of its effects, further information on the drug and its impact on child welfare can be found throughout this manual. Additional resources are available at **http://www.childwelfare. gov/systemwide/service_array/substance/drug_specifi c/meth.cfm** and **http://www. methresources.gov/**.

3. HOW PARENTAL SUBSTANCE USE DISORDERS AFFECT CHILDREN

IN THIS SECTION

- The impact of substance use on prenatal development
- The impact of substance use on childhood development

The lives of millions of children are touched by substance use disorders (SUDs). The 2007 National Survey on Drug Use and Health reports that 8.3 million children live with at least one parent who abused or was dependent on alcohol or an illicit drug during the past year. This includes 13.9 percent of children aged 2 years or younger, 13.6 percent of children aged 3 to 5 years, 12.0 percent of children aged 6 to 11 years, and 9.9 percent of youths aged 12 to 17 years.[48] These children are at increased risk for abuse or neglect, as well as physical, academic, social, and emotional problems.[49]

A predictable, consistent environment, coupled with positive caregiver relationships, is critical for normal emotional development of children. Parental substance abuse and dependence have a negative impact on the physical and emotional well-being of children and can cause home environments to become chaotic and unpredictable, leading to child maltreatment. The children's physical and emotional needs often take a back seat to their parents' activities related to obtaining, using, or recovering from the use of drugs and alcohol.[50]

This chapter discusses how prenatal and postnatal substance use by parents affects fetal and early childhood development. It is intended to help child protective services (CPS) caseworkers understand the behaviors and problems that some children in the child welfare system may exhibit and that hold implications for their potential need for services.

A DEFINITION OF CHILD MALTREATMENT

The Child Abuse Prevention and Treatment Act, reauthorized in the Keeping Children and Families Safe Act of 2003 (P.L. 108-36), provides the minimum standards for defining child physical abuse, neglect, and sexual abuse that States must incorporate into their statutory definitions in order to receive Federal funds. Under this Act, child maltreatment is defined as:

"Any recent act or failure to act on the part of a parent or caregiver, which results in death, serious physical or emotional harm, sexual abuse or exploitation, or an act or failure to act which presents an imminent risk of serious harm."[51]

A "child" under this definition generally means a person younger than age 18 or who is not an emancipated minor. In cases of child sexual abuse, a "child" is one who has not attained the age of 18 or the age specified by the child protection law of the State in which the child resides, whichever is younger.[52]

The Impact on Prenatal Development

In 2006 and 2007, an average of 5.2 percent of pregnant women aged 15 to 44 years used an illicit drug during the month prior to being surveyed, and 11.6 percent had consumed alcohol.[53] Nationwide, between 550,000 and 750,000 children are born each year after prenatal exposure to drugs or alcohol.[54] These children often are medically fragile or born with a low birth weight. Some are born prematurely and require intensive care.

Identifying the effects of drugs and alcohol on fetuses has posed challenges for researchers. While there has been some success researching the effects of alcohol on fetal development, securing accurate information regarding the use of illicit drugs from pregnant women or women who have given birth has proven to be very difficult. In addition, women who abuse substances often have other risk factors in their lives (e.g., a lack of prenatal care, poor nutrition, stress, violence, poor social support) that can contribute significantly to problematic pregnancies and births.

The sections that follow summarize some of what is known about the effects of substance use on prenatal development.

Pregnancy and SUDs

Women who use alcohol or illicit drugs may find it difficult or seemingly impossible to stop, even when they are pregnant. Moreover, pregnancy can be stressful and uncomfortable.

For someone who commonly uses drugs and alcohol to minimize pain or stress, this practice may not only continue, but also become worse. Pregnant women can face significant stigma and prejudice when their SUDs are discovered. For these reasons, some women avoid seeking treatment or adequate prenatal care. Other pregnant women, however, do seek treatment. According to the Substance Abuse and Mental Health Services Administration, 3.9 percent of the women admitted to State licensed or certified SUD treatment programs were pregnant at the time of admission.[55] In another study, pregnant women aged 15 to 44 years were more likely than nonpregnant women of the same age group to enter treatment for cocaine abuse.[56]

SCREENING NEWBORNS AT BIRTH

Opinions differ about how best to respond to prenatal substance exposure. Some hospitals are reconsidering whether they should test newborns for drugs, and some courts are treating prenatal substance exposure as a public health matter, turning to CPS only if they determine the child was harmed. Decisions regarding whether and when to screen newborns for prenatal substance exposure are beyond the purview of CPS.

Child welfare legislation has provided some guidance regarding how such cases should be handled. The Keeping Children and Families Safe Act of 2003 requires that health care providers notify CPS, as appropriate, to address the needs of infants born exposed to drugs, and requires the development of a plan of safe care for any affected infants. In 2006, statutes in 15 States and the District of Columbia specified reporting procedures when there is evidence at birth that an infant was exposed prenatally to drugs, alcohol, or other controlled substances. Additionally, 13 States and the District of Columbia included prenatal substance exposure in their definitions of child abuse or neglect.[57]

The Effects of Prenatal Exposure to Alcohol

Drinking alcohol during pregnancy can have serious effects on fetal development. Alcohol consumed by a pregnant woman is absorbed by the placenta and directly affects the fetus.[58] A variety of birth defects to the major organs and the central nervous system, which are permanent, can occur due to alcohol use during pregnancy, though the risk of harm decreases if the pregnant woman stops drinking completely.[59] Collectively, these defects are called Fetal Alcohol Syndrome (FAS). FAS is one of the most commonly known birth defects related to prenatal drug exposure. Children with FAS may exhibit:

- Growth deficiencies, both prenatally and after birth
- Problems with central nervous system functioning
- IQs in the mild to severely retarded range
- Small eye openings and poor development of the optic nerve
- A small head and brain
- Joint, limb, ear, and heart malformations.

Exhibit 3-1. Childhood Behavior and Characteristics Associated with FAS, ARND, and ARBD[60].

Developmental Stage	Typical Behaviors or Characteristics	FAS/ARND/ARBD Behaviors or Characteristics
Infants	• Develop mental and physical skills • Bond with caretakers	• Problems with spatial and depth perception, muscle coordination and development, facility with speech, and processing information • Attention deficit disorder • Inability to focus • Possible attachment disorders
Toddlers	• Develop sense of self • Assert independence by saying "no"	• Difficulty exercising self-control, which leads to self- doubt and feelings of inadequacy
5–7 year olds	• Try new things • Meet or exceed academic standards • Learn new social skills	• Overwhelmed with new situations and interactions with other children • Inability to pick up social skills by observation • Problems meeting academic standards
8–12 year olds	• Increased influence of peers • Games become important method of bonding and developing interpersonal skills	• Difficulty remembering rules of games • Lack of remorse in breaking rules • Become depressed and exhibit other behavior problems
Teenagers	• Continued detachment from parents • Development of individual identity • Learn to identify with larger community	• May lack skills to become good community members • Become socially isolated • May find their way to peer groups that engage in high- risk behaviors • May with draw altogether from groups

Alcohol-Related Neurodevelopmental Disorder (ARND) and Alcohol-Related BirThDefects (ARBD) are similar to FAS. Once known as Fetal Alcohol Effects, ARND and ARBD are terms adopted in 1996 by the National Academy of Sciences' Institute of Medicine. ARND and ARBD encompass the functional and physiological problems associated with prenatal alcohol exposure, but are less severe than FAS. Children with ARND can experience functional or mental impairments as a result of prenatal alcohol exposure, and children with ARBD can have malformations in the skeletal and major organ systems. Not all children who are exposed prenatally to alcohol develop FAS, ARND, or ARBD, but for those who do, these effects continue throughout their lives and at all the stages of development, although they are likely to present themselves diff erently at each developmental stage. Exhibit 3-1 compares typical childhood behavior at each developmental stage with behaviors and characteristics associated with FAS, ARND, and ARBD.

More information on FAS is available from the National Organization on Fetal Alcohol Syndrome (http://www.nofas. org) and the National Center on Birth Defects and Developmental Disabilities (http://www.cdc.gov/ncbddd/fas).

The Effects of Prenatal Exposure to Drugs

Similar to alcohol use, use of other substances can have significant effects on the developing fetus. For example, cocaine or marijuana use during pregnancy may result in premature birth, low birth weight, decreased head circumference, or miscarriage.[61] Prenatal exposure to marijuana has been associated with difficulties in functioning of the brain.[62] Even if there are no noticeable effects in the children at birth, the impact of prenatal substance use often can become evident later in their lives. As they get older, children who were exposed to cocaine prenatally can have difficulty focusing their attention, be more irritable, and have more behavioral problems.[63] Difficulties surface in sorting out relevant versus irrelevant stimuli, making school participation and achievement more challenging.

Pregnancy as a Motivation for Treatment

Given the dangers associated with substance use during pregnancy, women who abuse substances during pregnancy should receive treatment as early as possible. Research has found that women often are more amenable to entering treatment when they are pregnant.[67] CPS caseworkers and other professionals, therefore, should try to use the pregnancy to motivate women to change. CPS caseworkers may not have much opportunity to interact with women who have not yet given birth unless there are other children in the family who have entered the child welfare system.

Once their babies are born, significant changes can occur in the lives of women who abused alcohol or drugs during pregnancy. In the case of babies who test positive for substances at birth, the mothers may experience remorse and sadness over the actual or potential consequences of their substance use, which also can be a motivating factor to seek treatment. If CPS is involved, mothers may admit to enough drug use to explain the positive drug test, but not to an addiction, due to the fear of losing custody of their children. They may comply with treatment requirements in order to compensate for the problems their SUD may have caused their children. Nevertheless, new difficulties may begin when CPS closes the case and the pressure is off the mothers to stay clean. For instance, they may be tempted to use drugs and alcohol again. (For more information on treatment issues, see Chapter 5, *Treating Substance Use Disorders*.)

THE EFFECTS OF PRENATAL METHAMPHETAMINE USE

Prenatal exposure to methamphetamine can cause a wide range of problems, including birth defects, fetal death, growth retardation, premature birth, low birth weight, developmental disorders, and hypersensitivity to touch in newborns. Older children who were exposed prenatally to substances may exhibit cognitive deficits, learning disabilities, and poor social adjustment.[64]

Caseworkers should note that methamphetamine users might not be knowledgeable about the potential harm to themselves or to the fetus. Like cocaine and heroin users, methamphetamine users tend to avoid prenatal care clinics.[65] Caseworkers also should be careful of labeling children who have been exposed prenatally to methamphetamine. For example, labeling a child as a "methbaby" can cause the child or others to have lower expectations for academic and life achievements and to ignore other causes for the physical and social problems the child may encounter.[66]

The Impact on Childhood Development

Exposure to parental SUDs during childhood also can have dire consequences for children. Compared to children of parents who do not abuse alcohol or drugs, children of parents who do, and who also are in the child welfare system, are more likely to experience physical, intellectual, social, and emotional problems. Among the difficulties in providing services to these children is that problems affected or compounded by their parents' SUDs might not emerge until later in their lives.[68]

This section summarizes some of the consequences of SUDs on childhood development, including a disruption of the bonding process; emotional, academic, and developmental problems; lack of supervision; parentification; social stigma; and adolescent substance use and delinquency.

Disruption of the Bonding Process

When mothers or fathers abuse substances after delivery, their ability to bond with their child—so important during the early stages of life—may be weakened. In order for an attachment to form, it is necessary that caregivers pay attention to and notice their children's attempts to communicate. Parents who use marijuana, for example, may have difficulty picking up their babies' cues because marijuana dulls response time and alters perceptions. When parents repeatedly miss their babies' cues, the babies eventually stop providing them. The result is disengaged parents with disengaged babies. These parents and babies then have difficulty forming a healthy, appropriate relationship.

Neglected children who are unable to form secure attachments with their primary caregivers may:

- Become more mistrustful of others and may be less willing to learn from adults
- Have difficulty understanding the emotions of others, regulating their own emotions, or forming and maintaining relationships with others
- Have a limited ability to feel remorse or empathy, which may mean that they could hurt others with out feeling their actions were wrong
- Demonstrate a lack of confidence or social skills that could hinder them from being successful in school, work, and relationships
- Demonstrate impaired social cognition, which is awareness of oneself in relation to others as well as of others' emotions. Impaired social cognition can lead a person to view many social interactions as stressful.[69]

Emotional, Academic, and Developmental Problems

Children who experience either prenatal or postnatal drug exposure are at risk for a range of emotional, academic, and developmental problems. For example, they are more likely to:

- Experience symptoms of depression and anxiety
- Suffer from psychiatric disorders
- Exhibit behavior problems
- Score lower on school achievement tests
- Demonstrate other difficulties in school.

These children may behave in ways that are challenging for biological or foster parents to manage, which can lead to inconsistent caregiving and multiple alternative care placements.

Positive social and emotional child development generally has been linked to nurturing family settings in which caregivers are predictable, daily routines are respected, and everyone recognizes clear boundaries for acceptable behaviors.[70] Such circumstances often are missing in the homes of parents with SUDs. As a result, extra supports and interventions are needed to help children draw upon their strengths and maximize their natural potential despite their home environments. Protective factors, such as the involvement of other supportive adults (e.g., extended family members, mentors, clergy, teachers, neighbors), may help mitigate the impact of parental SUDs.

Lack of Supervision

The search for drugs or alcohol, the use of scarce resources to pay for them, the time spent in illegal activities to raise money for them, or the time spent recovering from hangovers or with drawal symptoms can leave parents with little time or energy to care properly for their children. These children frequently do not have their basic needs met and often do not receive appropriate supervision. In addition, rules about curfews and potentially dangerous activities may not be enforced or are enforced haphazardly. As a result, SUDs are often a factor in neglect cases.

Parentification

As children grow older, they may become increasingly aware that their parents cannot care for them. To compensate, the children become the caregivers of the family, often extending their caregiving behavior to their parents as well as younger siblings. This process is labeled "parentification."[71]

Parentified children carry a great deal of anxiety and sometimes go to great lengths to control or to eliminate their parents' use of drugs or alcohol. They feel responsible for running the family. These feelings are reinforced by messages from the parents that the children cause the parents' SUDs or are at fault in some way if the family comes to the attention of authorities. Sometimes these children must contact medical personnel in the case of a parent's overdose, or they may be left supervising and caring for younger children when their parents are absent while obtaining or abusing substances.

Social Stigma

Adults with SUDS may engage in behaviors that embarrass their children and may appear disinterested in their children's activities or school performance. Children may separate themselves from their parents by not wanting to go home after school, by not bringing friends to the house, or by not asking for help with homework. These children may feel a social stigma attached to certain aspects of their parents' lives, such as unemployment, homelessness, an involvement with the criminal justice system, or SUD treatment.

Adolescent Substance Use and Delinquency

Adolescents whose parents have SUDs are more likely to develop SUDs themselves. Some adolescents mimic behaviors they see in their families, including ineffective coping behaviors such as using drugs and alcohol. Many of these children also witness or are victims of violence. It is hypothesized that substance abuse is a coping mechanism for such traumatic events.[72] Moreover, adolescents who use substances are more likely to have poor academic performance and to be involved in criminal activities. The longer children are exposed to parental SUD, the more serious the negative consequences may be for their overall development and well-being.

CHILD ABUSE AS A PRECURSOR TO SUBSTANCE USE DISORDERS

Many people view SUDs as a phenomenon that leads to or exacerbates the abuse or neglect of children. Research also suggests, however, that being victimized by child abuse, particularly sexual abuse, is a common precursor of SUDs.[73] Sometimes, victims of abuse or neglect "self-medicate" (i.e., drink or use drugs to escape the unresolved trauma of the maltreatment).[74] One study found that women with a history of childhood physical or sexual abuse were nearly five times more likely to use street drugs and more than twice as likely to abuse alcohol as women who were not maltreated.[75] In another study, childhood abuse predicted a wide range of problems, including lower self-esteem, more victimization, more depression, and chronic homelessness, and indirectly predicted drug and alcohol problems.[76]

---

4. IN-HOME EXAMINATION, SCREENING, AND ASSESSMENT OF SUBSTANCE USE DISORDERS

IN THIS SECTION

- In-home examination
- Screening
- Assessment

The previous chapter described some of the effects of parental substance use disorders (SUDs) on children, but how does a child protective services (CPS) worker determine if SUDs exist in the family? This chapter discusses in-home examinations, SUD screening instruments, and SUD assessments, including their methods, benefits, and limitations, and how caseworkers can incorporate them into their practice.

In-Home Examination

An in-home examination includes observations by the CPS caseworker of the people and the environment in a home. When visiting a home as part of an investigation, the caseworker should check for the following indicators of possible SUDs:

- A report of substance use is included in the CPS call or report

- Drug paraphernalia (e.g., a syringe kit, charred spoons, a large number of liquor or beer bottles)
- The scent of alcohol or drugs
- A child or other family member reports alcohol or drug use by a parent
- A parent appears to be under the influence of a substance, admits to having an SUD, or shows other signs of addiction or abuse (e.g., needle marks).

This list can be used pre- or post-screening and can be incorporated into every home visit.[77]

Screening

Screening is the use of a simple, and usually brief, set of questions that have been validated (i.e., tested to show that they accurately indicate the presence of an SUD). Results are easy to interpret. Generally, individuals who are not trained SUD treatment providers use the instruments.

The goal of screening is to determine whether a family member requires further evaluation for SUDs.[78] CPS caseworkers can use screening as a part of their standard home visits or family assessments. This section describes the importance of screening, sample screening instruments, benefits and limitations of screening instruments, and what to do when an instrument indicates an individual may have an SUD.

SIGNS OF METHAMPHETAMINE USE AND MANUFACTURE[79]

With the increased use of methamphetamine, first responders are now more likely to work with clients who are users or manufacturers of this drug. The following information can assist them in identifying methamphetamine use or manufacturing.

Signs of possible methamphetamine use include:

- Increased breathing and pulse rate
- Sweating
- Rapid/pressured speech
- Euphoria (an exaggerated feeling of well-being)
- Hyperactivity
- Dry mouth
- Tremors (shaking hands)
- Dilated pupils
- Lack of appetite
- Insomnia or lack of sleep
- Bruxism (teeth-grinding)
- Depression
- Irritability, suspiciousness, paranoia
- Visual and auditory hallucinations
- Formication (the sensation of bugs crawling on the skin)

- The presence of white powder, straws, or injection equipment.

Signs that methamphetamine is possibly being manufactured in a home include:

- Laboratory equipment (e.g., flasks, rubber tubing, beakers, large amounts of coffee filters)
- Large quantities of pills containing ephedrine or pseudoephedrine (e.g., certain cold medicines)
- A chemical odor
- Chemicals not commonly found in a home (e.g., red phosphorous, acetone, liquid ephedrine, ether, iodine, phenylacetone [P2P])
- Unusually large quantities of household chemicals (e.g., lye, paint thinner)
- Chemicals usually found on a farm (e.g., anhydrous ammonia)
- Residue from the manufacture of methamphetamine (usually of a maroon color) in bathtubs, sinks, toilets, or on the walls
- Containers used for purposes not originally intended (e.g., glass milk or beer bottles with unfamiliar liquids)
- No visible means of income
- Unusual security precautions (e.g., extra locks, barred or blacked-out windows, expensive alarm systems).

Importance of Substance Use Disorder Screening

Screening for SUDs should be a routine part of CPS investigations, risk and safety assessments, and case planning and monitoring. Evidence of SUDs may not be noticeable upon initial investigation, but may emerge over time as caseworkers develop relationships with a family or notice that family members are unable to participate in program activities. Given the prevalence of SUDs among families involved in the child welfare system, CPS caseworkers should consider screening during all stages of the case.

SAFETY ISSUES WHEN ENCOUNTERING A SUSPECTED METHAMPHETAMINE LAB

First responders should use extreme caution and seek assistance from law enforcement, fire/rescue personnel, hazardous materials crews, or other appropriate individuals or groups if they are visiting a home that has a suspected methamphetamine lab because these homes may have:

- Individuals under the influence of methamphetamine or other drugs and/or who may be armed
- Defense systems, including explosive devices and other booby traps
- Vicious animals
- Dangerous and volatile chemicals. [80]

First responders who enter a methamphetamine lab that has not been properly ventilated and cleaned—or who are not properly equipped to avoid exposure to chemicals (i.e., have respirators, protective clothing)— may experience shortness of breath, coughing, chest pain, dizziness, vomiting, lack of coordination, burns, and, in some cases, death. If first responders do come into contact with possibly dangerous chemicals, they should wash the exposed skin with liquid soap and water or, depending on the type of chemical exposure, a chemical solution. They also should remove contaminated shoes and clothing. First responders should be knowledgeable about agency protocols for the evacuation, decontamination, and health screenings of children and others found at the home, including which, if any, of the child's possessions (e.g., medications, eyeglasses) should be retrieved from the home and how they should be decontaminated.

First responders who determine they are in a home that has a suspected methamphetamine lab should immediately leave the residence, taking care not to:

- Touch anything in the lab
- Turn on or off any electrical switches (e.g., lights)
- Eat or drink anything
- Open, move, or sniff containers with suspected chemicals
- Smoke anywhere near the home.
- Alarm or act in a way that could be perceived as aggressive by others in the home (i.e., suddenly running from a room, pushing someone aside), especially suspected methamphetamine users, who may experience paranoia and extremely aggressive behavior.[81]

CPS caseworkers understandably may be uncomfortable discussing SUDs with family members who already feel threatened because of being under investigation for child maltreatment. Abuse and addiction are not always visible, and family members are likely to be reluctant to disclose activities that may be illegal or that could further jeopardize custody of their children. As described in Chapter 2, *The Nature of Substance Use Disorders*, SUDs often are masked by other problems, such as mental illness or domestic violence, and can be overlooked if those other problems are more apparent. The opposite also can be true; an SUD may mask other problems, such as domestic violence or disabilities. Moreover, addiction often is characterized by denial, and family members may not recognize that they have an SUD. For example, they may feel that their drinking is with in an acceptable range or that their marijuana use is not problematic.

Screening is just one of many approaches used to identify SUDs. It is not completely accurate nor will it work all the time (i.e., not all positive responses will demonstrate an SUD, and not all negative responses will rule out a disorder). CPS caseworkers should also rely on additional techniques, such as observation, medical histories, reports from family members or friends, or arrest records. Nevertheless, using a brief screening instrument takes little time and provides an objective method for caseworkers to use in opening a discussion about sensitive issues. In this way, screening becomes part of a continuum of activities aimed at addressing families' problems with SUDs.

GENERAL HOME VISIT SAFETY TIPS

Families experiencing multiple issues (e.g., SUDs, mental health problems, domestic violence, criminal behavior) can make it more dangerous for CPS caseworkers going into homes to investigate cases of child maltreatment. While on a home visit, caseworkers should remember the following safety tips:

- Ensure that the CPS supervisor knows the time and place of the appointment and the expected time of return.
- Dress appropriately and in a manner that blends into the community.
- Walk close to buildings or close to the curb in an effort to have at least one safe side. Stay away from bushes, alleys, and dark corners, if possible.
- Know the route in and out of the area by examining a map or by talking with others beforehand. Do not wander or appear lost or confused.
- Park as close to the home as possible and in a way that helps ensure an easy exit. Keep the car keys in hand while entering and exiting the home so they are easily available.
- Be aware of your surroundings at all times. Enter and leave homes carefully, noticing doors, windows, neighbors, loiterers, and anything or anyone that may be a risk to safety.
- If unsure of the safety or surroundings of the location, move to another spot by suggesting taking a break or getting a cup of coffee and finish talking there.
- Attempt to keep a clear path to an exit.
- Be aware of dogs that may pose a threat.
- Follow intuition and take action if feeling afraid or threatened. Leave the home or call 911 if necessary.
- Have access, if possible, to technology that may assist with safety issues (e.g., GPS systems, cell phones).

In cases where drugs and alcohol may be an issue in the family or the surrounding community:

- Go to the home with another caseworker or law enforcement officer, particularly if the home is in an area known for drug dealing.
- Know the local signs that indicate a drug deal is occurring. In such situations, do not enter the home with out law enforcement personnel.
- Be aware of homes or other living environments that may be used as a clandestine drug factory. Do not attempt to investigate such places alone, and immediately contact the police or sheriff if such a lab is suspected. Anyone with out proper training and protective gear should stay at least 500 feet away from any suspected laboratory. The following are signs of a possible lab:
  - Strong or unusual chemical odors
  - Laboratory equipment, such as glass tubes, beakers, funnels, and Bunsen burners
  - Chemical drums or cans in the yard

> - A high volume of automobile or foot traffic, particularly at odd hours
> - New, high fences with no visible livestock or other animals.
>
> - If one or both parents appear to be intoxicated, high, incoherent, or passed out, ensure the safety and supervision of the children. Once that has been accomplished, it is appropriate to reschedule the appointment. It may be appropriate to call the supervisor for guidance.[82]

Sample Screening Instruments

Ideally, screening instruments used by CPS caseworkers should be brief, easily administered, inexpensive, and capable of detecting a problem or condition when it exists. Two screening tools available for CPS caseworkers are the CAGE and UNCOPE questionnaires, which are shown in Exhibit 4-1. These quick screens should be used with other information and observations.[85] For a list of screening instruments, see Appendix F, *Commonly Used Screening Instruments*. A sample instrument is available in Appendix G, *State of Connecticut Department of Children and Families Substance Abuse Screening and Information Form*.

EXHIBIT 4-1. SAMPLE SCREENING INSTRUMENTS FOR SUBSTANCE USE DISORDERS

The CAGE Questionnaire (Amended for Drug Use)

C Have you ever felt the need to **C**ut down on your drinking or drug use?

A Have you ever felt **A**nnoyed by people criticizing your drinking or drug use?

G Have you ever felt bad or **G**uilty about your drinking or drug use?

E Have you ever had a drink or used a drug first thing in the morning to steady your nerves or get rid of a hangover? (**E**ye-opener)

Scoring: If the answer is "yes" to one or more questions, the responder should receive a formal alcohol and drug assessment. Answering "yes" to one or two questions may indicate alcohol and drug-related problems. Answering "yes" to three or four questions may indicate alcohol or drug dependence.[83]

UNCOPE

U Have you spent more time drinking or **U**sing than you intended?

N Have you ever **N**eglected some of your usual responsibilities because of alcohol or drug use?

C Have you ever felt you wanted or needed to **C**ut down on your drinking or drug use in the past year?

O Has your family, a friend, or anyone else ever told you they **O**bjected to your alcohol or drug use?

P Have you found yourself thinking a lot about drinking or using? (**P**reoccupied)

E Have you ever used alcohol or drugs to relieve **E**motional discomfort, such as sadness, anger, or boredom?

Scoring: Two or more positive responses indicate possible abuse or dependence and a need for further assessment by an SUD treatment provider.[84]

Benefits and Limitations of Screening Instruments

Screening for SUDs is harder and requires more skill than screening for other problems among child welfare populations, such as barriers to work or stress. This is because SUDs often are characterized by stigma and denial and frequently involve illegal activities. Although screening instruments can provide useful information, they are not with out fl aws. With out informed interpretation and communication of their results, these instruments will not be effective. It is important to understand both the benefits and the limitations of screening instruments in order to use them properly.

The benefits of screening instruments include the following:

- Instruments provide a consistent structure for caseworkers to use in interviewing family members.
- Instruments can provide a starting point and context for further discussion and service planning.
- Instruments offer parents a chance to disclose an SUD and give caseworkers a chance to refer the parent to an SUD treatment provider for assessment.
- Screening instruments allow caseworkers to weigh an individual's responses to estimate whether SUDs might be a problem.
- Many instruments are widely available and accessible.
- Several instruments have been empirically tested for validity (i.e., the instrument is accurate) and reliability (i.e., the instrument is consistent).
- Many instruments take little time to administer and are not difficult to interpret.[86]

The limitations of screening instruments include the following:

- Screening instruments have been tested and found valid with a variety of populations, but every instrument may not be appropriate for every population. For example, some instruments may have been tested in settings where individuals go for health care and treatment, but not in public agencies or in situations where families know they risk losing their children. Before using a particular instrument in a CPS setting, it is important to check the literature regarding the appropriate use of that instrument.
- Screening instruments rely on self-disclosure. Even the best instruments administered under optimal circumstances will yield valid information only to the extent that families respond honestly.
- Denial is a characteristic of SUDs, and because of this, family members may not understand or acknowledge that their pattern of substance use represents abuse or addiction.
- Information obtained from the screening alone will be of little benefit unless it is part of a continuum of identification, assessment, and treatment.

Instruments are only one technique that caseworkers should use in exploring SUDs with family members. They should complement rather than replace other techniques to identify SUDs. Additionally, instruments are not always correct. If a caseworker suspects an SUD, but the screening instrument does not indicate a problem, the caseworker's best judgment always should take precedence.

What to Do When a Screen Indicates a Substance Use Disorder

If the results of a screening instrument or an in-home check indicate that a parent may have an SUD, the CPS caseworker should take the following steps:

- Ensure that the parent receives an SUD assessment from a qualified SUD treatment provider.
- If an SUD is present, address it in the case plans for both the parent and the child.
- Ensure that a qualified professional assesses the child for the impact of parental SUD or for the possibility of the child's own use of substances.
- Coordinate service plans with the treatment professional.[87]

Even if an SUD initially has been ruled out as an important factor in the family's case plan, the caseworker should reassess if the family is not making progress in dealing with other issues. An unidentified SUD can hamper a family's progress for years.

Assessment

Once screening indicates that an individual may have an SUD, an assessment is the next step in a continuum of activities to address the problem. An assessment is a detailed evaluation used to determine whether treatment is needed. If so, then the assessment is utilized to design an appropriate treatment or service plan. Assessments should include various aspects of family living, such as housing, health issues, child behavior problems, and family strengths. In general, only professionals who are trained in administering assessments and in interpreting their results should conduct them.

DRUG TESTING PARENTS

Physical drug testing of parents for evidence of substance use brings to the surface complicated and interrelated issues of public policy, science and technology, and ethics. Drug testing of adults has different goals in different contexts. For example, parole and probation officers use drug testing to monitor compliance with the conditions of parole and probation; employers use them to make hiring decisions; and alcohol and drug abuse treatment programs use tests to assess whether a person is complying with the treatment plan. Parents involved with CPS who are known to have an SUD are likely to be tested as part of their alcohol and drug abuse treatment or to meet court requirements. CPS may rely on the results of drug tests to inform decisions about providing services or reunification, or they may consider drug testing as a means of determining if there is an SUD. Whichever way drug testing is used, it is important for CPS caseworkers and administrators to understand the following uses and limitations:

- Drug tests do not demonstrate patterns of drug use or demonstrate if a person is abusing or is dependent on substances. Test results simply indicate the recent use of a substance and, for some substances, the amount used.
- Common drug tests do not provide accurate information about alcohol use because alcohol metabolizes quickly and is not detectable after approximately 8 hours.
- Whether drug use is detected by tests depends not only on the drug used, but also on other factors such as the characteristics of each drug, an individual's metabolism, and the cut-off levels established by the agency requesting the test or the laboratory analyzing it.
- Drug tests are typically physically invasive procedures, which raises questions about an individual's right to privacy.
- Individuals may be afraid to discuss problems if they believe they will be tested.
- Positive results from drug tests require that there be qualified and trained staffavailable to initiate careful and sensitive follow-up discussions with family members.[88]

Importance of Sharing Information

Ideally, the CPS caseworker and the SUD treatment provider who is conducting the assessment will share information. Information from the CPS caseworker about the case provides the context for the assessment. Likewise, results from the assessment can assist the CPS caseworker in developing a comprehensive and coordinated service plan. The caseworker should provide the following information, if available, to the SUD treatment provider along with the referral:

- The family member's arrest history related to substance use
- The condition of the home when home visits were conducted
- A history of SUD treatment participation by the family member
- Any other SUD-related information.

Key Points for Making Referrals and for Using Assessments

The following are key points to remember when making referrals for and conducting SUD assessments with in the context of CPS:

- **The quality of the assessment is directly related to the quality of the information provided to the counselor conducting the evaluation**. Frequently, counselors rely on self-reported data in their evaluations. Self-reports often are criticized because there is a perception that individuals with SUDs often lie. This issue can be addressed by comparing the client's view of the problem with information available from other sources, such as a CPS caseworker, other service providers, and family members.
- **A good assessment should address the following family and parenting issues**:
- How substance use affects the client's ability to be a good parent;
- The level of care or intervention that would be most appropriate for this individual to address the current level of substance use;
- What should be required of the parent in order to demonstrate the ability to rear the child safely in light of a problematic use of substances.

- **SUD treatment providers may feel that family-relevant assessments are beyond their professional scope of practice.** If a CPS caseworker encounters a situation in which the only SUD assessment available is conducted by someone with limited experience in addressing family issues, this should be stated explicitly in the caseworker's case notes and in court reports. Additionally, caseworkers should consult with a supervisor if they do not have confidence in the assessment.
- **Communication is critical.** Confidentiality issues surrounding SUD treatment records frequently are cited as a reason why CPS and SUD treatment agencies do not work well together. (Confidentiality is discussed in more detail in Chapter 8, *Putting It Together: Making the Systems Work for Families*.) Clear communication among the various parties is critical for ensuring that case plans and treatment plans are created properly and followed. Additionally, an understanding of each professional culture is crucial to working well together.

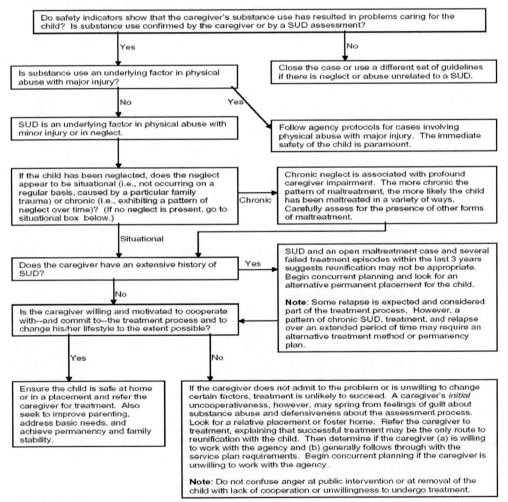

Adapted from *Tough Problems, Tough Choices: Guidelines for Needs-based ServicePlanning in Child Welfare*, a publication developed by Casey Family Programs, Ihe Annie E. Casey Foundation, and American Humane. It is available at http://www.americanhumane.org/protecting-children.

Exhibit 4-2. Decision Tree for Child Welfare Cases Involving Caregiver Substance Use Disorders[89].

See Chapter 8, *Putting It Together: Making the Systems Work for Families*, for more information on how CPS and SUD treatment systems can work together effectively. Additionally, refer to Exhibit 4-2 for more information regarding how SUD issues should be taken into consideration in child maltreatment cases.

For information about how the child welfare system, SUD treatment providers, and the courts can improve screening and assessment policies and protocols, refer to *Screening and Assessment for Family Engagement, Retention, and Recovery (SAFERR)* at **http://www.ncsacw.samhsa.gov/files/SAFERR.pdf**.

5. TREATING SUBSTANCE USE DISORDERS

IN THIS SECTION
• The goal of treatment • Treatment considerations • Common treatment approaches • Support services • Gender-sensitive treatment • Barriers to treatment

Substance use disorders (SUDs), like other chronic diseases, are treatable. Trained SUD treatment providers can determine the best treatment path for individuals to take and can enlist the assistance of other service providers, such as child protective services (CPS) caseworkers, in the treatment process. This chapter discusses the goal of SUD treatment, important treatment considerations, various approaches to treatment, issues related to gender-sensitive treatment, and barriers that may impede individuals from receiving treatment. This chapter is intended to help CPS caseworkers strengthen their understanding of treatment services available to help the families with whom they work. The role of CPS in supporting the treatment process is discussed in more detail in Chapter 6, *The Role of Child Protective Services When Substance Use Disorders Are Identified*.

The Goal of Treatment

An SUD is a medical condition with significant behavioral effects. These behaviors may frustrate, stymie, and anger treatment providers and CPS caseworkers. While individual experiences vary, persons with an SUD often have:

- Little experience or skills with which to cope with their feelings. Their substance use tends to numb discomfort, at least temporarily. Many of these individuals have been turning to drugs and alcohol since their teenage years.

- Difficulty escaping or solving everyday problems with out using substances. As a result, they can feel quite helpless when confronted with the day- to-day challenges of life.
- Poor communication skills. They may be ineffective in some areas and over-emote in others.
- Problematic behaviors, such as being manipulative or dishonest. These behaviors may be useful, however, in helping them obtain drugs and alcohol or hiding the use of these substances. Some individuals with SUDs may find it easy to be dishonest because they have buried or avoided their true feelings.

The goal of treatment is to help individuals break the cycle of addiction and dependence so that they may learn better ways of dealing with challenges in their lives. Caseworkers should keep in mind that treatment does not equal recovery. Recovery is a lifelong process, with treatment being one of the first steps. Recovery entails making lifestyle changes to regain control of one's life and accepting responsibility for one's own behavior.[90]

Research has demonstrated that SUD treatment works. A number of national studies over the past decades have shown that SUD treatment can result in abstinence from substance use, significant reduction in the abuse of substances, decreased criminal activity, and increased employment.[91] Recent studies also link SUD treatment for mothers with children in substitute care to improved child welfare outcomes, such as shorter stays in foster care for children and increased likelihood of reunification.[92] Furthermore, treatment has been shown to be cost-effective and to reduce costs in such areas as crime, health care, and unemployment.[93]

Treatment Considerations

SUD treatment is not a "one size fits all" service or one that remains static over time for a particular participant. For example, an individual who drank heavily for 10 years and is mentally ill is likely to have different treatment needs than an individual who recently became addicted to cocaine. When treatment is provided, the following should be considered:

DETOXIFICATION

Some individuals require detoxification services before they are able to participate effectively in ongoing treatment and recovery. Detoxification is a process whereby individuals are with drawn from alcohol and drugs, typically under the care of medical staff; it is designed to treat the acute physiological effects of ceasing the use of substances. It can be a period of physical and psychological readjustment that allows the individuals to participate in ensuing treatment. Medications are available to assist in detoxification. In some cases, particularly for alcohol, barbiturates, and other sedatives, detoxification may be a medical necessity, and untreated with drawal may be medically dangerous or even fatal.

The immediate goals of detoxification programs are:

- **To provide a safe with drawal from the substance of dependence and enable individuals to become alcohol- or drug-free**. Numerous risks are associated with with drawal, ranging from physical discomfort and emotional distress to death. The specific risks are affected by the substance on which the individual is dependent.

- **To provide with drawal that protects people's dignity**. A concerned and supportive environment, sensitivity to cultural issues, confidentiality, and appropriate detoxification medication, if needed, are important to individuals maintaining their dignity through an often difficult process.
- **To prepare individuals for ongoing alcohol and drug abuse treatment**. While in the detoxification program, individuals may establish therapeutic relationships with staff or other patients that help them to become aware of treatment options and alternatives to their current lifestyle. It can be an opportunity to provide information and motivate them for treatment.

Detoxification is not needed by all individuals and is not intended to address the psychological, social, and behavioral problems associated with addiction. With out subsequent and appropriate treatment, detoxification rarely will have a lasting impact on individuals' substance-abusing behavior. The appropriate level of care following detoxification is a clinical decision based on the individual's needs.[94]

- **Type and setting**. An individual should be placed in the type and setting of treatment that is most appropriate for the specific problems and needs. Just as a doctor may determine that a patient should receive medication instead of surgery to correct a problem, an SUD treatment provider must make decisions about the most appropriate course of treatment for an individual. The type, length, and duration of the treatment vary depending on the type and the duration of the SUD and the individual's support system and personal characteristics. The duration of the treatment may range from weeks or months to years.
- **Reassessment and modification of treatment plan**. An individual's treatment and service plan should be reassessed and continually modified to ensure that the plan meets the person's evolving needs.[95]
- **Involuntary treatment**. An individual does not have to "hit bottom" or "want to change" in order to benefit from treatment. Involuntary or mandated treatment can be just as effective as voluntary treatment. Sanctions or enticements in the family, work, or court setting can significantly increase treatment entry, retention, and success.[96]
- **Attorney involvement**. In instances where the parent has an attorney, the attorney also can play a key role in the early engagement of the client in treatment. CPS caseworkers and SUD treatment providers can facilitate this by reaching out to attorneys to help them understand the treatment process and clients' needs. This helps them represent the clients better and provides a better opportunity for reunification.
- **Timetables**. Because of the potential confl icts between child welfare and treatment timetables, treatment should begin as soon as possible so that there is time for family reunification. Often, however, there are delays in treatment either because it is not available or the need for treatment is not determined right away. CPS caseworkers and SUD treatment providers should work together to engage clients in treatment as early as possible.

Common Treatment Approaches

There are a number of ways to categorize treatment, based on the level of care (i.e., intensity of treatment and services offered) or the theoretical orientation and treatment approach. The following are some common treatment approaches:

- **Cognitive-behavioral approaches** address ways of thinking and behaving. Cognitive-behavioral treatment helps participants recognize situations in which they are most likely to use drugs, develop strategies for dealing with these situations, and build specific skills to address behaviors and problems that are associated with SUDs. For example, if a woman suggests that she is most likely to use cocaine after she has had a fight with her partner, the therapist would work with her to develop more positive ways of dealing with her anger and frustration following a fight. The treatment provider also may detail possible consequences to the individual, such as breaking parole and being forced to return to prison, as a means of changing behavior.

> **TIMETABLES IN CHILD WELFARE AND SUBSTANCE USE DISORDER TREATMENT**
>
> CPS agencies and SUD treatment providers have their own timetables for establishing family and individual well-being. The Adoption and Safe Families Act (P.L. 105-89) requires CPS agencies to:
>
> - Establish a permanency plan with in 12 months of a child entering the child welfare system
> - Initiate proceedings to terminate parental rights if a child has been in foster care for 15 of the most recent 22 months.
>
> SUD treatment can range from weeks or months to years. CPS caseworkers and treatment providers, therefore, should communicate frequently to make sure that this time is productive and to serve the children and families most effectively.[97]

- **Motivational enhancement treatment** incorporates some elements of cognitive-behavioral treatment, but focuses on increasing and then maintaining participants' motivations for change. Rather than forcing individuals to accept that they have a problem, this approach focuses on the individual's needs and the discrepancies between their goals and their current behaviors. This approach seeks to draw solutions from the treatment participants rather than having the solutions imposed by therapists.
- **Contingency management** includes both motivational enhancement treatment and an additional component of reinforcements and rewards. For example, credits may be offered as a reward for established positive behaviors, such as consistent attendance in group therapy or negative urinalysis testing. These credits then can be exchanged for items (such as baby products).
- **Therapeutic community** is an approach based on both cognitive-behavioral therapy and on the notion that treatment is best provided with in the context of a community of

individuals who have similar histories. This model was developed to provide treatment to individuals with antisocial character traits in addition to SUDs and tends to be highly confrontational. By having treatment participants confront each others' behaviors and attitudes, they learn a great deal about their own behaviors and also learn from the other participants. Often, therapeutic community models of treatment are found with in the correctional system. Given its confrontational nature, a therapeutic community may not be appropriate for some individuals. For example, women who have experienced intimate partner violence likely would not react well to this treatment approach.

- **Trauma-informed treatment services** generally follow one or more of the above treatment theories and reflect an understanding of trauma and its impact on SUDs and recovery. This approach acknowledges that a large percentage of SUD treatment participants have sustained physical, emotional, and sexual trauma in their lives and their disorder may be the result of self- medicating behaviors to deal with post-traumatic stress disorder symptoms.

MODEL TREATMENT AND PREVENTION PROGRAMS

The following Internet resources provide information about model SUD treatment and prevention interventions and their characteristics:

- The Substance Abuse and Mental Health Services Administration (SAMHSA) has compiled a list of evidenced-based programs that have prevented or reduced SUDs and other related behaviors. SAMHSA's National Registry of Evidence-based Programs and Practices has reviewed these programs rigorously and assessed their effectiveness. To view this list, go to **http:// modelprograms.samhsa.gov**.
- SAMHSA's *Guide to Evidence-Based Practices* provides listings for more than 35 websites that contain information and research on specific evidence-based programs and practices for the treatment or prevention of SUDs. Listings can be sorted and browsed by topic areas, target age groups, and settings. To view these listings, visit **http://www.samhsa.gov/ebpWebguide/index. asp**.
- The National Institute on Drug Abuse of the National Institutes of Health offers a list of principles for substance use prevention based on a number of long-term research studies. That list can be viewed at **http://www.nida.nih.gov/Infofacts/lessons.html.**

- **Trauma-specific treatment services** go a step further than trauma-informed treatment services and address the impact of the specific trauma on the lives of participants. This approach works to facilitate trauma healing and recovery as part of the treatment services. Several integrated, trauma-specific, treatment models for women have been developed in recent years.[98]
- **Treatment based upon the relational model of women's development** acknowledges the primacy of relationships in the lives of women and focuses upon the establishment and support of positive relationships. These positive relationships for the treatment participant may be with the therapist or with other significant figures, especially children and spouses.

Support Services

Along with SUD treatment, supplemental services often are provided to give additional support aimed at improving treatment outcomes. The following are important support services for treatment:

- **Case management services** are aimed at eliminating or reducing barriers to participation in treatment and include links to housing, food, medical care, financial assistance, and legal services. Case management also may include problem-solving sessions to assist individuals in establishing priorities among the many demands made upon them by multiple systems.
- **Twelve-step models** that incorporate the 12 steps of Alcoholics Anonymous into treatment. Participants "work the steps" and move through treatment by accomplishing each of the 12 steps with guidance from a sponsor and with emphasis on attendance at meetings. Spirituality or belief in a "higher power" is a central component of 12- step models.

TREATMENT EXAMPLE: METHADONE MAINTENANCE

Treatment can take many forms and can be multilayered and complex in attempting to address the nature of SUDs. For example, opioid replacement therapy is a treatment that substitutes a noneuphoria inducing and legally obtainable drug (e.g., methadone, buprenorphine) for heroin or another opiate. The treatment also provides counseling and other rehabilitation services. Methadone maintenance treatment is a type of opioid replacement therapy and is very effective. Along with preventing illicit opiate use, methadone has been shown to be effective in reducing criminal activity and increasing employment. Additionally, this treatment method reduces the risk of HIV-associated behaviors (e.g., needle use and sharing) and infection.[99]

Individuals engaged in methadone maintenance treatment can face heavy discrimination with in the child welfare system from judges, attorneys, and caseworkers who believe the ultimate goal of treatment should be a completely drug-free individual. Stopping the methadone treatment, however, leaves the individual at a very high risk for relapse to illicit opiate use and its associated high-risk factors, including unsafe injection practices and illegal behavior in order to support a habit. All of these can significantly increase the risk of abuse or neglect to children in the custody of these parents. Hence, the decision to require a detoxification from methadone must be considered carefully and based upon sound clinical principles rather than upon the stigma associated with methadone treatment.

TANF AND SUBSTANCE USE DISORDER TREATMENT

In 1996, the Personal Responsibility and Work Opportunity Reconciliation Act (PRWORA) fostered a new vision for public assistance. PRWORA established the Temporary Assistance for Needy Families (TANF) block grant, which treats welfare as short-term, time-limited assistance designed to help families move to work and self-sufficiency. Its work requirements and time limits allow little room for work exemption and, therefore, created an incentive for agencies to examine the needs of those recipients overcoming serious and more difficult challenges, such as SUDs.[100] National estimates of the welfare population who have substance abuse issues range from 16 to 37 percent.[101] The 2007 National Survey on Drug Use and Health (NSDUH) reports a rate of 8.0 percent for illicit drug use in the general population.[102]

Both TANF and substance abuse treatment program administrators recognize that treatment in the absence of work does not fully meet the needs of TANF clients with substance abuse issues.[103] Instead, TANF clients should receive treatment while concurrently pursuing work and work-related activities related to self-sufficiency.[104]

- **Recovery mentor or advocate programs** pair a person in recovery with individuals in need of treatment to support their engagement and retention in the process. Recovery mentors or advocates offer the unique perspective of having been through a similar experience and can offer the client insight to matters that CPS caseworkers and SUD treatment providers cannot.
- **Abstinence monitoring** includes urinalysis testing, breath testing for alcohol, and the use of the sweat patch and other technologies. This can be an important component of treatment as it provides opportunities for feedback to individuals who are working to change addictive behavior. Negative drug test results can be used for reinforcement of changed behavior, while positive test results can be a cue to the treatment participant and therapist that the treatment plan may need adjusting.

There also are numerous other support services (e.g., mental health counseling, medical care, employment services, child care) that may be provided to assist families.

Gender-Sensitive Treatment

Historically, SUD treatment has been focused on men, and fewer women had access to treatment services. In recent years, however, additional emphasis and funding have begun to address women's specific needs.[105]

Women

The ability to access and to remain in treatment can be difficult for anyone. Motivation, transportation, insurance coverage, and waiting lists all can impede an individual's attempts at recovery. Women, however, often face additional challenges when seeking treatment.

Both men and woman can have significant others who have SUDs. However, women with partners with SUDs are more likely to abuse substances themselves.[106] For instance, some women have partners with SUDs and face the loss of these relationships when they make the decision to seek help. These partners may discourage women's efforts to obtain treatment. Violence in these relationships is not uncommon. Not only do these women face the loss of a relationship, but many also face the loss of economic support. This has particular importance when the women are also mothers with young, dependent children.

Even if mothers do not have to contend with unsupportive partners, seeking treatment still can be difficult. Many women do not want to enter treatment because they fear their children will be taken away if it is discovered that they have an SUD. Women also may fear the social stigma of being considered a "bad mother" if others find out about their drug use. When women decide to enter treatment, child care frequently is a critical hurdle to overcome. Few residential programs allow children to remain with their mothers while in treatment, and few outpatient programs provide child care, leaving it up to the mothers to identify a safe, reliable place for their children or to pay for licensed child care services.

The profile of women who have SUDs differs from their male counterparts. Compared to men, a greater number of women who enter treatment have a history of physical or sexual abuse.[107] Additionally, among persons with AIDS, a greater percentage of females than males were exposed through injection drug use and may participate in risky sexual behavior or trade sex for drugs.[108] Additionally, women are more likely than men to have co-occurring mental healthproblems.[109]

Women receive the most benefit from treatment when the treatment program provides comprehensive services that meet their basic needs, such as transportation, job counseling and training, legal assistance, parenting training, and family therapy, as well as food, clothing, and shelter. Additionally, research shows that women benefit from a continuing relationship with the SUD treatment provider throughout treatment and that women, during times of lapse or relapse, often need the support of the community and the encouragement of close friends and family.[110] For more information on components of women-centered SUD treatment, visit **http:// www.nida.nih.gov/WHGD/WHGDPub.html.**

INVOLVING FATHERS IN CASE PLANNING

The importance of involving nonresidential fathers is particularly relevant when the mother is the perpetrator of child maltreatment, and the child has to be removed from the home. Fathers can be a source of support to the mother of their child, both financially and emotionally; are an irreplaceable figure in the lives of their children; and can be a supportive presence as the family deals with the problems that contributed to the maltreatment, especially when the mother is going through SUD treatment. If it is determined that the family is not a safe place for the child, the nonresidential father is a placement option that should be considered.

Of course, there may be times when involving the nonresidential father in the case planning process is impossible or ill-advised, including when the father is involved in illegal activities. More often than not, however, the nonresidential father can play a useful role, although bringing him into the process may require skilled negotiating on the part of the caseworker.

Men

Men face many of the same treatment hurdles as women, but while treatment historically has focused on men, there is still relatively little literature that discusses men's roles with in the family, particularly how their substance use affects their roles as fathers and partners. Most often, mothers are the focus of CPS cases and are involved in treatment. While some of these women may be reluctant to involve fathers in the treatment process, both parents should be involved whenever possible, provided it does not increase safety risks. In addition, CPS caseworkers usually are required by the court to seek and to involve absent parents. In some cases, it is the fathers of the children in the child welfare system who become the focus of intervention due to the presence of mothers in treatment. In these cases, men's roles as fathers and primary caregivers for their children warrant significant attention as they struggle to provide appropriate, nurturing, and consistent parenting.

Barriers to Treatment

Most people who have SUDs do not receive treatment. According to NSDUH, approximately 23.2 million people in 2007 needed SUD treatment. Of these, 2.4 million (10.4 percent) received treatment at a specialty facility (including hospitals, drug or alcohol rehabilitation facilities, and mental health centers), and the remaining 20.8 million did not. Of the individuals who were classified as needing but not receiving treatment, only an estimated 1.3 million reported that they perceived a need for treatment for their problem, and 380,000 reported that they had made an effort to receive treatment.[111] Among women of childrearing age (18 to 49 years) who needed treatment in the past year, only 10.4 percent received it, and only 5.5 percent felt they needed it.[112]

There are multiple and complex barriers to treatment. According to NSDUH, of those individuals who did not receive treatment even after making efforts to obtain it, the most commonly reported reason was because they were unable to afford it or lacked health coverage.[113] Other reasons that individuals may not be able to receive, or want to receive, SUD treatment include:

- Lack of available treatment spaces
- Not knowing where to go for treatment
- An ambivalence or fear about changing behavior
- A belief that they can handle the problem with out
- Concerns about negative opinions among neighbors, community members, or co-workers regarding treatment
- Relationships with partners and with family members who still may be using substances and who do not support the individual's efforts to change
- A perception of "giving in" when treatment is mandated by an outside source, such as the court or social services department
- Co-occurring mental health disorders exacerbated by the individual's attempts at abstinence
- A lack of transportation to and from treatment

- Economic difficulties in which the need to work takes priority over the participation in treatment
- A lack of available child care during treatment times.

CPS caseworkers can help clients who have SUDs identify barriers to participation in treatment and support the development of strategies to overcome these barriers.

6. THE ROLE OF CHILD PROTECTIVE SERVICES WHEN SUBSTANCE USE DISORDERS ARE IDENTIFIED

IN THIS SECTION

- Family assessment and case planning
- Supporting parents in treatment and recovery
- Supporting children of parents with SUDs

Once substance use disorders (SUDs) are identified as an issue to be addressed in a family's case plan, the child protective services (CPS) caseworker needs to have a discussion with the family to understand their perceptions of the role and the impact substance abuse or dependence has in their lives. This discussion should include what can be done about the issue and how the family can be motivated to change. Since a discussion about SUDs may be met with denial and even anger toward the caseworker, a focus on the needs of the children generally will align caseworkers and parents in determining the best way to improve the situation. This chapter discusses family assessments and how they can be used in case planning, how to support parents who are in treatment and recovery, and how to assist children whose parents have SUDs.

Family Assessment and Case Planning

During the initial family assessment or investigation, the CPS caseworker identifies the behaviors and conditions of the child, parent, and family that contribute to the risk of maltreatment, which may include a family member's SUD. During the family assessment, the caseworker engages the family in a process designed to gain a greater understanding of family strengths, needs, and resources so that children are safe and the risk of maltreatment is reduced.[114] In particular, the caseworkers work with the family to:

- Identify family strengths that can provide a foundation for change (e.g., support systems)
- Reduce the risk of maltreatment by identifying and by addressing the factors that place children at risk
- Help the children cope with the effects of maltreatment, parental SUDs, and other co-occurring problems.

A family-focused response to address family functioning issues is essential to an effective case plan. Families are involved with CPS because of serious breakdowns in functioning that can be influenced profoundly by a family member's SUD, as well as by the same family member's transition to recovery. Not only must the parents' substance use be addressed, but the behavioral problems and issues that have developed for children over the span of their parents' substance use also must be resolved. To cease substance abuse and to make positive changes in their lives, it is vital for parents to move toward full acceptance of their substance abuse or addiction and its consequences. When parents address their SUDs and other issues, positive changes in family functioning can be achieved while the families also receive services through CPS.

NORTH CAROLINA FAMILY ASSESSMENT SCALE

One recognized family assessment tool that addresses alcohol and drug issues is the North Carolina Family Assessment Scale (NCFAS). The following is a list of domains (i.e., areas of influence) that are measured by the NCFAS and could be used in any family assessment. The domain descriptions highlight ways in which alcohol and drug issues can be included in a CPS family assessment.

- **Environment**. This domain refers to the neighborhood and social environment in which the family lives and works. Risk factors in this domain may include the presence or use of drugs in the household or community.
- **Parental capabilities**. This domain refers to the parent or caregiver's capacity to function in the role of the parent. This includes overall parenting skills, the supervision of children, disciplinary practices, the provision of developmental opportunities for children, and the parent's mental and physical health. The caseworker should assess whether, how, and to what extent the client uses alcohol and drugs and how this may affect the ability to parent the children.
- **Family interactions**. This domain addresses interactions among family members as well as the roles played by family members with respect to one another. Many family interactions can be affected by the use of alcohol and drugs. Items in this domain that may point to the possibility of an SUD include a parent's nonresponsiveness to the children or children serving as the primary caretakers of younger siblings.
- **Family safety**. This domain includes any previous or current reports or suspicions regarding physical, emotional, or sexual abuse of children, as well as neglect.
- **Child well-being**. This domain refers to the physical, emotional, educational, and relational functioning of the children in the family. Parental SUDs can negatively affect various areas of child well-being, such as mental and physical health, academic performance, behavior, and social skills. Caseworkers also should assess if the children are using drugs or alcohol.[115]

For more information about the NCFAS, visit http://www.nfpn.org/images les/ncfas_scale_ defs.pdf or http://www.friendsnrc.org/ download/outcomeresources/ toolkit/annot/ncfas.pdf.

Despite the positive nature of these changes, however, both children and parents may find change difficult. For example, a parent newly in recovery can find coping with a child's needs very taxing. The problems in family functioning that have developed over time can be overwhelming as the parent notices them for the first time. Similarly, children experiencing a parent's recovery may have trouble accepting the parent's attempt to function in a role that he previously was unable to perform due to an SUD (e.g., disciplining the child). Caseworkers and SUD treatment providers should encourage progress, reward success, and support the newly sober parents in their efforts to make changes in all areas of family functioning and in being substance free.

Exhibit 6-1. Stages of Change and the CPS Caseworker's Tasks[116].

Parent's Stage	Stage Description	Tasks
Precontemplation	No perception of having a problem or needing to change	Increase parent's understanding of risks and problems with current behavior; raise parent's doubts about behavior
Contemplation	Initial recognition that behavior may be a problem and uncertain about change	Discuss reasons to change and the risks of not changing (e.g., removal of child)
Decision to change	Conscious decision to change; some motivation for change identified	Help parent identify best actions to take for change; support motivation for change
Action	Takes steps to change	Help parent implement change strategy and take steps
Maintenance	Actively works on sustaining change strategies and maintaining long-term change	Help parent to identify triggers of SUD and use strategies to prevent relapse
Relapse	Slips (lapses) from change strategy or returns to previous problem behavior patterns (relapse)	Help parent re-engage in the contemplation, decision, and action stages

Supporting Parents in Treatment and Recovery

While SUD treatment should be provided only by trained professionals, CPS caseworkers can maintain an integral role in the process for both the parents and the children.

Providing Support During the Stages of Change
A common theory in the field of SUD treatment is that individuals transition through different stages of thought and behavior during the treatment process. Exhibit 6-1 describes the stages and how CPS caseworkers can assist their clients during each stage.

A FAMILY-CENTERED RESPONSE TO METHAMPHETAMINE USE

The North Carolina Division of Family Services and the Family and Children's Resource Program recently compiled a list of practice guidelines for establishing a safe, family-centered response to methamphetamine use. The following suggestions may be useful to CPS caseworkers in assisting families who are affected by methamphetamine use:

- **Family engagement**. Working with clients who use methamphetamine can be frustrating, but the caseworker should avoid prejudging or demonizing them. Assess each family individually and help build upon their strengths.
- **Case decisions**. Parental SUDs do not necessarily constitute child maltreatment. Each case needs to be assessed individually.
- **Collaboration**. Collaborate with other professionals, such as substance abuse treatment providers, law enforcement, medical personnel, and mental heal The xperts.
- **Placement**. Placement in foster care never should be automatic, even in the case of finding a child in a methamphetamine lab. The caseworker should assess each situation thoroughly and explore the possibility of placement with kin. However, the caseworker should keep in mind that methamphetamine use is sometimes a problem for extended families.
- **Permanence** . It can be a challenge to achieve family reunification with in the time frames set forThin the Adoption and Safe Families Act. This is often because of the time required to recover from methamphetamine use and the fact that some users may be involved in the criminal justice system.
- **Education**. Ensure that foster parents and others involved in the case are knowledgeable about methamphetamine use.[117]

Once the parent is in treatment, the CPS caseworker can coordinate with the SUD treatment provider to monitor progress, to develop ongoing supports, and to intervene in times of crisis. Ongoing communication allows both systems to obtain a more complete picture of the family, which will allow for the development and modification of appropriate service plans.

When working with parents who are in treatment or who are in the process of recovery, CPS caseworkers should be mindful of the process that the parent is going through and address the relevant issues or needs. In early recovery, the client still may be detoxifying from drugs or alcohol and experiencing mood swings. The issues the client may need to address (or may need help in addressing) in order to stay sober typically include employment, housing, transportation, and a connection with an affirmative support system. Further along in recovery, the client may demonstrate several positive life changes that the caseworker can acknowledge, build upon, and encourage.

Throughout the recovery process, the caseworker, as well as the client, should have a clear understanding of the possibility of relapse and have a plan to address the situation if it occurs. Some frequently identified factors that contribute to lapse and to relapse include:

- Feeling complacent in recovery
- Feeling overwhelmed, confused, stuck, or stressed

- Having strong feelings of boredom, loneliness, anger, fear, anxiety, or guilt
- Engaging in compulsive behaviors such as gambling or sexual excess
- Experiencing relationship difficulties
- Failing to follow a treatment plan, quitting therapy, or skipping doctor appointments
- Being in the presence of drugs or alcohol.

Using Motivational Interviewing

Motivation can be defined as a willingness or a desire to change behavior.[118] Parents in the CPS system who have SUDs may be ambivalent about addressing their issues. They may be comfortable with their substance-related behaviors and believe that they serve a useful function in their lives.[119] Caseworkers and SUD treatment providers often find that motivating these parents to make behavioral changes is one of the most challenging aspects of their jobs.

Motivational interviewing is one approach CPS caseworkers can use to increase individuals' willingness to change. This type of interviewing accepts that ambivalence toward change is normal and seeks to engage and to mobilize the treatment participant on this basis.[120]

The four general principles of motivational interviewing are:

- Ambivalence about substance use is normal and is an obstacle in recovery.
- Ambivalence can be overcome by working with the client's motivations and values.
- The relationship between the caseworker or treatment provider and the client should be collaborative with each participant bringing his own expertise.
- Argument and aggressive confrontation should be avoided.[121]

> More information on how to support and to facilitate treatment and recovery is available in *Understanding Substance Abuse and Facilitating Recovery: A Guide for Child Welfare Workers*, a publication prepared by the National Center for Substance Abuse and Child Welfare under contract for the Substance Abuse and Mental Health Services Administration and the Administration for Children and Families with in the U.S. Department of Health and Human Services. The publication is available at http://www.ncsacw.samhsa.gov/files/UnderstandingSAGuide.pdf.

The connections, realizations, new understandings, and solutions should come from the client rather than from the CPS caseworker.

> For more information on motivational interviewing, go to **http://www.motivationalinterview.org** or **www.americanhumane.org/rmqic**.

Supporting Children of Parents With Substance Use Disorders

Caseworkers also have a key role in supporting children as their parents seek treatment for SUDs. As discussed earlier, children in the child welfare system whose parents have SUDs are at risk for a number of developmental and emotional problems. One of the difficulties in providing services to these children is that their problems, which are affected or compounded by their parents' SUDs, might not emerge until later in their lives. In addition, these children also are more likely than children of parents who do not have SUDs to remain in foster care for longer periods of time.[122] Because of their greater risks and longer stays in out-of-home care, it is particularly important for CPS caseworkers to assess thoroughly the needs (e.g., developmental, emotional, behavioral, educational) of these children and to link them with appropriate services in a timely manner. Both the assessments and service provision should be matched to the children's developmental levels and abilities. Children from families affected by SUDs do not always move through the developmental continuum in the normal sequential phases.

Children often have misperceptions about their role in their parents' problems. One approach to helping children deal with issues associated with a parent's SUD is to talk through lessons, such as the three Cs:

- You did not *cause* it (the parent's SUD).
- You cannot *control* it.
- You cannot *cure* it (which addresses the issue of the child taking on the role of the parent in the parent-child relationship).

Similarly, caseworkers can discuss a number of other important issues with children whose parents have an SUD, including:

- **Addiction is a disease**. Their parents are not bad people; they have a disease and may show inappropriate behavior when using substances.
- **The child is not the reason that the parent has an SUD.** Children do not cause the disease and cannot make their parents stop.
- **There are many children in situations like theirs**. There are millions of children whose parents have an SUD. They are not alone.
- **They can talk about the problem**. Children do not have to be scared or be ashamed to talk about their problems. There are many individuals and groups they can talk to and receive assistance.[123]

Services for children, such as those offered through the Strengthening Families Program, include problem-solving models that emphasize how to prevent the child from developing an addictive disorder later in life (with an emphasis on abstinence).

TITLE IV-E WAIVER PROJECTS TARGETING FAMILIES AFFECTED BY SUBSTANCE ABUSE

Since 1996, several States have implemented waiver demonstration projects that allow Title IV-E foster care funds to be used to pay for services for families in the child welfare system with substance abuse problems. The following describes some of these projects:

- Illinois began its demonstration project in 2000, and with a recent 5-year extension, it is scheduled to continue through 2011. Through this project, recovery coaches engage substance-affected families during the treatment process, work to remove treatment barriers, and provide ongoing support. The project emphasized treatment retention for caregivers who already had been referred to substance abuse treatment and whose children already had received out-of-home placements.

    An evaluation of the first phase of the Illinois demonstration project found that compared to parents who received standard services, the parents who worked with recovery coaches:
    - Accessed treatment more quickly
    - Experienced lower rates of subsequent maltreatment
    - Achieved family reunification faster.[124]

    The evaluation also identified barriers to reunification, including domestic violence, mental health issues, and inadequate housing. The extension addresses these co-occurring problems and broadens the geographic scope of the demonstration.
- From 1999 to 2005, New Hampshire's Project First Step placed licensed alcohol and drug abuse counselors in two district CPS offices. The counselors conducted substance abuse assessments concurrently with CPS maltreatment investigations, facilitated access to treatment and other services, assisted with case planning, and provided intensive case management services. The evaluation findings were modest, yet they showed some promising trends.[125]
- From 1996 to 2002, substance abuse specialists in Delaware were co-located in local CPS offices. The specialists accompanied CPS workers on home visits, consulted on case planning, and provided referrals to treatment and support services. Division of Family Services officials found that the addition of specialists on site was helpful to caseworkers in recognizing the signs of substance abuse, exploring addiction-associated issues with family members, and making appropriate referrals.

For additional information on the substance abuse waivers, visit http://www.acf.hhs.gov/programs/cb/programs_fund/cwwaiver/substanceabuse/index.htm.

7. CHILD PROTECTIVE SERVICES AND SUBSTANCE USE DISORDE TREATMENT PROVIDERS: SIMILARITIES AND DIFFERENCES

IN THIS SECTION

- Areas of similarity
- Areas of diff erence

Just as there often is an overlap between the clients who child protective services (CPS) and substance use disorder (SUD) treatment agencies serve, there also is common ground in the structures and the principles that guide these two systems. CPS caseworkers and SUD treatment providers should understand the similarities and the differences between the two systems so that they can offer the most comprehensive services possible to children and families. This chapter traces the areas of similarity and difference between the CPS and SUD treatment systems.

Areas of Similarity

There are many areas in which CPS and SUD treatment agencies overlap, including programmatic goals, the characteristics of the families served, management challenges, and new demands regarding outcomes.

Shared Goals

Though their primary emphases may differ, both CPS and SUD treatment agencies want family members to stop abusing substances and want children to be safe. In addition, they serve many families in common, even though they may be working with different family members. Professionals in each field should recognize that involving and providing appropriate services to the entire family is the most effective way of addressing the family's issues.

Since both systems have common goals, they also should share the responsibility for achieving them. CPS caseworkers need to know whether parents are sufficiently recovered from SUDs before recommending that their children live at home, but CPS caseworkers cannot treat SUDs. SUD treatment providers know that children provide an important incentive for parents to enter and remain in treatment, but SUD treatment providers cannot make decisions regarding where children will live. When each agency only emphasizes its own particular objective, it is unlikely that either will succeed. When both focus on the broader goals of helping the entire family, despite pressures and forces that make that focus difficult, the odds are better that the agencies and the families will succeed.

Shared Characteristics of Families Served

As discussed earlier, individuals with SUDs and parents who maltreat their children often have many other problems (e.g., mental illness, health issues, histories of domestic violence, poverty). They require services that are beyond the scope of either CPS or SUD treatment agencies. Many of these problems overlap, so both CPS and SUD treatment agencies find themselves trying to address problems, such as a serious mental disorder, criminal records, HIV/AIDS, and limited job skills. Too often, each agency tries to tackle these varied problems on its own, overlooking opportunities to share this enormous responsibility with others.

Shared Management and Operational Challenges

CPS and SUD treatment program administrators and staff often face similar challenges in managing their agencies and operating their programs. These challenges may be external, such as locating services that families need, coordinating with agencies that provide those services, navigating complex bureaucracies, and responding to political opinions or media coverage that portray families as unworthy of support. Other challenges are internal, such as difficulties in hiring and training staff, high staffturnover and burnout, low pay, and outdated computer record- keeping systems.

To the extent that administrators and staffcan design strategies that build on their common management challenges, they may ease some of these burdens. For example, both CPS and SUD treatment managers spend time locating and coordinating services, such as housing or mental health counseling, frequently for the same families. Time could be saved, and possibly outcomes improved, if managers collaborated in securing these services. In addition, managers could design joint training programs for stafffrom both agencies and seek continuing education units for staffwho participate.

Shared Pressures to Attain Measurable Outcomes

Federal legislation requires both CPS and SUD treatment agencies to achieve measurable results, such as employment for adults and permanency decisions for children. Therefore, managers from both systems are required to design and to monitor their programs to attain those results. This means that managers in both systems have to:

- Establish clear goals for staff
- Create internal monitoring and progress review systems
- Identify problems early and resolve them quickly.

CPS and SUD treatment program managers can share ideas for establishing processes that lead to measurable results. They also can collaborate in designing monitoring and tracking systems in a way that provides useful information between their agencies as well as with in them.

Areas of Difference

Notwith standing these similarities, CPS and SUD treatment agencies may become confused or frustrated when trying to work together, even when they share overarching goals. The two systems diff er in some fundamental ways, including how families enter programs, the choices available to families while they are participating, and the consequences for families if they cannot meet the standards required for completion. These different contexts lead to different experiences for families involved with each system. Likewise, staffin each system face disparate experiences and challenges.

Parents can be angry or frightened when CPS caseworkers come to their homes and question their children and neighbors, especially when caseworkers determine that their children have to be removed. When families come to the attention of CPS agencies, they often become involved with the courts, SUD treatment agencies, and other service providers. If they refuse to comply with the requirements established by these agencies, or if they cannot make adequate progress, they know they risk losing their children permanently.

In contrast, people generally enter SUD treatment voluntarily when they decide they are ready, and they leave when they want, even if they still are using substances. At times, however, courts order treatment as a condition of probation or parole. Coercive treatment has increased over the past several years, in part due to the increase in the use of drug courts, which are special courts designed for arrestees who have SUDs.

CPS and SUD treatment agencies also differ in the following ways:

- The primary focus of CPS is on the safety and well-being of children, and the primary focus of SUD treatment is on adult recovery. Staff of the two systems may see themselves as serving different clients, even if the clients are from the same family.
- The two systems operate under different laws and regulations.
- Funding for the two systems comes from different sources and with different conditions, even while often serving the same family.
- CPS caseworkers and SUD treatment providers may have different training, professional backgrounds and credentials, and disciplines. They also commonly use different terms and have different definitions of certain terms. For example, CPS caseworkers usually do not differentiate between substance use, abuse, or addiction. Caseworkers generally only want to know if the substance use affects an individual's ability to parent.
- Data collection requirements, computer systems, and management reporting requirements are often inconsistent or incompatible between the two systems.

Both systems operate with in strict confidentiality guidelines and staff can be uncomfortable sharing information with each other, which can cause frustration. (See Chapter 8, *Putting It Together: Making the Systems Work for Families*, for a more detailed discussion of confidentiality issues.)

8. PUTTING IT TOGETHER: MAKING THE SYSTEMS WORK FOR FAMILIES

IN THIS SECTION

- Principles to guide collaboration
- Collaboration at all levels
- Techniques for promoting collaboration
- Confidentiality and information sharing

While many child protective services (CPS) and substance use disorder (SUD) treatment agencies find collaboration challenging, it is crucial to achieving positive outcomes for families involved with both systems. This chapter presents principles to guide CPS agencies in forming collaborative relationships with SUD treatment and other agencies. It proposes techniques to improve collaboration at both the policy and the frontline levels. This chapter also discusses confidentiality issues, which often determine what types of information can be shared during the collaborative process.

Setting the Stage: Principles to Guide Collaboration

As discussed earlier, CPS and SUD treatment agencies often have different structures, funding streams, and definitions of success. These diff erences affect collaboration at the Federal level as well as at the administrative and frontline levels in States and counties.

Families whose members have SUDs and who are involved with the child welfare system have multiple and complex needs as well as strengths. Their needs often span many social service disciplines. No single person, agency, or profession has the capacity to address all of their circumstances. Collaboration builds on the individual strengths of each agency and family member, forging shared approaches that are more effective than an individual response.

Collaboration is grounded in interdependent relationships and is more important when the problems are complex, the needs are varied, and the systems are different. In order to be effective, collaborative relationships should include the following:

- **Trust** that enables individuals to share information, to speak honestly with each other, and to respect other points of view
- **Shared values** that are honored by all participants
- **A focus on common goals** in spite of the fact that participants come from agencies that have different missions, philosophies, or perceptions
- **A common language** that all participants can understand and that is not unnecessarily technical or filled with acronyms
- **Respect** for the knowledge and experience that each participant and each profession brings to the relationship, which includes recognizing the strengths, needs, and limitations of all participants
- **A collective commitment** to working through conflict that encourages participation by all group members
- **A desire to share decision-making, risk taking, and accountability** that supports group members in participating in important decisions and assuming responsibility for the outcome of group decisions.[126]

One of the biggest challenges facing both CPS caseworkers and SUD treatment providers is securing services from other social service agencies with whom relationships may not exist. For example, families involved with either CPS or SUD treatment agencies most likely will need some combination of the following services: mental health, domestic violence, income support, housing, transportation, health care, child care, and early childhood education. While collaboration with all these service providers is important, the need for mental health, domestic violence, and income support services among families receiving child welfare services and affected by substance abuse is especially critical and warrants special attention.

CPS, SUDs, AND COURT INVOLVEMENT

The court system is a key partner of both the child welfare and the SUD treatment systems. The courts ultimately decide if a child should be removed from or returned to a home. Therefore, judges and other court staff should have a general knowledge of SUDs and child welfare issues and how those issues are relevant to each case. This requires cross-training as well as ongoing communication and collaboration among the three systems. Along with making decisions to remove from or to return a child to the home, courts also may be involved with these same families through the criminal justice system or the drug courts.

If families also are involved in the criminal justice system, caseworkers may want their case plans to require the completion of all conditions of probation or parole in order for the parents to care for their children. However, the criminal justice system and the juvenile court system may have very different goals with respect to parental SUDs, with one focusing on the prevention of further criminal behavior (an emphasis on public safety) and the other focusing on the welfare of the children in the family.

Many States and communities are utilizing drug courts, which serve as an alternative to a strictly punitive, non-treatment oriented approach. Drug courts integrate public health and public safety and make treatment a priority.[127] They use ongoing, active involvement by judges to provide structure and support, and they hold both families and agencies, such as CPS, accountable for the commitments they make. Drug courts steer individuals with SUDs who commit nonviolent crimes, such as larceny or drug dealing, to treatment instead of jail; follow sentencing guidelines that set standards to ensure equity for jail time based on the crime; and utilize community partnership programs that encourage police, probation and parole officers, treatment providers, and citizens to work together to create healthy and safe environments that benefit everyone. Additionally, drug courts:

- Assess the substance user's needs
- Create an effective, mandated treatment plan
- Provide the necessary follow-up to assist with the treatment process.

Accountability for the participant attending treatment rests with the drug court. In one study, more than two-thirds of participants mandated by drug courts to attend treatment completed it, which is a completion rate six times greater than most previous efforts.[128]

Drug courts are becoming an increasingly popular alternative for responding to methamphetamine use. The ability to respond quickly and consistently to violations of the treatment plan, coupled with the accountability measures and the ever-present threat of going to jail due to a violation, make drug courts one of the most effective mechanisms for dealing with methamphetamine use.[129] For additional information on drug courts and methamphetamine use, visit **http://www.ojp.usdoj.gov/BJA/pdf/ MethDrugCourts.pdf**.

Family Treatment Drug Courts (FTDCs) are specialized drug courts designed to work with parents with SUDs who are involved in the child welfare system. A national evaluation found that FTDCs were more successful than traditional child welfare case processing in helping substance-abusing parents enter and complete treatment and reunite with their children.[130]

For more information on drug courts in general, refer to the National Drug Court Institute/National Association of Drug Court Professionals website at **http://www.ndci.org** and the Office of Justice Programs Drug Court Clearinghouse and Technical Assistance Project publication, *Juvenile and Family Drug Courts: An Overview*, available at **http://www.ncjrs.org/html/bja/jfdcoview/welcome.html**.

For more information on the courts and CPS, refer to the *User Manual Series* publication, *Working with the Courts in Child Protection*, at **http://www.childwelfare.gov/pubs/usermanuals/courts/**.

In many States, CPS and social welfare are housed with in one umbrella social services agency. While this configuration does not guarantee that collaboration will occur, it eliminates some of the structural problems often encountered when agencies do not share a common organizational context.

Collaboration at All Levels

Collaboration among agency officials at the highest levels is a necessary, but not always sufficient, condition for collaboration on the frontline. Suggestions for fostering collaboration are discussed below.

Collaboration at the State Level
There are several steps that State CPS and other officials can take to promote collaboration among their agencies:

- **Establish ongoing interagency task forces and authorize members to make decisions**. The task forces should be charged with addressing issues that make it difficult for staff to coordinate services. Topics might include designing integrated screening or assessment instruments, developing mechanisms to track participants across different agencies, or proposing methods for staff to share information under the rules of confidentiality.
- **Create joint mission statements** with SUD treatment and other agencies and promote the mission statement through notices, memos, or policy directives that are signed by officials from each agency.
- **Prepare integrated funding requests** to support integrated programming activities. Develop and execute shared advocacy strategies for securing those funds.
- **Require cross-training of staff** and schedule staff from other systems to deliver that training. Hold these training sessions at other agencies.
- **Co-locate staff** in each other's agency.
- **Create interagency agreements** such as Memorandums of Understanding (MOUs). For more information about MOUs, see Appendix H, *Memorandums of Understanding*.

Collaboration on the Frontline
There are several steps that frontline staff and supervisors can take to promote collaboration among their agencies:

- **Visit each other's programs**, talk to program participants, and meet each other's staff. CPS caseworkers should visit SUD treatment programs, observe activities, and hear from families who are in recovery. Similarly, SUD treatment professionals should visit CPS offices and accompany caseworkers on some home or field visits.
- **Convene multidisciplinary case staffings**, some of which should include family members. During these meetings, caseworkers and families should develop shared plans for services, allocate tasks, and discuss ways they can share responsibility for activities and outcomes.
- **Discuss diff erences** in a way that helps everyone understand each other's point of view, the rules, each one's limitations, and the scope of authority.

Techniques for Promoting Collaboration

Collaboration is not likely to occur unless stafffrom participating agencies have opportunities to understand their partners and to work together to solve shared problems. SUDs and child maltreatment are complicated issues; staffwho work in one field generally know little about the other field. In addition, both SUDs and maltreatment are clouded by sensational media stories, shame, and stigma, making it especially important that frontline practitioners have access to accurate information. Information sharing, professional development and training, and co-location are examples of techniques that can promote collaboration.

Information Sharing

The easiest way for CPS caseworkers and SUD treatment providers to collaborate is to share information. Information sharing between colleagues can range from general information about each system (e.g., agency protocols) to case-specific information (e.g., a permanency plan or strategy for handling a parent's possible relapse). CPS caseworkers should be knowledgeable, however, of any confidentiality laws that restrict what information they are allowed to share. Confidentiality issues are discussed later in this chapter.

Professional Development and Cross-training

Professional development provides structured learning experiences that go beyond teaching about new rules or forms. Professional development allows caseworkers to understand their discipline better, to advance their careers, and to feel part of an important human services system. Cross-training means teaching workers from one field, such as CPS, about the fundamental concepts and practices of another field, such as SUD treatment.

CPS agencies can design professional development and cross-training programs in ways that mirror the interagency relationships they want to develop— relationships in which individuals are encouraged to explore and to discuss values, ideas, and policies.

Co-location

Some CPS agencies have SUD treatment providers on site. Co-location demonstrates that agency officials consider cooperation and collaboration to be agency. Priorities and integral elements of agency culture. If senior officials decide to co-locate staff, they are more likely to realize that collaboration is an expected method of conducting business, not merely an agency buzzword.

ONLINE TUTORIALS FOR KNOWLEDGE-BUILDING AND CROSS-SYSTEMS WORK

The National Center on Substance Abuse and Child Welfare, an initiative of the Administration for Children and Families and the Substance Abuse and Mental Health Services Administration, has developed four free online self-tutorials to build knowledge about SUDs and child welfare and to support and facilitate cross-systems work. The tutorials are each intended for a specific audience: child welfare professionals, substance abuse treatment professionals, judicial officers and attorneys in the dependency system, and legislators. A certificate for claiming Continuing Education Units is available upon successful completion of each tutorial. The tutorials are available at **http://www. ncsacw.samhsa.gov/ tutorials/ index.asp**.

For more information on training resources, visit **http://www.childwelfare. gov/ systemwide/training/**.

Co-location can be highly effective in helping CPS caseworkers and SUD treatment providers develop relationships that are essential to delivering comprehensive and well-organized services. It can change what are often a series of sequential referrals into concurrent discussions (case staffings) that bring greater expertise to case planning. Caseworker stress and burnout can be reduced if several people participate in making difficult and sensitive decisions regarding child placement. Co-location also may make it easier for family members to participate in designing their service plan, to comply with requirements that come from both treatment and CPS agencies, and to understand the roles that different caseworkers perform in helping them succeed.

Co-location, however, is not a perfect solution. It does not automatically create relationships or guarantee collaboration. Co-location can introduce management challenges related to supervision, space, pay differences, performance requirements, or work expectations. Furthermore, it can be administratively complex and, at times, programmatically inappropriate when too many people are involved with one family. When this happens, families may feel overburdened, they may worry that their confidences have been violated, or they may think that decisions are being made with out their involvement.

Confidentiality and Information Sharing

As CPS and SUD treatment agencies work more closely, they are faced with deciding how and when to share information about families. Both agencies recognize the importance of allowing families to have privacy to discuss and to address such difficult, sensitive problems as SUDs and child maltreatment. Both also must adhere to a variety of laws and regulations that govern disclosure of information and protect family privacy.

At times, staff with in each agency may feel that laws regarding confidentiality make it difficult to share or to receive information, and confidentiality rules may be put forth as a reason for their inability to communicate. For example, a CPS caseworker may become frustrated if an SUD treatment provider cannot share information regarding a parent's progress in treatment; the caseworker may feel that this information might inform child custody decisions. On the other hand, an SUD treatment provider may become frustrated when decisions regarding a child's placement are made with out a CPS caseworker discussing how it may affect the parent's progress in treatment. However, a study of seven innovative CPS agencies and SUD treatment programs noted that while Federal and some State laws are obstacles to information exchange, these laws did not create insurmountable barriers to collaboration.[131] This section discusses confidentiality laws and ways to share information appropriately.

Confidentiality Laws

Laws addressing various aspects of confidentiality involving professional relationships, communications, and situations vary. These laws may focus on:

- SUD treatment privacy requirements
- Mandated reporting of child abuse and neglect
- Privacy of CPS records
- Client-therapist confidentiality statutes
- Research programs and data collection on human subjects.[132]

SUD treatment confidentiality laws are based on the view that individuals with SUDs are more likely to seek treatment if they know that information about them will not be disclosed unnecessarily to others. With out the assurance of privacy, the fear of public disclosure of their problem possibly could prevent some individuals from obtaining needed treatment.

At times, however, there are important reasons for agencies to share information when working with the same families. Federal SUD treatment regulations specify circumstances under which it is appropriate that information be shared, including if the information relates to reports of child abuse or neglect.

See Appendix I, *Confidentiality and the Release of Substance Use Disorder Treatment Information*, for a list of circumstances in which patient record information can be released. Additionally, the Child Abuse Prevention and Treatment Act of 1974 (P.L. 93–247) requires that States allow for the public disclosure of information regarding a death, or near death, of a child when it is the result of maltreatment.

SUD treatment providers are subject to mandatory child abuse reporting laws in their States, requiring treatment staff to report incidents of suspected child abuse and neglect. However, this exemption from standard confidentiality requirements applies only to initial reports of child abuse or neglect. It does not apply to requests or even subpoenas for additional information or records, even if the records are sought for use in civil or criminal investigations. Thus, patient files and patient-identifying information protected by the Federal confidentiality law still must be with held from CPS agencies and the court unless there is some other authorization such as patient consent, an appropriate court order, or in some cases, a Qualified Service Organization Agreement (QSOA). Consent forms and QSOAs are discussed later in this chapter.

Key considerations related to the types of information that can be shared between CPS caseworkers and SUD treatment providers include:

- **CPS case information**. Factors surrounding the case, any previous case history, the family environment, and other factors that are informative to the SUD treatment provider in conducting the assessment and in developing the treatment plan. CPS caseworkers must obtain appropriate consent to share this information.
- **SUD screening information**. Federal law and regulations allow CPS caseworkers to share with SUD treatment personnel information gathered during a screening for the purpose of referring an individual for an assessment.
- **SUD diagnosis and treatment information**. An SUD treatment agency may not disclose this information with out written consent or court order. This is true even if the CPS agency referred the family member to the treatment program and mandated the assessment. For an example of a consent form, see Appendix J, *Sample Qualified Service Organization Agreement and Consent Form*.
- **Attendance in treatment programs**. SUD treatment programs may report a family member's attendance at treatment, or their failure to attend, as long as the patient has signed a written consent that has not expired or been revoked. Attendance is often a key component of the family's case plan.
- **A treatment participant's relapse.** SUD treatment programs may report information about relapse to CPS caseworkers if that information is covered by a valid written consent signed by the patient. However, for many CPS agencies, the key information may be whether the family member is making satisfactory progress in treatment, even if relapse has occurred.
- **Combined case plan**. Most of the discussion between SUD treatment providers and CPS caseworkers will be permissible as long as the information discussed is covered by a valid written consent form. It is advisable to tell family members that their case will be discussed at periodic meetings or telephone calls and specifically who will participate in the discussions.

SUBPOENAS

A subpoena to testify in court is not sufficient to require the release of confidential information, as specified under Federal regulations related to confidentiality, nor is a police search warrant. If subpoenaed to court to testify, an SUD treatment provider should first refuse, citing Federal regulations related to confidentiality. Only with a judge's subsequent court order that finds a just cause to ignore this law in this particular case may a counselor testify with out a client's written consent.

If CPS caseworkers release the results of a substance abuse evaluation or any information regarding a client's treatment, they violate Federal regulations related to confidentiality. Everyone, not just SUD treatment providers, is bound by Federal confidentiality statutes, and CPS caseworkers can be prosecuted for violating these laws. Caseworkers should clarify with their supervisor or their agency's attorney any questions they may have about this statute and should document any legal advice given that pertains to this statute.

Ways to Share Information Appropriately

In order for the CPS caseworker and SUD treatment provider to communicate, it is important to obtain the client's consent early, preferably at the time of the referral to treatment. Clients involved with CPS agencies may consent voluntarily to information disclosures in order to aid investigations of child maltreatment because their refusal to cooperate may result in losing custody of their children. However, information that has been disclosed through consent may not be used in criminal investigations or to prosecute the person. A consent form is only valid until the date, event, or condition on which it expires, or at any time when the treatment participant or client revokes consent. Therefore, it is a good idea to set the expiration date far enough into the future to ensure that needed information can be retrieved by the other agency. It is permissible to have the consent form contain an end date that fits circumstances.[133] (See Appendix I, *Confidentiality and the Release of Substance Use Disorder Treatment Information*, for details about what should be included in a voluntary consent form.)

Another way that information can be shared between systems is through a QSOA. SUD treatment providers may disclose information under a QSOA with out the patient's consent. A QSOA is an agreement between two service organizations to share information about and to protect the confidentiality of individuals they serve. A QSOA should not be confused with an MOU, which usually is an agreement between two or more organizations to provide services to a common set of clients.

A qualified service organization is one that provides services to the SUD treatment program. CPS agencies meet this definition if they provide services that help the SUD treatment agency serve the client. The heads of both the SUD treatment agency and the CPS agency must sign this agreement. Once signed, QSOAs permit disclosure of information to enable the organization to provide a service to the alcohol and drug abuse treatment program. QSOAs cannot be used for other purposes, such as obtaining reimbursement. Information obtained as part of a QSOA may not be re-disclosed to any other agency with out permission.[134] See Appendix J, *Sample Qualified Service Organization Agreement and Consent Form*, for a sample QSOA form.

Confidentiality is an important part of communication. The parameters and limitations of communication have to be established locally. Furthermore, administrative procedures need to be put in place to encourage communication among staff. When approached with care, confidentiality rules do not automatically limit communication. Rather, they set the context with in which staffcan share important information, and families can be assured that sensitive aspects of their lives will be protected.

It is important to note, however, that regardless of privacy rules and confidentiality of information under Federal laws, mandatory reporters of child abuse and neglect are required to report suspected cases of child maltreatment, according to an Information Memorandum issued by the U.S. Department of Health and Human Services in September 2005. The memorandum "to affirm the obligation of mandatory reporters to report child abuse and neglect under State and Federal laws" refers specifically to exceptions to the confidentiality and privacy rules in the Health Insurance Portability and Accountability Act (HIPAA), the

Public Health Service Act Title X family planning program, and the confidentiality rules relating to patient records in federally funded alcohol and drug abuse treatment services.[135]

FEDERAL GUIDELINES REGARDING CONFIDENTIALITY

The following are examples of Federal guidelines for patient confidentiality in cases involving SUDs or child maltreatment:

- **The Code of Federal Regulation, Alcohol and Drug Abuse Treatment Confidentiality , 42 C.F.R., Part II**, provides guidelines for maintaining patient confidentiality, including rules for information sharing, for SUD treatment agencies. They can be viewed at **http://www.access**
- **The Child Abuse and Neglect Prevention and Treatment Act (CAPTA), 45 C.F.R. 1340.14** , requires States to have guidelines for maintaining confidentiality of child abuse and neglect reports. It can be viewed at **http://www.access. html**.
- **HIPAA of 1996 (P.L. 104–191)** provides standards for health plans, health care providers, and health care clearinghouses to ensure the security and privacy of health information, including access to records. HIPAA also upholds mandatory child abuse reporting laws. For more information on HIPAA and its relationship to SUD treatment, visit the Substance Abuse and Mental Health Services Administration website at **http://www.hipaa.samhsa.gov/hipaa.html**.

For more information on child maltreatment legal issues and laws, visit **http://www.childwelfare.gov/ systemwide/laws_policies/**.

CONCLUSION

For staff in any agency, it is easy to lose sight of the other systems and agencies that share a common client base. Families that experience SUDs and child maltreatment have needs, problems, and strengths that are diverse and complex. As a result, they often require the services of multiple agencies. It is critical that CPS caseworkers and SUD treatment providers have an understanding of the other system as well as the skills and desire to work toward a common goal. It is equally important that families are consulted in order to make certain that the collaborative structure helps them to address their SUDs and to ensure the safety and well-being of their children. With all of the parties committed to working jointly toward the same goals and being open to innovative approaches, successful outcomes can be achieved.

APPENDIX A. GLOSSARY OF TERMS

Addiction – the overpowering physical or psychological urge to continue alcohol or drug use in spite of adverse consequences. Often, there is an increase in tolerance for the drug and with drawal symptoms sometimes occur if the drug is discontinued.

Adjudicatory Hearings – held by the juvenile and family court to determine whether a child has been maltreated or whether another legal basis exists for the State to intervene to protect the child.

Adoption and Safe Families Act – signed into law November 1997 and designed to improve the safety of children, to promote adoption and other permanent homes for children who need them, and to support families. The law requires child protective services (CPS) agencies to provide more timely and focused assessment and intervention services to the children and families who are served with in the CPS system.

Alcoholism – a dependency on alcohol characterized by craving and loss of control over its consumption, physical dependence and with drawal symptoms, and tolerance.

AOD – alcohol and other drugs.

Assessment – evaluation or appraisal of a candidate's suitability for substance use disorder (SUD) treatment and placement in a specific treatment modality or setting. This evaluation includes information regarding current and past SUDs; justice system involvement; medical, familial, social, education, military, employment, and treatment histories; and risk for infectious diseases (e.g., sexually transmitted diseases, tuberculosis, HIV/AIDS, and hepatitis).

CASA – court-appointed special advocates (usually volunteers) who serve to ensure that the needs and interests of a child in judicial proceedings are fully protected.

Case Closure – the process of ending the relationship between the CPS worker and the family that often involves a mutual assessment of progress. Optimally, cases are closed when families have achieved their goals and the risk of maltreatment has been reduced or eliminated.

Case Plan – the casework document that outlines the outcomes, goals, and tasks necessary to be achieved in order to reduce the risk of maltreatment.

Caseworker Competency – demonstrated professional behaviors based on the knowledge, skills, personal qualities, and values a person holds.

Central Registry – a centralized database containing information on all substantiated/founded reports of child maltreatment in a selected area (typically a State).

Child Abuse Prevention and Treatment Act (CAPTA) – see Keeping Children and Families Safe Act.

Child Protective Services (CPS) – the designated social services agency (in most States) to receive reports, investigate, and provide intervention and treatment services to children and families in which child maltreatment has occurred. Frequently, this agency is located with in larger public agencies, such as departments of social services.

Cognitive Behavioral Therapy – a school of psychotherapy that originated in the United States and subscribes to a behavioral emphasis on stimulus- response relationships and psychological learning theory.

Concurrent Planning – identifies alternative forms of permanency by addressing simultaneously both reunification and legal permanency with a new parent or caregiver, should reunification efforts fail.

Craving – a powerful, often uncontrollable, desire for drugs, alcohol, or other substances.

Cultural Competence – a set of attitudes, behaviors, and policies that integrates knowledge about groups of people into practices and standards to enhance the quality of services to all cultural groups served.

Denial – a psychological defense mechanism disavowing the significance of events. Denial also can include a range of psychological maneuvers designed to reduce awareness of the fact that using a substance (or engaging in a behavior) is the cause of an individual's problems rather than a solution to those problems. Denial can be a major obstacle to recovery.

Detoxification – process in a structured medical or social milieu in which the individual is monitored for with drawal from the acute physical and psychological effects of drug or alcohol addiction.

Differential Response – an area of CPS reform that offers greater flexibility in responding to allegations of abuse and neglect. Also referred to as "dual track" or "multi-track" response, it permits CPS agencies to respond differentially to children's needs for safety, the degree of risk present, and the family's needs for services and support. See "dual track."

Disclosure – a communication of client- or patient- identifying information or the communication of information from the record of a client or patient who has been identified.

Dispositional Hearings – held by the juvenile and family court to determine the disposition of children after cases have been adjudicated, such as whether placement of the child in out-of-home care is necessary and the services the children and family will need to reduce the risk of maltreatment and to address its effects.

Drug – a substance that, by its chemical nature, affects the structure or function of a living organism.

Dual Diagnosis (also Dual Disorder) – a term used to describe a condition in which a single person has more than one major clinical psychological or psychiatric diagnosis. Often, this phrase is used to describe people who have a severe mental illness as well as a co-existing SUD.

Dual Track – term reflecting new CPS response systems that typically combine a nonadversarial service-based assessment track for cases in which children are not at immediate risk with a traditional CPS investigative track for cases where children are unsafe or at greater risk for maltreatment. See "diff erential response."

Evaluation of Family Progress – the stage of the CPS case process during which the CPS caseworker measures changes in family behaviors and conditions (risk factors), monitors risk elimination or reduction, assesses strengths, and determines case closure.

Family Assessment – the stage of the child protection process during which the CPS caseworker, community treatment provider, and the family reach a mutual understanding regarding the behaviors and conditions that must change to reduce or eliminate the risk of maltreatment, the most critical treatment needs that must be addressed, and the strengths on which to build.

Family Group Conferencing – a family meeting model used by CPS agencies to optimize family strengths in the planning process. This model brings the family, extended family, and others important in the family's life (e.g., friends, clergy, neighbors) together to make decisions regarding how best to ensure the safety of the family members.

Family Unity Model – a family meeting model used by CPS agencies to optimize family strengths in the planning process. This model is similar to the Family Group Conferencing model.

Full Disclosure – CPS information to the family regarding the steps in the intervention process, the requirements of CPS, the expectations for the family, the consequences if the family does not fulfill the expectations, and the rights of the parents to ensure that the family completely understands the process.

Guardian ad Litem – a lawyer or lay person who represents a child in juvenile or family court. Usually this person considers the best interest of the child and may perform a variety of roles, including those of independent investigator, advocate, advisor, and guardian for the child. A lay person who serves in this role is sometimes known as a court-appointed special advocate or CASA.

Habituation – the result of repeated consumption of a drug that produces psychological, but not physical, dependence. The psychological dependence produces a desire (not a compulsion) to continue taking drugs for the sense of improved well-being.

Home Visitation Programs – prevention programs that offer a variety of family-focused services to pregnant women and families with new babies. Activities frequently encompass structured visits to the family's home and may address positive parenting practices, nonviolent discipline techniques, child development, maternal and child health, available services, and advocacy.

Immunity – established in all child abuse laws to protect reporters from civil law suits and criminal prosecution resulting from filing a report of child abuse and neglect.

Initial Assessment or Investigation – the stage of the CPS case process during which the CPS caseworker determines the validity of the child maltreatment report, assesses the risk of maltreatment, determines if the child is safe, develops a safety plan if needed to ensure the child's protection, and determines services needed.

Intake – the stage of the CPS case process in which the CPS caseworker screens and accepts reports of child maltreatment.

Interview Protocol – a structured format to ensure that all family members are seen in a planned strategy, that community providers collaborate, and that information gathering is thorough.

Involuntary Commitment – process by which patients who have not committed any crime are brought to SUD treatment against their wishes by relatives, police, or through a court proceeding. Also known as "protective custody" or "emergency commitment."

Juvenile and Family Courts – established in most States to resolve conflict and to otherwise intervene in the lives of families in a manner that promotes the best interest of children. These courts specialize in areas such as child maltreatment, domestic violence, juvenile delinquency, divorce, child custody, and child support.

Keeping Children and Families Safe Act – The Keeping Children and Families Safe Act of 2003 (P.L. 108-36) included the reauthorization of CAPTA in its Title I, Sec. 111. CAPTA provides minimum standards for defining child physical abuse and neglect and sexual abuse that States must incorporate into their statutory definitions in order to receive Federal funds. CAPTA defines child abuse and neglect as "at a minimum, any recent act or failure to act on the part of a parent or caretaker, which results in death, serious physical or emotional harm, sexual abuse or exploitation, or an act or failure to act which presents an imminent risk of serious harm."

Kinship Care – formal child placement by the juvenile court and child welfare agency in the home of a child's relative.

Liaison – a person with in an organization who has responsibility for facilitating communication, collaboration, and coordination between agencies involved in the child protection system.

Mandated Reporter – individuals required by State statutes to report suspected child abuse and neglect to the proper authorities (usually CPS or law enforcement agencies).

Mandated reporters typically include professionals, such as educators and other school personnel, health care and mental health professionals, social workers, child care providers, and law enforcement officers. Some States identify all citizens as mandated reporters.

Memorandum of Understanding – an agreement between two or more organizations to define a given relationship and each party's responsibilities with in the agreement.

Multidisciplinary Team – established between agencies and professionals with in the child protection system to discuss cases of child abuse and neglect and to aid in decisions at various stages of the CPS case process. These teams also may be designated by different names, including child protection teams, interdisciplinary teams, or case consultation teams.

Neglect – the failure to provide for a child's basic needs. Neglect can be physical, educational, or emotional. *Physical neglect* can include not providing adequate food or clothing, appropriate medical care, supervision, or proper weather protection (heat or coats). *Educational neglect* includes failure to provide appropriate schooling, failure to address special educational needs, or allowing excessive truancies. *Psychological neglect* includes the lack of any emotional support and love, chronic inattention to the child, or exposure to spouse, drug, or alcohol abuse.

Neurotransmitters – a group of chemicals in the brain that transmit nerve impulses from one neuron to another across a space called a synapse. Drugs act on the brain at the neurotransmitter level. The presence of a drug in the brain changes how many neurotransmitters are available to send nerve impulses from one neuron to the next. The level or amount of a drug in the brain affects how well diff erent kinds of chemical signals are transmitted, changing how an individual thinks and feels.

Out-of-home Care – child care, foster care, or residential care provided by persons, organizations, and institutions to children who are placed outside their families, usually under the jurisdiction of juvenile or family court.

***Parens Patriae* Doctrine** – originating in feudal England, a doctrine that vests in the State a right of guardianship of minors. This concept gradually has evolved into the principle that the community, in addition to the parent, has a strong interest in the care and nurturing of children. Schools, juvenile courts, and social service agencies all derive their authority from the State's power to ensure the protection and rights of children as a unique class.

Parent or Caretaker – person responsible for the care of the child.

Patient Placement Criteria – standards of, or guidelines for, SUD treatment that describe specific conditions under which patients should be admitted to a particular level of care, under which they should continue to remain in that level of care, and under which they should be discharged or transferred to another level. They generally describe the settings, staff, and services appropriate to each level of care and establish guidelines based on diagnosis and other specific areas of patient assessment.

Physical Abuse – the inflicting of a nonaccidental physical injury. This may include burning, hitting, punching, shaking, kicking, beating, or otherwise harming a child. It may, however, have been the result of over-discipline or physical punishment that is inappropriate to the child's age.

Prevention – the theory and means for reducing the harmful effects of drug use in specific populations. Prevention objectives are to protect individuals before signs or symptoms of substance use problems appear, to identify persons in the early stages of substance abuse and intervene, and to end compulsive use of psychoactive substances through treatment.

Primary Prevention – activities geared to a sample of the general population to prevent child abuse and neglect from occurring. Also referred to as "universal prevention."

Protective Factors – strengths and resources that appear to mediate or serve as a buffer against risk factors that contribute to vulnerability to maltreatment or against the negative effects of maltreatment experiences.

Protocol – an interagency agreement that delineates joint roles and responsibilities by establishing criteria and procedures for working together on cases of child abuse and neglect.

Psychological Maltreatment – a pattern of caregiver behavior or extreme incidents that convey to children that they are worthless, flawed, unloved, unwanted, endangered, or only of value to meeting another's needs. This can include parents or caretakers using extreme or bizarre forms of punishment or threatening or terrorizing a child. Psychological maltreatment also is known as emotional abuse or neglect, verbal abuse, or mental abuse.

Recovery – achieving and sustaining a state of healThin which the individual no longer engages in problematic behavior or psychoactive substance use and is able to establish and accomplish goals.

Relapse – the return to the pattern of substance abuse or addiction, as well as the process during which indicators appear before the client's resumption of substance use.

Response Time – a determination made by CPS and law enforcement regarding the immediacy of the response needed to a report of child abuse or neglect.

Review Hearings – held by the juvenile and family court to review dispositions (usually every 6 months) and to determine the need to maintain placement in out-of-home care or court jurisdiction of a child.

Risk – the likelihood that a child will be maltreated in the future.

Risk Assessment – the measurement of the likelihood that a child will be maltreated in the future; frequently carried out through the use of checklists, matrices, scales, and other methods.

Risk Factors – behaviors and conditions present in the child, parent, or family that likely will contribute to child maltreatment occurring in the future.

Safety – absence of an imminent or immediate threat of moderate to serious harm to the child.

Safety Assessment – a part of the CPS case process in which available information is analyzed to identify whether a child is in immediate danger of moderate or serious harm.

Safety Plan – a casework document developed when it is determined that the child is in imminent or potential risk of serious harm. In the safety plan, the caseworker targets the factors that are causing or contributing to the risk of imminent serious harm to the child, and identifies, along with the family, the interventions that will control them and ensure the child's protection.

Secondary Prevention – activities targeted to prevent breakdowns and dysfunctions among families who have been identified as being at risk for abuse and neglect.

Service Agreement – the casework document developed between the CPS caseworker and the family, which outlines the tasks necessary to achieve risk reduction goals and outcomes.

Service Provision – the stage of the CPS casework process during which CPS and other service providers off er specific services to reduce the risk of maltreatment.

Sexual Abuse – inappropriate adolescent or adult sexual behavior with a child. It includes fondling a child's genitals, making the child fondle the adult's genitals, intercourse, incest, rape, sodomy, exhibitionism, sexual exploitation, or exposure to pornography. To be considered child abuse, these acts have to be committed by a person responsible for the care of a child (for example a babysitter, a parent, or a day care provider) or related to the child. If a stranger commits these acts, it would be considered sexual assault and handled solely by the police and criminal courts.

Substance Abuse – a pattern of substance use resulting in clinically significant physical, mental, emotional, or social impairment or distress, such as failure to fulfill major role responsibilities, or use in spite of physical hazards, legal problems, or interpersonal and social problems.

Substance Dependence – see "addiction."

Substance Use – consumption of low or infrequent doses of alcohol and other drugs, sometimes called experimental, casual, or social use, such that damaging consequences may be rare or minor.

Substance Use Disorder (SUD) – a medical condition that includes the abuse of or addiction to (or dependence on) alcohol or drugs.

Substantiated – an investigation disposition concluding that the allegation of maltreatment or risk of maltreatment was supported or founded by State law or State policy. A CPS determination means that credible evidence exists that child abuse or neglect has occurred.

System of Care – a comprehensive continuum of child welfare, SUD, and other support services coordinated to meet the multiple, evolving needs of clients.

Tertiary Prevention – treatment efforts geared to address situations in which child maltreatment already has occurred, with the goals of preventing child maltreatment from occurring in the future and of avoiding the harmful effects of child maltreatment.

Tolerance – a state in which the body's tissue cells adjust to the presence of a drug in given amounts and eventually fail to respond to ordinarily effective dosages. Consequently, increasingly larger doses are necessary to produce desired effects.

Treatment – the stage of the child protection case process during which specific services are delivered by CPS and other providers to reduce the risk of maltreatment, support families in meeting case goals, and address the effects of maltreatment.

Universal Prevention – activities and services directed toward the general public with the goal of stopping maltreatment before it starts. Also referred to as "primary prevention."

Unsubstantiated (also Not Substantiated) – an investigation disposition that determines that there is not sufficient evidence under State law or policy to conclude that the child has been maltreated or is at risk of maltreatment. A CPS determination means that credible evidence does not exist that child abuse or neglect has occurred.

Withdrawal – symptoms that appear during the process of stopping the use of a drug that has been taken regularly.

APPENDIX B. RESOURCE LISTINGS OF SELECTED NATIONAL ORGANIZATIONS CONCERNED WITH CHILD MALTREATMENT AND/OR SUBSTANCE USE DISORDERS

The following are several representatives of the many national organizations and groups dealing with various aspects of child maltreatment and substance use disorders. Visit http://www.childwelfare.gov to view a more comprehensive list of resources and visit http://www.childwelfare.gov/organizations/index.cfm to search an organization database. Inclusion on this list is for information purposes only and does not constitute an endorsement by the Office on Child Abuse and Neglect or the Children's Bureau.

National and Federal Substance Use Disorder Organizations

Addiction Technology Transfer Centers
address: National Office
University of Missouri–Kansas City
5100 Rockhill Road
Kansas City, MO 64110-2499
phone: (816) 235-6888
fax: (816) 235-6580
email: no@nattc.org
website: http://www.nattc.org

A nationwide, multidisciplinary resource that draws upon the knowledge, experience, and latest work of recognized experts in the field of addictions.

Community Anti-Drug Coalitions of America
address: 625 Slaters Lane, Suite 300
Alexandria, VA 22314
phone: (800) 54-CADCA
fax: (703) 706-0565
email: info@cadca.org
website: http://cadca.org

Builds and strengthens the capacity of community coalitions to create safe, healthy, and drug-free communities. Supports its members with technical assistance and training, public policy, media strategies and marketing programs, conferences, and special events.

Join Together Online
address: 715 Albany Street, 580-3rd Floor
Boston, MA 02118
phone: (617) 437-1500
fax: (617) 437-9394
email: info@jointogether.org
website: http://www.jointogether.org

Supports community-based efforts across the country to reduce, prevent, and treat substance use disorders. Focuses attention on strengthening community capacity to expand the demand for and supply of high-quality substance use disorder treatment.

National Alliance for Drug Endangered Children (DEC)/National DEC Resource Center
address: 1942 Broadway, Suite 314
Boulder, CO 80302
phone: (303) 413-3064
fax: (303) 938-6850
website: http://www.nationaldec.org/

Promotes the DEC team concept and public awareness for the problems faced by DEC through multidisciplinary training for communities. It supports a nationwide network of professionals serving DEC by providing referrals to experts, updated research, and best practice information.

National Health Information Center
address: P.O. Box 1133
Washington, DC 20013-1133
phone: (301) 565-4167
(800) 336-4797
fax: (301) 984-4256
email: info@nhic.org
website: http://www.health

A health information referral service that links consumers and health professionals to organizations best able to answer their questions.

National Institutes of Health
address: 9000 Rockville Pike
Bethesda, MD 20892
phone: (301) 496-4000
email: nihinfo@od.nih.gov
website: http://www.nih.gov

Seeks to acquire knowledge to help prevent, detect, diagnose, and treat disease and disability, from the rarest genetic disorder to the common cold. Relevant institutes include the National Institute on Drug Abuse and the National Institute on Alcohol Abuse and Alcoholism.

National Organization on Fetal Alcohol Syndrome
address: 900 17th Street, NW, Suite 910
Washington, DC 20006
phone: (202) 785-4585
(800) 66-NOFAS
fax: (202) 466-6456
email: information@nofas.org
website: http://www.nofas.org

Dedicated to eliminating birth defects caused by alcohol consumption during pregnancy and improving the quality of life for those individuals and families affected by fetal alcohol syndrome.

Office of National Drug Control Policy
address: Drug Policy Information Clearinghouse
P.O. Box 6000
Rockville, MD 20849–6000

phone: (800) 666–3332
fax: (301) 519–5212
website: http://www.whitehousedrugpolicy.gov

Establishes policies, priorities, and objectives for the Nation's drug control program to reduce illicit drug use, manufacturing, and trafficking; drug-related crime and violence; and drug-related health consequences. Produces the National Drug Control Strategy, which directs the Nation's anti-drug efforts and establishes a program, a budget, and guidelines for cooperation among Federal, State, and local entities.

Substance Abuse and Mental Health Services Administration
address: 1 Choke Cherry Road
Rockville, MD 20857
phone: (240) 276-2000
fax: (240) 276-2010
website: http://www.samhsa.gov

Seeks to improve the quality and availability of prevention, treatment, and rehabilitative services in order to reduce illness, death, disability, and cost to society resulting from substance use disorders and mental illnesses.

Child Welfare Organizations

American Humane Association Children's Division
address: 63 Inverness Drive, East
Englewood, CO 80112-5117
phone: (303) 792-9900
fax: (303) 792-5333
website: www.americanhumane.org

Conducts research, analysis, and training to help public and private agencies respond to child maltreatment.

American Professional Society on the Abuse of Children
address: 350 Poplar Avenue
Elmhurst, IL 60126
phone: (630) 941-1235
(877) 402-7722
fax: (630) 359-4274
email: apsac@apsac.org
website: www.apsac.org

Provides professional education, promotes research to inform effective practice, and addresses public policy issues. Professional membership organization.

American Public Human Services Association
address: 810 First Street, NE, Suite 500
            Washington, DC 20002-4267
phone: (202) 682-0100
fax: (202) 289-6555
website: www.aphsa.org

Addresses program and policy issues related to the administration and delivery of publicly funded human services. Professional membership organization.

AVANCE Family Support and Education Program
address: 118 N. Medina
            San Antonio, TX 78207
phone: (210) 270-4630
fax: (210) 270-4612
website: www.avance.org

Operates a national training center to share and disseminate information, materials, and curricula to service providers and policymakers interested in supporting high-risk Hispanic families.

Child Welfare League of America
address: 2345 Crystal Drive, Suite 250
            Arlington, VA 22202
phone: (703) 412-2400
fax: (703) 412-2401
website: www.cwla.org

Provides training, consultation, and technical assistance to child welfare professionals and agencies, while educating the public about emerging issues affecting children.

National Black Child Development Institute
address: 1313 L Street, NW
            Suite 110
            Washington, DC 20005-4110
phone: (202) 833-2220
fax: (202) 833-8222
email: moreinfo@nbcdi.org
website: www.nbcdi.org

Operates programs and sponsors a national training conference through Howard University to improve and protect the well-being of African-American children.

National Children's Advocacy Center
address: 210 Pratt Avenue
            Huntsville, AL 35801

phone: (256) 533-KIDS
fax: (256) 534-6883
website: http://www.nationalcac.org

Provides prevention, intervention, and treatment services to physically and sexually abused children and their families with in a child-focused team approach.

National Indian Child Welfare Association
address: 5100 SW Macadam Avenue, Suite 300
Portland, OR 97239
phone: (503) 222-4044
fax: (503) 222-4007
website: www.nicwa.org

Disseminates information and provides technical assistance on Indian child welfare issues. Supports community development and advocacy efforts to facilitate Tribal responses to the needs of families and children.

National Resource Center for Child Protective Services
address: 925 #4 Sixth Street, NW
Albuquerque, NM 87102
phone: (505) 345-2444
fax: (505) 345-2626
website: http://www.nrccps.org

Focuses on building State, local, and Tribal capacity through training and technical assistance in child protective services, including meeting Federal requirements, strengthening programs, eligibility for the Child Abuse Prevention and Treatment Act grant, support to State Liaison Officers, and collaboration with other national resource centers.

Child Abuse Prevention Organizations

National Alliance of Children's Trust and Prevention Funds
address: 5712 30th Avenue, NE
Seattle, WA 98105
phone: (206) 526-1221
fax: (206) 526-0220
email: alliance@psy.msu.edu
website: www.ctfalliance.org

Assists State children's trust and prevention funds in strengthening families and protecting children from harm.

Prevent Child Abuse America
address: 500 N. Michigan Avenue, Suite 200
Chicago, IL 60611
phone: (312) 663-3520
fax: (312) 939-8962
email: mailbox@preventchildabuse.org
website: www.preventchildabuse.org

Conducts prevention activities such as public awareness campaigns, advocacy, networking, research, and publishing. Also provides information and statistics on child abuse.

For the General Public

Childhelp
address: 15757 North 78th Street
Scottsdale, AZ 85260
phone: (800) 4-A-CHILD (child abuse hotline)
(800) 2-A-CHILD (TDD child abuse hotline)
(480) 922-8212
fax: (480) 922-7061
website: http://www.childhelp.org/

Provides crisis counseling to adult survivors and child victims of child abuse, offenders, and parents, and operates a national hotline.

National Center for Missing and Exploited Children
address: Charles B. Wang International Children's Building
699 Prince Street
Alexandria, VA 22314-3175
phone: (800) 843-5678 (24-hour hotline)
(703) 274-3900
fax: (703) 274-2220
website: www.missingkids.com

Provides assistance to parents, children, law enforcement, schools, and the community in recovering missing children and raising public awareness about ways to help prevent child abduction, molestation, and sexual exploitation.

Parents Anonymous
address: 675 West Foothill Blvd., Suite 220
Claremont, CA 91711
phone: (909) 621-6184
fax: (909) 625-6304
email: Parentsanonymous@parentsanonymous.org
website: www.parentsanonymous.org

Leads mutual support groups to help parents provide nurturing environments for their families.

For More Information

Child Welfare Information Gateway
address:	1250 Maryland Avenue, SW
	Eighth Floor
	Washington, DC 20024
phone:	(800) 394-3366
	(703) 385-7565
fax:	(703) 385-3206
email:	info@childwelfare.gov
website:	http://www.childwelfare.gov/

Collects, stores, catalogs, and disseminates information on all aspects of child maltreatment and child welfare to help build the capacity of professionals in the field. A service of the Children's Bureau.

National Center for Substance Abuse and Child Welfare
address:	4940 Irvine Blvd., Suite 202
	Irvine, CA 92620
phone:	(714) 505-3525
fax:	(714) 505-3626
email:	ncsacw@cff utures.org
website:	www.ncsacw.samhsa.gov

Disseminates information, provides technical assistance, and develops knowledge that promotes effective practice, organizational, and system changes related to substance use disorder and child welfare issues at the local, State, and national levels.

National Clearinghouse for Alcohol and Drug Information
address:	P.O. Box 2345
	Rockville, MD 20847
phone:	(240) 221-4019
	(800) 729-6686
	(877) 767-8432 (En Español)
	(800) 487-4889 (TDD)
fax:	(240) 221-4292
email:	info@health
website:	http://ncadi.samhsa.gov

Serves as the world's largest resource for current information and materials concerning substance use disorder prevention and addiction treatment. A service of the Substance Abuse and Mental Health Services Administration's Center for Substance Abuse Prevention.

APPENDIX C. STATE TELEPHONE NUMBERS FOR REPORTING CHILD MALTREATMENT

Each State designates specific agencies to receive and investigate reports of suspected child abuse and neglect. Typically, this responsibility is carried out by child protective services (CPS) with in a Department of Social Services, Department of Human Resources, or Division of Family and Children Services. In some States, police departments also may receive reports of child abuse or neglect.

Many States have local or toll-free telephone numbers for reporting suspected maltreatment. **The reporting party must be calling from the same State where the child is allegedly being maltreated for most of the following numbers to be valid.**

For States not listed, or when the reporting party resides in a different State from the child, please call **Childhelp, 800-4-A-Child** (800-422-4453), or your local CPS agency. States may occasionally change the telephone numbers listed below. To view the most current contact information, including State Web Addresses, visit **http://www.childwelfare.gov/pubs/reslist/rl_dsp.cfm?rs_id=5&rate_chno=11-11172.**

Alabama (AL)
334-242-9500

Alaska (AK)
800-478-4444

Arizona (AZ)
888-SOS-CHILD
(888-767-2445)

Arkansas (AR)
800-482-5964

Colorado (CO)
303-866-5932

Connecticut (CT)
800-842-2288
800-624-5518 (TDD)

Delaware (DE)
800-292-9582

District of Columbia (DC)
202-671-SAFE (7233)

Florida (FL)
800-96-ABUSE
(800-962-2873)

Hawaii (HI)
808-832-5300

Idaho (ID)
800-926-2588

Illinois (IL)
800-252-2873
217-524-2606

Indiana (IN)
800-800-5556

Iowa (IA)
800-362-2178

Kansas (KS)
800-922-5330

Kentucky (KY)
800-752-6200

Maine (ME)
800-452-1999
800-963-9490 (TTY)

Massachusetts (MA)
800-792-5200

Mississippi (MS)
800-222-8000
601-359-4991

Missouri (MO)
800-392-3738
573-751-3448

Montana (MT)
866-820-KIDS (5437)

Nebraska (NE)
800-652-1999

Nevada (NV)
800-992-5757

New Hampshire (NH)
800-894-5533
603-271-6556

New Jersey (NJ)
877-652-2873
800-835-5510 (TDD/TTY)

New Mexico (NM)
800-797-3260
505-841-6100

New York (NY)
800-342-3720
518-474-8740
800-369-2437 (TDD)

Oklahoma (OK)
800-522-3511

Pennsylvania (PA)
800-932-0313

Puerto Rico (PR)
800-981-8333
787-749-1333

Rhode Island (RI)
800-RI-CHILD
(800-742-4453)

South Carolina (SC)
803-898-7318
Tennessee (TN)
877-237-0004

Texas (TX)
800-252-5400

Utah (UT)
800-678-9399

Vermont (VT)
800-649-5285 (after hours)

Virginia (VA)
800-552-7096
804-786-8536

Washington (WA)
866-END-HARM
(866-363-4276)
800-562-5624 (after hours)
800-624-6186 (TTY)

West Virginia (WV)
800-352-6513

APPENDIX D. DIAGNOSTIC AND STATISTICAL MANUAL OF MENTAL DISORDERS CRITERIA[136]

Criteria for Substance Dependence

A maladaptive pattern of substance use, leading to clinically significant impairment or distress, as manifested by three (or more) of the following, occurring at any time in the same 12-month period:

1. Tolerance, as defined by either of the following:
   a. A need for markedly increased amounts of the substance to achieve intoxication or desired effect.
   b. Markedly diminished effect with continued use of the same amount of the substance.
2. With drawal, as manifested by either of the following:
   a. The characteristic with drawal syndrome for the substance (refer to criteria A and B of the criteria sets for with drawal from the specific substances).
   b. The same (or a closely related) substance is taken to relieve or avoid with drawal symptoms.
3. The substance often is taken in larger amounts or over a longer period than was intended.
4. There is a persistent desire or unsuccessful efforts to cut down or control substance use.

5. A great deal of time is spent in activities necessary to obtain the substance (e.g., visiting multiple doctors or driving long distances), use the substance (e.g., chain-smoking), or recover from its effects.
6. Important social, occupational, or recreational activities are given up or reduced because of substance use.
7. The substance use is continued despite knowledge of having a persistent or recurrent physical or psychological problem that is likely to have been caused or exacerbated by the substance (e.g., current cocaine use despite recognition of cocaine-induced depression, or continued drinking despite recognition that an ulcer was made worse by alcohol consumption).

Specify if

a. With physiological dependence—evidence of tolerance or with drawal (i.e., either Item 1 or 2 is present).
b. Without physiological dependence—no evidence of tolerance or with drawal (i.e., neither Item 1 nor 2 is present).

Criteria for Substance Abuse

A maladaptive pattern of substance use leading to clinically significant impairment or distress, as manifested by one (or more) of the following, occurring with in a 12-month period:

1. Recurrent substance use resulting in a failure to fulfill major role obligations at work, school, or home (e.g., repeated absences or poor work performance related to substance use; substance-related absences, suspensions, or expulsions from school; neglect of children or household).
2. Recurrent substance use in situations in which it is physically hazardous (e.g., driving an automobile or operating a machine when impaired by substance use).
3. Recurrent substance-related legal problems (e.g., arrests for substance-related disorderly conduct).
4. Continued substance use despite having persistent or recurrent social or interpersonal problems caused or exacerbated by the effects of the substance (e.g., arguments with spouse about consequences of intoxication, physical fights).

The symptoms never have met the criteria for substance dependence for this class of substance.

APPENDIX E. COMMONLY ABUSED SUBSTANCES

This appendix presents information about some of the most commonly abused types of substances and the drugs affiliated with those types. A table provides additional information on commonly abused substances, including street names and methods of use.

Types of Commonly Abused Substances

Cannabinoids (e.g., marijuana, hashish) can produce feelings of euphoria, anxiety, or depression as well as distort perception and slow reaction time. Marijuana, the most commonly used illicit drug, has been associated with automobile and industrial accidents as well as physical ailments, most notably cancer.[137] It is usually smoked, making its health risks similar to those of tobacco in terms of pulmonary and cardiac effects.

Club Drugs (e.g., GHB, ketamine, MDMA, flunitrazepan, yaba) include a variety of drugs from other drug categories (e.g., hallucinogens, depressants). The name is derived from the fact these substances often are used by younger people at nightclubs and parties. Some club drugs, gamma hydroxyl butyrate (GHB) and Rohypnol in particular, have gained notoriety for use in drug-assisted sexual assault cases and, therefore, are referred to as "predatory drugs."

Certain club drugs, such as ketamine, have medical or veterinary uses, but are used in a significantly diff erent quantity or by a population other than for whom they are intended. Yaba, which means "crazy medicine" in Thai, is a combination of methamphetamine and caffeine and is becoming increasingly available at rave parties. Like methamphetamine, use of yaba can result in a rapid heart rate and damage to the small blood vessels in the brain, which can lead to stroke. Its use also can lead to violent behavior, paranoia, confusion, or insomnia.

Depressants (e.g., barbiturates) include some drugs that are prescribed to reduce anxiety or act as a sedative or anticonvulsant. Depressants are used illicitly to produce feelings of well-being and to lower inhibitions. Signs of use include fatigue, confusion, and impaired coordination and memory. Alcohol, the most commonly abused substance, is categorized as a depressant.

Hallucinogens (e.g., acid, mescaline, psilocybin, phencyclidine) have no known medical use and are illegal. These substances produce altered states of perception and feeling. Users often are disoriented or inattentive. The effects of hallucinogens are unpredictable and depend on several factors, including the user's personality, the surroundings in which they are used, the quantity taken, and the drug's purity.

Users may experience a "bad trip" that can include terrifying thoughts and feelings, fear of insanity or death, and deep despair. An observable, long-term effect for some users is persistent perception disorder, which is commonly referred to as flashbacks.

Inhalants (e.g., aerosol sprays, nitrous oxide, butyl nitrate) usually are legal and readily available household and commercial products whose chemical vapors are inhaled to produce mind-altering effects. Observable effects of use include runny nose, watery eyes, and headaches. Users can ingest the substances by inhaling directly from product containers, sniffing a cloth saturated with the substance, or sniffing the substance from a plastic bag that is placed over the nose and mouth. Deeply inhaling vapors or using large amounts over a short time may result in disorientation, violent behavior, unconsciousness, or even death. High concentrations of inhalants can cause suffocation by displacing oxygen in the lungs. One of the significant factors in the use of inhalants is their accessibility, particularly for children. National surveys indicate inhaling dangerous products is becoming a widespread problem.[138]

Opioids and Narcotic Pain Relievers (e.g., heroin, morphine, oxycodone, hydrocodone) are used illegally for their euphoric effects. Many opioids and narcotic pain relievers originally were developed to relieve pain, and doctors still prescribe some for that purpose. The pain of with drawal from heroin and other opioids is made worse by the fact that these drugs medicate pain. Therefore, individuals in with drawal may experience pain they did not feel while using opiates and may not be able to deal with pain as they normally would. Signs of use include needle marks as well as decreased pulse and respiration rates.

Stimulants (e.g., cocaine, amphetamines, methamphetamine) can produce effects such as increased alertness, over-activity, depression, and insomnia. Cocaine is a powerful stimulant that primarily affects the dopamine system—the part of the brain that regulates feelings of pleasure and excitement. Cocaine use can cause violent or hypersexual behavior, paranoid thinking, and agitation or anxiety. Prenatal exposure to cocaine can cause premature labor, low birth weight, and fetal death. Studies also indicate that exposure to cocaine leads to problems in school-aged children in such areas as problem solving, inhibition, impulse control, and abstract reasoning.[139] The effects of methamphetamine and amphetamines, which are other types of stimulants, are similar, although methamphetamine often has a greater impact on the central nervous system. Methamphetamine is generally less expensive than cocaine, and because the body metabolizes it more slowly, its effects may last as much as 10 times longer than a high from cocaine.[140] Individuals who use methamphetamine may experience serious health and psychiatric conditions, including memory loss, aggression, violence, psychotic behavior, and potential coronary and neurological damage.[141]

COMMONLY ABUSED COMMERCIAL PRODUCTS

Adhesives: Model airplane glue, household glue, rubber cement.

Aerosols: Spray paint, hair spray, air freshener, fabric protector.

Anesthetics: Nitrous oxide, ether, chloroform.

Cleaning agents: Dry cleaning fluid, spot remover, degreaser.

Gases: Nitrous oxide, butane, propane, helium.

Solvents: Nail polish remover, paint thinner, lighter fluid, gasoline.

The types of substances used by adolescents and adults change faster than current literature can document, and families may mention drugs that are unknown to child protective services caseworkers. Three valuable Federal Internet resources for current information on a variety of substances are:

- The National Clearinghouse for Alcohol and Drug Information (**http://ncadi.samhsa.gov/**)
- The National Institute on Drug Abuse (**www.drugabuse.gov**)
- The Office of National Drug Control Policy (**www.whitehousedrugpolicy.gov**).

Table Commonly Abused Substances.

Drug Group	Drug	Street Names	Method of Use
Cannabinoids	Hashish	Hash	Smoked in hand-rolled cigarettes, pipes, or water pipes (i.e., "bongs").
	Marijuana	Grass, pot, weed	
Club Drugs	Gamma hydroxy butyrate	GHB, "G"	Mixed into drinks or injected.
	Ketamine	Special K, "K," Kit Kat, vitamin K	Mixed into drinks, injected, added to smokable materials, snorted, or consumed in pill form.
	MDMA (3,4-methylenedioxy methamphetamine)	Ecstasy, X, XTC, E	Consumed in pill form, mixed into drinks, or injected.
	Flunitrazepan	Rohypnol (commercial name), roofies	Mixed into drinks or injected.
	Yaba	Crazy medicine, Nazi speed	Consumed in pill form, inhaled (by melting tablets and inhaling vapors), snorted, or injected.
Depressants	Alcohol	Booze, juice, hooch	Swallowed in liquid form.
	Barbiturates, methaqualone, benzodiazepines	Downers, ludes	Consumed in capsules, tablet, or pill form; mixed into drinks; or injected.
Hallucinogens	Lysergic acid diethylamide	Acid, LSD	Swallowed in tablet or capsule form, or placed into thin squares of gelatin, paper, sugar cubes, gum, candy, or crackers.
	Mescaline	Peyote, cactus, mesc	Chewed, swallowed in capsule or pill form, or ground and infused in hot water and consumed as tea.
	Psilocybin/Psilocyn	Mushrooms, shrooms	Chewed, smoked, or ground and infused in hot water and consumed as tea.

Table Commonly Abused Substances (Continued).

Drug Group	Drug	Street Names	Method of Use
	Phencyclidine	Angel dust, crystal, PCP	Snorted, injected, applied to leafy material and smoked, or swallowed in liquid, capsule, tablet, or pill form.
Inhalants	Airplane glue, aerosol sprays, gasoline, paint thinner	Air blast, highball	Inhaled or sniffed, sometimes using a paper bag, rag, gauze, or ampoule.
	Cyclohexyl, amyl nitrate, or butyl nitrate	Poppers, snappers	
	Nitrous oxide (N_2O)	Whippets	
Opioids and narcotic pain relievers	Heroin	Smack, junk	Injected, snorted, or smoked.
	Morphine	M, monkey, white stuff	Injected, snorted, or smoked.
	Opium	Black stuff, block, gum, hop	Swallowed or smoked.
	Oxycodone	Oxycontin (commercial name), O.C.	Swallowed, injected, or snorted.
	Hydrocodone	Vicodin (commercial name)	Swallowed.
Stimulants	Amphetamines	Speed, uppers	Swallowed in capsule, tablet, or pill form; injected; smoked; or snorted.
	Cocaine	Coke, blow, Connie	Snorted or injected.
	Crack cocaine	Crack, rock	Smoked.
	Methamphetamine	Meth, crystal, crystal meth, Tina, T, crank, speed	Snorted, injected, smoked, or swallowed.
Other compounds	Anabolic steroids	Anadrol (commercial name), Oxandrin (commercial name), roids, juice	Injected, swallowed, applied to skin
	Dextromethorphan (DXM)	Robotripping, robo, triple C (Note: DXM is found in some cough and cold medications)	Swallowed

For more information on commonly used drugs and their effects and health consequences, visit **http://www.nida.nih.gov/drugpages/drugsofabuse.html.**

APPENDIX F. COMMONLY USED SCREENING INSTRUMENTS

The substance use disorder treatment field has developed and tested several screening instruments. The following table provides a short description of the more commonly used instruments that have been found valid when used in appropriate settings. It is essential to review the materials accompanying the instruments before using them. These materials provide practical guidance, such as how many positive responses indicate that alcohol or drug use may be a problem, and they may suggest alternative wording of questions that might work better in child welfare settings.

Table Selected Substance Use Disorder Screening Instruments.

Instrument	Purpose	Summary	For More Information
Adult Substance Use Survey (ASUS) *(For use with the Self-Appraisal Survey)*	Screens for an individual's perceived alcohol and drug use and abuse, mental health concerns, motivation for treatment, anti-social attitudes and behaviors, and level of defensiveness.	• Sixty-four questions that can be self-administered or asked by another person. Available in Spanish. • Takes 8–10 minutes to administer. Training is required and available. A user's guide is available. • Free for use in Colorado but permission is required.	Kenneth Wanberg, Ph.D. Center for Addiction Research and Evaluation, Inc. 5460 Ward Road, Suite 140 Arvada, CO 80002 (303) 421-1261
Alcohol Use Disorders Identification Test (AUDIT)[1]	Designed to identify individuals whose alcohol use has become a danger to their health. Includes three subscales that assess amount and frequency of drinking, alcohol dependence, and problems caused by alcohol.	• Ten questions that can be self-administered or asked by another person. • Takes about 1 minute to complete. • Targeted at adults. • Free except for training materials.	Thomas Babor Alcohol Research Center University of Connecticut 263 Farmington Avenue Farmington, CT 06030-2103
CAGE Questionnaire[2]	Related to drinking behavior.	• Four questions that can be self-administered or asked by another person. • Targeted at individuals 16 years of age or older. • Questions can be incorporated into other questionnaires. • Free.	Available through numerous publications, websites, and treatment and prevention programs, including: http://pubs.niaaa.nih.gov/publications/Assesing%20Alcohol/InstrumentPDFs/1 6_CAGE.pdf
CAGE-AID[3]	Similar to the CAGE Questionnaire, but this expanded version includes questions about the use of illicit drugs as well as alcohol.	• Nine questions that can be self-administered or asked by another person. • Targeted at individuals 16 years of age or older. • Questions can be incorporated into other questionnaires. • Free.	Available through numerous publications, websites, and treatment and prevention programs.
Drug Abuse Screening Test (DAST)[4]	Designed to screen for the use of illegal drugs.	• Twenty questions (short version has 10) whose cumulative score indicates whether there is a drug problem, whether the person should be monitored, or whether the person should be assessed further.	The Addiction Research Foundation Center for Addiction and Mental Health 33 Russell Street Toronto, M5S2S1 Ontario, Canada (415) 595-6111 (800) 463-6273

Table Selected Substance Use Disorder Screening Instruments. (Continued)

Instrument	Purpose	Summary	For More Information
Michigan Alcoholism Screening Test (MAST)[5]	Designed to screen for lifetime alcoholism-related problems.	• Twenty-five questions that can be self-administered or asked by another person. Shorter version also available. • Takes 5 minutes to administer. • Targeted at adults. • Minor cost for original, then can be copied.	Melvin L. Selzer, M.D. 6967 Paseo Laredo La Jolla, CA 92037 (619) 459-1035
Self-Appraisal Survey (SAS) (*For use with the Adult Substance Use Survey*)	Designed to screen for alcohol and chemical dependency and to determine both the extent of use and the effects of use on aspects of life.	• Twenty-four questions that can be self-administered by participants and 12 items for caseworkers to complete using observations and other information. • Takes about 15 minutes. • Free in Colorado, but permission is required.	Kenneth Wanberg, Ph.D. Center for Addiction Research and Evaluation, Inc. 5460 Ward Road, Suite 140 Arvada, CO 80002 (303) 421-1261
Substance Abuse Subtle Screening Inventory (SASSI)[6]	Designed to screen for chemical dependency and efforts to fake or conceal problems. It has eight subscales that can assess defensiveness and other dependency characteristics.	• Eighty-eight questions. • Takes 10–15 minutes. • Requires training to administer, but can be self-administered. • Requires training to interpret and score. • Must be purchased.	The SASSI Institute 201 Camelot Lane Springville, IN 47462 (800) 726-0526 http://www.sassi.com
Triage Assessment for Addictive Disorders (TAAD)	Designed for both drug and alcohol use in face-to-face interviews where time commitment is minimal.	• Thirty questions. • Takes 12–13 minutes to administer and score. • Can be administered by anyone with good interviewing skills. • Requires expertise to score. • Must be purchased.	Norman G. Hoffmann, Ph.D. Evince Clinical Assessments P.O. Box 17305 Smithfield, RI 02917 (800) 755-6299 http://www.evinceassessment.com
TWEAK Alcohol Screen	Developed and validated for women. Recommended by the California Institute of Mental Health.	• Five questions that can be self-administered or asked by another person. • Takes 5 minutes to administer and score. • No training is required. • Free	Marcia Russell, Ph.D. Research Institute on Addictions 1021 Main Street Buffalo, NY 14203 (716) 887-2507 http://www.ria.buffalo.edu
UNCOPE	Designed to detect alcohol or drug problems.	• Six questions found in existing instruments and research reports. • Can be self-administered or asked by another person. • No training is required. • Free.	Norman G. Hoffmann, Ph.D. Evince Clinical Assessments P.O. Box 17305 Smithfield, RI 02917 (800) 755-6299 http://www.evinceassessment.com/research.html

[1] Babor, T., de la Puente, J. R., Saunders, J., & Grant, M. (1992). *AUDIT: The Alcohol Use Disorders Identification Test: Guidelines for use in primary health care.* Geneva, Switzerland: World Health Organization.

[2] Mayfield, D., McLeod, G., & Hall, P. (1974). The CAGE questionnaire: Validation of a new alcoholism instrument. *American Journal of Psychiatry, 131*(10), 1121–1123.

[3] Brown, R. L., & Rounds, L. A. (1998). Conjoint screening questionnaires for alcohol and other drug abuse: Criterion validity in primary care practice. *Wisconsin Medical Journal, 94*(3), 13 5–140.

[4] Skinner, H. A. (1982). The Drug Abuse Screening Test (DAST). *Addictive Behavior, 7*(4), 363–371.

[5] Selzer, M. (1971). The Michigan Alcoholism Screening Test: The quest for a new diagnostic instrument. *American Journal of Psychiatry, 127*(12), 1653–1658.

[6] Miller, G. (1985). *The Substance Abuse Subtle Screening Inventory (SASSI) manual*. Bloomington, IN: Spencer Evening World.

Many of these screening instruments are available from Federal websites, especially the National Institute on Alcohol Abuse and Alcoholism (**http:// www.niaaa.nih.gov**) and the National Institute on Drug Abuse (**http://www.nida.nih.gov**). Some are available in Spanish. For screening instruments in other languages, it may be necessary to work with a translator who is not a friend or a relative of the family.

Although screening tools are a great resource, they are not meant to be the sole source of decision-making. Rather, child protective services caseworkers must rely on multiple sources of information as well as their professional training and experience to help them decide whether substance use is a problem for a specific family.

APPENDIX G. STATE OF CONNECTICUT DEPARTMENT OF CHILDREN AND FAMILIES SUBSTANCE ABUSE SCREENING AND INFORMATION FORM

Date: ____/____/____

DCF Worker: _____ Phone: _____

DCF Supervisor: _____ Phone: _____

Client Name: _____ SAFE #: _____

Date client referred to SAFE, if applicable: _____

This form shall be completed by the social worker upon return to the office. Please check **every** box either "yes" or "no," as appropriate. If there is any "yes" box checked for questions 1-13, a referral for an evaluation shall be made to Project Safe.

1. Yes ☐ No ☐ Client appeared to be under the influence of drugs and/or alcohol.
2. Yes ☐ No ☐ Client showed physical symptoms of trembling, sweating, stomach cramps, or nervousness.
3. Yes ☐ No ☐ Drug paraphernalia was present in the home, i.e., pipes, charred spoons, foils, blunts, etc.
4. Yes ☐ No ☐ Evidence of alcohol abuse was present in the home, i.e., excessive number of visible bottles/cans whether empty or not.
5. Yes ☐ No ☐ There was a report of a positive drug screen at birth for mother and child.
   List drugs detected: _____
6. Yes ☐ No ☐ There was an allegation of substance abuse in the CPS report.
7. Yes ☐ No ☐ The child(ren) reports substance abuse in the home. When? _____

8. Yes ☐ No ☐ The client has been in substance abuse treatment. When? _____

Appendix G. (Continued)

9. Yes ☐ No ☐   The client has used the following in the last 12 months:

                 Marijuana/Hashish ☐   Heroin/Opiates ☐   Cocaine/Crack ☐

                 Other drugs: _____

10. Yes ☐ No ☐   Client shared that he/she has experienced negative consequences from the misuse of alcohol.

                 DWI/DUI ☐   Domestic Fights ☐   Job Loss ☐   Arrests ☐

                 Other: _____

11. Yes ☐ No ☐   Client shared he/she has experienced trouble with the law due to the use of alcohol or other drugs.

                 DWI/DUI ☐   Domestic Violence ☐   Drug Possession Charge ☐

                 Other: _____

12. Yes ☐ No ☐   There are adults who may be using drugs and/or misusing alcohol who have regular contact with the client's children.

13. Yes ☐ No ☐   The client acknowledged medical complications due to the use of substances.

14. Other Comments:

Adapted from Young, N. K., & Gardner, S. L. (2002). *Navigating the pathways: Lessons and promising practices in linking alcohol and drug services with child welfare, Technical Assistance Publication (TAP) Series 27*, p. 131–132. (SAMHSA Publication No. SMA-02-3639). Rockville, MD: Department of Health and Human Services, Substance Abuse and Mental HealthServices Administration, Center for Substance Abuse Treatment.

APPENDIX H. MEMORANDUMS OF UNDERSTANDING[142]

What is a Memorandum of Understanding (MOU)?
An MOU is a written agreement that serves to clarify relationships and responsibilities between two or more organizations that share services, clients, and resources.

Why is it important to have an MOU?

MOUs help strengthen community partnerships by delineating clear roles between individuals, agencies, and other groups. Communities with MOUs report that the strengthened partnerships resulted in enhanced services for children and families.

What is actually included in an MOU?

Generally, MOUs can address a variety of issues and topics. Content areas to consider including in an MOU are:

- Clarification of agency roles;
- Referrals across agencies;
- Assessment protocols;
- Parameters of confidentiality;
- Case management intervention;
- Interagency training of staff;
- Agency liaison and coordination;
- Process for resolving interagency confl icts;
- Periodic review of the MOU.

How do we know our community is ready to develop an MOU?

Communities that are concerned about reducing the incidence of child maltreatment are excellent candidates for creating an MOU. In communities that are experiencing strained relationships between potential partners, the process of writing an MOU provides a unique opportunity to address misperceptions and differences and to work jointly to resolve gaps in service delivery.

What strategies should we undertake as we begin the MOU process?

Depending on existing relationships with in communities, one strategy may include inviting key supporters to meetings to explore the feasibility of MOU development. Communities have reported that once they had the commitment and investment from the various agencies, the MOU process quickly crystallized and resulted in a written MOU. An additional strategy may include inviting an outside consultant to facilitate a partnership that leads to the development of an MOU.

What are the problems that might arise during the MOU process?

Problems may arise concerning misperceptions about each other's goals, missions, and philosophy. Professionals from child welfare agencies report that the MOU meetings helped them understand each other's language and history and provided a context in which to view other philosophies and missions. Additional problematic issues may include confidentiality policies, assessment decisions, levels of intervention, and out-of-home placement for children. The MOU provides an opportunity to address these critical issues to meet the needs of the community.

How does the MOU actually help families and children?

Families affected by child maltreatment report that they are reluctant to request assistance, are required to participate in services that do not address the underlying issues, and frequently feel misunderstood by professionals. Communities with existing MOUs have reported that children who are maltreated were less likely to be placed in out-of-home settings and that families were more motivated to work with professionals to reduce the risk of future child abuse and neglect. Families in communities where MOUs have been established reported a higher level of satisfaction in working with professionals.

APPENDIX I. CONFIDENTIALITY AND THE RELEASE OF SUBSTANCE USE DISORDER TREATMENT INFORMATION

The Comprehensive Alcohol Abuse and Alcoholism Prevention, Treatment, and Rehabilitation Act (1970) and the Drug Abuse Office and Treatment Act (1972) regulate the disclosure of confidential information by substance use disorder treatment programs that receive Federal assistance. Generally, a provider cannot release any information that identifies an individual in the program and cannot acknowledge the presence of an individual in the treatment program. The following are exceptions under which client information can be released:

- It will be used in internal communications between or among those with a legitimate interest who need the information in connection with their duties that arise out of the provision of diagnosis, treatment, or referral for treatment of substance use disorders if the communications are with in the program or between a program and an entity that has direct administrative control over the program.
- It relates to a medical emergency requiring assistance.
- It relates to research or an audit of the program or service.
- It relates to a crime on the premises involving drug use or a mental condition.
- It relates to reports of suspected child abuse and neglect.
- A court order has been obtained.
- It will be used by qualified organizations providing services to the program.
- Proper consent, by way of a criminal justice consent form, has been obtained from the individual in the program (in the case of a minor, the consent must be obtained from the patient, the parents, or both). This consent must be in writing and must contain each of the following items:
  - The name and general description of the program(s) making the disclosure;
  - The name of the individual or organization that will receive the disclosure;
  - The name of the patient who is the subject of the disclosure;
  - The purpose or need for the disclosure;
  - How much and what kind of information will be disclosed;
  - A statement regarding revocation of consent;
  - The date, event, or condition upon which the consent will expire;
  - The signature of the patient;
  - The date on which the consent is signed.[143]

APPENDIX J. SAMPLE QUALIFIED SERVICE ORGANIZATION AGREEMENT AND CONSENT FORM

XYZ Service Center ("the Center") and

_____

(Name of the alcohol/drug program)

(the "Program") hereby enter into an agreement whereby the Center agrees to provide:

_____

(Nature of services to be provided to the program)

Furthermore, the Center:

(1) Acknowledges that in receiving, transmitting, transporting, storing, processing, or otherwise dealing with any information received from the Program identifying or otherwise relating to the patients in the Program ("protected information"), it is fully bound by the provisions of the Federal regulations governing the Confidentiality of Alcohol and Drug Abuse Patient Records, 42 CFR, Part 2; and the Health Insurance Portability and Accountability Act (HIPAA), 45 CFR, Parts 142, 160, 162, and 164, and may not use or disclose the information except as permitted or required by this Agreement or by law;

(2) Agrees to resist any efforts in judicial proceedings to obtain access to the protected information except as expressly provided for in the regulations governing the Confidentiality of Alcohol and Drug Abuse Patient Records, 42 CFR, Part 2.

(3) Agrees to use appropriate safeguards (*can define with more specificity*) to prevent the unauthorized use or disclosure of the protected information;

(4) Agrees to report to the Program any use or disclosure of the protected information not provided for by this Agreement of which it becomes aware (*insert negotiated time and manner terms*);

(5) Agrees to ensure that any agent, including a subcontractor, to whom the Center provides the protected information received from the Program, or created or received by the Center on behalf of the Program, agrees to the same restrictions and conditions that apply through this agreement to the Center with respect to such information;*

(6) Agrees to provide access to the protected information at the request of the Program, or to an individual as directed by the Program, in order to meet the requirements of 45 CFR § 164.524, which provides patients with the right to access and copy their own protected information (*insert negotiated time and manner terms*);

(7) Agrees to make any amendments to the protected information as directed or agreed to by the Program pursuant to 45 CFR § 164.526 (*insert negotiated time and manner terms*);

(8) Agrees to make available its internal practices, books, and records, including policies and procedures, relating to the use and disclosure of protected information received from the Program, or created or received by the Center on behalf of the Program, to

the Program or to the Secretary of the Department of Health and Human Services for purposes of the Secretary determining the Program's compliance with HIPAA (*insert negotiated time and manner terms*);

(9) Agrees to document disclosures of protected information, and information related to such disclosures, as would be required for the Program to respond to a request by an individual for an accounting of disclosures in accordance with 45 CFR § 164.528 (*insert negotiated time and manner terms*);*

(10) Agrees to provide the Program or an individual information in accordance with paragraph (9) of this agreement to permit the Program to respond to a request by an individual for an accounting of disclosures in accordance with 45 CFR § 164.528 (*insert negotiated time and manner terms*);

Termination

(1) The program may terminate this agreement if it determines that the Center has violated any material term;

(2) Upon termination of this agreement for any reason, the Center shall return or destroy all protected information received from the Program, or created or received by the Center on behalf of the Program. This provision shall apply to protected information that is in the possession of subcontractors or agents of the Center. The Center shall retain no copies of the protected information.

(3) In the event that the Center determines that returning or destroying the protected information is infeasible, the Center shall notify the Program of the conditions that make return or destruction infeasible (*insert negotiated time and manner terms*).

Upon notification that the return or destruction of the protected information is infeasible, the Center shall extend the protections of this Agreement to such protected information and limit further uses and disclosures of the information to those purposes that make the return or destruction infeasible, as long as the Center maintains the information.

Executed this _____ day of _____, 20 ___.

_____   _____
President   Program Director
XYZ Service Center   [Name of the Program]
[address]   [address]

---

*Although HIPAA requires these paragraphs to be included in Business Associate agreements, 42 C.F.R. § 2.11 requires qualified service organizations to abide by the Federal drug and alcohol regulations, which prohibit such organizations from redisclosing any patient-identifying information even to an agent or subcontractor. Legal Action Center has asked the U.S. Department of Health and Human Services for an opinion on this issue.

Obtained from Legal Action Center. (n.d.). *Sample qualified service organization/ business associate agreement* [Online]. Available: http://www.lac.org/doc_library/ lac/publications/QSO-BA%20Agreement%20Form.pdf.

Sample Consent Form Consent
for the Release of Confidential Information

I, _____, authorize _____
　　　(Name of patient)　　　　　　　(Name or general designation of program making disclosure)

to disclose to _____
　　　　　　(Name of person or organization to which disclosure is to be made)

the following information: _____
　　　　　　(Nature and amount of information to be disclosed; as limited as possible)

The purpose of the disclosure authorized in this is to:

_____
(Purpose of disclosure, as specific as possible)

I understand that my substance use disorder treatment records are protected under the Federal regulations governing Confidentiality and Drug Abuse Patient Records, 42 CFR, Part 2, and the Health Insurance Portability and Accountability Act of 1996, 45 CFR, Parts 160 and 164, and cannot be disclosed with out my written consent unless otherwise provided for by the regulations. I also understand that I may revoke this consent in writing at any time except to the extent that action has been taken in reliance on it, and that in any event this consent expires automatically as follows:

_____
(Specification of the date, event, or condition upon which this consent expires)

_____

I understand that generally (*insert name of program*) may not condition my treatment on whether I sign a consent form, but that in certain limited circumstances I may be denied treatment if I do not sign a consent form.

_____　　　　_____
Date　　　　　　　　　　　　　　　Signature of Patient

　　　　　　　　　　　　　　　　　_____
　　　　　　　　　　　　　　　　　Signature of parent, guardian, or uthorized
　　　　　　　　　　　　　　　　　representative where required.

Adapted from Legal Action Center. (n.d.). *Sample consent - basic* [On-line]. Available: http://www.lac.org/doc_library/lac/publications/Consent-Basic.pdf.

End Notes

[1] U.S. Department of Health and Human Services, Substance Abuse and Mental Health Services Administration (SAMHSA), Office of Applied Studies (OAS). (2009, April). Children living with substance-dependent or substance-abusing parents: 2002–2007. *The NSDUH Report* [On-line]. Available: http://oas.samhsa.gov/2k9/SAparents/SAparents.htm.

[2] DeBellis, M. D., Broussard, E. R., Herring, D. J., Wexler, S., Moritz, G., & Benitez, J. G. (2001). Psychiatric co-morbidity in caregivers and children involved in maltreatment: A pilot research study with policy implications. *Child Abuse & Neglect, 25(7)*, 923–944; Dube, S. R., Anda, R. F., Felitti, V. J., Croft, J. B., Edwards, V. J., & Giles, W. H. (2001). Growing up with parental alcohol abuse: Exposure to childhood abuse, neglect, and household dysfunction. *Child Abuse & Neglect, 25(12)*, 1627–1640; Chaffin, M., Kelleher, K., & Hollenberg, J. (1996). Onset of physical abuse and neglect: Psychiatric, substance abuse, and social risk factors from prospective community data. *Child Abuse & Neglect, 20*(3), 191–203.

[3] Kelleher, K., Chaffin, M., Hollenberg, J., & Fischer, E. (1994). Alcohol and drug disorders among physically abusive and neglectful parents in a community-based sample. *American Journal of Public Health, 84*(10), 1586–1590.

[4] U.S. Department of Health and Human Services, Administration for Children and Families (ACF). (2008). *Child maltreatment 2006* [On-line]. Available: http://www.acf.hhs.gov/programs/cb/pubs/cm06/index.htm.

[5] U.S. Department of Health and Human Services, ACF. (1999). *Blending perspectives and building common ground. A report to Congress on substance abuse and child protection* [On-line]. Available: http://aspe.hhs.gov/hsp/subabuse99/subabuse.htm.

[6] U.S. Department of Health and Human Services, ACF. (1999); Hans, S. (1995). Diagnosis in etiologic and epidemiologic studies. In C. Jones & M. De La Rosa (Eds.), *Methodological issues: Etiology and consequences of drug abuse among women.* Washington, DC: U.S. Department of Health and Human Services, National Institutes of Health (NIH), National Institute on Drug Abuse (NIDA); Tarter, R., Blackson, T., Martin, C., Loeber, R., & Moss, H. (1993). Characteristics and correlates of child discipline practices in substance abuse and normal families. *American Journal on Addictions, 2*(1), 18–25; Kumpfer, K. L., & Bayes, J. (1995). Child abuse and drugs. In J. H. Jaffe (Ed.), *The encyclopedia of drugs and alcohol* (Vol. 1, pp. 217–222). New York, NY: Simon & Schuster.

[7] U.S. Department of Health and Human Services, ACF. (1999).

[8] Young, N. K., & Gardner, S. L. (2002). Navigating the pathways: Lessons and promising practices in linking alcohol and drug services with child welfare. *Technical Assistance Publication (TAP) 27.* Rockville, MD: U.S. Department of Health and Human Services, SAMHSA.

[9] American Psychiatric Association. (1994). *Diagnostic and statistical manual of mental disorders, 4ThEd., Text Revision (DSM-IV-TR).* Washington, DC: Author.

[10] U.S. Department of Health and Human Services, SAMHSA. (2008). *Results from the 2007 National Survey on Drug Use and Health: National findings* [On-line]. Available: http://www.oas.samhsa.gov/nsduh/2k7nsduh/2k7Results.cfm#TOC.

[11] U.S. Department of Health and Human Services, SAMHSA. (2008); U.S. Department of Health and Human Services, Centers for Disease Control and Prevention (CDC). (2008). *Alcohol and public health* [On-line]. Available: http://www.cdc.gov/alcohol/ index.htm; U.S. Department of Health and Human Services, & U.S. Department of Agriculture. (2005). *Dietary guidelines for Americans 2005* [On-line]. Available: http://www.health dga2005/document/html/chapter9.htm.

[12] U.S. Department of Health and Human Services, SAMHSA. (1 999a). *Drug abuse and addiction research: 25 years of discovery to advance the healThof the public* [On-line]. Available: http://www.drugabuse.gov/STRC/STRCindex.html; Leshner, A. I. (2001). Addiction is a brain disease. *Issues in Science and Technology Online* [On-line]. Available: http:// www.nap.edu/issues

[13] Straussner, S. L. A., & Attia, P. R. (2002). Women's addiction treatment through a historical lens. In S. L. A. Straussner & S. Brown (Eds.), *The handbook of addiction treatment for women* (pp. 3–25). San Francisco, CA: Jossey-Bass; Musto, D. F. (1997). Historical perspectives. In J. H. Lowinson, P. Ruiz, R. B. Millman, & J. G. Langrod (Eds.), *Substance abuse: A comprehensive textbook* (pp. 1–10). Baltimore, MD: Williams & Wilkins.

[14] U.S. Department of Health and Human Services, NIH, NIDA. (2008). *Drugs, brains, and behavior: The science of addiction* [On-line]. Available: http://www. drugabuse.gov/Scienceofaddiction/.

[15] U.S. Department of Health and Human Services, NIH, NIDA. (2005a). *Addiction is a chronic disease* [On-line]. Available: http://www.nida.nih.gov/ about/welcome/aboutdrugabuse/chronicdisease; World Health Organization. (2004). *Neuroscience of psychoactive substance use and dependence: Summary* [On-line]. Available: http://www.who.int/substance_abuse/publications/en/Neuroscience_E.pdf; U.S. Department of Health and Human Services, NIH, NIDA. (2008).

[16] Anthenelli, R. M., & Schuckit, M. A. (1997). Genetics. In J. H. Lowinson, P. Ruiz, R. B. Millman, & J. G. Langrod (Eds.), *Substance abuse: A comprehensive textbook* (pp. 41–51). Baltimore, MD: Williams & Wilkins.

[17] World Health Organization. (2004); U.S. Department of Health and Human Services, SAMHSA. (1 999b). *Mental health: A report of the surgeon general* [On-line]. Available: http://www.surgeongeneral. gov/library/mentalhealth/home.html; Anthenelli, R. M., & Schuckit, M. A. (1997).

[18] U.S. Department of Health and Human Services, NIH, NIDA. (2008).

[19] Alcoholics Anonymous. (1972). *A brief guide to Alcoholics Anonymous* [On-line]. Available: http:// www.alcoholics abriefguidetoaa.pdf; Alcoholics Anonymous. (2001). *The big book* [On-line]. Available: http://www.aa.org/ bigbookonline/.

[20] U.S. Department of Health and Human Services, NIH, NIDA. (2005b) *Principles of drug addiction treatment: A research based guide* [On-line]. Available: www.nida.nih.gov/PODAT/PODATindex.html; U.S. Department of Health and Human Services, NIH, NIDA. (n.d.) *The brain and addiction* [On-line]. Available: http://teens brain2.asp#voluntary.

[21] Semidei, J., Radel, L., & Nolan, C. (2001). Substance abuse and child welfare: Clear linkages and promising responses. *Child Welfare, 80*(2), 69–128.

[22] U.S. Department of Health and Human Services, SAMHSA. (2008).

[23] U.S. Department of Health and Human Services, SAMHSA. (2008).

[24] U.S. Department of Health and Human Services, SAMHSA. (1999b).

[25] Wright, S. (2000). Women's use of drugs: Gender- specific factors. In H. Klee, M. Jackson, & S. Lewis (Eds.), *Drug use and motherhood* (pp. 15–31). New York, NY: Routledge.

[26] Pagliaro, A. M., & Pagliaro, L. (2000). *Substance use among women: A reference and resource guide*. Philadelphia, PA: Brunner/Mazel.

[27] Daly, J. E., & Pelowski, S. (2000). Predictors of dropout among men who batter: A review of studies with implications for research and practice. *Violence and Victims, 15*(2), 137–160; Barrerra, M., Palmer, S., Brown, R., & Kalaher, S. (1994). Characteristics of court involved men and non-court involved men who abuse their wives. *Journal of Family Violence, 9*(4), 333–345; Gelles, R. (1993). Alcohol and other drugs are associated with violence— ey are not its causes. In R. Gelles & D. Loseke (Eds.), *Current controversies in family violence* (pp. 182–196). Newbury Park, CA: Sage.

[28] Bragg, H. L. . *Child protection in families experiencing domestic violence* [On-line]. Available: http://www. childwelfare.gov/pubs/usermanuals/domesticviolence/ domesticviolence.pdf.

[29] Cunradi, C. B., Caetano, R., & Schafer, J. (2002). Alcohol-related problems, drug use, and male partner violence severity. *Alcoholism: Clinical and Experimental Research, 26*(4), 493–500; Brickley, M. R., & Shephard, J. P. (1995). The relationship between alcohol intoxication, injury severity and Glasgow coma scores in assault patients. *Injury, 26*(5), 311–314; Shephard, J. P., & Brickley, M. R. (1996). The relationship between alcohol intoxication, stressors and injury in urban violence. *British Journal of Criminology, 36*(4), 546–566.

[30] Najavits, L. M. (2001). *Seeking safety: A treatment manual for PTSD and substance abuse*. New York, NY: Guilford Press.

[31] Kessler, R. C., Sonnega, A., Bromet, E., Hughes, M., & Nelson, C. B. (1995). Posttraumatic stress disorder in the National Comorbidity Survey. *Archives of General Psychiatry, 52*(12), 1048–1060.

[32] Resnick, H. S., Kilpatrick, D. G., Dansky, B. S., Saunders, B. E., & Best, C. L. (1993). Prevalence of civilian trauma and posttraumatic stress disorder in a representative sample of women. *Journal of Consulting and Clinical Psychology, 61*(6), 984–991.

[33] Smyth, N. (1998). Exploring the nature of the relationship between poverty and substance abuse: Knowns and unknowns. *Journal of Human Behavior in the Social Environment, 1*(1), 67–82.

[34] Drake, B., & Pandy, S. (1996). Understanding the relationship between neighborhood poverty and specific types of child maltreatment. *Child Abuse & Neglect, 20*(11), 1003–1018; Sedlak, A. J., & Broadhurst, D. D. (1996). *Third National Incidence Study of Child Abuse and Neglect (NIS-3)*. Washington, DC: U.S. Department of Health and Human Services, National Center on Child Abuse and Neglect; Boney-McCoy, S., & Finkelhor, D. (1995). Prior victimization: A risk factor for child sexual abuse and for PTSD-related symptomatology among sexually abused youth. *Child Abuse & Neglect, 19*(12), 1401–1421; Pelton, L. H., & Milner, J. S. (1994). Is poverty a key contributor to child maltreatment? In E. Gambrill & T. J. Stein (Eds.), *Controversial issues in child welfare* (pp. 16–28). Needham Heights, MA: Allyn & Bacon; Coulton, C., Korbin, J., Su, M., & Chow, J. (1995). Community level factors and child maltreatment rates. *Child Development, 66*(5), 1262–1276; Jones, L. (1990). Unemployment and child abuse. *Families in Society, (71)*10, 579–587.

[35] U.S. Department of Health and Human Services, SAMHSA. . *Homelessness: Provision of mental health and substance abuse services* [On-line]. Available: http://www.mentalhealth.org/publications/allpubs/ homelessness; The United States Conference of Mayors. (2006). *Hunger, homelessness still a challenge in America according to Mayors/Sodexho* [On-line]. Available: http://www.usmayors.org/uscm/ us%5F mayor%5Fnewspaper/documents/01_1 6_06/ hunger.asp.

[36] Columbia University, National Center on Addiction and Substance Abuse. (1998). *Behind bars: Substance abuse and America's prison population* [On-line]. Available: http://www.casacolumbia.org/pdshopprov/ files/5745.pdf.

[37] U.S. Department of Health and Human Services, SAMHSA, OAS. (2005). *Illicit drug use among persons arrested for serious crimes* [On-line]. Available: http:// www.oas.samhsa.gov/2k5/arrests

[38] Abram, K. M., & Teplin, L. A. (1991). Co-occurring disorders among mentally ill jail detainees. *American Psychologist, 46*(10), 1036–1045.

[39] Beck, A. J., Karberg, J. C., & Harrison, P. M. (2002). Prison and jail inmates at midyear 2001. *Bureau of Justice Statistics Bulletin* [On-line]. Available: http:// www.ojp.usdoj.gov/bjs/pub/pdf/pjim01.pdf; Sabol, W. J., Minton, T. D., & Harrison, P. M. (2007). Prison and jail inmates at midyear 2006. *Bureau of Justice Statistics Bulletin* [On-line]. Available: http:// www.ojp.usdoj.gov/bjs/pub/pdf/pjim06.pdf.

[40] Greenfield, L. A., & Snell, T. L. (2000). *Women off enders* [On-line]. Available: http://www.ojp.usdoj.gov/bjs/pub/pdf/wo.pdf; Snell, T. L. (1994). *Women in prison* [On-line]. Available: http://www.ojp.usdoj.gov/bjs/pub/pdf/wopris.pdf.

[41] Snell, T. L. (1994).

[42] Otero, C., Boles, S., Young, N. K., & Dennis, K. (2004). *Methamphetamine: Addiction, treatment, outcomes and implications*. Rockville, MD: U.S. Department of Health and Human Services, SAMHSA.

[43] U.S. Department of Health and Human Services, SAMHSA. (2008).

[44] U.S. Department of Justice, Drug Enforcement Administration. (n.d.). *Methamphetamine* [On-line]. Available: http://www.usdoj.gov/dea/concern/meth.html#3.

[45] Office of National Drug Control Policy. (2006). *Drug Endangered Children (DEC)* [On-line]. Available: http://www.whitehousedrugpolicy.gov/enforce/ dr_endangered_child.html.

[46] Otero, C., et al. (2004).

[47] National Association of Counties. (2005). *The methepidemic in America: Two surveys of U.S. counties: The criminal effect of methon communities & the impact of methon children* [On-line]. Available: http://www.naco.org.

[48] U.S. Department of Health and Human Services, SAMHSA, OAS. (2009).

[49] U.S. Department of Health and Human Services, ACF. (1999).

[50] Zuckerman, B. (1994). Effects on parents and children. In D. Besharov (Ed.), *When drug addicts have children*. Washington, DC: Child Welfare League of America.

[51] Child Abuse Prevention and Treatment Act, 42 U.S.C. 5106g, §Sec.111-2.

[52] Child Abuse Prevention and Treatment Act, 42 U.S.C. 5106g, §Sec.111-2.

[53] U.S. Department of Health and Human Services, SAMHSA. (2008).

[54] Landdeck-Sisco, J. (1997). *Children with prenatal drug and/or alcohol exposure* [On-line]. Available: http://www.archrespite.org/archfs49.htm.

[55] U.S. Department of Health and Human Services, SAMHSA. (2007). *Treatment Episode Data Set (TEDS) 1995–2005: National admissions to substance abuse treatment services* [On-line]. Available: http://wwwdasis.samhsa.gov/teds05/tedsad2k5web.pdf.

[56] U.S. Department of Health and Human Services, SAMHSA. (2002). *Pregnant women in substance abuse treatment. The DASIS report* [On-line]. Available: http://www.oas.samhsa.gov/2k2/pregTX/pregTX. htm.

[57] Child Welfare Information Gateway. (2006). *Prenatal drug use as child abuse* [On-line]. Available: www.childwelfare.gov/systemwide/laws drugexposedall.pdf.

[58] University of California-Santa Barbara, School of Sociology. (n.d.). *Effects of drugs taken during pregnancy* [On-line]. Available: http://www.soc.ucsb. edu/sexinfo/?article=pregnancy&refi d=003.

[59] National Organization on Fetal Alcohol Syndrome. (2004). *Frequently asked questions* [On-line]. Available: http://www.nofas.org/faqs.aspx?id=9.

[60] McCreight, B. (1997). *Recognizing and managing children with fetal alcohol syndrome/fetal alcohol effects: A guidebook* (pp. 9–15). Washington, DC: Child Welfare League of America.

[61] Phibbs, C. S., Bateman, D. A., & Schwartz, R. M. (1991). The neonatal costs of maternal cocaine use. *Journal of the American Medical Association, 266*(11), 1521–1 526; Zuckerman, B., Frank, D. A., Hingson, R., Amaro, H., & Levenson, S. M. (1989). Effects of maternal marijuana and cocaine use on fetal growth. *New England Journal of Medicine, 320*(14), 762–768; Canadian Health Network, Canadian Centre on Substance Abuse. (2004). *What are the effects of alcohol and other drugs during pregnancy?* [On-line]. Available: http://www.canadian-health.

[62] Noland, J. S., Singer, L. T., & Arendt, R. E. (2003). Executive functioning in preschool-aged children prenatally exposed to alcohol, cocaine, and marijuana. *Alcoholism: Clinical & Experimental Research, 27*(4), 647–656.

[63] Vogel, A. (1997). Neurodevelopment: Cocaine wreaks subtle damage on developing brains. *Science, 278*(5335), 38–39.

[64] Otero, C., et al. (2004).

[65] Irwin, K. (1995). Ideology, pregnancy, and drugs: Differences between crack-cocaine, heroin, and methamphetamine users. *Contemporary Drug Problems, 22*(4), 613-638.

[66] Join Together Online. (2005). *Methscience not stigma: Open letter to the media* [On-line]. Available: http://www.jointogether.org.

[67] Finfgeld, D. (2001). Emergent drug abuse resolution models and their implications for childbearing and childrearing women. *HealthCare for Women International, 22*(8), 723–733.

[68] U.S. Department of Health and Human Services, ACF. (1999).

[69] Goldman, J., & Salus, M. K. (2003). *A coordinated response to child abuse and neglect: The foundation for practice* [On-line]. Available: http://www.childwelfare. gov/pubs/usermanuals/foundation/index.cfm; Sullivan, S. (2000). *Child neglect: Current definitions and models—A review of child neglect research, 1993– 1998.* Ottawa, Canada: National Clearinghouse on Family Violence; Perry, B. D. (1997). *Incubated in terror: Neurodevelopmental factors in the 'cycle of violence'* [On-line]. Available: http://www.childtrauma. org/CTAMATERIALS/incubated.asp; Kraemer, G. W. (1992). A psychobiological theory of attachment. *Behavioral and Brain Sciences, 15*(3), 493–511.

[70] Shonkoff, J., & Phillips, D. (Eds.). (2000). *From neurons to neighborhoods: The science of early childhood development.* Washington, DC: National Academy Press; Kagan, J. (1999). The role of parents in children's psychological development. *Pediatrics, 104*(1), 164–167.

[71] Boszormenyi-Nagy, I., & Spark, G. M. (1973). *Invisible loyalties: Reciprocity in intergenerational family therapy.* New York, NY: Harper & Row.

[72] Kilpatrick, D., Acierno, R., Saunders, B., Resnick, H., & Best, C. (2000). Risk factors for adolescent substance abuse and dependence: Data from a national sample. *Journal of Consulting and Clinical Psychology, 68*(1), 19–30.

[73] National Research Council, Panel on Research on Child Abuse and Neglect. (1993). *Understanding child abuse and neglect.* Washington, DC: National Academy Press; Dembo, R., Dertke, M., La Voie, L., Borders, S., Washburn, M., & Schmeidler, J. (1987). Physical abuse, sexual victimization and illicit drug use: A structural analysis among high-risk adolescents. *Journal of Adolescence, 10*(1), 13–34.

[74] National Research Council, Panel on Research on Child Abuse and Neglect. (1993).

[75] McCauley, J., Kern, D. E., Kolodner, K., Dill, L., Schroeder, A. F., DeChant, H. K., et al. (1997). Clinical characteristics of women with a history of childhood abuse. *Journal of the American Medical Association, 277*(17), 1362–1368.

[76] Stein, J. A., Leslie, M. B., & Nyamathi, A. (2002). Relative contributions of parent substance use and childhood maltreatment to chronic homelessness, depression, and substance abuse problems among homeless women: Mediating roles of self-esteem and abuse in adulthood. *Child Abuse & Neglect, 26*(10), 1011–1027.

[77] Breshears, E. M., Yeh, S., & Young, N. K. (2004). *Understanding substance abuse and facilitating recovery: A guide for child welfare workers* [On-line]. Available: http://www.ncsacw.samhsa.gov/fi les/508/ UnderstandingSAGuideDW.htm.

[78] Nakashian, M., & Moore, E. A. (2001). *Identifying substance abuse among TANF eligible families.* Rockville, MD: U.S. Department of Health and Human Services, SAMHSA.

[79] Illinois State University, School of Social Work. (2001). *Signs of client methamphetamine use and caseworker safety procedures* [On-line]. Available: http://www.drugfreeinfo.org/PDFs/ strengthensupervision.pdf.

[80] Society for Public Health Education, U.S. Department of Health and Human Services, Agency for Toxic Substances and Disease Registry, & The American College of Medical Toxicology. (2007). *Helping communities combat clandestine methamphetamine laboratories* [On-line]. Available: http://www.sophe.org/ upload/Meth%20Toolkit_ final_997254035_3242008 14271 9.pdf.

[81] Society for Public Health Education, U.S. Department of Health and Human Services, Agency for Toxic Substances and Disease Registry, & The American College of Medical Toxicology. (2007).

[82] California Attorney General's Office, Crime and Violence Prevention Center. (n.d.). *Recognizing clandestine meThlabs* [On-line]. Available: http:// www.stopdrugs.org/recognizinglabs.html; KCI The Anti-MethSite. (n.d.). *Is there a meThlab cookin' in your neighborhood?* [On-line]. Available: http:// www.kci.org/meth_info/neighborhood_lab.htm; Salus, M. K. (2004*). Supervising child protective services caseworkers* [On-line]. Available: http:// www.childwelfare.gov/pubs/usermanuals/supercps/ supercps.pdf.

[83] Ewing, J. A. (1984). Detecting alcoholism: The CAGE Questionnaire. *Journal of the American Medical Association, 252*, 1905–1907

[84] Hoffman, N. G. (n.d.). *UNCOPE* [On-line]. Available: http://www.evinceassessment.com/ UNCOPE_for_web. pdf.

[85] Breshears, E. M., et al. (2004).

[86] Wanberg, K. W. (2000). *User's guide to the Self- Assessment Survey—SAS: Preliminary screening for substance abuse problems.* Arvada, CO: Center for Addiction Research and Evaluation; Nakashian, M. (2003). *Talk and trust: Identifying substance abuse among Colorado Works families* [On-line]. Available: http://www.ncsacw.samhsa.gov/fi les/508/ talkAndTrust.htm.

[87] Breshears, E. M., et al. (2004).

[88] Nakashian, M. (2003).

[89] Feild, T., & Wintefeld, A. P. (2003). *Tough problems, tough choices: Guidelines for needs-based service planning in child welfare* [On-line]. Available: http:// www.americanhumane.org/protecting-children resources/casey-decision-making-guidelines/products. html.

[90] Breshears, E. M., et al. (2004).

[91] National Association of State Alcohol and Drug Abuse Directors. (2001, March). *Alcohol and other drug treatment effectiveness: A review of state outcome studies* [On-line]. Available: http://www.nasadad.org/ resource.php?base_id=9 1; Hubbard, R. L., Craddock, S. G., Flynn, P. M., Anderson, J., & Etheridge, R. M.

(1997). Overview of one-year follow-up outcomes in DATOS. *Psychology of Addictive Behavior, 11*(4), 261–278; University of Chicago, National Opinion Research Center. (1997). *National treatment improvement evaluation study. Final report* [On-line]. Available: http://www.icpsr.umich.edu/SAMHDA/ NTIES/NTIES-PDF/ntiesfnl.pdf; Gerstein, D. R., Johnson, R. A., Harwood, H., Fountain, D., Suter, N., & Malloy, K. (1994). *Evaluating recovery services: The California Drug and Alcohol Treatment Assessment (CALDATA)*. Sacramento, CA: California Department of Alcohol and Drug Programs; Hubbard, R., Mardsen, M., Rachal, J., Harwood, H., Cavanaugh, E., & Ginzburg, H. (1989). *Drug abuse treatment: A national study of effectiveness*. Chapel Hill, NC: University of North Carolina Press; Simpson, D. (1981). Treatment for drug abuse: Follow-up outcomes and length of time spent. *Archives of General Psychiatry, 38*(8), 875–880.

[92] Green, B. G., Rockhill, A. M., & Furrer, C. J. (2007). Does substance abuse treatment make a difference for child welfare case outcomes? A statewide longitudinal analysis. *Children and Youth Services Review, 29*(4), 460–473.

[93] Gerstein, D. R., et al. (1994).

[94] U.S. Department of Health and Human Services, NIH, NIDA. (2005b).

[95] U.S. Department of Health and Human Services, NIH, NIDA. (2005b).

[96] U.S. Department of Labor. (2006). *Treatment* [Online]. Available: http://www.dol.gov/asp/programs/drugs/workingpartners/sab/treatment.asp.

[97] Breshears, E. M., et al. (2004).

[98] Finklestein, N., VandeMark, N., Fallot, R., Brown, V., Cadiz, S., & Heckman, J. (2004). *Enhancing substance abuse recovery through integrated trauma treatment*. Sarasota, FL: National Trauma Consortium.

[99] Sorensen, J. L., & Copeland, A. L. (2000). Drug abuse treatment as an HIV prevention strategy: A review. *Drug and Alcohol Dependence, 59*(1), 17–31.

[100] Palla, S., Kakuska, C., Myles, B., & Hercik, J. (2003). *Achieving common goals: Final report* [Online]. Available: http://peerta.acf.hhs.gov/pdf/ common_goals.pdf.

[101] Child Welfare League of America. (2002). *CWLA testimony submitted to the Senate Finance Subcommittee on Social Security and Family Policy for the hearing on issues in TANF reauthorization: Helping hard-to-employ families* [On-line]. Available: http://www.cwla.org/ advocacy/tanf020425.htm.

[102] U.S. Department of Health and Human Services, SAMHSA. (2008).

[103] Palla, S., et al. (2003); Wetzler, S. (2000). *An innovative approach to welfare reform: The University Behavioral Associates Bronx Demonstration Project*. Unpublished manuscript.

[104] Kirby, G., Pavetti, L., Kauff, J., & Tapogna, J. (1999). *Integrating alcohol and drug treatment into a work-oriented welfare program: Lessons from Oregon* [On-line]. Available: http://www.mathematica-mpr.com/PDFs/oregon.pdf; Rivera, J. A. (2003). *Defining and operationalizing work in the substance abuse treatment setting*. Brooklyn, NY: Rivera, Sierra & Company; Palla, S., et al. (2003).

[105] Breshears, E. M., et al. (2004).

[106] Wright, S. (2000).

[107] U.S. Department of Health and Human Services, SAMHSA. (2000). *Substance abuse treatment for persons with child abuse and neglect issues* [On- line]. Available: http://ncadi.samhsa.gov/govpubs/ BKD343/; U.S. Department of Health and Human Services, SAMHSA. (1997). *Substance abuse treatment and domestic violence* [On-line]. Available: http:// ncadi.samhsa.gov/govpubs/BKD239/.

[108] U.S. Department of Health and Human Services, CDC. (2001). *HIV/AIDS surveillance report* [Online]. Available: http://www.cdc.gov/hiv/stats/ hasr1 302.htm.

[109] U.S. Department of Health and Human Services, SAMHSA, OAS. (2003). *Admissions of persons with co-occurring disorders: 2000. The DASIS report* [On- line]. Available: http://oas.samhsa.gov/2k3/dualTX/dualTX.htm.

[110] U.S. Department of Health and Human Services, NIH, NIDA. (2005c). *NIDA InfoFacts: Treatment methods for women* [On-line]. Available: http://www. drugabuse.gov/Infofacts/TreatWomen.html.

[111] U.S. Department of Health and Human Services, SAMHSA. (2008).

[112] U.S. Department of Health and Human Services, SAMHSA, OAS. (2007). *The NSDUH Report: Substance use treatment among women of childrearing age* [On-line]. Available: http://www.oas.samhsa.gov/2k7/womenTX/womenTX.cfm.

[113] U.S. Department of Health and Human Services, SAMHSA. (2008).

[114] DePanfilis, D., & Salus, M. K. . *Child protective services: A guide for caseworkers* [On-line]. Available: http://www.childwelfare.gov/pubs/usermanuals/cps/ cps.pdf.

[115] National Family Preservation Network. (2005). *North Carolina Family Assessment Scale* [On-line]. Available: http://www.nfpn.org/preservation. php.

[116] Breshears, E. M., et al. (2004).

[117] North Carolina Division of Social Services, & The Family and Children's Resource Program. (2005). *Crafting a safe, family-centered response to meth* [Online]. Available: http://www.practicenotes.org/vol10_n2/familycentered.htm.

[118] Miller, W., & Rollnick, S. (1992). *Motivational interviewing: Preparing people to change addictive behavior*. New York, NY: Guilford Press.

[119] Breshears, E. M., et al. (2004).
[120] Rollnick, S., & Miller, W. (1995). What is motivational interviewing? *Behavioral and Cognitive Psychotherapy, 23*(4), 325–334.
[121] Miller, W. R. (1999). *Enhancing motivation for change in substance abuse treatment (Treatment Improvement Protocol Series 35)* [On-line]. Available: http:// www.ncbi.nlm.nih.gov/books/bv.fcgi?rid=hstat5. chapter.61 302.
[122] U.S. Department of Health and Human Services, ACF. (1999); U.S. Department of Health and Human Services, ACF, Children's Bureau. (1997). *National Study of Protective, Preventive and Reunification Services Delivered to Children and Their Families*. Washington, DC: U.S. Government Printing Office.
[123] National Association for Children of Alcoholics. (n.d.). *Facts for you* [On-line]. Available: http://www.nacoa.org/facts4u.htm.
[124] Ryan, J. (2006). *Illinois alcohol and other drug abuse (AODA) waiver demonstration: Final evaluation report* [On-line]. Available: http://cfrcwww.social.uiuc.edu/ pubs/Pdf.files/AODA.01 .06.pdf.
[125] Kantor, G. K. (2006). *Evaluation of New Hampshire's Title IV-E waiver demonstration project: 1999 –2005. Executive summary* [On-line]. Available: http://pubpages.unh. edu/thgkk/Papers(pdf)+Presentations(ppt)/FirstStepExecSummary. pdf pdf.
[126] Stark, D. R. (1999). *Collaboration basics: Strategies from six communities engaged in collaborative efforts among families, child welfare and children's mental health*. Washington, DC: Georgetown University, Center for Child and Human Development.
[127] Huddleston, C. W. (2005). *Drug courts: An effective strategy for communities facing methamphetamine* [On-line]. Available: http://www.ojp.usdoj.gov/BJA/pdf/ MethDrugCourts.pdf.
[128] Marlowe, D. B., DeMatteo, D. S., & Festinger, D. S. (2003). A sober assessment of drug courts. *Federal Sentencing Reporter, 16*(2), 153–1 57.
[129] Huddleston, C. W. (2005).
[130] NPC Research. (2007). *The National Family Treatment Drug Court Evaluation: Key outcome findings* [On-line]. Available: http://www.npcresearch. com/Files/FTDC_Evaluation_Key_Outcome_ Findings.pdf.
[131] Young, N. K., & Gardner, S. L. (2002).
[132] Young, N. K., & Gardner, S. L. (2002); U.S. Department of Health and Human Services, ACF. (1999).
[133] U.S. Department of Health and Human Services, SAMHSA. (2004). *The confidentiality of alcohol and drug abuse patient records regulation and the HIPAA privacy rule: Implications for alcohol and substance abuse programs* [On-line]. Available: http://www. hipaa.samhsa.gov/Part2privacyrule.htm.
[134] U.S. Department of Health and Human Services, SAMHSA. (1 999c). *Welfare reform and substance abuse treatment confidentiality: General guidance for reconciling need to know and privacy*. Rockville, MD: Author.
[135] U.S. Department of Health and Human Services, ACF. (2005). *Information memorandum ACYF-CB- IM-05-07* [On-line]. Available: http://www.acf.hhs.gov/programs/cb/laws_policies/policy/im/im0507.htm.
[136] American Psychiatric Association. (1994). Diagnostic and statistical manual of mental disorders (4thed.) Text Revision (DSM-IV-TR). Washington, DC: Author.
[137] U.S. Department of Health and Human Services, Substance Abuse and Mental Health Services Administration. (2003). *Marijuana: Facts for teens* [On-line]. Available: http://www.nida.nih.gov/MarijBroch/Marijteens.html.
[138] UNational Inhalant Prevention Coalition. (2004). *About inhalants* [On-line]. Available: http://www.inhalants.org/about.htm.
[139] Lester, B. M., LaGasse, L. L., & Siefer, R. (1998). Cocaine exposure and children: The meaning of subtle effects. *Science, 282*(5389), 633–634.
[140] American Council for Drug Education. (1999). Basic facts about drugs: Methamphetamine [On-line]. Available: http://www.acde. org/common/Meth.htm.
[141] Otero, C., Boles, S., Young, N. K., & Dennis, K. (2004). Methamphetamine: Addiction, treatment, outcomes and implications. Rockville, MD: U.S. Department of Health and Human Services, Substance Abuse and Mental Health Services Administration.
[142] Bragg, H. L. (2003). *Child protection in families experiencing domestic violence* [On-line]. Available: http://www.childwelfare.gov/ pubs/usermanuals/domesticviolence/.
[143] Adapted from U.S. Department of Justice, Office of Juvenile Justice and Delinquency Prevention. (2000). Legal issues. *Juvenile Accountability Incentive Block Grants Program Bulletin* [On-line]. Available: http://www.ncjrs.org/html/ ojjdp/jiabg_blltn_03_1_00/6.html.

In: Parents with Substance Use Disorders and Child Protection... ISBN: 978-1-60692-400-6
Editor: Thomas P. Brouwer © 2011 Nova Science Publishers, Inc.

Chapter 2

PARENTAL SUBSTANCE USE AND THE CHILD WELFARE SYSTEM

United States Department of Health and Human Services

Parental substance use continues to be a serious issue in the child welfare system. Maltreated children of parents with substance use disorders often remain in the child welfare system longer and experience poorer outcomes than other children (U.S. Department of Health and Human Services [HHS], 1999). Addressing the multiple needs of these children and families is challenging.

What's inside:

- Statistics and costs
- Impact of parental substance use on parenting
- Impact on child outcomes
- Methamphetamine
- Other substances
- Service delivery issues
- Promising practices
- Resources for further information

This bulletin provides a brief overview of some of the issues confronting families affected by parental substance use who enter the child welfare system, and it examines some of the service barriers as well as the innovative approaches child welfare agencies have developed to best meet the needs of these children and families.

STATISTICS AND COSTS

It is estimated that 9 percent of children in this country (6 million) live with at least one parent who abuses alcohol or other drugs (Substance Abuse and Mental Health Services

Administration [SAMHSA], 2003). Studies indicate that between one-third and two-thirds of child maltreatment cases involve substance use to some degree (HHS, 1999).

It is difficult to determine the numbers of child welfare cases that involve substance-using parents. One article notes that not all child welfare agencies systematically record information on parental substance use disorders, and many substance abuse treatment programs do not routinely ask patients if they have children (Young, Boles, & Otero, 2007). The article goes on to summarize available data from a number of national studies, estimating that 22,440 children receiving in-home services for maltreatment and 128,640 to 211,720 children in out-of-home care had a parent with a substance use disorder in 2004. In that same year, approximately 295,000 parents receiving treatment for substance use had one or more children removed by child protective services.

Expenditures related to substance use are significant, because maltreated children of parents with a substance use disorder may experience more severe problems and remain in the foster care system longer than maltreated children from other families (HHS, 1999). One study estimates that of the more than $24 billion States spend annually to address different aspects of substance use, $5.3 billion (slightly more than 20 percent) goes to child welfare costs related to substance abuse (National Center on Addiction and Substance Abuse at Columbia University, 2001).

IMPACT OF PARENTAL SUBSTANCE USE ON PARENTING

Parents with substance use disorders may not be able to function effectively in a parental role. This can be due to:

- Impairments (both physical and mental) caused by alcohol or other drugs
- Domestic violence, which may be a result of substance use
- Expenditure of often limited household resources on purchasing alcohol or other drugs
- Frequent arrests, incarceration, and court dates
- Time spent seeking out, manufacturing, or using alcohol or other drugs
- Estrangement from primary family and related support

Families in which one or both parents have substance use disorders, and particularly families with an addicted parent, often experience a number of other problems that affect parenting, including mental illness, unemployment, high levels of stress, and impaired family functioning, all of which can put children at risk for maltreatment (National Center on Addiction and Substance Abuse at Columbia University, 2005). The basic needs of children, including nutrition, supervision, and nurturing, may go unmet due to parental substance use, resulting in neglect. Depending on the extent of the substance use and other circumstances (e.g., the presence of another caregiver), dysfunctional parenting can also include physical and other kinds of abuse (HHS, 1999).

IMPACT ON CHILD OUTCOMES

The impact of parental substance use disorders on a child can begin before the child is born. While the full effects of prenatal drug exposure depend on a number of factors, alcohol or drug use during pregnancy has been associated with infant mortality, premature birth, miscarriage, low birth weight, and a variety of behavioral and cognitive problems in the child (National Institute on Drug Abuse, n.d.; Maternal Substance Abuse and Child Development Project, n.d.). A 2007 study of children in foster care found that prenatal maternal alcohol use predicted child maltreatment, and combined prenatal maternal alcohol and drug use predicted foster care transitions (Smith, Johnson, Pears, Fisher, & DeGarmo).

Fetal alcohol spectrum disorders (FASD) are among the most well-known consequences, affecting an estimated 40,000 infants born each year. Children with FASD may experience mental, physical, behavioral, and learning disabilities (National Organization on Fetal Alcohol Syndrome, 2006). Children with the most severe disorders may suffer from fetal alcohol syndrome, alcohol-related neurodevelopmental disorder, or alcohol- related birth defects.

Research has demonstrated that children of parents with substance use disorders are more likely to experience abuse (physical, sexual, or emotional) or neglect than children in other households (DeBellis et al., 2001; Dube et al., 2001; Hanson et al., 2006). As infants, they may suffer from attachment difficulties that develop because of inconsistent care and nurturing, which may interfere with their emotional development (Tay, 2005). As growing children, they may experience chaotic households that lack structure, positive role models, and adequate opportunities for socialization (Hornberger, 2008).

In addition, children of parents who use or abuse substances have an increased chance of experiencing a variety of other negative outcomes (HHS, 1999):

- Maltreated children of parents with substance use disorders are more likely to have poorer physical, intellectual, social, and emotional outcomes.
- They are at greater risk of developing substance use problems themselves.
- They are more likely to be placed in foster care and to remain there longer than maltreated children of parents without substance use problems.

METHAMPHETAMINE

Over the last decade, there has been an increase in the manufacture and use of methamphetamine. From 1995 to 2005, the percentage of substance abuse treatment admissions for primary abuse of methamphetamine/amphetamine more than doubled from 4 percent to 9 percent (National Clearinghouse for Drug and Alcohol Information, n.d.).

Parental use of methamphetamine has many of the same effects on children as other kinds of drug use. Prenatal exposure can produce birth defects and low birth weight and may lead to developmental disorders (Brown University, 2006). Parents who use methamphetamine may suffer physical and psychological effects that lead to abuse and neglect of their children (National Institute on Drug Abuse, 2006). In addition, some methamphetamine users also are producers of the drug, which can be manufactured using common household products. These home "labs" put children in additional danger from exposure to the drugs and the conditions under which they are manufactured and distributed (Swetlow, 2003).

Surveys conducted by the National Association of Counties indicate that methamphetamine has increased the burden of child welfare agencies in many areas of the country (National Association of Counties, 2005). In addition to increasing caseloads in some areas, the unique dangers of methamphetamine labs have prompted many jurisdictions to develop specific protocols for meeting the needs of children who may have been exposed to the drug (Swetlow, 2003).

OTHER SUBSTANCES

While methamphetamine continues to garner much attention, other drugs actually account for the bulk of substance use disorders. According to SAMHSA (2007):

- Marijuana was the most commonly used illicit drug in 2006, accounting for 72.8 percent of illicit drug use.
- In 2006, there were 2.4 million cocaine users, a figure that remained the same from 2005 but was an increase from 2002 (at 2.0 million).
- The number of heroin users increased from 136,000 in 2005 to 338,000 in 2006, and the corresponding prevalence rate increased from 0.06 to 0.14 percent.
- The most widely used substance continues to be alcohol. In 2006, heavy drinking was reported by 6.9 percent of the population (17 million people), while binge drinking was reported by 23 percent (57 million people).

SERVICE DELIVERY ISSUES

Child welfare agencies face a number of difficulties in serving children and families affected by parental substance use disorders:

- Inadequate funds for services and/or dependence on client insurance coverage
- Insufficient service availability or scope of services to meet existing needs
- Lack of training for child welfare workers on substance use issues
- Lack of coordination between the child welfare system and other services and systems, including hospitals that may screen for drug exposure, the criminal justice system, and the courts
- Conflicts in the time required for sufficient progress in substance abuse recovery to develop adequate parenting potential, legislative requirements regarding child permanency, and the developmental needs of children (Young & Gardner, 2003)

Agencies are faced with timeframes imposed by the Adoption and Safe Families Act of 1997 (ASFA) that may not coincide with substance abuse treatment. Although ASFA requires that an agency file a petition for termination of parental rights if a child has been in foster care for 15 of the past 22 months, unless it is not in the best interest of the child, many States cannot adhere to this timeframe due to problems with accessing substance abuse services in a timely manner. This results in delayed permanency decisions for children in the foster care system (U.S. General Accounting Office [GAO], 2003). For example, despite a Federal mandate that pregnant and parenting women receive priority for accessing substance abuse treatment services, States report it is often difficult for these parents to access an open treatment slot quickly (GAO, 2003). Once a slot is available, treatment itself may take many months, and achieving sufficient stability to care for their children may take parents even longer. In addition, relapse is often part of the recovery process for parents undergoing treatment, especially in the early phases, so it is especially important that parents access treatment quickly (HHS, 1999). Custodial parents who require residential treatment may face an additional barrier since many of these programs do not allow children to live in the facility.

PROMISING PRACTICES

There is a growing movement toward collaboration among the child welfare, substance abuse, courts, and other systems that provide services for children and families affected by substance use by their parents. Communication, understanding, and active collaboration among service systems are vital to ensuring that child welfare-involved parents in need of substance abuse treatment are accurately identified and receive appropriate treatment in a timely manner (Child Welfare League of America, 2001; HHS, 1999).

Some examples of effective approaches include:

Prevention and Treatment

- Focusing on early identification of at-risk families in substance abuse treatment programs so that prevention services can be provided to ensure children's safety and well-being in the home
- Providing coaching or mentoring to parents for their treatment, recovery, and parenting (Ryan, 2006)
- Offering shared family care in which a family experiencing parental substance use and resulting child maltreatment is placed with a host family for support and mentoring (National Abandoned Infants Assistance Resource Center, n.d.)
- Giving mothers involved in the child welfare system priority access to substance abuse treatment slots
- Providing inpatient treatment for mothers in facilities where they can have their children with them
- Motivating parents to enter and complete treatment by offering such incentives as support groups or housing (Voices for America's Children, November 2004).

Systems Changes

- Stationing addiction counselors in child welfare offices or forming ongoing teams of child welfare and substance abuse workers

- Developing or modifying dependency drug courts to ensure treatment access and therapeutic monitoring of compliance with court orders
- Developing cross-system partnerships to ensure coordinated services (e.g., formal linkages between child welfare and other community agencies to address each family's needs)
- Providing wraparound services that streamline the recovery and reunification processes
- Conducting cross-system training
- Recruiting and training a diverse workforce and including training in cultural competence (National Center on Substance Abuse and Child Welfare, 2005)
- Exploring various funding streams to support these efforts (e.g., using State or local funds to maximize child welfare funding for substance abuse-related services or using Temporary Assistance to Needy Families [TANF] funds to support substance abuse treatment for families also involved with the child welfare system) (Young and Gardner, 2002)

The Children's Bureau has funded a number of discretionary grants to promote demonstration projects with a goal of improved outcomes for children growing up in families in which one or more parents has a substance use problem. These grants have included:

- Family Support Services for Grandparents and Other Relatives Providing Care for Children and Substance Abusing and HIV-Positive Women (awarded in 2001 with six grantees)
- Family Support Services for Grandparents and Other Relatives Providing Caregiving for Children of Substance Abusing and/ or HIV-Positive Women (awarded in 2004 with four grantees)
- Model Development or Replication to Implement the CAPTA Requirement to Identify and Serve Substance Exposed Newborns (awarded in 2005, with four grantees)
- Targeted Grants to Increase the Well- Being of, and to Improve the Permanency Outcomes for, Children Affected by Methamphetamine or Other Substance Abuse (awarded in 2007, with 53 grantees under four program options)

(For more information on these awards, visit the Children's Bureau Discretionary Grants Library online at http://basis.caliber GrantHome.)

Replication or adaptation of any of the above approaches requires a careful assessment of State or local capacity, including needs and strengths of families served, as well as a careful assessment of the evaluation findings to ensure funds are targeted toward effective programs. Agencies also should focus on the specific needs of the families they serve when selecting among these (and other) approaches.

RESOURCES FOR FURTHER INFORMATION

Child Welfare Information Gateway
www.childwelfare.gov/systemwide/ service_array/substance/

The Substance Abuse web section of the Information Gateway website links to information on prevention and treatment services for families affected by parental substance use and involved with the child welfare system.

Children's Bureau
www.acf.hhs.gov/programs/cb
The Children's Bureau funds a variety of programs and initiatives that promote the safety, permanency, and well-being of children and their families, including initiatives designed to address parental substance use.

Children and Family Futures
www.cffutures.com
Children and Family Futures' mission is to improve the lives of children and families, particularly those affected by substance use disorders. CFF advises Federal, State, and local government and community-based agencies, conducts research on the best ways to prevent and address the problem, and provides comprehensive and innovative solutions to policy makers and practitioners.

MethResources.Gov
www.methresources.gov
This agency is part of the White House Office of National Drug Control Policy, U.S. Department of Justice, & the U.S. Department of Health and Human Services. The website offers factsheets, FAQs, and information and resources on prevention, intervention, and treatment for methamphetamine use.

National Abandoned Infants Assistance Resource Center
http://aia.berkeley.edu
The National Abandoned Infants Assistance Resource Center's mission is to enhance the quality of social and health services delivered to children who are abandoned or at-risk of abandonment due to the presence of drugs and/or HIV in the family. The Resource Center, which is funded by the Children's Bureau, provides training, information, support, and resources to service providers who assist these children and their families.

National Center on Substance Abuse and Child Welfare
www.ncsacw.samhsa.gov
NCSACW was formed to improve systems and practice for families with substance use disorders who are involved in the child welfare and family judicial systems by assisting local, State, and Tribal agencies. NCSACW is jointly funded by the Children's Bureau and SAMHSA.

National Clearinghouse for Alcohol & Drug Information
http://ncadi.samhsa.gov
Sponsored by SAMHSA, NCADI is a one-stop resource for information about substance abuse prevention and addiction treatment; resources include the Prevention Materials database, with more than 8,000 prevention- related materials, and the Treatment Resources database, available to the public in electronic form.

National Institute on Alcohol Abuse and Alcoholism
www.niaaa.nih.gov
Part of the National Institutes of Health, the NIAAA is the primary U.S. agency for conducting and supporting research on the causes, consequences, prevention, and treatment of alcohol abuse, alcoholism, and alcohol problems and disseminates research findings to general, professional, and academic audiences.

National Institute on Drug Abuse
www.nida.nih.gov
The National Institute on Drug Abuse supports over 85 percent of the world's research on the health aspects of drug abuse and addiction. NIDA works to ensure that the foundation for the nation's drug abuse reduction efforts are based on science.

National Organization on Fetal Alcohol Syndrome
www.nofas.org
NOFAS works to raise public awareness of Fetal Alcohol Syndrome (FAS) and to develop and implement innovative ideas in prevention, intervention, education, and advocacy in communities throughout the nation.

National Registry of Evidence-Based Programs and Practices
www.nrepp.samhsa.gov
SAMHSA sponsors this searchable database of interventions for the prevention and treatment of substance abuse and mental health disorders.

The Rocky Mountain Quality Improvement Center
www.americanhumane.org/site/PageServer?pagename=pc_best_practice_rmqic_homepage
The Rocky Mountain Quality Improvement Center (RMQIC) has completed its Children's Bureau-funded project, but the website continues to offer resources and information on providing safety, permanency, and well-being for children of families with substance abuse problems.

Self-Help Groups
http://ncadistore.samhsa.gov/catalog/ referrals.aspx?topic=83&h=resources
SAMHSA provides this list of national self-help groups with contact information so that local meetings and resources can be identified. Groups include Alcoholics Anonymous, Al-Anon, National Association for Children of Alcoholics, Women for Sobriety, and more.

Substance Abuse and Mental Health Services Administration
www.samhsa.gov
SAMHSA is the Federal agency charged with improving the quality and availability of prevention, treatment, and rehabilitative services in order to reduce illness, death, disability, and cost to society resulting from substance abuse and mental illnesses.

REFERENCES

[1] Brown University (2006, September 16). Methamphetamine use restricts fetal growth, study finds. *ScienceDaily*. Retrieved May 27, 2008, from www.sciencedaily.com/ releases/2006/09/0609 1520505 6.htm

[2] Child Welfare League of America. (2001). *Alcohol, other drugs, & child welfare*. Washington, D.C.: Author. Retrieved January 28, 2008, from www.cwla.org/ programs/bhd/aodbrochure.pdf

[3] DeBellis, M. D., Broussard, E. R., Herring, D. J., Wexler, S., Moritz, G. & Benitez, J. G. (2001). Psychiatric co-morbidity in caregivers and children involved in maltreatment: A pilot research study with policy implications. *Child Abuse & Neglect*, 25, 923-944.

[4] Dube, S. R., Anda, R. F., Felitti, V. J., Croft, J. B., Edwards, V. J. & Giles, W. H. (2001). Growing up with parental alcohol abuse: Exposure to childhood abuse, neglect, and household dysfunction. *Child Abuse & Neglect*, 25, 1627-1640.

[5] Hanson, R. F., Self-Brown, S., Fricker-Elhai, A. E., Kilpatrick, D. G., Saunders, B. E. & Resnick, H. S. (2006). The relations between family environment and violence exposure among youth: Findings from the National Survey of Adolescents. *Child Maltreatment, 11(1)*, 3-15.

[6] Hornberger, S. (2008, May). *Children and families impacted by alcohol and drug dependency: What do we know and what are we learning*. PowerPoint presented at Child Welfare Information Gateway, Fairfax, VA.

[7] Maternal Substance Abuse and Child Development Project. (n.d.). *Facts about drug use in pregnancy*. Retrieved January 28, 2008, from www.psychiatry Drugs%20Fact% 20Sheet.pdf

[8] National Abandoned Infants Assistance Resource Center. (n.d.). (2008). Shared family care (webpage). Downloaded May 27, from http://aia.berkeley.edu information_ resources/shared_family_ care.php

[9] National Association of Counties. (2005). *The meth epidemic in America. Two surveys of U.S. counties: The criminal effect of meth on communities; the impact of meth on children*. Retrieved January 28, 2008, from www.naco.org/Template. cfm?Section= Media_Center&template=/ContentManagement/ContentDisplay.cfm&   ContentID=1 7216

[10] National Center on Addiction and Substance Abuse at Columbia University. (2001). *Shoveling up: The impact of substance abuse on state budgets*. New York: Author. Retrieved January 28, 2008, from www. casacolumbia.org/absolutenm/templates/ articles.asp?articleid=239&zoneid=3 1

[11] National Center on Addiction and Substance Abuse at Columbia University. (2005). *Family matters: Substance abuse and the American family*. New York: Author. Retrieved March 7, 2008, from www.casacolumbia.org/Absolutenm/ articlefiles/380-family_matters_report.pdf

[12] National Clearinghouse for Drug and Alcohol Information. (n.d.) Retrieved April 24, 2008, from http://ncadistore. samhsa.gov/catalog/productDetails. aspx?ProductID=1 7801

[13] National Institute on Drug Abuse (n.d.). *Prenatal effects*. Retrieved January 28, 2008, from www.drugabuse.gov/ consequences/prenatal/

[14] National Institute on Drug Abuse. (2006). *Methamphetamine abuse and addiction*. Retrieved January 28, 2008, from www.drugabuse.gov/PDF/RRMetham.pdf

[15] National Organization on Fetal Alcohol Syndrome. (2006). *FASD: What everyone should know*. Retrieved December 19, 2007, from www.nofas.org/MediaFiles/PDFs/factsheets/everyone.pdf

[16] National Center on Substance Abuse and Child Welfare. (2005). *Understanding substance abuse and facilitating recovery: A guide for child welfare workers*. Retrieved January 28, 2008, from www.ncsacw. samhsa.gov/files/UnderstandingSAGuide. pdf

[17] Ryan, J. P. (2006). *Illinois Alcohol and Other Drug Abuse (AODA) waiver demonstration: Final evaluation report*. The State of Illinois Department of Children and Family Services. Retrieved April 25, 2008, from www.cfrc.illinois.edu/pubs/Pdf.files/AODA.01.06.pdf

[18] Smith, D. K., Johnson, A. B., Pears, K. C., Fisher, P. A. & DeGarmo, D. S. (2007). Child maltreatment and foster care: Unpacking the effects of prenatal and postnatal substance use. *Child Maltreatment, 12(2)*, 150-160.

[19] Substance Abuse and Mental Health Services Administration. (2003). *Children living with substance-abusing or substance- dependent parents*. (National Household Survey on Drug Abuse). Rockville, MD: Office of Applied Studies. Retrieved January 28, 2008, from www.oas.samhsa. gov/2k3/children

[20] Substance Abuse and Mental Health Services Administration. (2007). *Results from the 2006 national survey on drug use and health: National findings*. Rockville, MD: Office of Applied Studies (NSDUH Series H-32, DHHS Publication No. SMA 07-4293). Retrieved April 25, 2008, from www.oas.samhsa.gov/ nsduh/2k6nsduh/2k6Results.pdf

[21] Swetlow, K. (June 2003). Children at clandestine methamphetamine labs: Helping meth's youngest victims. *OVC Bulletin*. Retrieved January 28, 2008, from the website of the Office for Victims of Crime, U.S. Department of Justice: www. ojp.usdoj.gov/ovc/publications/bulletins/ children/19 7590.pdf

[22] Tay, L. (2005). *Attachment & recovery: Care for substance affected families*. Retrieved May 22, 2008, from the Child Health and Development Institute of Connecticut, Inc. website: www.chdi.org/admin/ uploads/220863825493d45d5e 790e.pdf

[23] U.S. Department of Health and Human Services. (1999). *Blending perspectives and building common ground: A report to Congress on substance abuse and child protection*. Washington, DC: U.S. Government Printing Office. Retrieved January 28, 2008, from http://aspe.hhs. gov/HSP/subabuse99/subabuse.htm

[24] U.S. General Accounting Office [GAO]. (2003). *Foster care: States focusing on finding permanent homes for children, but long-standing barriers remain*. Washington, D.C.: Author. Retrieved January 28, 2008, from www.gao.gov/new.items/d03626t.pdf

[25] Voices for America's Children. (November 2004). *Child welfare cases with substance abuse factors: A review of current strategies*. Retrieved January 28, 2008, from www.nadec.org/user_files/3538_1401049.pdf

[26] Young, N. K., Boles, S. M. & Otero, C. (2007). Parental substance use disorders and child maltreatment: Overlap, gaps, and opportunities. *Child Maltreatment, 12(2)*, 137-149.

[27] Young, N. & Gardner, S. (2003). *A preliminary review of alcohol and other drug issues in the states' children and family service reviews and program improvement plans.* Retrieved April 14, 2003 from www.ncsacw.samhsa.gov/files/ SummaryofCFSRs.pdf

[28] Young, N. & Gardner, S. (2002). *Navigating the pathways: Lessons and promising practices in linking alcohol and drug services with child welfare. Technical Assistance Publication (TAP) 27.* Rockville, MD: Substance Abuse and Mental Health Services Administration, Center for Substance Abuse Treatment.

Chapter 3

DRUG TESTING IN CHILD WELFARE: PRACTICE AND POLICY CONSIDERATIONS

United States Department of Health and Human Services

ACKNOWLEDGMENTS

This document was prepared by the National Center on Substance Abuse and Child Welfare (NCSACW) under Contract No. 270-027108 for the Substance Abuse and Mental Health Services Administration (SAMHSA) and the Administration for Children and Families (ACF), both within the U.S. Department of Health and Human Services (HHS). Nancy K. Young, Ph.D. developed the document with assistance from SAMHSA's Center for Substance Abuse Prevention (CSAP). Sharon Amatetti, M.P.H. served as the Government Project Officer from the SAMHSA Center for Substance Abuse Treatment (CSAT) and Irene Bocella, M.S.W. served as the Project Officer from the ACF Children's Bureau.

I. INTRODUCTION

Alcohol and other drug use can impair a parent's judgment and ability to provide the consistent care, supervision, and guidance that all children need. For child welfare workers who are charged with ensuring the safety of children, it is often difficult to determine what level of functional improvement will enable a parent with a substance use disorder to retain or resume his or her parental role without jeopardizing the child's well-being. Child welfare professionals are faced with the difficult task of collecting adequate information about families, making informed and insightful decisions based on this information, and taking timely and appropriate action to safeguard children.

The Adoption and Safe Families Act (P.L. 105-89) of 1997 requires that child welfare agencies and courts ensure that permanency in children's caregiving relationship is provided consistent with statutory timelines. These timelines, including a court hearing to oversee that a permanent placement is obtained twelve months after a child is placed in out-of-home-care, created a renewed urgency for finding effective ways to address concurrent substance abuse and child maltreatment in families whose children have been placed in protective custody.

Drug testing is one tool that child welfare workers often use to facilitate decision-making with these families. Drug testing refers to the use of various biologic sources such as urine, saliva, sweat, hair, breath, blood and meconium to determine the presence of specific substances and/or their metabolites in an individual's system. Child welfare workers use test results to make informed decisions regarding child removal, family support services, family reunification, or termination of parental rights. However, limited information has been available to child welfare workers, judges, and attorneys on the utility of drug testing and how to correctly interpret the results in the context of child welfare practice.

A drug test alone cannot determine the existence or absence of a substance use disorder. In addition, drug tests do not provide sufficient information for substantiating allegations of child abuse or neglect or for making decisions about the disposition of a case (including decisions regarding child removal, family reunification, or termination of parental rights). Child welfare workers, judges, and attorneys must make these decisions using information from the child abuse investigation, child safety and risk assessments, family assessments, and a comprehensive substance abuse assessment. It is helpful for these practitioners and policymakers to establish partnerships with their local substance abuse treatment counterparts, who can assist in the decision making that is critical to successful development and implementation of drug testing policies.

A drug test alone cannot determine the existence or absence of a substance use disorder. In addition, drug tests do not provide sufficient information for substantiating allegations of child abuse or neglect or for making decisions about the disposition of a case.

Organization and Purpose of This Paper

The purpose of this paper is to guide child welfare agency policymakers in developing practice and policy protocols regarding the use of drug testing in child welfare practice. This guidance describes the practice and policy issues that policymakers must address to include drug testing in the comprehensive assessment and monitoring that child welfare agencies provide.

The paper focuses primarily on drug testing of parents who come to the attention of child welfare agencies and courts through reports of child abuse or neglect. However, court practices and policies might use testing in other child welfare contexts. For example, drug testing might be useful for conducting home studies for prospective foster or adoptive parents, understanding drug use patterns among teens in out-of-home care, or evaluating older youth in independent living programs.

Throughout the paper, we identify key action steps to help child welfare agencies implement drug testing. We also include an appendix describing the Sacramento County, California, Divisions of Child Protective Services and Alcohol and Drug Services drug testing policy and procedures as an illustration of a well-developed policy.

II. CONSIDERATIONS FOR USING DRUG TESTING

Agency Values and Mandates

Policy discussions about drug testing often focus on technical testing methods, verification of test results, costs, staffing issues, and legal issues related to confidentiality. The values that shape drug testing policy are discusssed less often. However, the values of child welfare, substance abuse agencies, and courts deserve adequate attention at the beginning of the policy-making process to clarify the reasons for using drug testing.

Substance abuse treatment agencies and child welfare agencies commonly use drug testing for different purposes because they have different mandates and different underlying values and missions. These agencies' and professionals' values include attitudes about the nature of addiction, abstinence, and relapse, and about the effects of substance use and abuse on parenting.

These attitudes influence approaches to identifying and working with parents with substance use disorders, beyond drug testing. However, drug testing policies typically reflect agency mandates and values as well. The National Center on Substance Abuse and Child Welfare (NCSACW), funded by the Substance Abuse and Mental Health Services Administration and the Administration for Children and Families, has adopted the Collaborative Values Inventory (CVI) developed by Children and Family Futures. Partner agencies can administer the inventory anonymously to a group and then review the results to explore group members' values. Several of the questions address values related to drug testing. We recommend that partners explore these values when they begin forming policies and procedures governing drug testing. For information about the CVI, visit http:// www.ncsacw.sa mhsa .gov.

Key Action Step: Partner agencies need to understand value differences across systems concerning approaches to families affected by substance use disorders.

THE SPECIAL ISSUES OF TESTING FOR PRENATAL SUBSTANCE EXPOSURE

Several factors influence policies regarding the testing of newborns for evidence of prenatal substance exposure. These factors include cost and privacy concerns as well as societal, systems, and organizational values. Very few hospitals test newborns routinely, and studies have indicated that hospitals do not usually inform child welfare or other State agencies about the number of infants tested at birth, test results, or referrals to child welfare agencies (Young et al., 2008). However, recent legislation in some States requires a referral of children to a child welfare agency when drug exposure is detected, based on States' efforts to follow the Federal policy stated in the 2003 amendments to the Child Abuse Prevention and Treatment Act. Children with fetal alcohol spectrum disorders have also received increased attention in some States including the development of State policy committees. In addition, some States and localities have significantly expanded prenatal screening, rather than relying solely on testing at birth.

Establishing a Collaborative Approach before Implementing Drug Testing

Drug testing by child welfare agencies is not a stand-alone activity. It should be part of a larger effort to address substance use by parents and must therefore fit into the agency's and community's approach to substance abuse and take into consideration any State law or prior court cases affecting practice or policy. For additional information about creating a comprehensive, collaborative approach to address the screening and assessment needs of families with substance use disorders who are involved in the child welfare system, consult *Screening and Assessment for Family Engagement, Retention, and Recovery (SAFERR)*, a guidebook developed by the National Center on Substance Abuse and Child Welfare (Young, et al., 2007).

Drug Testing in Substance Abuse Treatment and Child Welfare Programs

Historically, child welfare agencies and substance abuse treatment agencies have used drug testing for different purposes. Both types of agencies conduct drug testing because it provides information about a client's drug use behavior that can confirm or contradict what the agency has learned through other assessments and observations. Agencies test people who might underreport or deny substance use due to fear of real or perceived negative reprisals.

Drug test results indicate only that the drug or its metabolite is present at or above the established concentration cutoff level in the test specimen. They do not reveal whether a parent abuses or is dependent on illicit drugs or alcohol. Conversely, child welfare agency professionals should not rely on a negative drug test result as the sole determining factor for ruling out substance use, abuse, or dependence. A negative drug test result only indicates that the test did not detect the drug or its metabolite or that its concentration is below the established cutoff level in that particular specimen at that time. Similarly, a drug test on a newborn at birth does not determine whether the mother's use or the extent of the mother's use has compromised her infant's growth or development.

> *Key Action Step: Complete training on recognizing signs and symptoms of substance use disorders.*

The best way to evaluate the probability that someone is not using drugs is by using a combination of random drug tests, self-reports, and observations of behavioral indicators by substance abuse treatment providers or professionals and child welfare workers. Observations include positive changes in hygiene and grooming; improved functioning in daily life; improved work behavior; avoidance of people, places, and things associated with drug use; and improved consistency in complying with child welfare and substance abuse treatment case plan requirements.

Drug Testing in Substance Abuse Treatment Settings

Substance abuse treatment providers commonly use drug testing as a tool to help clinically diagnose substance use disorders, plan treatment, monitor progress, and support recovery. Substance abuse treatment professionals use behavioral indications, such as those described above, to determine whether a parent is sustaining recovery, and they view drug testing as a useful test to confirm drug use.

Specifically, substance abuse treatment providers use drug testing to:

- Provide objective data in assessing and diagnosing substance use disorders and monitoring progress during treatment;[1]
- Provide an opportunity to address a parent's denial, inability, or unwillingness to recognize a need for intervention or treatment services and to address their motivation to stop using drugs;
- Provide an additional measure of accountability for clients and agencies by monitoring treatment efficacy; and
- Present objective evidence to the courts, child welfare agencies, criminal justice agencies, and other involved agencies that a parent is not using drugs, particularly when testing is conducted randomly over a period of time.

Drug Testing in Child Welfare Settings

Child welfare settings employ drug tests for different purposes than substance abuse treatment settings. Some of the more frequent uses for child welfare drug testing, in concert with other tools, are to:

- Provide proof of or rule out substance abuse as part of a child maltreatment or child abuse investigation and determine whether substance abuse is associated with child risk;
- Monitor whether a parent is continuing to use during an open child welfare case;
- Provide evidence that family reunification is warranted or unwarranted; and,
- Provide documented evidence that the parent is drug free (courts often order such documentation).

Key Action Step: Identify a clear purpose for using drug testing.

Child welfare agencies can also use drug testing to motivate parents who use substances to become involved in treatment and to provide motivation and positive reinforcement for parents in the early stages of recovery.

Drug testing in child welfare settings should be one component of a comprehensive family assessment to identify or eliminate substance abuse as a contributing factor to maltreatment.

Key Action Step: Determine how drug testing currently fits with the child welfare agency's overall risk and safety assessment protocols.

Situations in which drug testing is not appropriate in child welfare practice and policy include:

- The parent is an active participant in a substance abuse treatment program that already requires frequent random drug testing.
- The parent informs the case manager, treatment provider, or both of a relapse. In this circumstance, the case manager or treatment provider should assess the child's safety and risk. The provider should also consider assessing the parent's current drug use patterns and need for a treatment or alternative intervention. If the parent is under the court's jurisdiction, providers should also ask the parent to sign a drug use acknowledgement form as is common practice in criminal justice probation agencies.

III. DRUG TESTING CONSIDERATIONS

Policymakers must make several decisions to launch a drug testing program in a child welfare setting. These decisions include whether to test all parents reported to the agency, as well as where to conduct tests, the types of specimen to collect, and which substances to test for. Administrative considerations are important as well and include staff training and qualification requirements and costs associated with testing. Each of these issues is addressed below.

Determine Whom to Test

Due to the high rates of substance use disorders in parents reported to child welfare agencies for suspected child abuse or neglect, some child welfare agencies have decided to conduct drug tests on all parents under court jurisdiction. However, given the limitations of drug testing, this might not be cost effective. Selective testing is an alternative to testing all parents by providing the option to choose which parents need to undergo a drug test. This option potentially reduces the overall cost of the testing program by reducing the total number of tests.

When only testing selected parents, child welfare staff members should base decisions on which individuals to test using information from the child abuse investigation, child safety and risk assessments, and family assessments. Other considerations in determining who to drug test may involve mothers of babies who were identified at birth as having been prenatally exposed to drugs. Remember, drug testing can be a component of the child welfare assessment process, but is not a substitute for a substance abuse assessment.

A comprehensive substance abuse assessment involves a review of an individual's drug use pattern and areas of life affected by substance abuse such as family and social relationships, criminal justice, and psychological distress.

Specimen Types

Drugs and/or their metabolites can be detected in several different biological matrices. Drug testing facilities use the term "matrix" to refer to the specimen type analyzed in a drug test. Each specific specimen matrix including urine (the most common matrix used), saliva, sweat, hair, breath, blood, and meconium has a unique set of considerations during testing. Due to the serious implications of testing, every possible precaution should be in place to ensure the accuracy of the testing procedures.

The Substance Abuse and Mental Health Services Administration (SAMHSA) certifies drug testing laboratories for the Federal Workplace Drug Testing Program. This certification is currently only available for urine specimen testing, but proposed Federal guidelines are under consideration that may extend the process to hair, oral-fluid, and sweat-patch testing. Child welfare agencies are not bound by the Federal Employee Drug Testing Program requirements, but they might want to adopt this model program to ensure a high level of accuracy. For more information about the Federal drug testing program, as well as a list of certified laboratories, visit http://workplace

---

Key Action Step: Decide which individuals to test.

The following section provides a description of the various types of specimen tests and some of their implications based on information from the U.S. Department of Justice (2000) and Office on National Drug Control Policy (2007).

Urine specimens are the most widely used, cost effective, and well-researched specimens for detecting drugs in adults, older children, and youth. Most illicit drugs are excreted into urine during the 48 hours after use. For some drugs, frequent and multiple drug use can result in an extended detection period. For example, chronic, high dose marijuana users may produce confirmed positive results in urine for up to 30 days (Ellis, Mann, Judson, Schramm & Tashchian, 1985). To deter the individual who is undergoing the drug test from tampering with or adulterating his/her urine specimen, or from substituting his/her specimen with a specimen from someone else, agencies must use a supervised collection method. At this time, urine is the only biological specimen for which Federal guidelines are available.

Oral fluid, or saliva, is a more recently used matrix for drug testing. An oral fluid specimen is collected on a swab placed inside the cheek within the mouth. The advantages of testing oral fluids include the ease of collecting a sample, the noninvasive sample collection method, and the ability to identify drugs used within the previous 24 hours. Drug testing on oral fluid specimens can be performed either with a point-of-collection device or a laboratory test. Oral-fluid tests may be unable to detect use after 48 hours with some metabolites or drugs and may be less effective than urine tests in detecting past marijuana use. In addition, although studies have demonstrated that oral-fluid testing has clinically useful levels of accuracy, not all commercial drug testing products for oral fluids are equally reliable.

Sweat specimens are collected by applying a gauze patch with a tamper-evident adhesive seal directly to the skin for typically a 7-day period. The patch is usually applied to the upper arm or upper back. The sweat patch is analyzed by the laboratory for drugs and/or their metabolites. The sweat patch specimen provides a cumulative record of the individual's drug use during the time frame that the patch is worn. The advantages of using sweat patch tests include its cumulative record of drug use. Although this type of collection is noninvasive, it may be unsuitable for people with sensitive skin. External contamination from drugs is possible due to improper skin cleansing prior to patch application. Individual differences in amounts of sweat produced can also affect drug test results.

The use of **hair** specimens to detect drugs has become more common in recent years. Hair specimen tests can detect drug use over several months, depending on the length of the hair specimen. Other advantages of hair testing include the ability to pinpoint long-term changes in drug use patterns, difficulty of substituting specimens or invalidating results, and the noninvasive specimen collection method. Disadvantages include the test's inability to detect single-drug use within the last 3 days. Hair specimen testing is not effective for monitoring compliance on a regular basis because it cannot discriminate between recent drug use and use that occurred months earlier. Differences in hair structure, porosity, use of hair-color products, and external contamination can affect drug test results.

Breath specimens are collected using a device that estimates a person's blood-alcohol content. For forensically valid use, breath testing devices, commonly known as "breathalyzers" must be calibrated according to the U.S. Department of Transportation standards and State statutes or regulations (U.S. Department of Transportation, 2007). The major advantages of this specimen collection method include that it is inexpensive, noninvasive, and reliable for detecting the presence and concentration of alcohol. A limitation of breath specimen testing is that it only provides information about recent alcohol use but not drug use.

Blood specimens are collected to detect use of both alcohol and drugs. However, the process for obtaining blood specimens is invasive and qualified personnel must collect these specimens.

Meconium (contents of fetal intestines) specimens are collected from early newborn stools. Meconium testing detects the presence of drugs and alcohol, which helps determine if the infant has been prenatally exposed to these substances, indicating that the mother used drugs after 13 weeks of pregnancy. Meconium testing can detect use of alcohol, cocaine, marijuana, opiates, barbiturates, benzodiazepines, amphetamines, and phencyclidine (PCP) during pregnancy.

When deciding which specimen(s) to collect, child welfare agencies should determine which types of testing devices or instruments used to analyze specimens are available from vendors. They should choose the most accurate and cost-effective testing device for their program.

> *Key Action Step: Select the type of specimen to collect and the testing device to use.*

Detection Window

Timing is a critical factor in drug testing. The specific drug used, amount of drug in the person's body, the frequency of drug use, and metabolism affect how long the drug remains in the body. The detection window determines the type of specimen to collect because different types of specimens have different detection timeframes. Table 1 provides additional information from the Office of National Drug Control Policy (Office of National Drug Control Policy, 2002) on the pros and cons of various drug testing specimen matrices. The table also provides general guidelines from SAMHSA (Center for Substance Abuse Treatment [CSAT], 2006) on the detection period for each specimen matrix to help in the selection of the appropriate specimen type. The table also includes information on breath, blood, and meconium testing.

Table 1. Pros and Cons of Different Specimen Sources.

Specimen	Window of Detection	Pros	Cons
Urine	• Up to 2–4 days	• Most accurate results • Least expensive • Most flexibility for testing different drugs • Most likely to withstand legal challenge	• Specimen can be adulterated, substituted, or diluted • Limited detection window • Collection can be invasive or embarrassing • Specimen handling and shipping can be hazardous
Oral Fluid	• Up to 48 hours	• Collecting the oral fluid specimen can be observed • Minimal risk of tampering • Noninvasive • Can be collected easily in virtually any environment • Can be used to detect alcohol use • Can be used to detect recent drug use	• Drugs and drug metabolites do not remain in saliva as long as in urine • Less efficient than other testing methods for detecting marijuana use • pH changes can alter specimen • Moderate to high cost
Sweat	• FDA ceared for 7 days	• Relatively noninvasive • Sweat patch typically worn for 7 days • Quick application and removal of sweat patch • Patch seal tampering minimized • Longer window of drug detection than urine and blood	• Only a few laboratories offer sweat patch testing • Those with sensitive skin may react to the patch • Possible time-dependent drug loss from the patch • Possible external drug contamination from improper skin cleansing prior to application
		• Relatively resistant to specimen adulteration • No specimen substitution possible	• For marijuana, current use by a naïve user may not be detected • For marijuana, positive sweat results are possible in current abstinent, but previously chronic high dose, users • Sweat production dependent • Moderate to high cost

Table 1. (Continued).

Specimen	Window of Detection	Pros	Cons
Hair	• Up to 4–6 mnths	• Collecting the hair specimen can be observed • Long detection window • Does not deteriorate • Can be used to measure chronic drug use • Convenient shipping and storage; needs no refrigeration • Noninvasive • More difficult to adulterate than urine	• Moderate to high cost • Cannot be used to detect alcohol use • Cannot be used to detect drug use 1–7 days prior to drug test • Not effective for compliance monitoring • External contamination
Breath	• Up to 12–24 hours	• Minimal cost • Reliable detector of presence and amount of alcohol • Noninvasive	• Very limited detection window for alcohol • Can only be used to detect presence of alcohol
Blood	• Up to 12-24 hours	• Can be used to detect presence of drugs and alcohol • Test produces accurate results	• Invasive • Moderate to high cost
Meconium	• Up to 2-3 days	• Can be used to detect long-term use • Can be used to detect presence of drugs and alcohol • Easy to collect and highly reliable	• Short detection window after infant's birth

(Office of National Drug Control Policy, 2002; Substance Abuse and Mental Health Services Administration, Center for Substance Abuse Treatment, 2006).

Drug Testing Methods

Point of Collection and Laboratory Testing

Drug testing of specimens can be conducted at the point of collection or the specimen can be transported to a laboratory for testing.

Point-of-collection tests are screening tests conducted in the field at such locations as treatment facilities, child welfare offices, and courts. Field tests should be confirmed by a laboratory. Results from point-of-collection screening tests are usually visually interpreted by an analyst but many new technologies are using laboratory instruments to verify color differences. Some point-of-collection tests produce results in the form of a color on a dip stick. Differences in color acuity, color perception, and lighting can lead to misinterpretation of results. Staff conducting point-of-collection tests must be qualified in interpreting test results. If the results are to be used in court proceedings for purposes other than monitoring case progress, agencies should have the specimen confirmed using a laboratory test or procedure (see below).

Point-of-collection drug testing devices can only be used with urine, saliva, and breath specimens. The U.S. Food and Drug Administration (FDA) has approved several urine point-of-collection devices but only one saliva point-of-collection device. To find out more information about which point-of-collection devices are FDA approved, visit http://www.accessdata.fda.gov/scripts PCDSimpleSearch.cfm.

> *Key Action Step: Determine when to use point-of collection versus laboratory testing.*

Laboratory tests usually involve two phases—an instrumented screening test and a confirmatory test. The screening test can detect the presence of a substance, but the quantitative confirmatory test distinguishes the presence of a specific drug and/ or metabolite in the presence of other various drugs and determines the drug's concentration. Screening tests are used initially to determine if a confirmatory test should be conducted. Laboratories use confirmatory tests to clearly identify the drugs that are present. Details on the types of tests conducted for screening and confirmatory testing and common terminology and acronyms used in these processes are often found on laboratory test reports.

Screening for a specified panel of drugs typically involves the use of immunoassay technology (a laboratory technique that makes use of the binding between an antigen (i.e., drug) and its homologous antibody to identify and quantify the specific antigen or antibody in a sample). Common immunoassay technologies that are utilized for laboratory screening testresults include the enzyme multiplied immunoassay technique (EMIT), fluorescence polarization immunoassay (FPIA), radioimmunoassay (RIA), and kinetic interaction of microparticles in solution (KIMS). These screening assays are very sensitive to the presence of a drug or its metabolites. Immunoassay technologies have become less expensive, provide results rapidly, and are sufficiently sensitive to detect targeted drugs, their metabolites, or both.

However, chemical reactions that occur during this process can make it difficult to distinguish a given drug from other drugs, such as a prescription drugs with a similar chemical structure. Therefore the potential for cross reactivity with another substance to create a misleading drug test results always exists. For example, some over-the-counter cold medications (e.g., pseudo-ephedrine and ephedrine) have chemical structures very similar to amphetamine metabolites and therefore may cross react with the drug assay and cause a positive amphetamine screen result. For this reason, immunoassay manufacturers recommend confirming all positive drug screening results with a more specific confirmatory test that uses an analytically different technology (U.S. Department of Justice, 1999). Laboratories perform this quantitative level of drug testing to confirm positive drug test results on the same specimen, typically using gas chromatography/mass spectrometry (GC/MS) technology (a method which identifies and quantifies compounds that can be vaporized without decomposition). The results of the GC/MS test must agree with the initial drug screen result to confirm a positive drug test result (HHS, 2008). Confirmatory analyses can be significantly more expensive than screening tests but are much more sensitive and accurate for detecting a specific analyte or drug. A positive screening drug test result is considered a "presumptive positive" until confirmed by GC/MS methodology. Agencies should use a SAMHSA-certified laboratory to confirm drug test results that will be used in court proceedings. http://workplace

When child welfare agencies present drug test results in court that could result in serious consequences for the parent and his or her children (such as requiring substance abuse treatment for the parent or removal of the children from the parent's custody), agencies should perform confirmatory instrument testing to ensure the drug test's accuracy. Tests results used in case decisions require the greatest accuracy possible.

Specimen Integrity

To ensure the testing program's integrity, agencies must ensure that parents do not tamper with or alter their specimens and that they correctly match each specimen to the parent who provided it. The likelihood that a parent can tamper with a specimen depends on the specimen type. Unfortunately, tampering attempts are not uncommon with the type of specimen tested most frequently—urine.

> *Key Action Step: Establish the procedure for specimen collection and observation.*

Agencies must take steps to minimize specimen tampering to obtain an accurate drug test result.

When a staff member of the same sex as the parent is not available to monitor urine collection, the agency must implement other measures to reduce the likelihood that the parent will adulterate or substitute the specimen. These measures might include checking the specimen's temperature and adding a tint to the toilet water to prevent the parent from giving toilet water as a specimen or diluting the specimen with toilet water. Random testing reduces the possibility that parents will bring another individual's clean specimen as a substitute for their own. In addition, agencies must make every effort to ensure that they identify each specimen with the name of the person who provided the specimen. A chain of custody protocol helps document the specimen's handling and storage. For more information on preventing tampering and maintaining the chain of custody, visit http://www.drugfreeworkplace.org.

Which Drugs to Test For

In deciding which drugs to test for, the agency should consider the prevalence of different drugs in the community, which drugs are prone to be abused, and the history of the individual undergoing the test. Single drug tests can screen for the presence of only one drug, whereas panel testing screens for multiple drugs. Panel testing is particularly useful for testing parents because most parents who use drugs may use several different drugs. The National Institute on Drug Abuse (NIDA) suggests testing for a panel of five drugs: marijuana, cocaine, opioids, amphetamines, and phencyclidine (PCP) (NIDA, 2007). Some jurisdictions modify these five drug panels to reflect their local drug use patterns. With panel drug tests, parents can provide one specimen and obtain multiple drug test results. For example, a typical six-panel test might include marijuana, cocaine, opiates, benzodiazepines, amphetamines, and barbiturates. Agencies can also use tests to detect alcohol, but due to its short duration in the bloodstream and its short detection window in urine, agencies do not usually include alcohol in these panel tests unless they have reason to believe that the person has consumed alcohol in the past 12 hours. However, many agencies supplement the panel test with a breathalyzer to detect alcohol use.

Many laboratories also offer a wider set of screening and confirmatory tests for additional drugs that might be prevalent in a given geographic area. These could include pain management medications, such as oxycodone and hydrocodone, and benzodiazepines (Valium®, Xanax®, and others). Some drugs, such as steroids and d-lysergic acid diethylamide (LSD), require special laboratory testing procedures at a considerably higher cost.

> *Key Action Step: Determine which drug(s) to include in the test panel.*

Costs

Cost is an important consideration in developing the agency's drug testing protocol. When planning a drug testing program, agencies must determine how much staff time, space for collecting specimens, and storage space they will need, as well as how they will transport specimens. These considerations are especially important if the agency anticipates a high volume of drug testing. Costs have been reduced in some sites that have established guidelines that, in most cases, do not include conducting a drug test if the parent admits drug use and by implementing random testing protocols, which allow for less frequent tests.

The costs of drug tests depend on the number of drugs tested for, the drug testing matrix, the specimen collection method, the vendor, and the volume of tests conducted. Testing a specimen for a panel of drugs costs more than testing a specimen for one drug. Tests that use specialized laboratory equipment or extensive laboratory procedures are more costly. Agencies must consider these factors before implementing a drug testing program and must continually evaluate their program's cost effectiveness.

> *Key Action Step: Consider cost implications of the drug testing protocoland choice of a vendor.*

Laboratories and vendors charge less per test for point-of-collection tests as the total volume of tests conducted for an agency increases. If the agency's drug test volume is high, an investment in point-of-collection devices might be cost effective. Furthermore, many State correctional agencies negotiate statewide contracts with vendors for testing by all probation staff throughout the State. Although multi- agency contracts might not be feasible for community-based child welfare agencies, negotiating with vendors in partnership with a local substance abuse treatment agency or criminal justice agency might yield better prices than separate contracts with vendors. Considerations in contracting with vendors include specifying which services will be included in their responsibilities such as data collection and reporting, scheduling with clients for testing times, testifying in legal proceedings, and responsibilities for communicating with child welfare and the courts.

Staff Skills and Qualifications

Staff need training to perform different drug testing procedures and to collect the different kinds of specimens. The agency's vendor should provide adequate staff training on the use of their equipment and testing procedures. Staff who administer drug tests should have experience in laboratory drug testing and point-of-collection drug testing, as well as documented training.

With the increased use and abuse of opiate-derivative pain killers, such as oxycodone and hydrocodone, additional precautions against false positives need to be taken when testing for misuse of opiates, such as heroin or prescription medications. Unlike illegal drugs, where any use is always a red flag, use of prescription medication is often under a physician's care. Agencies should consult a Medical Review Officer (MRO) to establish appropriate drug testing procedures and to interpret drug test results for prescription drugs.

> *Key Action Step: Determine the type of staff training to provide on drug testing and the type of qualifications needed to administer the tests.*

An MRO is a physician with expertise in substance abuse who receives, interprets, and evaluates drug test results. General information about MROs is available at the U.S. Department of Transportation's Web site at http://www.dot.gov/ost/dapc/mro.html.

DRUG ENFORCEMENT ADMINISTRATION GUIDELINES

The U.S. Drug Enforcement Administration provides guidelines on Drug-Free Workforce Programs http://www.alwaystestclean.com/dea_guidelines.htm. DEA suggests the following guidelines for drug testing programs:

- Contract with a reliable, professional drug testing vendor who will ensure quality control and chain of custody for drug test samples. More information on factors to consider when contracting with a vendor is provided in Appendix C of this paper. SAMHSA maintains a list of federally approved laboratories at http://www.drugfreeworkplace.gov/DrugTesting.
- To obtain certification from the HHS National Laboratory Certification Program, drug testing laboratories must successfully complete three rounds of performance testing on samples, undergo a laboratory inspection, and ensure that the personnel providing the services are trained in the drug testing procedures. Laboratories must document this training and maintain and test the equipment according to the manufacturer's instructions (H HS, 2007).
- Implement drug testing in as fair, accurate, and legally defensible a manner as is reasonable. Ensure that the collection, handling, and drug testing procedures are reliable and accurate and that they reduce the risk of misidentification.
- Establish legal counsel's approval of the drug testing methods.
- Perform a confirmation drug test when an initial drug test result is positive, preferably using GC/MS, and have a Medical Review Officer review the results.
- Provide timely notification of drug test results to the parent and other interested agencies.

IV. INCORPORATING DRUG TESTING INTO CHILD WELFARE CASEWORK

Discussing Drug Testing With Parents

When an agency's drug testing protocol calls for testing a parent, agency staff should:

- Discuss drug testing with the parent, allowing the parent to self-disclose what the drug test results are likely to reveal and his or her past use of illicit drugs and the misuse of prescription drugs, including previous patterns of drug use and specific drugs used. This discussion should be conducted in an effort to engage the parent in services without using pejorative terms such as "clean or dirty" test results.
Discuss with the parent the need for complete disclosure of medical conditions and prescription and over-the-counter drugs and medication. With the increase in prescription drug misuse and abuse, it is important to get an accurate history of current and recent prescription medications. Provide the information that the parent discloses to the Medical Review Officer at the drug testing laboratory.
- Advise the parent of the purpose of the drug testing, which is to assist in case planning and to monitor progress if substance abuse treatment services are warranted. The parent needs to understand the consequences of positive and negative test results, how the agency will interpret a refusal to undergo a test, and how the agency will use the results in assessing child safety and risk.
- Describe the agency's drug testing procedures, including the testing location and date and the need for the parent to bring identification to the testing site and if the protocol includes random testing, the procedures for how random specimens are collected. It is helpful to provide a calendar that lists the parent's drug testing appointments and requirements and it is important to provide this information in writing so that it is easily understood.

> *Key Action Step: Develop a parent-engagement strategy.*

Frequency of Testing

Recovery from drug use can be a long-term process and requires a disease management approach to recovery which acknowledges the chronic nature of substance use disorders. Parents might need several months of substance abuse treatment to reach stability and integrate recovery into their lives sufficiently to ensure their children's safety.

Drug testing can help child welfare workers assess the effectiveness of substance abuse interventions in reducing threats to child safety and risks of future maltreatment. Early in the parents' participation in child welfare services and a treatment and drug testing program, drug test results may likely be positive. Helping the parent understand the scope and implications of his or her substance use disorder is an important task in this phase of treatment engagement and agencies should consider positive initial drug test results in this context when implementing consequences.

After initial drug testing, a randomized or ongoing drug testing program could be beneficial to provide evidence of success for parents, monitor compliance and evaluate progress in treatment. For example, Table 2 describes the frequency and intensity of the State of Arizona's testing services for parents undergoing a substance abuse treatment program (Arizona Department of Economic Security Child Protective Services, 2007).

Agencies should make decisions to modify drug testing frequency and intensity with input from the parent, supervisor, substance abuse treatment provider, and other professionals working with the family, particularly when drug testing is being conducted in multiple settings or agencies.

> Key Action Step: Establish frequency of testing.

When making such decisions, child welfare workers should take into account the following:

- The type of drug used and how long it can be detected;
- Clinical diagnosis, including the severity of the substance use disorder, the parent's historical patterns of use, and changes in affect and physical appearance;
- Whether the parent is participating in a residential treatment program (because testing is not usually beneficial until the individual has left the campus or otherwise has access to alcohol or drugs);
- Whether the parent consistently attends or participates in service delivery, particularly substance abuse treatment, self-help groups, or other recovery-support activities, and his or her level of cooperation with the case plan;
- Parent's denial or minimization, which can indicate that the parent does not understand the seriousness of his or her substance use and its consequences; and
- The parent's relapse-prevention plan, including the coping skills that the parent will use in unsafe environments in which he or she might face pressure to use, and whether the parent has made changes in the people, places, and things associated with his or her substance use.

Table 2. Drug Testing Service.

Timeframe	Suggested Frequency
0-60 days	Twice weekly
61-120 days	Twice per month
121 days or when behaviors indicate no further use	Monthly

Child welfare case workers may discontinue testing, with supervisor approval and input from the substance abuse treatment provider, if the parent no longer exhibits substance use behavior or the parent has received consistent negative drug testing results. With supervisory approval, the parent might need additional drug tests after the agency has stopped testing the parent if a staff member suspects that the parent has relapsed and is not admitting to resumed use. If a court has ordered the drug testing, child welfare workers should consult their supervisor and legal counsel for guidance regarding modification of drug testing.

SUBSTANCE-EXPOSED INFANTS

Substance-exposed infants are exposed to alcohol and other drugs that the mother ingested during pregnancy. This exposure may or may not be detected by drug testing.

Clear, standardized procedures for newborn testing are not available and policies vary among hospitals. In an estimated 90–95% of babies born who have been exposed to alcohol or illegal drugs, the exposure is not detected at birth and the infants go home with their birth parents without any interventions (Young et al., 2008). Some people perceive efforts to identify infants who have been prenatally exposed to conflict with privacy rights and others are concerned that detection will not lead to effective treatment, but only to punitive action. Recent prenatal screening and prevalence surveys have documented that 10-20% of all babies born have been exposed prenatally to illicit drugs or alcohol (Young et al., 2008). The 2003 amendments to the Child Abuse Prevention and Treatment Act required States receiving funding through the Act to provide a "plan of safe care" for infants determined to be "drug-affected" and to report such cases to a child protective services agency. A review of State policies on substance-exposed infants is available from the SAMHSA document, *Substance Exposed Infants: State Responses to the Problem*, available at http ://www.ncsacw. samhsa.gov.

Addressing Drug Test Results and Refusals

Agencies must make policy decisions regarding how to address a parent's negative drug test result, positive test result, refusal to submit to a drug test, and adulteration or dilution of a specimen. These decisions should include consideration of the differences in responses to parents under a court order and to parents who are not court ordered for drug testing. For parents under a court order, all drug test results and refusals should be reported to the courts for any implications this may have in the parent's case.

Drug tests serve as a mechanism to enhance discussions about recovery. Negative drug test results provide an opportunity to offer the parent positive reinforcement, recognize the parent's accomplishments, and offer continued support and encouragement. Parents often have difficulty being forthright about relapses, even when they are unlikely to suffer any punitive responses. Also, parents under a court order who demonstrate negative test results may receive certain incentives that parents without a court order may not receive.

A positive drug test result might mean a one-time lapse, or it might signal a return to chronic use. Child-welfare workers should view positive drug test results as indicators that the substance abuse treatment plan needs adjusting. As with the initial child safety assessment, child welfare workers should assess positive drug test results along with other indicators (such as a change in the parent's behavior or appearance, missed appointments, or failure to follow through with case plan objectives) to determine its potential impact on a child's safety and risk. A positive drug test result can also create an opportunity for intervention that the parent might have resisted previously.

Finally, a positive drug test result can provide an opportunity to employ strength- based or motivational-enhancement techniques to encourage the parent to continue to work on completing the case plan, particularly if he or she under a court order. Information about the use of motivational enhancement techniques can be found in a SAMHSA Treatment Improvement Protocol on the SAMHSA website at http://www.ncbi.nlm.nih.gov/bookshelf/br.fcgi?book=hssamhsatip&part=A61302.

When a parent receives a positive drug test result, the child welfare worker should:

- Discuss the results in a timely manner with the parent, preferably within 1-2 days of obtaining the results, giving the parent the opportunity to explain the results;
- Obtain an assessment by a substance abuse professional if the parent is not receiving substance abuse treatment or recovery services;
- Consult with the parent's substance abuse treatment provider; this consultation should include a review of the parent's relapse prevention plan and a reassessment of the array of services and interventions in which the parent is currently participating, as well as modifications of the parent's relapse prevention plan as needed; and
- Consider modifying the frequency of current drug testing for the parent.

Agencies might consider a parent's refusal to submit as a failure to test on that given day. Policies can also be developed to specifically address parents who tamper with or adulterate the drug test specimen. At a minimum, substance abuse treatment staff should record refusals in the parent's case file and should notify the judge and appropriate attorneys about parents under the court's jurisdiction.

> *Key Action Step: Develop a procedure to notify child welfare agencies and courts of drug test results.*

Coordination and Collaboration

Child welfare agencies expect most of the families they serve to complete numerous tasks as part of their case plan. Agencies should coordinate these services with the family and the service agencies responsible for providing these services to prevent unrealistic burdens on families. When a child welfare agency initiates ongoing drug testing for the parent, it needs to inform case workers whether the substance abuse treatment or probation agency is also requiring the parent to participate in drug testing. When health insurance pays for the testing, considerations for the protection of health information under the Health Insurance Portability and Accountability Act (HIPAA) of 1996 (P.L.104-191) must be addressed.

When parents must pay for drug testing, agencies should avoid duplicative drug tests. Sacramento County, California, pays for drug tests for parents with an open child welfare case because the financial cost could create a barrier to reunification. Depending on the jurisdiction, courts might decide who has to pay for a drug test and, in some circumstances, they might require parents to pay for their drug test at a local service provider. The use of valid information-release forms can enable these agencies to share drug test results, minimize costs to parents and agencies, and increase the likelihood of the parent's compliance. This coordination can ensure that drug testing contributes to child safety assessments and evaluations.

> *Key Action Step: Establish drug testing coordination and monitoring strategies with treatment agencies and courts.*

In 2007, the NCSACW published the Screening and Assessment for Family Engagement, Retention and Recovery (SAFERR) Model. This model provides guidance on strengthening cross-system collaborations to improve outcomes for families with substance use disorders who are involved with the child welfare system and those who are also involved with the court system (Young et al., 2007). NCSACW conducted an extensive review of the literature and concluded that, at present, no definitive research-driven or evidence-based method exists to determine whether drug use is contributing to child maltreatment. However, research and practical experience repeatedly indicate that parental substance use disorders and child maltreatment are highly correlated and that many, if not most, children under the jurisdiction of child welfare agencies and the courts come from families with substance use disorders (Young, Nakashian, Yeh & Amatetti, 2007). NCSACW examined the wide variety of available screening and assessment methodologies to identify the best tools for identifying child maltreatment or risk and for screening for potential substance abuse and dependence. The Center found that the quality of the teamwork among the agencies involved is much more important than the quality of any tool or set of tools (Young, Nakashian, Yeh & Amatetti, 2007).

This message has powerful implications for this discussion of the role of drug testing in child protection. The tool, in this case the drug test, cannot by itself convey a full picture of the strengths and needs of the family being served. A single tool screens for only one set of challenges and therefore requires additional input from multiple agencies with a broader perspective on the whole family to enable an agency to assess the child's safety and the parent's progress in recovery. Joint case staffing or family case conferencing with appropriate training can enhance this effort to share important information, continuously assess a family's progress in meeting case plan goals, and change case plans accordingly with the family's progress and evolving needs. More information on improving collaborative practice for families affected by substance use disorders and child maltreatment can be found at http://ncsacw.samhsa.gov.

V. SUMMARY

Throughout this document, we have identified key action steps to help child welfare and substance abuse agencies develop comprehensive policies and protocols covering several critical dimensions. These key steps are summarized here:

- Understand value differences between partner agencies concerning approaches to families affected by substance use disorders.
- Complete training on recognizing signs and symptoms of substance use disorders.
- Identify a clear purpose for using drug testing.
- Determine how drug testing fits with the child welfare agency's overall risk and safety assessment protocols.
- Decide which individuals to test.

- Select the type of specimen to collect and the testing methodology to use.
- Determine when to use point-of-collection versus laboratory testing.
- Establish the procedure for specimen collection and observation.
- Determine which drug(s) to include in the drug testing panel.
- Consider cost implications of the drug testing protocol and choice of a vendor.
- Determine what type of staff training to provide on drug testing and the qualifications needed to administer the tests.
- Develop a parent engagement strategy.
- Establish frequency of testing.
- Decide how to address confirmed positive drug results, negative results, refusals to undergo testing, and adulterated specimens.
- Develop a procedure to notify child welfare agencies and courts of drug test results.
- Establish drug testing coordination and monitoring strategies with treatment agencies and courts.

Drug testing can be an important addition to a child safety and risk assessment, family assessment, comprehensive substance abuse assessment, case planning, and substance abuse intervention and treatment services. Test results can provide useful information for determining whether a parent is using or abstaining from the use of illicit drugs or misuse or abuse of legal drugs. Agencies should not use drug testing as the sole or primary measure of the existence or absence of a substance use disorder, degree of impairment, or parent's ability to effectively care for his or her child; agencies can best make these determinations using a combination of ongoing assessment, random drug tests, observations of the parent's behavior and participation in the case plan, and parent self-reports. Before implementing drug testing, child welfare agencies need to develop policies and procedures for testing, provide adequate staff training, and procure the services of a drug testing laboratory and Medical Review Officer.

When used effectively, drug testing can serve as a catalyst for the individual to stop using drugs, a deterrent to continued drug use, and positive reinforcement for continued abstinence. Drug testing results contribute to the full spectrum of client monitoring and support needed to ensure a child's safety, permanency, and wellbeing, as well as family recovery.

APPENDIX A: DRUG TESTING POLICY EXAMPLE, SACRAMENTO COUNTY, CA

The following is a detailed description of the drug testing protocol that Sacramento County, California implemented. The county has more than a decade-long history of service system reforms to address parental substance use in the child welfare population. This description includes the county's decisions and agreements among the substance abuse, child welfare, and court agencies to use drug testing results most effectively and efficiently in conjunction with other behavioral signs and symptoms to monitor progress in treatment and family case plans.

Policy Environment and Purposes

The Specialized Treatment and Recovery Services (STARS) program conducts a model drug testing program in accordance with the county's collaboratively established drug testing policies and procedures. STARS workers (referred to as recovery specialists) provide recovery-management services to all parents with substance use disorders and an open child welfare case in two settings: (1) voluntary services programs in which the child has not been removed from parental custody, and (2) family reunification programs for families whose child is in protective custody.

STARS recovery specialists ensure immediate access for the parent to substance abuse treatment services. They also offer monitoring and accountability for the parent's treatment requirements. In addition, the recovery specialists communicate drug test results and compliance with treatment requirements to the child welfare agency and the court under a negotiated protocol among all three parties.

The STARS program offers parents a supportive environment with an emphasis on honesty and recovery and uses drug testing to assist parents in their recovery process. The goal of drug and alcohol testing is to hold parents accountable for their substance use and to provide opportunities for intervention at critical points in the recovery process. Observed urine collection can be invasive and embarrassing for parents, so recovery specialists are trained to put parents at ease. Most STARS workers are in recovery themselves, and they quickly develop trusting, supportive relationships with parents.

The STARS program philosophy is based on helping parents improve their lives and the well-being of their children; the program's purpose is not to "catch" parents using drugs. Rather, the drug testing program is presented to parents as an effective way for them to gather evidence about their successes and ability to care for their children.

The STARS drug testing model is intended to significantly reduce costs to the county by reducing the number of drug tests required for each parent as he or she progresses in recovery by eliminating duplication of testing across county agencies. The model also reduces the number of tests required by not testing parents who admit to substance use.

Funding

The STARS program is a 501(c)(3) nonprofit organization, funded by general funds from Sacramento County's Child Welfare Services and Alcohol and Drug Services. STARS also receives financial support from its parent company, BRIDGES, Inc. A toxicology laboratory has a contract with the county's Division of Child Protective Services (CPS) to provide testing equipment and laboratory services for all STARS parents involved with CPS. The STARS program contracts directly with another vendor for laboratory tests that the primary contractor cannot provide, such as benzodiazepine panels.

Drug Testing Procedures

All STARS parents are required to undergo observed drug and alcohol testing on a random schedule. The recovery specialists determine the appropriate number of tests according to STARS protocol. The recovery specialists can do the drug and alcohol testing and can send specimens for confirmations. Parents must sign an authorization form for release of health care information and the client drug screening agreement form prior to submitting a specimen for drug testing. Parents must also review the STARS "Client Guide for the Safe Use of Medications in Your Recovery" and sign the medication management agreement form. All forms used in the STARS program are included at the end of this appendix.

Random Tests

Recovery specialists are required to assign all drug and alcohol testing in a random manner, implementing irregular testing patterns in consecutive bimonthly reporting periods. However, recovery specialists may direct parents to undergo an alcohol or drug test if they suspect that a parent has used a substance.

Color Code System

In addition to testing requested directly by recovery specialists, STARS parents are required to submit to observed drug and alcohol tests according to a color code system. The system assigns parents to one of four testing colors at enrollment intake. Men are assigned to the green group (about 30% of parents in STARS are fathers) and women are assigned to the red or yellow group. All STARS parents who have participated in the program for 6 months are assigned to the blue group. The system assigns all of the parents in a recovery specialist's case load to the same group. The system develops a color code calendar each month and distributes it to STARS recovery specialists to help them schedule appointments and contact the parents. A sample monthly calendar is included in this appendix.

Parents must call the STARS office every Sunday, Tuesday, and Thursday after 6:00 p.m. to find out if their group needs to be tested. If so, the parents must appear at a testing site by the end of the following business day to submit a specimen for drug testing.

STARS calls in parents for testing in irregular patterns. Recovery specialists monitor the frequency and reporting of alcohol and drug tests from both the color code scheme and the additional random tests that they order.

Frequency

The number of drug tests that each parent must undergo depends on how long the parent has participated in STARS, his or her progress in recovery, relevant court orders, CPS mandates, and the STARS support service plan which details the substance abuse treatment requirements. Typically, parents are tested at least twice per week initially; the frequency decreases over time to about twice per month after 6 months in most cases.

Testing Equipment

Recovery specialists use two types of point-of-collection devices, the Intoximeter breathalyzer and the ValTox specimen bottle and urine drug test strip, also known as a dipstick.[2] Specialists use the breathalyzer tests and test strips because of their low cost and because they provide immediate results that can form the basis of a therapeutic intervention.

- Intoximeter breathalyzer: Each recovery specialist uses an Intoximeter breathalyzer to determine the presence of alcohol in the parent's breath. The vendor services and recalibrates the Intoximeters weekly to ensure test reliability. Parents blow into the breathalyzer mouthpiece, and results are instantaneous.
- ValTox specimen bottle and urine drug test strips: The recovery specialist transfers each urine specimen into the ValTox specimen bottle provided by the contracted vendor. The specimen bottles contain a preservative, a temperature strip, a lid, and a label. A STARS worker dips a test strip into the urine specimen and reads the results within 5 minutes. This strip tests for the presence of amphetamine/methamphetamine, cocaine, tetrahydrocannabinol, phencyclidine (PCP), and opiates.

Chain of Custody

STARS require each recovery specialist to maintain custody of the instant test strips, breathalyzer mouthpieces, and specimen bottles. To obtain testing equipment, recovery specialists must request the items they need in the STARS inventory log. Only authorized STARS personnel are allowed to distribute test devices and kits.

If the ValTox test result is positive, the recovery specialist asks the parent if he or she wants to have laboratory confirmation testing. When sending a urine specimen to the laboratory, the recovery specialist indicates the date, time, and temperature of the specimen on the label. After signing the label, the recovery specialist places the specimen in the laboratory envelope, which contains information about the parent, test date, recovery specialist signature, and parent signature. The recovery specialist then places the envelope in a secure specimen lock box located in the STARS offices.

Whenever recovery specialists send specimens for further testing, they must record the specimen transfer in the laboratory testing logbook. The STARS building has two logbooks, one near each of the two locked specimen containers.

Therapeutic Intervention and Experience

Negative Drug Test Result

When the results of a STARS screening drug dipstick and alcohol breathalyzer test are negative, the parent and the recovery specialist sign a negative results receipt and each receives a copy of the receipt. A sample receipt is included in this appendix. In most cases, parents with a negative urine drug test strip result do not undergo further drug testing. A recovery specialist might order a confirmatory laboratory analysis, however, if the parent's behavior is not consistent with point-ofcollection test results or if the specimen temperature suggests laboratory testing is warranted.

Positive Drug Test Result

If the result of the breathalyzer or screening dipstick drug test is presumptively positive for any substance, the recovery specialist offers the parent the opportunity to admit to recent use and sign a statement of noncompliance with their case plan.

If the parent denies drug use and requests that a confirmation test be conducted, the recovery specialist labels the bottle, deposits the bottle into the laboratory- provided envelope, records the test in a laboratory-testing logbook and parent file, and sends the specimen for confirmation testing. In such cases, the program considers the point-of-collection-testing results to be presumptive until confirmatory results are available.

If the parent admits to use, the recovery specialist asks the parent to sign a statement of noncompliance, which the recovery specialist also signs. The recovery specialist discusses the use with the parent and develops a plan to address any barriers to success and to prevent additional substance use. The recovery specialist encourages the parent to call his or her CPS social worker immediately to inform him or her of the noncompliance and describe the plan for continuing recovery.

The statement of noncompliance specifies the substance used and date of last use. The parent, CPS, and recovery specialist receive copies of the form. A sample form is provided in this appendix. Depending on the substance(s) that the parent reports using and other behavioral indicators, the recovery specialist might order a confirmatory laboratory test.

Voluntary Positive Reports

STARS recovery specialists give parents the opportunity to admit to recent drug or alcohol use at any time, without the need for a drug test. If a parent admits recent use, the recovery specialist discusses the use with the parent and develops a plan to address any barriers and prevent future use. The recovery specialist encourages the parent to call his or her CPS social worker immediately to inform him or her of the noncompliance and describe the plan for continuing recovery.

The recovery specialist also asks the parent to sign and date a statement of noncompliance. The recovery specialist also signs and dates the statement, which specifies the substance used and date of last use. The parent, social worker and recovery specialist receive copies of the statement.

Tests that are Considered Not Compliant with Court Orders

- STARS does not consider any test not directed by STARS personnel, either directly or via the color code call-in system, to be a valid authorized test for their reporting to the court or CPS.
- STARS considers any specimen left unattended or not handled according to chain-of-custody guidelines to be invalid.

- STARS considers any failure to provide a specimen to be a failure to test.
- Recovery specialists use the test temperature gauge included on the bottle and visual checks to evaluate if the specimen may have been diluted. If so, they send the urine specimen to the laboratory for verification of test strip results. These confirmatory tests are paid for by the STARS program.
- STARS recovery specialists report to the court and to CPS any tests involving diluted urine specimens and urine specimens whose temperature is out of the normal range as the parent is noncompliant with the testing requirements of their case plan.

Notification of Confirmed Positive Drug Tests and Failures to Test

STARS requires recovery specialists to inform the CPS social worker, treatment provider, and STARS supervisor of all positive test strip results and failure-to-test incidents. If a parent has a positive test result for alcohol or drugs or fails to test and the parent has a child in his or her care or has unsupervised visits with the child, the recovery specialist is required to notify a CPS staff member within 30 minutes of the test. The notification must be made directly to a CPS staff member; a message cannot be left on an answering service.

In the fall of 2009, confirmation test procedures were changed in that CPS now considers all positive strip results as positive and specimens are only sent for confirmation if the parent states that the strip test is not accurate and requests that a confirmation be conducted. The parent must pay the $20 for the confirmation test to be conducted and if the result is negative, the parent receives a refund from CPS. If the test confirms that there is a positive result, the parent is responsible for the $20 confirmation test fee.

For more information about the STARS program, please contact Jeff Pogue, STARS program director:

Jeff Pogue, Director
STARS Program
3600 Power Inn Road, Suite D3
Sacramento, CA 95826
Phone: 916/453-2704, Ext. 17
E-mail: jeff@bridgesinc.net

The following forms are provided as samples to assist organizations in developing drug testing policies and procedures.

- Client Drug Screening Agreement
- Client Drug Screening Agreement Track III
- Authorization for Release of Health Care Information
- Medication Management Agreement
- Drug and Alcohol Screening Test – Negative Results
- Drug and Alcohol Screening Test – Presumptive/Altered Results
- Color Code System Calendar

(Bridges, Inc., 2001).

> **S. T.A.R.S.**
>
> *Specialized Treatment And Recovery Services A program of Bridges Inc.*

CLIENT DRUG SCREENING AGREEMENT

All STARS clients are required to submit to random observed drug and alcohol screenings unless otherwise instructed. With the prior approval of both the client's social worker and the director of STARS, clients may be assigned to a blanket-testing schedule, which will consist of testing on each:

_____Monday, Wednesday, and Friday
OR
_____Tuesday, Thursday, and Saturday

If the client fails to test on the day that they are instructed to test on, they will receive an administrative positive which will automatically make them non-compliant during that report period. Clients directed to Valley Toxicology to test must obtain proof of test and submit it to their Recovery Specialist by the last day of the report period to receive credit for the test. Clients in residential treatment are excused from participating in the process described above while in treatment but must begin doing so on the first day following discharge.

The Recovery Specialist, apart from the process described above, will also direct clients to test on a random basis. The Recovery Specialist may direct the client to test on any day either with the Recovery Specialist or at a Valley Toxicology testing site. If a client fails to test as directed by their Recovery Specialist, they will receive an administrative positive which will make them automatically non-compliant during that report period.

Upon completing any test at Valley Toxicology or the Effort, all clients are required to call and report the test to their Recovery Specialist's phone extension. If any client fails to test as required by the this agreement or directed by their Recovery Specialist they must immediately call their Recovery Specialist and they are required to appear at the STARS Program office the next day before 10:00 AM.

Clients are to be ready to test at all scheduled Treatment sessions. Clients are required to be on site at the Treatment Provider 15 minutes before their scheduled treatment session and then wait 15 minutes after the treatment session in case the Recovery Specialist shows up to test the client. Failure to show at a scheduled treatment session will result in an administrative positive if the Recovery Specialist shows up to test the client and the client is not present. Recovery Specialists are required to wait up to 15 minutes for the client to produce a specimen and to furnish the client with a receipt.

_____1. **I understand that I am required to follow the above testing instructions and that a failure to test as directed will result in an administrative positive.**
_____2. **I understand that I am required to submit to random observed drug and alcohol screening as directed by the Recovery**

Specialist and that I should be ready to test 15 minutes before and after all scheduled Treatment sessions.

_____ _____
Client   Date

_____ _____
Treatment Coordinator   Date

TRACK III. CLIENT DRUG SCREENING AGREEMENT

All Track III STARS clients are still required to submit to random observed drug and alcohol screenings. *Each Level III client will be assigned the color Blue.* They will be required to call the STARS telephone number (916) 453-2704) every Sunday, Tuesday and Thursday evening after 6:00 pm to receive instructions whether they are supposed to go to a Valley Toxicology testing site the next day to be tested based upon their color assignment. If the client fails to test on the day that they are instructed to test on the recorder, they will receive an administrative positive which will automatically make them non-compliant during that report period. Clients directed to Valley Toxicology to test must obtain proof of test and submit it to their Recovery Specialist by the last day of the report period to receive credit for the test. Clients in residential treatment are excused from participating in the call in process described above while in treatment but must begin calling in on the first day following discharge.

Clients will also be directed to test on a random basis by their Recovery Specialist apart from the call in process described above. The Recovery Specialist may direct the client to test on any day either with the Recovery Specialist or at a Valley Toxicology testing site. If a client fails to test as directed by their Recovery Specialist, they will receive an administrative positive which will make them automatically non-compliant during that report period.

Upon completing any color code or directed test all clients are required to call and report the test to their Recovery Specialist's phone extension. If any client fails to test as required by the color code or as directed by their Recovery Specialist they must immediately call their Recovery Specialist and they are required to appear at the STARS Program office the next day before 10:00 AM.

Clients are to be ready to test at all scheduled Treatment sessions. Clients are required to be on site at the Treatment Provider 15 minutes before their scheduled session and then wait 15 minutes after the session in case the Recovery Specialist shows up to test the client. Failure to show at a scheduled Treatment session will result in an administrative positive if the Recovery Specialist shows up to test the client and the client is not present. Recovery Specialists are required to wait up to 15 minutes for the client to produce a specimen and to furnish the client with a receipt.

_____ 1. I understand that I am required to call STARS every Sunday, Tuesday, and Thursday evening after 6:00 pm to receive testing instructions and that failure to call or to test as directed on the recorder will result in an administrative positive.

_____ 2. I understand that I am required to submit to random observed drug and alcohol screening as directed by the Recovery Specialist and that I should be ready to test 15 minutes before and after all scheduled Treatment sessions.

_____   _____
Client   **Date**

_____   _____
Recovery Specialist   **Date**

Specialized Treatment and
Recovery Services
3600 Power Inn Rd. Suite C
Sacramento, CA 95826
Office 916 453-2704
Fax 916 453-2708

Authorization for Release of Health Care Information

To: Dr. _____

Your patient _____ is receiving services from the Specialized Treatment and Recovery Services (STARS) program. This program provides case management for your patient for the purposes of recovery from substance abuse. As a part of the program, your patient is subject to random urine drug testing for controlled substances. For that reason your patient has been asked to provide us with a list of prescribed medications.

It is our hope that in the treatment of your patient, non-narcotic medications can be prescribed whenever possible to help your patient continue in recovery and eliminate potential positive drug tests.

Occasionally, it is necessary to contact the prescribing physician to confirm that a participant is receiving a prescribed medication that has resulted in a positive drug screening. Your patient has signed this release of information so that the specified recovery specialist may contact you for this information. PLEASE KEEP THIS RELEASE IN YOUR PATIENT'S RECORDS.

Thank you for your assistance
Sincerely,

Jeff Pogue
Director/Drug Court Coordinator
Specialized Treatment and Recovery Services

RELEASE OF MEDICAL INFORMATION

I hereby authorize the release of information regarding any medication, which could result in a positive test on a drug screening that is currently being prescribed for my medical use. The information is to be released only to STARS Director Jeff Pogue or to Recovery Specialist _____.

This authorization will be effective for one year from the date of my signature or until my STARS case is closed.

Signature_____Date_____

Witness_____Date_____

Medication Management Agreement

This agreement between_____and Specialized Treatment and Recovery Services (STARS) is for the purpose of establishing an agreement and to clarify the conditions upon which STARS is willing to accept the use of mind-altering prescription medications. This agreement is a necessary factor in establishing and maintaining the trust and confidence necessary to accurately report your progress to the Dependency Court. The patient agrees to and accepts the following conditions for the use of prescription medications:

I will not use any illegal or uncontrolled drugs.

I will not share, sell, or trade my medications for money, goods, or services.

I will not attempt to obtain additional pain type medications or other mind-altering medications from any other health care provider without notifying this office. I understand that doing so may result in a non-compliant report from this program.

I agree to safeguard my medications in such a manner that it will prevent loss or theft.

I agree that I will use my medications exactly as prescribed, at a rate no greater than prescribed.

I understand that unless otherwise specified by my physician, my prescription is only valid for thirty (30) days from the date the prescription is filled. The only exception to this is a chronic pain diagnosis or other medically documented reason. The STARS director must approve these exceptions.

I have read & understand all of the above policy.
This agreement is entered into on this day _____, _____.

Client Signature: _____

Please Print Name: _____

Witness: _____

Sacramento County
Department of Health and Human Services
Specialized Treatment and Recovery Services (STARS)
Drug and Alcohol Screening Test – Negative Results

Client Name _____

Test Date _____ / _____ / _____ **Temperature** _____

Social Worker _____ **Worker Code** _____

Test Location

STARS___ Treatment Provider___ Field___ Home___ Other___

I submitted to a breath and urine sample on the above stated date and the results were negative

_____   _____
[Date]   *Client Signature*

_____   _____
[Date]   *Recovery Specialist Signature*

Sacramento County
Department of Health and Human Services
Specialized Treatment and Recovery Services (STARS)
Drug and Alcohol Screening Test – Presumptive/Altered Results

Client Name _____

Test Date _____ / _____ / _____ **Temperature** _____

Social Worker _____ **Worker Code** _____

Test Location
STARS___ Treatment Provider___ Field___ Home___ Other___

I understand that I submitted a breath/urine sample on the above stated date and that the breath/urine sample has indicated a presumptive positive result for the following:

Alcohol Breathalyzer Result:	**Cocaine**	**Opiates**
_____	Marijuana/THC	Benzodiazepines
Methamphetamine/Amphetamine	PCP	**Sample Diluted/Altered**

_____I waive my option of a confirmation test and accept the positive result of the initial screen. I recognize that this acceptance constitutes a full admission of drug use and further admit using the above drugs on the date listed_____.

_____I waive my option of providing a breath and urine sample and admit that I used the above noted drug/alcohol on the date listed_____.

_____I do not accept the result of the initial screen that resulted in the presumptive positive and/or diluted/altered test. I hereby request a confirmation test to be completed.

_____

_____

[Date]   *Client Signature*

_____

[Date]   *Recovery Specialist Signature*

JUNE 2008

Sun	Mon	Tue	Wed	Thu	Fri	Sat
1	2 Purple, Blue, Yellow	3	4 Red	5	6 Green	7
8 Note: Yellow is called 2x this week>>	9 Green, Red, Yellow	10	11 Purple	12	13 Yellow	14
15	16 Yellow	17	18 Green	19	20 Purple, Red	21
22	23 Green, Red	24	25 Purple, Yellow	26	27 Blue	28
29	30 Purple					

STARS COLOR CODE CALENDAR

APPENDIX B: ESTABLISHING CUTOFF LEVELS

Established cutoff levels are preset thresholds that laboratories use to determine whether a drug test result is negative or positive. Positive drug test results have concentration levels above the cutoff levels, whereas the levels in negative results are below the cutoff levels. Laboratories set the levels at a value designed to indicate whether a certain amount of an illicit drug is present. Depending on the purpose of the drug testing program, these values may vary between laboratories or for specific clients of the laboratories.

The Mandatory Guidelines for Federal Workplace Drug Testing Programs have established cutoff levels for Federal workplace settings (HHS, 2004). Table 3 displays standards that can serve as the basis for developing child welfare testing protocols, although local jurisdictions might want to adapt these standards for their child welfare or treatment practices. These levels reflect the 5.1.2010 Guidelines.

Another example of established cutoff levels comes from the Professional Health Monitoring Programs (personal communication, 2009). Table 4 shows drug testing program standards for compliance monitoring for physicians, nurses, dentists, lawyers, social workers, psychologists, pharmacists, and health paraprofessionals.

Table 3. Cutoff Level Standards for Federal Workplace Drug Testing Programs, in Nanograms per Milliliter.

Cutoff Levels	Initial Screen	Confirmatory Test
Amphetamines	1000	500
Cocaine Metabolites	300	150
Marijuana Metabolites	50	15
Opiate Metabolites	2,000	2,000
Phencyclidine (PCP)	25	25

Table 4. Cutoff Level Standards for Professional Health Monitoring Programs, in Nanograms per Milliliter.

Cutoff Levels	Initial Screen	Confirmatory Test
Amphetamines	1,000	200
Antidepressants	100	100
Antihistamines	100	100
Barbiturates	300	200
Benzodiazepines	50	10-50
Narcotics/Opiates	100-750	100-500
Stimulants	500	500

Child-welfare and substance-abuse treatment agencies should consult their laboratories to determine the cutoff levels used to indicate a positive drug test result. These cutoff levels might be lower than the Federal standards for drug- free workplaces, resulting in a higher likelihood of positive drug test results. For example, cutoff levels for amphetamines, including methamphetamine, might be 200 nanograms per milliliter (ng/mL), which is well below the Federal Drug Free Workplace standards. However, 300 ng/mL would be a confirmed positive drug test result based on the cutoff levels used by the Professional Health Monitoring Programs with a confirmatory cutoff of 200 ng/ml. Although using Federal Drug-Free Workplace cutoff levels is more defensible than other cutoff levels in court, these levels might under-indentify individuals who have used an illicit drug.

Determining appropriate cutoff levels in child welfare practice is a local implementation issue for policymakers. We recommend that the child welfare agencies consult with their general counsel and local alcohol and drug treatment administration when determining what cutoff thresholds to use. Some local jurisdictions set common cutoff levels for multiple systems, including criminal justice and probation, child welfare, and substance abuse treatment agencies. If the laboratory does not use the same levels as those that the systems use, the courts and each system should train its staff members to ensure that they give parents common messages and use the same approaches to drug testing.

APPENDIX C: CONSIDERATIONS IN CONTRACTING WITH A VENDOR FOR DRUG TESTING

In 2003, the U.S. Drug Enforcement Administration developed *Guidelines for a Drug-Free Workforce*. Agencies should consider these guidelines when contracting with a vendor to implement drug testing:

- The vendor should provide guidance in developing collection procedures to ensure that agencies obtain specimens properly and that parents do not tamper with their specimens.
- The vendor should provide all of the materials that the agency needs for specimen collection and written instructions for collecting specimens. These materials might include containers, chain-of-custody and report forms, evidence tape, prepaid tamper-proof mailers, and labels. The contract price should include these items as well as courier service. An agency might need to make separate financial arrangements if it requires a urine-collection vendor in addition to the laboratory services. If an agency uses a separate collection vendor, this vendor should be a facility that specializes in specimen collection for workplace drug testing.
- Containers should be sterile and not contain preservatives that might alter the drugs or metabolites being tested for or interfere with the drug test result. Containers should also include a built-in temperature strip that can measure the urine specimen's temperature. This is useful for detecting specimen substitutions or other attempts to tamper with the specimen.
- The vendor and its drug testing analysts must comply with State and Federal licensing and certification requirements.
- The vendor must provide a clear, up-to-date procedure manual for laboratory drug testing and point-of-collection methods. Laboratories certified by the National Laboratory Certification Program follow the procedural guidelines approved by HHS (HHS, 2007).

- The laboratory must furnish an analytical plan to ensure that it confirms all screened positive drug test results with a GC/MS confirmatory test and that it does not transmit any results to the agency based solely on the initial screening drug test result. In other words, the vendor should automatically submit all initial screening positive drug test specimens for GC/MS confirmation and quantization testing.
- The vendor should define the analytical sensitivity and specificity for each drug test procedure. Most employers, including non-regulated employers, follow the cutoff levels established by the U.S. Department of Transportation's drug testing program. However, the agency and the vendor should agree on any change from the drug test laboratory's normal thresholds for detection in writing.
- The vendor's drug testing procedures should differentiate between legitimate therapeutic drug, illegal drug use or misuse, and illicit drug use. Thus, the tests should rule out legal medications that parents use for legitimate medical reasons before declaring a drug test result to be positive. Agencies should consider contracting with a Medical Review Officer to determine whether the parent might have used prescription medications for legitimate purposes.
- The vendor should be able to identify any of the normally abused illegal drugs or their metabolites and offer several drug panel tests as a cost effective option.
- Once the specimen has arrived at the laboratory via an approved courier, the vendor should deliver a confirmed written drug test result within 2–3 days. Agencies should never base their child-placement actions on oral notification of drug test results. The vendor and child welfare agency or substance abuse provider should establish procedures to maintain confidentiality, and the laboratory should offer refrigerated storage for confirmed positive specimens.
- With timely notification, the vendor should make available expert testimony in the form of written records and personal appearances to describe results, drug testing methodology, and opinions.
- Technical and managerial laboratory personnel should be trained and qualified to conduct all point of collection and laboratory drug testing.

APPENDIX D: DEFINITIONS AND TERMS

Adulterated Specimen. A specimen that has been altered, as evidenced by test results showing either a substance that is not a normal constituent for that type of specimen or showing an abnormal concentration of an endogenous substance.

Aliquot. A fractional part of a specimen used for testing, representing the whole specimen.

Calibrator. A solution of known concentration in the appropriate matrix that is used to define expected outcomes of a measurement procedure or to compare the response obtained with the response of a test specimen aliquot/sample. The concentration of the analyte of interest in the calibrator is known within limits ascertained during its preparation. Calibrators may be used to establish a calibration curve over a concentration range.

Chain of Custody (COC). Procedures to account for the integrity of each specimen or aliquot by tracking its handling and storage from point of specimen collection to final disposition of the specimen and its aliquots.

Control. A sample used to evaluate whether an analytical procedure or test is operating within predefined tolerance limits.

Cutoff. The decision point or value used to establish and report a specimen as negative, positive, adulterated, substituted, or invalid.

Donor. The individual from whom a specimen is collected.

HHS. The U.S. Department of Health and Human Services.

Initial Drug Test. The test used to differentiate a negative specimen from one that requires further testing for drugs or drug metabolites.

Invalid Result. The result reported by an HHS-certified laboratory in accordance with the criteria established in Section 3.8 when a positive, negative, adulterated, or substituted result cannot be established for a specific drug or specimen validity test.

Laboratory. A permanent location where initial and confirmatory testing, reporting of results, and recordkeeping is performed under the supervision of a responsible person.

Medical Review Officer (MRO). A licensed physician who reviews, verifies, and reports a specimen test result to the agency.

Negative Result. The result reported by an HHS-certified laboratory, IITF, or POCT tester to an MRO when a specimen contains no drug or the concentration of the drug is less than the cutoff concentration for that drug or drug class and the specimen is a valid specimen.

Positive Result. The result reported by an HHS-certified laboratory when a specimen contains a drug or drug metabolite equal to or greater than the cutoff concentration.

Sample. A performance testing sample, quality control material used for testing, or a representative portion of a donor specimen.

Specimen. Fluid or material collected from a donor at the collection site for the purpose of a drug test. Urine is the only specimen allowed for Federal workplace drug testing programs.

Standard. Reference material of known purity or a solution containing a reference material at a known concentration.

REFERENCES

[1] Arizona Department of Economic Security Child Protective Services. (2007). *Practice guidelines for utilizing drug testing*. Retrieved December 5, 2008, from https://egov.azdes.gov/CMS400Min/InternetFiles/InternetProgrammaticForms/pdf/ ACY-1173G.pdf.

[2] Center for Substance Abuse Treatment. (2006). *Substance abuse: Clinical issues in intensive outpatient treatment. Treatment Improvement Protocol (TIP) Series 47*. HHS Publication No. (SMA) 06-4182. Rockville, MD: Substance Abuse and Mental Health Services Administration.

[3] Ellis, Jr G. M., Mann, M. A., Judson, B. A., Schramm, N. T. & Tashchian, A. (1985). Excretion patterns of cannabinoid metabolites after last use in a group of chronic users. *Clinical Pharmacology & Therapeutics, 38*, 572-8.

[4] National Institute on Drug Abuse. (2007, September). *Frequently asked questions about drug testing in schools*. Retrieved April 2, 2008, from http://www.nida.nih.gov/DrugPages/testi ngfaqs. html.

[5] Office of National Drug Control Policy. (2002, July). *What you need to know about drug testing in schools*. Retrieved September 26, 2007, from http://www.ncjrs.gov/ondcppu bs/pu blications/pdf/drug_testing . pdf.

[6] U.S. Department of Transportation. (2007, December). *Conforming products list of evidential breath measurement devices*. Washington, DC: Department of Transportation, National Highway Traffic Safety Administration. Retrieved April 1, 2008, from http://www.dot.gov/ost/dapc/testingpubs/20071217_CPL_EBT.pdf.

[7] U.S. Department of Health and Human Services. (2007, October). *National laboratory certification program*. Retrieved April 3, 2008, from http://www. workplace Backg round 1007.pdf.

[8] U.S. Department of Health and Human Services, Substance Abuse & Mental Health Services Administration. (2004). *Mandatory guidelines for Federal workplace drug testing programs*. Retrieved September 26, 2007, from http://www.workplace.samhsa.gov/DrugTesting/Files_Drug_Testing/Federal/HHS Guidelines%20(Effective%20Novem ber%20 1,%202004). Pdf.

[9] U.S. Department of Health and Human Services, Substance Abuse and Mental Health Services Administration, Center for Substance Abuse Prevention, Division of Workplace Programs. (2008, March). *Making your workplace drug-free: A kit for employers*. Retrieved March 21, 2008, from http://download.ncadi.samhsa.gov/ Prevli ne/pdfs/SMA07-4230. Pdf.

[10] U.S. Department of Justice, Office of Justice Programs, Bureau of Justice Assistance. (1999, July). *Integrating drug testing into a pretrial services system: 1999 update*. Retrieved April 10, 2009, from http://www.ncjrs.gov/pdffiles1/ bja/176340-1 .pdf.

[11] U.S. Department of Justice, Office of Justice Programs, Drug Court Clearinghouse and Technical Assistance Project. (2000, May). *Drug testing in a drug court environment: Common issues to address*. Retrieved April 10, 2009, from http:// www.ncjrs.gov/pdffiles1/ojp/181103.pdf.

[12] U.S Drug Enforcement Agency. (2003). Guidelines for a Drug-Free Workforce.

[13] Young, N. K., Gardner, S., Otero, C., Dennis, K., Chang, R., Earle, K. & Amatetti, S. (2009). *Substance-Exposed Infants: State Responses to the Problem*. HHS Pub. No. (SMA) 09-4369. Rockville, MD: Substance Abuse and Mental Health Services Administration.

[14] Young, N. K., Nakashian, M., Yeh, S. & Amatetti, S. (2007). *Screening and assessment for family engagement, retention, and recovery (SAFERR)*. HHS Publication No. (SMA) 07-4261. Rockville, MD: Substance Abuse and Mental Health Services Administration.

End Notes

[1] Although drug testing has several uses, it has limited value for diagnosing a parent's current substance use, abuse, or dependence on substances. Biological, genetic, and clinical research findings have shown that *substance dependence* is a chronic disorder and, unlike *substance abuse*, is associated with tolerance or withdrawal, loss of control of the frequency and/or amount of substance use, and continued use despite adverse consequences (American Psychiatric Association, 2000). Drug testing is only one component that addiction professionals use to establish a diagnosis. Other information sources include parent interviews, generally using standardized instruments, as well as a review of the parent's pertinent history. Although an addiction professional can conduct an assessment to identify a substance use disorder, in most States, only a licensed practitioner (such as a physician, registered nurse practitioner, psychologist, or licensed clinical social worker) can make a diagnosis in accordance with the American Psychiatric Association's *Diagnostic and Statistical Manual of Mental Disorders, 4th Edition* (DSM-IV) (2000).

[2] The Intoximeter and ValTox brands that the STARS program uses are only some of the many devices available. Agencies need to determine which brands their vendors provide and choose the brand that is best for their drug testing program.

Chapter 4

SUBSTANCE ABUSE SPECIALISTS IN CHILD WELFARE AGENCIES AND DEPENDENCY COURTS: CONSIDERATIONS FOR PROGRAM DESIGNERS AND EVALUATORS

United States Department of Health and Human Services

ACKNOWLEDGMENTS

This document was prepared by the National Center on Substance Abuse and Child Welfare (NCSACW) under Contract No. 270-027108 for the Substance Abuse and Mental Health Services Administration (SAMHSA) and the Administration for Children and Families (ACF), both within the U.S. Department of Health and Human Services (HHS). Nancy K. Young, Ph.D., developed the document. Sharon Amatetti, M.P.H., served as the Government Project Officer from SAM HSA's Center for Substance Abuse Treatment (CSAT) and Irene Bocella, M.S.W., served as the Project Officer from Children's Bureau within the Administration for Children and Families.

INTRODUCTION

For more than a decade, studies have suggested that a sizable majority of the families involved in child welfare services are affected by parental substance use disorders. With the passage of the Federal Adoption and Safe Families Act (ASFA, Public Law 105-89, 1997), the complex issues of parents with a substance use disorder who are involved with the child welfare system have become the focus of increased attention. Under ASFA, parents have limited time to comply with reunification requirements, including attaining and demonstrating recovery from their addiction and safely care for their children, or face permanent termination of their parental rights. Given the historical low rates of reunification and extended duration of foster care placements for families with substance use disorders, these families are likely to compose most of the families affected by this legislation.[1,2] In addition, since substance abuse treatment can be a lengthy process and the recovery process often takes longer than is allowed under the ASFA timelines, it is important that substance-abusing parents be engaged in treatment as soon as possible. As a result, finding effective ways to address concurrent substance use and child maltreatment problems in families has taken on renewed importance.

Historically, a lack of coordination and collaboration has hindered the ability of child welfare, substance abuse treatment, and family/dependency court systems to support these families.[3,4] Although the courts that have jurisdiction in cases of child abuse and/or neglect operate under various names (e.g., dependency, family, or juvenile), for the purposes of this paper they are referred to as dependency courts. The systems operate under different, even conflicting, mandates, priorities, timelines, and definitions of the primary parent, and each system has different goals and definitions of success. One of the primary emphases in discussions of how to best meet the needs of families affected by substance use disorders under ASFA has been on strengthening the collaborative relationships between the child welfare system, the substance abuse treatment agencies, and the courts. Coordinated efforts among child welfare caseworkers, treatment providers, and dependency courts are proposed as keys to timely access to appropriate treatment services, parent participation in child welfare and treatment services, and quality follow-up support.[5,6]

Models of collaborative intervention vary widely in emphasis. They include such innovations as co-location of substance abuse specialists in child welfare offices or dependency courts, dependency drug courts, joint case management and planning, official committees to guide collaborative efforts, wraparound services, improved cross-system communication protocols, and cross-agency training of staff.

However, there are few empirical studies on the effectiveness of these collaborative models. Available research suggests that the collaborative process functions to provide a variety of supports to parents and has an important impact on service systems. A recent study by Green and colleagues[7] found that successful collaboration helps to ensure that parents are not overwhelmed by the multiple demands and requirements of their case plans. In addition, collaboration indirectly supports parents by improving the ability of providers to work together on the parents' behalf. This collaborative process includes such functions as providing a bigger resource base from which to offer needed services, helping providers to better monitor case progress, providing additional services and supports when parents are struggling, improving the coordination and timing of services, and holding providers accountable to each other. Successful collaboration has also been found to influence case outcomes by improving the ability of key stakeholders to make good decisions because of the availability of timely, comprehensive, and accurate information.[8]

To generate new knowledge about innovative and effective child welfare practices, Public Law 103-432 (authorized by Congress in 1994) introduced the concept of Federal waivers to child welfare programs. The introduction of Federal child welfare waivers mainly impacts Title IV-E, which is the Foster Care and Adoption Assistance Program. Since 1996, 17 States have implemented 25 child welfare waiver demonstrations. Four of those States (Delaware, New Hampshire, Illinois, and Maryland) were granted waivers to demonstrate new approaches to families with substance use disorders. Delaware co-located privately contracted substance abuse counselors with child protection managers in county child welfare offices. The substance abuse counselors were responsible for linking parents to treatment and for providing support services to parents while they awaited treatment. Through New

Hampshire's waiver demonstration, licensed substance abuse counselors worked with child welfare workers in an advisory and supportive capacity and used their skills to provide training, assessment, treatment, and case management services. Illinois's demonstration focused on treatment retention and recovery for parents who lost custody of their children because of substance abuse disorders. The Illinois model incorporated a proactive intensive services model in which privately contracted case management specialists directly engaged families throughout the treatment process and provided post-treatment support. Maryland planned to implement a collaborative case management model in which privately contracted substance abuse specialists would work with child welfare workers, parent aides, and volunteer mentors to assess the needs of family members and to determine appropriate treatment options. The Maryland demonstration waiver was terminated before its full implementation because of various competing priorities and implementation issues. Table 1 at the end of the Appendix describes additional characteristics of the first three waiver demonstration sites, Delaware, New Hampshire, and Illinois.

Results from the Federal waiver demonstrations found that substance abuse-child welfare collaborations were most successful when backed by strong managerial support. Successful demonstrations were found to require careful service coordination and consistent communication between substance abuse specialists and child welfare staff. The mere co-location of substance abuse specialists in child welfare offices did not ensure that workers communicated about their cases. Successful collaboration requires the establishment of formal systems to share case information and to keep all staff informed about caregiver progress. In addition, adequate and appropriate substance abuse treatment resources need to be available to parents.

PURPOSE OF THIS PAPER

This paper focuses on one particular model of collaboration, the placing of substance abuse specialists in either child welfare offices or dependency courts. The purpose of co-locating substance abuse specialists is to ensure that parents are assessed as quickly as possible, to improve parent engagement and retention in treatment, to streamline entry into treatment, and to provide consultation to child welfare and dependency court workers.[9] In addition to briefly describing substance abuse specialist programs and their various components, this paper includes findings from eight qualitative interviews of programs that place substance abuse specialists in child welfare offices or dependency courts. The interviews highlight ways in which early decisions about the program's collaborative structure influence other design decisions. Understanding how design decisions are related to one another can help jurisdictions to systematically create substance abuse specialist programs that best meet their specific needs and use resources most efficiently. This information is intended to provide those interested in creating a substance abuse specialist program with valuable data on programmatic and collaborative structures, lessons learned about program design, problems or challenges faced by these programs, and how the issues were resolved. Table 1 at the end of the appendix includes a summary of key components of the programs.

Programmatic and Collaborative Structures of Substance Abuse Specialist Programs

Co-located substance abuse specialist programs vary, each having their own unique programmatic and collaborative structures. The programmatic structure is based on a variety of underlying concepts and arrangements, such as the overall purpose of the program, the roles and responsibilities of substance abuse specialist staff, and the locations and settings of the programs. The collaborative structure includes concepts such as the underlying values and principles guiding the program; funding; staff development, training, and supervision; and joint accountability, outcomes, and evaluation. A more detailed description of each programmatic and collaborative structure follows.

Programmatic Structure

Purpose of the Program
The type of substance abuse specialist program that is designed and implemented varies depending on its purpose. Some programs are begun with the purpose of building linkages and improving communication and collaboration between systems. Other programs hope to improve parents' access to assessment and treatment, whereas others might design substance abuse specialist programs to improve the ability of child welfare and court staff to manage their caseloads. Some programs are designed with all three purposes in mind.

Roles and Responsibilities
The roles and responsibilities of the substance abuse specialist vary and depend on the purpose of the program. If the purpose is building linkages and improving communication and collaboration between systems, the substance abuse specialist often serves as a formal liaison and is responsible for building and enhancing the relationships between the systems. If the purpose is to improve parents' access to assessment and treatment, the specialist may serve as a treatment broker or as a front-line service provider. If the purpose of the program is to improve the ability of child welfare and court staff to manage caseloads in which substance abuse is a factor, the substance abuse specialist may serve as an advisor about the nature of substance use disorders as they relate to all parents and, at times, individual families.

Locations and Settings
Some programs have chosen to assign a substance abuse specialist to regional child welfare offices, for example Connecticut's Project SAFE (Substance Abuse and Family Education). This specialist, who is a child welfare employee, provides consultation and training to child welfare workers, as well as interventions with parents. Similarly, Delaware's Title IV-E Waiver Demonstration used Title IV-E funds to hire substance abuse specialists in each of its three child welfare offices. These specialists conduct substance abuse assessments, identify treatment options, monitor parent treatment entry to improve retention, and provide consultation to child welfare workers. In contrast, some programs place substance abuse specialists in units within the agency for specific functions. Examples of these arrangements include workers placed in child welfare investigation units.

Substance abuse specialists are also located in child welfare offices or dependency courts as full- or part-time substance abuse treatment agency employees or contract staff. This type of connection with the substance abuse treatment agency can facilitate the service integration and treatment referral process. As dedicated staff, the specialists are the direct linkage to treatment provider agencies that can strengthen relationships with treatment providers, facilitate ongoing case monitoring, and maintain cross-system professional relationships.

Collaborative Structure

Underlying Values and Principles

Each partner enters the collaboration with its own perspective and particular assumptions about the mission and mandates of the other partners. Agencies seeking a partnership often have different perspectives on whether substance abusers can be effective parents; whether the client is the parent, child, or family; and whether the goal is child safety, family preservation, or economic self-sufficiency. Unless these differences are identified and addressed, collaborative agencies may find it difficult to reach agreement on issues related to the program-structured elements. Often the values and definitional issues, such as who is viewed as the primary parent, affect the ways in which staff work across agencies' boundaries. Developing common principles of how the child welfare and substance abuse treatment agencies and staff will work together to best serve the parents in each of their caseloads is critical. Program designers must consider how they will secure each system's buy-in to a shared set of values and principles that drive the outcomes to be measured.

> *States' experience indicates that successful collaboration requires the establishment of formal systems to share case information and to keep all staff informed about caregiver progress. Adequate and appropriate substance abuse treatment resources also need to be available to parents.*

Funding

As jurisdictions move to create substance abuse specialist programs, professionals engaged in program design find that they are dealing with scarce resources. Contracting with a local substance abuse treatment provider may provide some cost efficiencies rather than having the specialist be employed by the child welfare agency. However, the financing strategies employed to provide the specialist program are often locally determined based on unique community influences. The strategies have included State funds, Federal child welfare and substance abuse treatment funds, and local investments.

Staff Development, Training, and Supervision

Child welfare, dependency court, and substance abuse treatment workers must address the complex needs and build on the strengths of their shared parents. To accomplish these goals, they need to continually improve their knowledge and skills through staff development and to receive ongoing interdisciplinary training and supervision. Conventional training in which professionals learn about their own roles and responsibilities without an appreciation for the cross-system roles and the ways to work appropriately in interdisciplinary teams may deepen any divisions between agency staff. Therefore, workers may participate in the cross-agency training program. For example, substance abuse staff may attend the child welfare New Worker Training. Staff supervision is also an important aspect of the programs, and various relationships have been implemented. Some programs have used a dual supervision approach with both agencies, others have contracted with service providers for supervision, and others use child welfare staff for supervision.

Joint Accountability, Outcomes, and Evaluation

Jointly developed outcomes are the best indicators that the agencies agree on the goals of their partnership and how to measure their progress toward achieving those goals. Agreement on accountability and outcomes means that the partners continue to measure their progress using their own, different measures of program success (e.g., treatment retention or child safety) while also agreeing to measure and report their collective effectiveness (e.g., family stability or reduction in reoccurrence of child neglect). The extent of focus on both the outcomes and the issues for data collection and monitoring varies significantly across programs.

Programs Interviewed

There were seven programs included in our review: (1) Connecticut's Substance Abuse Specialists; (2) Massachusetts' Substance Abuse Regional Coordinators Program; (3) Washington's Substance Abuse Services Initiative; (4) Sacramento County's Early Intervention Specialists and Specialized Treatment and Recovery Services; and, programs that were Title IV-E Waiver Demonstrations; (5) Delaware's Substance Abuse Counselors Program; (6) New Hampshire's Project First Step, and (7) Illinois's Recovery Coach Program. These programs were selected for interviews because they are some of the Nation's most well-established substance abuse specialist programs.

Methodology

Qualitative interviews were conducted with key informants from the child welfare, substance abuse treatment, and dependency court systems. The key informants were those responsible for managing the substance abuse specialist program in their jurisdictions. Respondents were contacted by telephone and asked to participate in a 1-hour telephone interview.

The semi-structured interview was generally based on open-ended questions including a number of questions related to programmatic structure (i.e., purpose, roles and responsibilities, and locations and settings), collaborative structure (i.e., underlying values and principles; funding; staff development, training, and supervision; and joint accountability, outcomes, and evaluation), and lessons learned. Table 1, on page 45, provides a matrix of commonalities and differences among programs based on the programmatic and collaborative structures identified.

Results

This section describes the lessons learned in the sites with substance abuse specialist programs that were interviewed for this paper and examines 10 key areas or "critical factors" in the operation of the substance abuse specialist program.

1. Training: Understanding How to Use the Specialist

Child welfare offices and courts use the substance abuse specialist in a number of ways. In each program, the teams have determined the community's specific needs for the program. In some sites, the specialist provides initial screening to all new parents and then conducts follow-up evaluations as clinically indicated; other systems require that all parents participate in an evaluation by the specialist. In at least one program, the specialist is responsible for conducting face-to-face evaluations only for those parents who are referred by either the court or the child welfare system. It is important that the child welfare and court professionals who interact with the specialists clearly understand and receive training on how and when to access the specialist's expertise.

In many sites, substance abuse specialists work closely with a multidisciplinary team to assist the child welfare worker and/or the court in managing parent cases and ensuring that parents are receiving needed resources. Specialists may be involved in the day-to-day communication with the parent and often serve as content experts in child welfare investigations. Interviewees in two sites noted the importance of having the same substance abuse specialist involved with parents throughout the length of their cases. Regardless of the way in which the specialist is used, it is important that each program retain the flexibility to develop the system that works for its local community needs.

2. Training: Cross-Training Multisystem Staff

Cross-training the multisystem providers (child welfare professionals, court staff, and substance abuse coaches and counselors) is of vital importance to the success of the program. Cross-training supports team building, sets the context within which the providers are to operate, and establishes mutual expectations. This is separate from training child welfare and court professionals on the mechanics of how to use the specific services of substance abuse specialists. Cross-training promotes the success of a substance abuse specialist program because all cross- trained participants agree on joint accountability, outcomes, and evaluation. All team members also should have an overall understanding of ASFA and how the deadlines affect the treatment timeline, as well as their professional role in helping the parent navigate the timeline successfully. Cross-training for all team members generally includes providing information and promoting skills to work with trauma and its effects on women and children, as well as providing appropriate screening, assessment, and access to community resources.

3. Specialists' Background and Expertise

In addition to their high level of commitment to the position and to the multidisciplinary team, the skill set and attributes of the specialist are critical to the success of the program. It is important that each specialist have knowledge about, and respect for, the child welfare system and the court, including the institutional history and the core values of both partners. Interviewees also recommended that specialists receive specific ongoing training in their field of expertise. Personal characteristics of a successful substance abuse specialist included having a "never give up" attitude, expertise in substance use and related disorders, expertise in children and family issues including relevant laws, close ties to the community, and excellent communication and follow-through skills. One difficulty noted by interviewees from three sites was that hiring qualified specialists can be time consuming.

Interviewees agreed that the placement of a substance abuse specialist should not be a random assignment of counselors who are sent to conduct treatment assessments in the child welfare office or the court. Finding the right specialist who has a strong background in substance use disorders and its related conditions, and who possesses the preferred attributes described by these seven programs, can make a significant impact on the success of the programs.

4. Support of Leadership Across Systems

All of the seven program interviewees expressed the importance of having the support of top leadership across each of the agencies. Program success and sustainability requires that buy-in for the cross-system collaboration occur at all levels of each department and organization. This requirement was noted as especially important in the child welfare system. In most sites, the system administrators worked together to develop an overall framework for their staff to build on during program development, including a set of shared outcomes.

In addition to the top-level agency support, program coordinators ensure that their department supervisors stay informed about the work and utility of the substance abuse specialist. Regular communication between systems can ensure that the leadership understands the roles and responsibilities of the staff who are carrying out the day-to-day activities of the program.

5. Collaborative Relationships

Interviewees also stated that it is imperative that the systems involved in operating and monitoring a substance abuse specialist program develop a set of joint values and principles to formalize and guide the collaborative relationships. They found these joint values and principles were essential to the ongoing planning and implementation of the programs. Whenever possible, there were formal partnerships whereby agencies and community organizations have written agreements to collaborate and share responsibility for ensuring that parents have access to needed resources.

It is crucial to involve stakeholders such as the courts, domestic violence counselors, and other community providers in the process as early as possible and to engage them in the dialogue about cross-system collaboration. Involvement of the different systems that are typically needed by the target population, including mental health treatment agencies, child care, housing, and vocational and educational resources, is also important. Interviewees noted that generating the necessary buy-in from each of the different systems to develop joint values and principles and to formalize collaborative relationships can be a slow process. However, the result of this process sets the context within which substance abuse specialists and other providers are to operate and be successful.

6. Space and Location of the Specialist

The multisystem program development team often decides on the space and location of the substance abuse specialist. In many situations, the substance abuse specialist is co-located in the child welfare office and strategically placed in a visible location. In other situations, the specialist is co-located in the court and has a visible presence in the child welfare office on a regular basis. One interviewee stressed that the host office, generally the child welfare office, must be willing to take deliberate steps to incorporate the specialist into the office environment. These steps may include introducing the specialists and clarifying their roles and responsibilities to supervisors and other staff members and disseminating information on how to access the services of the specialist.

7. Communication and Information-Sharing Protocols

Regular and effective communication between the substance abuse specialist, the child welfare staff, court staff and attorneys, and the other community providers is essential to the success of the program. The demands of the position should allow time for regular contact with other team members including time for information sharing through scheduled meetings, daily communication, and team building. In addition, clear understanding of the roles and responsibilities of the various team members, as well as a communication protocol, was suggested as essential for effective communication.

8. Sustainable and Flexible Funding Sources

It is important to ensure that there are adequate and reliable resources to operate the program and to create a strong sense of ownership in its ongoing success. Budgeting and sustainability planning for this type of collaboration should include representatives and funding from each of the systems involved.

There is a need to ensure sufficient stability in the program funding to attract full-time professionals who are passionate about their investment in the multidisciplinary team concept and in the target population they serve. Staffing the substance abuse specialist positions with either short-term funding allocations or grants will make it difficult to attract and hire well-qualified and motivated personnel. In addition, funding for the program needs to be flexible and allow for program revisions that arise as the needs of the system change over time.

9. Evaluation

Interviewees noted the importance of evaluation in two key ways. First, evaluation is critical to understanding the successes and challenges of the substance abuse specialist program and allows for program revisions as needed. Second, positive evaluation results justify the existence of the substance abuse specialist program and generate continued and additional support for the program.

Funding must include the resources needed to support data collection and outcomes management. Standardizing certain instruments, such as screening or evaluation, can reduce costs and provide valuable information necessary for a thorough evaluation. The evaluation of the substance abuse specialist program will provide a solid foundation for quality improvement and for building program sustainability.

10. Access to Treatment Services

Access to treatment services after the initial evaluation or assessment is a critical component for success. Interviewees described access as the general availability of appropriate treatment services in the community, and emphasized the role that substance abuse specialists can play in directly or indirectly facilitating parent screening, assessment, and engagement in services. In at least one program, eligibility periods for accessing the services of the specialists were extended from the first 90 days of the case to 6 months to allow for the establishment of relationships between the parent and the caseworker, and with multiple systems.

If planning and initial implementation of the substance abuse specialist program indicate a potential increased number of individuals accessing services, it is also important that treatment services have the resources and capacity to meet the potential increases. These treatment services also need to include ancillary services that address families' needs. Table 1 summarizes the substance abuse specialist programs across the sites interviewed for this paper.

APPENDIX A: CASE STUDIES

Connecticut: Substance Abuse Specialists

Background and Purpose

In 1989, a class action lawsuit [Juan F. v. O'Neill] was filed against the Connecticut Department of Children and Families (DCF) alleging that DCF was grossly underfunded and understaffed, child abuse complaints were not investigated, high caseloads overwhelmed social workers, and the dwindling supply of foster parents was underpaid and inadequately trained. Plaintiffs brought claims under the reasonable efforts provisions of Title IV-E, the Due Process Clause. The lawsuit resulted in a comprehensive consent decree in 1991 covering all areas of policy, management, procedures, and operation of the department's child protective services.

Connecticut addressed these issues by, in part, developing and implementing Project SAFE (Substance Abuse and Family Education) in 1995 to improve the child protection system. Project SAFE provides a direct link between the child protection system and the adult substance abuse treatment system statewide. The program provides centralized intake procedures and priority access to substance abuse evaluations, drug screenings, and outpatient treatment services. Because of this collaborative program, direct-line social work staff in DCF have the ability to secure timely substance abuse evaluations and screenings for cases in which substance abuse issues are identified.

At the time Project SAFE was created, DCF began hiring substance abuse specialists to serve as consultants and provide expertise and training to its social workers.

Roles and Responsibilities

Substance abuse specialists provide consultation, expertise, and training to child welfare workers to improve the workers' practice and to provide brief interventions for families. The roles and responsibilities vary to meet the different needs of the population served in each area of the State. Examples of roles and responsibilities include (1) home visiting with child welfare workers, (2) collaborating with adolescent and adult treatment providers, (3) interpreting drug screening results for the child welfare workers, and (4) consulting with the workers about referrals to treatment providers. Specialists were involved in 70–80 percent of the 1,978 DCF neglect cases in 2006 for which substance abuse treatment was indicated.

Connecticut has been exploring Illinois' recovery coach model as a way to better engage clients and provide more outreach. This exploration arises from concern about how to help more DCF clients engage in and complete treatment. Currently, child welfare workers and substance abuse specialists work together to provide clients with treatment referrals, but subsequent treatment entry is not ensured.

Locations and Settings

Connecticut is a State-administered child welfare system comprising 15 area offices, divided according to towns, cities, and population clusters. Each area office director determines the number of substance abuse specialists needed for his or her area. There are eight to nine total substance abuse specialists in Connecticut. A specialist may serve more than one area.

In each area, the substance abuse specialist is one member of the Area Resource Group, a clinical team that includes a registered nurse and children's mental health professionals, including at least one clinical social worker and a psychologist.

Underlying Values and Principles

Under Project SAFE, a Memorandum of Agreement between DCF and the Department of Mental Health and Addiction Services (DMHAS) was developed that provides policy-level guidance for specialists and child welfare workers when working with DMHAS-funded treatment providers. Through the agreement, DCF clients receive assistance from the specialists and workers with gaining access to drug tests, evaluations, and outpatient treatment.

On the practice level, however, philosophical differences may remain in whether the client is the parent, child, or family, and whether the goal is child safety, family preservation, or parent recovery. Because of the differing values, some child welfare workers avoid substance abuse specialists, whereas others have productive relationships with them. Successful collaborations result in child welfare workers and substance abuse specialists working on cases together, focused on the children's needs, the family's needs, and the parents' treatment needs.

Funding

Because of the consent decree, the State of Connecticut allocates funds to DCF to pay for 67 unionized clinical specialists with expertise in clinical social work, nursing, substance abuse, children's mental health, and family and clinical psychology. Specialists' salaries range from $45,000–$68,000 plus benefits negotiated in the collective bargaining agreement.

Substance abuse specialists are hired by DCF and are employed by the State of Connecticut. DCF pays the specialists from the State allocation. Specialists have the same job class as clinical social workers and are members of the health care union.

Staff Development, Training, and Supervision

DCF State substance abuse specialists must be licensed clinical social workers with additional licensure or certification in alcohol and other drug counseling. The requirement for additional certification can be waived if the candidate has experience working with the substance abuse treatment system. Statewide, there is a shortage of licensed professionals who are qualified to fill these positions, which has led to DMHAS and treatment providers hiring staff without substance abuse credentials.

When substance abuse specialists were first introduced in the early 1990s, child welfare workers and providers experienced a learning curve on how to use the specialists appropriately. The specialists provided cross-training to child welfare workers and providers to help them understand the role and functions of the specialists. Today, many DCF area offices view the worker, provider, and specialist as a "treatment team." In addition, DCF is moving toward a model of training that will provide child welfare workers with an understanding of substance use disorders, treatment, and recovery.

Specialists report to their respective DCF area office director, who is responsible for determining the specialist's responsibilities. The DCF area office directors supervise the specialists, which includes providing ongoing training, coaching, improving knowledge and clinical skills, and providing other necessary support to improve clinical outcomes for children and families. Specialists are required to maintain their licensure and certifications.

Joint Accountability, Outcomes, and Evaluation

Since introducing substance abuse specialists, DCF has collected activity data including the number, frequency, and type of consultations provided by the substance abuse specialists on each case. In addition, DCF collects data on triage, case conferencing, tracking, and case management.

Each area office collects data at the area level. However, the data are not standardized and are therefore difficult to analyze on a statewide, aggregate basis. To address this challenge, DCF has implemented the use of the Global Assessment of Individual Needs - Short Screener (GAIN-SS), a standardized screening for co- occurring disorders to be conducted by child welfare workers. Substance abuse specialists train child welfare workers to use the GAIN-SS instrument. Recently, DCF began providing specialists information on the extent of GAIN-SS usage and the training and technical assistance needs among workers in specific area offices.

CONTACT: Peter Panzarella, Director of Substance Abuse Services
Connecticut Department of Children and Families
Phone: 860-550-6527
E-mail: peter.panzarella@po.state.

Delaware: Substance Abuse Counselors Program

Background and Purpose

In 1996, the U.S. Department of Health and Human Services granted the Delaware Department of Services for Children, Youth, and Their Families' Division of Family Services (DFS) approval to implement a Title IV-E Waiver Demonstration Project. The purpose of Delaware's 5-year waiver demonstration was to reduce the cost of out-of-home care by focusing on early identification of parental substance use disorders and substance abuse treatment service referrals. Before the demonstration project, DFS had limited access to substance abuse counselors. DFS applied for the waiver demonstration with the intent of using the expertise of substance abuse treatment counselors to reduce removals of children from the home or facilitate reunification of families with substance use disorders.

Although all child welfare workers received 3 days of training related to substance abuse, they had limited hands-on experience in working with these issues. The substance abuse counselors, however, were familiar with the treatment network, both within and outside of Delaware (e.g., Philadelphia and Maryland), had contacts in an array of treatment agencies, and understood the variety of programs offered by each agency (e.g., perinatal, methadone, and adolescent). With the support of the substance abuse treatment counselors, parents were provided with referrals that better reflected their individual and treatment needs.

In addition, child welfare workers experienced difficulty in negotiating the managed care system that governs a significant portion of the substance abuse treatment network. One of the biggest challenges was navigating Medicaid and managed care preauthorization specifications regarding treatment length and coverage and determining which treatment agencies accepted Medicaid. The Title IV-E waiver provided an opportunity for DFS to use substance abuse counselors who were familiar with the managed care system.

In the evaluation results, the Waiver Demonstration Project was not cost-neutral, nor did it demonstrate cost savings. As a result, the demonstration project was terminated in December 2001. Although Federal funding for the project ceased, DFS, substance abuse treatment agencies, child welfare workers, and courts saw the value in using substance abuse counselors who could assess and connect clients to appropriate treatment in a timely manner. The juvenile court wrote letters to DFS praising the expertise of counselors in helping parents to complete treatment. DFS also received letters from clients testifying to the positive impact the counselors made on their lives. As a result, DFS decided to continue the Substance Abuse Counselors Program using non-Federal Title IV-E sources.

Roles and Responsibilities

The primary roles and responsibilities of the substance abuse counselors include providing consultation, evaluations, referrals, linkages, and case management services to adult DFS clients who may have a substance use disorder. Specifically, the substance abuse counselors fulfill the following responsibilities:

1. Collaborate with treatment units;
2. Provide consultation services to child welfare investigation units;
3. Identify clients with suspected or documented substance use disorders;
4. Conduct home visits with the DFS social worker or on their own;
5. Refer clients with suspected or documented substance use disorders to a substance abuse treatment agency for an assessment;
6. Link and monitor substance abuse treatment services provided by substance abuse treatment agencies;
7. Provide continued support to clients while the client is engaged in treatment;
8. Coordinate services and case monitoring with the DFS social worker;
9. Keep DFS informed of activities and status of the client;
10. Participate in child safety decisions;
11. Participate in case conferences and jointly develop case plans with DFS;
12. Enter notes summarizing client contacts into the DFS computerized case management system known as FACTS (Family and Child Tracking System);
13. Conduct or arrange random urine screenings for clients as needed (to be determined by either the substance abuse counselor or the DFS social worker);

14. Testify in court as needed (if proper subpoenas have been issued); and
15. Provide quarterly "brown bag" seminars to DFS staff to cover a variety of timely substance abuse issues. Recently, seminar topics have included how to recognize whether clients may be using methamphetamine or heroin. Attendance is voluntary; however, many DFS staff attend because of the useful information provided.

DFS and treatment unit supervisors emphasize the need for the counselors to work flexible hours to accommodate the child welfare aspects of the case (i.e., visitations and home visits). Substance abuse counselors consult with an average of 15 DFS caseworkers and carry caseloads ranging from 26–37 families.

Locations and Settings

Delaware has three counties and four regional child welfare offices—one office each in Sussex and Kent counties and two offices in New Castle county. There is one substance abuse counselor assigned to each region. DFS contracts with community-based substance abuse treatment agencies in each region to employ the substance abuse counselors and to provide clinical oversight. The DFS treatment program manager is involved in interviewing these potential substance abuse counselors.

The substance abuse counselors are co-located in the community-based substance abuse treatment and agency with DFS treatment staff in each of the four regional DFS offices. DFS provides each substance abuse counselor with office space, a computer, a telephone, and a State vehicle. By co-locating the substance abuse counselors with DFS staff, the counselors are available either to accompany DFS staff on home visits and to case conferences or to provide consultation to DSF staff. The counselors are considered part of their respective DFS treatment units and are included in all unit meetings.

Underlying Values and Principles

In 1998, DFS signed a Memorandum of Understanding with Delaware Health and Social Services, Division of Substance Abuse and Mental Health (DSAMH), to ensure that every DFS client is given priority status to receive a substance abuse assessment. Although this arrangement was made independently of the demonstration project, it provided the foundation for building shared values and principles between agencies.

Several aspects of the program design have helped build a shared set of values between child welfare and substance abuse systems. For example, new substance abuse counselors must complete a 6-month DFS New Worker Training protocol before they can carry a caseload. Through the DFS New Worker Training, the substance abuse counselors learn child welfare and safety issues as well as DFS policies and procedures. The counselors, having gone through New Worker Training, understand where differences in values can easily cause misunderstandings between the child welfare and substance abuse treatment systems. The DFS treatment program manager conducts trainings for all treatment agencies in the State on DFS's Child Protection Registry, child welfare timeframes (Adoption and Safe Families Act), substance abuse, treatment, and recovery.

Funding

DFS contracts with these substance abuse agencies to hire the certified substance abuse counselors. DFS transfers funds to the agencies in exchange for their employment, training, and supervision of counselors. Since DFS funds the Substance Abuse Counselors Program, DFS establishes the terms and conditions of contracts with the agencies. When the Title IV-E Waiver Demonstration Project ended, DFS reallocated funding from other treatment contracts to continue the Substance Abuse Counselors Program.

DFS spends approximately $150,000 annually on the substance abuse counselors' salaries, health insurance, Federal Insurance Contributions Act taxes, association dues, conference fees, and urinalysis screenings. The contracts between DFS and the substance abuse treatment agencies are the cost-reimbursement type. As such, the agencies submit invoices to DFS each month to cover monthly expenses incurred by the substance abuse counselors. The substance abuse counselors have access to a State vehicle; DFS absorbs the cost of State vehicle use.

Staff Development, Training and Supervision

Substance abuse counselors must maintain a current certification in drug and alcohol counseling (CDAC) and must receive clinical supervision by a credentialed supervisor. The treatment agencies that employ the counselors have their own desired qualifications and requirements based on the populations they serve.

As discussed previously, new substance abuse counselors must complete the DFS New Worker Training protocol. The DFS treatment program manager provides opportunities for additional in-service training as well. All counselors must maintain their CDAC certification, and some treatment agencies require additional training.

Delaware uses a dual supervision model to train and supervise counselors. The substance abuse treatment agencies provide a credentialed supervisor to conduct ongoing clinical supervision and training of the counselors. DFS provides supervision for the child welfare aspects of each counselor's cases. The DFS treatment program manager and the DSAMH director of drug and alcohol services coordinate and facilitate quarterly meetings with all parties involved in the Substance Abuse Counselors Program (DFS, DSAMH, treatment agencies, and counselors). At the quarterly meetings, these parties review and discuss any systemic issues and concerns and develop programmatic improvement strategies.

Joint Accountability, Outcomes and Evaluation

Since 1996, the DFS Treatment Program Manager has collected data monthly, from the substance abuse counselors, summarizing their caseload and the status of each client. The data collected are as follows:

- Date each case is referred by child welfare to the substance abuse counselor;
- Date of the counselor's first contact with the client;
- Whether the client was referred to a treatment agency;
- Whether the client attended treatment/scheduled appointments;
- Duration of treatment episode;
- Existence of co-occurring mental health disorders and domestic violence issues;
- Whether the client was in substance abuse treatment at the time of referral;

- Whether the children were placed in out-of-home care;
- Identified barriers to success; and
- The client's current prognosis.

In evaluating a client's current prognosis, the counselors select one of the following choices:

- Excellent: Client connected to treatment, consistent negative urines, and improvement in functioning noted;
- Good: Client attended evaluation, appears to be motivated toward treatment, mostly negative urines, and little improvement in functioning noted;
- Fair: Client attended evaluation, little motivation toward treatment, some negative urines, and little improvement in functioning noted; and
- Poor: Client did not attend evaluation, no motivation toward treatment, no negative urines, and no improvement in functioning noted.

If a counselor gives a client a prognosis of "fair" or "poor," the counselor will increase efforts to engage the client through more frequent contact and potentially increasing the level of structure in the substance abuse treatment program for the parent.

DFS's budget does not allocate money for an independent program evaluation. Thus, given limited evaluation resources, the first analysis of the post- demonstration project data was completed in 2006 by a graduate student/research assistant. The results indicated that in 2005, 24 percent of parents working with the substance abuse counselors completed a treatment program. Because of the evaluation, DFS, the treatment agencies, and the substance abuse counselors are developing strategies to improve the treatment retention rates among DFS clients. For example, peer mentors have been suggested as a possible additional component of the program.

CONTACT: JoAnn Bruch, Treatment Program Manager
Division of Family Services
Delaware Department of Services for Children, Youth, and Their Families
Phone: 302-633-2690
E-mail: Joann.Bruch@state.

Illinois: Recovery Coach Program

Background and Purpose

The Recovery Coach Program in Illinois emerged from a history of collaborative efforts focused on improving services for substance-affected families in child welfare. In 1986, the Department of Children and Family Services (DCFS) and the Department of Human Services (DHS), Division of Alcoholism and Substance Abuse (DASA), launched Project SAFE (Substance and Alcohol-Free Environment.) This pilot project was launched to learn whether DCFS and DASA could increase the number of women with substance use disorders engaged and retained in treatment if their unique needs, such as child care, transportation, and lack of insurance for treatment, were met.

In 1998, DCFS launched a second pilot project, the Intact Family and Recovery Program, in Cook county. The cornerstone of the project is the collaboration between child welfare workers and alcohol and other drug abuse (AODA) workers in serving mothers of prenatally exposed infants. This collaboration allows the engagement of mothers into treatment immediately after the birth of their child with the goal of keeping the family intact. This pilot project revealed that there was a further need for cross-training of child welfare and AODA workers and that these workers needed the ability to address clients' co-occurring issues (i.e., domestic violence and mental health issues). The project also revealed that clients benefited when they had an advocate to assist them in progressing through treatment.

When presented with an opportunity to apply for a Title IV-E Waiver Demonstration, DCFS believed that its experience in addressing substance abuse issues among child welfare clients would help the agency create and implement an effective waiver demonstration program. The waiver demonstration program began in April 2000 in Cook county (Chicago and suburban areas) and continued until June 2005. The purpose of the waiver demonstration program in Illinois was to test a model of intensive case management in the form of a recovery coach. The use of a recovery coach was intended to increase access to substance abuse services, improve substance abuse treatment outcomes, shorten the length of time in out-of-home care for the child, and affect child welfare outcomes, including increasing rates of family reunification and decreasing the risk of continued maltreatment.

At the conclusion of the demonstration program, an independent evaluator determined that the program met all of its intended outcomes. The program also provided a cost savings of $5.6 million over the 5 years of the demonstration, which DCFS was able to reinvest in State child welfare services. As a result, DCFS received a 5-year extension to expand the program into the southern, more rural, part of the State, including Madison and St. Clair counties. The new project began in December 2006 and will end in December 2011. The purpose of the current Title IV-E waiver project continues to be the use of a recovery coach.

Roles and Responsibilities

The role of the recovery coach is to be an advocate for DCFS clients in working with their child welfare workers, the courts, the substance abuse treatment agencies, and their family members. As an advocate, the recovery coach assists the parent in obtaining benefits and in meeting the responsibilities and mandates related to the parent's child welfare case and recovery treatment plan. Recovery coach services are provided for the duration of the case and may be continued for a period of time after the child welfare case closes.

Recovery coaches engage DCFS clients in all activities related to the substance abuse aspects of a case, including comprehensive clinical assessments, service planning, outreach, and case management. The following paragraphs describe some of these activities.

The clinical assessments focus on a variety of problem areas, such as housing, domestic violence, parenting, mental health, and family support needs. Recovery coaches also conduct urinalysis to help demonstrate to the court whether the client has tested negatively for substance use.

In service planning, recovery coaches coordinate DCFS and other services. They also arrange for the appropriate level of care and ensure that there are no gaps in service.

In conducting outreach, recovery coaches work with substance-abusing families in their community. The coaches improve communication between the child welfare worker and substance abuse treatment facilities to ensure a seamless delivery of services. Recovery coaches also transport clients to appointments and court hearings, arrange and attend meetings with families and treatment providers, and make joint home visits with child welfare caseworkers and/or treatment agency staff. At least one recovery coach is always on call during evenings, weekends, and holidays to respond to any emergencies that may arise. Recovery coaches engage in information sharing with child welfare, treatment providers, and juvenile court personnel. The information sharing is intended to help inform permanency decisions. To ensure recovery, child welfare workers and treatment providers contact recovery coaches if they sense a client is about to relapse.

Locations and Settings

The offices of recovery coaches are located in a Treatment Alternatives for Safe Communities (TASC) office, the organization initially responsible for providing recovery coach services to clients in the demonstration group. This office is close to the Cook county juvenile court, a location found to be effective, particularly if the recovery coach is unable to locate a client. Thus, if the client appears in court, Juvenile Court Assessment Project (JCAP) professionals are able to identify his or her recovery coach and immediately re-link the client to that recovery coach. Recovery coaches, however, often spend most of their time in the field.

Clients receiving recovery coach services meet the recovery coach liaison at JCAP immediately after their substance abuse assessment. DCFS contracts with Caritas, a central intake service organization, to perform the initial JCAP assessment, make a treatment recommendation, and set up an intake appointment at one of the treatment agencies participating in the interagency agreement between DCFS and DASA.

There are four recovery coach teams that each focus on clients and/or specific issues (e.g., men, women, or co-occurring disorders). Each team has one supervisor and four to five recovery coaches and each team includes outreach workers, sometimes known as trackers, who are responsible for finding clients who have become difficult to locate at some point during the recovery process. There are two trackers in Cook County, and one of the team supervisors works with both trackers.

Underlying Values and Principles

Since 1995, DCFS has had in place a formal interagency agreement with DHS and DASA. Periodically, DCFS, DHS, and DASA review this interagency agreement to ensure that DCFS clients continue to receive priority treatment admission. DCFS contracts with approximately 60 private agencies (such as Catholic Charities and Lutheran Social Services of Illinois) to provide child welfare case management for about 80 percent of Illinois families with open child welfare cases. The contracts and interagency agreements with private agencies outline DCFS policy and procedures for serving substance-affected families. The agreements clearly outline procedures for working productively and collaboratively with child welfare workers and recovery coaches. In addition, the DCFS contracts with TASC and Caritas specify DCFS' expectations for assessment, referral, recovery coach services, and data collection.

Funding

DCFS spends approximately $2.2 million annually on the Recovery Coach Program, including costs for the JCAP services, the computer-based data collection integrated system, and the recovery coaches. Recovery coaches receive the same benefits as TASC employees. Recovery coaches are required to use their own vehicle, but they receive the Federal rate allotment for mileage reimbursement.

Staff Development, Training and Supervision

Recovery coaches must be either a Certified Alcohol and Drug Counselor (CADC) or a Certified Assessment/Referral Specialist (CARS). Recovery coaches have 1 year after hiring to obtain the required certification. Supervisors are required to have a master's degree as well as experience in the child welfare and substance abuse treatment systems. Caritas and TASC are responsible for hiring, training, and supervising recovery coaches. DCFS contracts with TASC to provide supervision and training of recovery coaches. Recovery coaches are required to participate in a variety of DCFS and DASA trainings that cover various topics, including addiction, relapse prevention, the *Diagnostic and Statistical Manual of Mental Disorders (Fourth Edition)*, the American Society of Addiction Medicine, fundamentals of assessment, ethics, service hours, client-tracking systems, service planning, case management, and counseling.

Since the first waiver project, DCFS personnel have provided training on the role of recovery coaches to child welfare agencies and substance abuse treatment providers. DCFS emphasized to child welfare agencies that the recovery coach was not to replace the child welfare worker, but would instead provide a bridge to the client and the treatment community regarding all substance-related aspects of the child welfare case. The intention of the training was to emphasize the expertise of the recovery coach in assisting the parents through the recovery process.

In addition, the DCFS AODA Waiver coordinator provides cross-training to ensure collaboration between JCAP, Caritas, TASC, and other collaborating agencies. DCFS has also extended its training into courts to inform judges about the recovery process and the role of recovery coaches.

The DCFS AODA Waiver coordinator meets monthly with supervisors from TASC, JCAP, and Caritas to discuss the recovery coach program and any data collection issues. Cross-training about the various roles in the collaboration also occurs during these monthly meetings.

Joint Accountability, Outcomes and Evaluation

DCFS contracts with Caritas to coordinate a computer-based data collection integrated system called TRACCS (Treatment Record and Continuing Care System). Caritas collects data from child welfare workers, recovery coaches, and treatment agencies. The database includes a variety of client (e.g., demographics and placement history) and social service (e.g., placement records) information.

The current waiver demonstration project requires that an independent evaluator determine whether the project has met its outcomes and whether the project is cost-neutral. The Children and Family Research Center at the University of Illinois at Urbana-Champaign

School of Social Work analyzes the collected data to measure whether the following outcomes are being met:

(1) increased rates of reunification; (2) shorter lengths of stay in foster care; (3) a reduction in reallegations of child abuse and neglect; and (4) higher success rates for completion of parental substance abuse treatment among demonstration group participants. According to the Center's January 2006 evaluation report, DCFS has achieved its first three outcomes, with statistically significant differences between the control group and the demonstration group. Although no comparison was available for the fourth outcome, beginning in April 2004, 22 percent of clients in the demonstration group had completed treatment.

DCFS realized a cost savings of $5.6 million over the 5-year span of 2000–2005, which it reinvested in State child welfare services.

CONTACT: Rosie Gianforte, Alcohol and Other Drug Abuse Waiver Coordinator
Illinois Department of Children and Family Services
Phone: 312-814-2440
E-mail: Rosie.Gianforte@illinois.gov.

Massachusetts: Substance Abuse Regional Coordinators Program

Background and Purpose

In 1998, the Massachusetts Department of Social Services (DSS) Child Welfare Department created a strategic plan entitled "The Project on Addressing Substance Abuse," in collaboration with the Massachusetts Department of Public Health's (DPH) Bureau of Substance Abuse Services (BSAS). The plan included six recommendations for improving substance abuse services for child welfare clients.

One recommendation was to establish a Substance Abuse Unit to focus exclusively on building child welfare's capacity and expertise in responding to substance abuse allegations. In 2000, DSS and DPH created and co-funded a managerial position at the child welfare central office. The two departments also hired the first substance abuse director with the agreement that DSS would be responsible for administrative oversight. In 2001, DSS and DPH used additional funding to create a central office assistant to the substance abuse director.

From 2001–2004, the substance abuse director and the assistant were responsible for training, policies, and projects related to substance abuse, including drug testing policies and procedures. In 2004, because of budgetary constraints, DPH could no longer co-fund the director position. The resulting budgetary considerations for DSS led to staffing changes that presented an opportunity to reflect on the strengths and weaknesses of the Substance Abuse Unit's activities and to configure a new program design and staffing plan.

Several factors led to DSS's continued support of the Substance Abuse Unit, including (1) the Substance Abuse Unit had demonstrated the value of and demand for its services to DSS; (2) governmental leadership, including the support of the DSS commissioner at the time, for integration and system changes in child welfare and substance abuse was in place;

and (3) the Massachusetts Child and Family Services Review, completed in fiscal year 2001, highlighted the need for DSS to improve substance abuse services.

However, two issues were highlighted for program and staffing revision. First, standardized drug testing services provided from 2002–2004 demonstrated that child welfare workers needed more training and support for cases in which substance abuse is a factor. During this timeframe, all drug testing was provided at one laboratory location, and results were reported to child welfare. Child welfare workers, partially from a lack of knowledge about when testing is appropriate, were unnecessarily referring large numbers of cases for drug testing. Second, with responsibility for all six regions, the two-person Substance Abuse Unit struggled to provide services in the field. There was a need to add and reconfigure staff to allow the Substance Abuse Unit to provide services on a regional level. For example, each of the six regions had received a mental health specialist in 2001.

With funding from DSS, the Substance Abuse Unit created six regional positions in 2004 and called the effort the Substance Abuse Regional Coordinators Program. The purpose of the program is to build child welfare's capacity and expertise to address substance abuse, create linkages between child welfare and the substance abuse provider community, and collaborate with colleagues in mental health and domestic violence.

Roles and Responsibilities

The roles and responsibilities of the coordinators were developed by the DSS substance abuse director. In developing coordinator roles, the director wanted to exclude responsibilities that would involve coordinators in extensive clinical work, which would hinder their ability to focus on system-level change, promote interagency collaboration, and build caseworkers' capacity and expertise to address substance abuse in their cases. Thus, case management and home visiting were intentionally excluded from the coordinator's role, though the coordinators regularly consult and provide expertise and guidance to DSS staff regarding substance abuse-related cases. Coordinators also attend multidisciplinary meetings and case staffing to provide their expertise and to ensure that DSS workers are adequately supported to address substance abuse.

Within these boundaries, DSS was intentionally broad in developing the various possible roles for the coordinator. Central administration wanted to give regional administration shared power to prioritize the various roles. Although central administration wanted to provide overall expertise and a common language and purpose among coordinators, the regional administrators could determine which roles would best serve the needs of the clients and caseworkers in that particular region. DSS also intentionally established common responsibilities between coordinators. For example, the substance abuse director planned to hold weekly meetings with all the coordinators, providing a venue for coordinators to learn from one another's experiences.

The roles and responsibilities listed in the coordinator job description are as follows:

- Conduct a capacity needs assessment on substance abuse for the assigned region and its corresponding area offices;
- Develop and implement substance abuse capacity building and action plans. Provide resources, support, and training to increase the level of substance abuse expertise in the assigned region;

- Implement regional and area objectives outlined in "The Project on Addressing Substance Abuse," in conjunction with regional leadership;
- Provide case consultation to assigned area offices as needed;
- Monitor ongoing pilot project efforts on substance abuse within assigned regions;
- Participate in regional and area team meetings, including continuous quality improvement teams, family group conferencing, and other clinical meetings;
- Work with community-based substance abuse providers to establish working relationships between the provider and the local DSS area office. This work includes improving communication with the provider and developing protocols to improve DSS clients' access to services and to streamline service provision;
- Participate in regional and area interagency or community-based substance abuse or child welfare meetings;
- Collect regional and area data on substance abuse when needed; and
- Participate on regional and statewide projects and committees as needed.

DSS works with approximately 20,000 families on any given day. The coordinators do not work directly with families in their case consultation role, but conduct a total of 50–75 consultations with the child welfare worker per month.

All the coordinators have a substance abuse treatment background, which has been invaluable as they build relationships with treatment providers. Their treatment background is also a challenge for the program, because the coordinators enjoy and may prefer to focus on the case consultation part of their work. Although the coordinators understand their role in promoting system change, most do not have a background in building interagency relationships. They also face the challenge of frequent misperceptions about their role from within both DSS and BSAS. For example, people often assume the coordinators are to be directly involved with cases. When the coordinators become involved in casework, as many DSS and BSAS staff believe is the coordinator role, keeping system change and capacity building at the forefront becomes a challenge.

Locations and Settings

Massachusetts child welfare services are State administered. DSS provides services through six regions and through area offices within each region. The DSS Substance Abuse Director works with each regional director to select the coordinator. The positions are known technically as regional positions (not central administrative office positions). There is one substance abuse coordinator for each region, working in his or her respective regional office while also providing services to area offices.

Underlying Values and Principles

A joint value for interagency collaboration between DSS and DPH/BSAS predated the Substance Abuse Regional Coordinators Program. The collaboration was developed during the creation of the 1998 strategic plan to address substance abuse and continues to exist in the Massachusetts Family Recovery Collaboration (MFRC). MFRC is an effort launched in 2006 to develop an integrated, coordinated system of care for families in which parental substance use disorders result in the maltreatment and/or neglect of children or increase the risk of such maltreatment or neglect. Its goal is improved well-being of children and strengthened families. MFRC is governed by a Memorandum of Understanding between DSS, DPH/BSAS, the Administrative Office of the Trial Court Juvenile Department, and the Wampanoag Tribe of Gay Head Aquinnah. The memorandum specifically explains joint values and principles for those involved in the MFRC collaboration.

The substance abuse director's weekly meetings with coordinators also reinforce the program's purpose and underlying values and principles. In the program's first 6 months, the leadership from the substance abuse director and weekly meetings were critical to help the coordinators form relationships with the child welfare workers and substance abuse treatment providers. The meetings continue to be important for helping the coordinators lead their regions to continue building their own capacity to address substance abuse.

Funding

The Substance Abuse Unit created six regional positions in 2004. Since the coordinators are technically regional positions, DSS allocates State funds to the regions to cover the coordinators' salaries, workspace, travel, and parking. The coordinators are State union positions, not funded by grants or legislative allocations. The DSS Substance Abuse Unit, however, does not have a program budget for other aspects of the program, such as purchasing equipment or funding conference participation.

Staff Development, Training and Supervision

Each coordinator is required to have at least a bachelor's degree in human services, social work, or a related field. Licensed professionals are encouraged to apply. Four years of full-time or equivalent part-time professional experience in social work, social casework, health care administration, public health, program administration, hospital administration, or program management is also required. However, either a bachelor's degree holder with 2 years of experience or a master's degree holder with 1 year of experience is also qualified.

Massachusetts has filled all six positions. All have master's degrees (one is in nursing, two are in social work, and two are Licensed Mental Health Counselors), and one has a Ph.D. It was difficult to find the right candidates for these positions for several reasons. These positions require professionals who are able to meet the relatively new challenge of working across governmental systems (including navigating the politics). And DSS strongly believed that the program's success depended on identifying candidates who have a background in working with families.

New coordinators participate in the 1-month-long child welfare New Worker Training, which is the key to understanding how child welfare operates. They typically receive a basic introduction to the program and job responsibilities from the substance abuse director. New hires also shadow experienced coordinators.

The director hosts a weekly meeting of the coordinators in which they are able to learn from one another's experiences. In the initial implementation of this program, these weekly meetings provided coordinators with support and direction as they worked to become integrated into the child welfare system. They gained a mutual sense of belonging and trust and built relationships with substance abuse treatment providers. Coordinators have recently started arranging meetings between themselves, representatives from the child welfare offices where they work, and local substance abuse treatment providers to build relationships and initiate cross- training.

Under a matrix-management model for supervision, the primary supervision for each coordinator is at the regional level. The DSS substance abuse director provides clinical supervision and technical support. Two factors may influence the supervisory relationships in the future. First, Massachusetts intends to hire a co-director of integrated practice for substance abuse and mental health, who will take over management of the program. Second, at the regional level, new clinical managers have recently been put into place, and some have substantial substance abuse experience.

Joint Accountability, Outcomes and Evaluation

The program does not track outcomes, but there are ways in which DSS is evaluating progress. In the weekly meetings, the substance abuse director can consistently gather information about coordinators' success. The director uses the following indicators to determine whether the purpose of the Substance Abuse Unit and the Substance Abuse Regional Coordinators Program is being effectively carried out:

- High utilization of the coordinator by caseworkers and external providers;
- Stronger linkages between child welfare and substance abuse treatment providers; and
- Increased capacity of child welfare to address cases in which substance abuse is a factor.

CONTACT: Kim Bishop-Stevens, Substance Abuse Manager
Massachusetts Department of Social Services
Phone: 617-748-2049
E-mail: kim.bishop-stevens@state.

New Hampshire: Project First Step

Background and Purpose

During the late 1990s, New Hampshire's Statewide Automated Child Welfare Information System, known as New Hampshire Bridges, documented a number of co-occurring issues facing child welfare clients, including substance abuse. Both the data and the opportunity to apply for a Title IV-E Waiver Demonstration Project led professionals from the New Hampshire Department of Health and Human Services (HHS), including representatives from the Division for Children, Youth and Families (DCYF) and what is now the Division of Alcohol and Drug Abuse Prevention and Recovery (DADAPR), to come together to determine how to better address the needs of families affected by substance use disorders who are involved in child welfare services. DCYF adapted Delaware's Substance Abuse Counselors Program, also funded as a Title IV-E Waiver Demonstration (see page 15).

In May 1998, New Hampshire DCYF received approval to run its proposed Title IV-E Waiver Demonstration Project, known as Project First Step. New Hampshire implemented its demonstration project in two of the State's most populated district office areas, which serve the majority of Hillsborough county. The waiver allowed New Hampshire to demonstrate whether spending the funds to increase capacity to provide parents with substance abuse treatment could improve reunification and other family permanency and safety outcomes for children from substance-affected families. HHS involved the University of New Hampshire (UNH) Family Research Lab, as well as field supervisors, caseworkers, and stakeholder groups, to provide its expertise during the program design phase.

Four factors influenced the demonstration project design in New Hampshire:

- Compared with many other States, the rate of substantiated child abuse and neglect referrals is relatively low. This factor is due, in part, to the State's stringent due process requirements for substantiation of allegations of child abuse and neglect. New Hampshire's Child Protection Act provides for a relatively long, 60-day assessment before substantiation. Substance abuse screening is conducted before substantiation, which has documented that one-fifth to one-fourth of all reports assigned for face-to-face assessments have an identified substance abuse issue. However, since 1996, just 10–11.5 percent of all DCYF cases have been substantiated. Upon investigation, 50 percent of those substantiated assessments that resulted in temporary removal or in-home services had parental substance abuse identified;
- Although heroin use is substantial in some areas, alcohol is the primary substance used by clients;
- New Hampshire is involved with most referrals on a short-term basis, but repeatedly (sometimes for a few months out of a year, over a period of years); and
- The program designers made an assumption that with children being removed from homes in only about 10 percent of cases, the actual number of children who would be traditionally eligible for Title IV-E funding in New Hampshire's demonstration project would be relatively small. Most families would be receiving in-home services.

HHS decided to co-locate Licensed Alcohol and Drug Counselors (LADCs) in two Child Protective Services (CPS) district offices, one in Nashua and the other in Manchester. From November 1999 through December 2004, reports that DCYF accepted for assessment were randomly assigned to experimental (enhanced services) or control (standard services) groups. Child Protective Service Workers (CPSWs) and LADCs were mutually assigned to families in the experimental group. Families in the control group received standard child protection and community- based assessment and treatment services.

By July 2003, a total of 435 families had enrolled in the demonstration, with 222 families in the experimental group and 213 in the control group. Children from families in the enhanced services group were more likely to remain with kin and had fewer foster care placements than children from families in the standard services group. Further, the average number of foster care placements for enhanced group children was significantly lower than the average number of similar placements for standard group children. Those children in the enhanced group who could not be safely reunified, reached the concurrent goal identified by Termination of Parental Rights sooner than those in the standard group. Regardless of substantiation of placement, children and their parents in the enhanced group demonstrated improved outcomes in the area of well-being.[10]

At the conclusion of the demonstration project, New Hampshire found that the cost of the enhanced LADC/CPSW services to families remained constant, so the project did not demonstrate savings in Title IV-E funds. Nevertheless, the addition of LADCs improved reunification and permanency rates and allowed the CPSWs to focus on all aspects of their cases by having a better connection with substance abuse treatment and recovery. By 2004, DCYF viewed the project as extremely important and genuinely believed that approaches like Project First Step were necessary to meet the needs of its clients. Thus, Project First Step was allowed to continue its efforts to increase clients' access to quality assessment and timely treatment and to encourage child protection, substance abuse treatment, and community services to create a system of integrated services.

The demonstration had two lasting effects that contributed to the program's continuation. First, families in the enhanced services group experienced improved kinship care as an alternative to foster care placement. In identified cases, LADCs worked with kinship caregivers to increase their awareness of the dynamics of addiction and recovery. LADCs also served as mediators between parents and kinship caregivers to obtain mutual support of the visitation and reunification plan.

Second, these counselors were able to engage parents in the enhanced group with the understanding that information shared with LADCs was subject to State and Federal confidentiality laws. Thus, parents were more open to the notion that the services of the LADCs would be helpful.

Roles and Responsibilities

During the Title IV-E demonstration, LADCs worked with CPSWs in an advisory and supportive capacity by providing training, assessment, treatment, and case management services. LADCs conducted an initial drug and alcohol assessment concurrently with the CPS maltreatment investigation and were involved from the outset in the risk and safety assessment to facilitate better decisions regarding child safety and out-of-home placement. LADCs could provide direct outpatient treatment or facilitate treatment access, thereby improving the timeliness of access to substance abuse treatment services and increasing the likelihood of positive treatment outcomes. In addition, LADCs had the option to continue working directly with parents for an additional 2 months after completion of the maltreatment assessment or CPS case opening.[11]

After the demonstration project concluded in 2004, DCYF expanded the duties of the LADCs. LADCs are now involved with all referrals in their respective district offices where substance abuse is indicated as a contributing factor. LADCs are involved as consultants with CPSWs, or they become involved directly with parents or caretakers when assessment and family service supervisors determine that substance abuse is a contributing factor to alleged or substantiated child abuse or neglect. If there are primary indicators of significant parent or caretaker substance abuse, LADCs may provide a direct substance abuse assessment and initiate referrals to community-based treatment.

LADCs help CPSWs reduce such barriers as access to treatment facilities and provide direct individual treatment for parents or caretakers who are receptive to treatment, but have not yet accessed treatment. LADCs currently train CPSWs to incorporate substance abuse screening questions in all abuse and neglect assessments to helpclarify the existence or extent of substance abuse. During the assessment process,LADC services result in enhanced community-based family support. In open DCYF cases, LADCs are involved, both as substance abuse treatment case managers for parents and caretakers and as readily available consultants for CPSWs and supervisors. For cases that involve in-home services, LADCs provide services consistent with family preservation. For those cases in which children are in temporary out-of-home care, LADC services help to expedite reunification or placement into kinship care, consistent with services attributed to time-limited family reunification.

For those situations in which the concurrent permanency plan is adoption, LADCs continue to be consultants in the case-planning process and to provide direct service to parents or caretakers if treatment resources are not available.[12]

Locations and Settings

In New Hampshire, the State HHS manages all child welfare and substance abuse services through district offices arranged by population and accessibility (e.g., ease of transportation). During the Title IV-E demonstration, LADCs were located in the Nashua and Manchester offices (one per office), serving most of Hillsborough County, the most populated area in New Hampshire. Today, Project First Step is expanding to a third office. Placing the LADCs in district offices allows LADCs to work directly with CPSWs in the field. DCYF would like to add more LADCs to increase the project's capacity.

Underlying Values and Principles

DCYF expected ongoing, respectful discussion and disagreements between the LADCs and the CPSWs, particularly with regard to determining the primary client and the goals. There was a learning period during which CPSWs developed an understanding that LADCs were bound to Federal confidentiality laws and that certain information could or could not be shared. Over time, the nature of discussions surrounding each case has changed from debating whether children should be removed from the home to what can be done to provide clients with integrated treatment. CPSWs have become well-versed in treatment terminology, and they have come to trust that the LADCs are providing information relevant to the case while maintaining client confidentiality.

Funding

The demonstration project was funded by Title IV-E funds. Since 2004, DCYF has funded Project First Step with grants from the Promoting Safe and Stable Families (PSSF) program, which is supported by Title IV-B funds, and the Child Abuse Prevention and Treatment Act (CAPTA). A line item in DCYF's budget allocates Project First Step $120,000–$150,000 per year. The funding covers salaries, furniture, telephones, mileage compensation, and administration.

New Hampshire has very little State funding for early intervention and for cross-training to promote service integration. In expanding Project First Step, district office staff will not want to commit energy to the learning curves necessary to develop such a program without knowing it will exist for at least 3–5 years. To expand Project First Step to areas outside Hillsborough County, for example, DCYF had to assure the district office new to the program that funding would be available for at least that long.

Staff Development, Training and Supervision

LADCs are certified to provide substance abuse counseling and mental health treatment. LADCs are self-employed, and the State considers them to be independent treatment providers. This arrangement helps DCYF to identify LADCs who are well-educated in the substance abuse and mental health treatment fields and who can consistently provide this perspective to CPSWs.

New Hampshire's HHS certifies LADCs as treatment providers and hires them. Local district office CPS supervisors select and interview candidates with oversight by the DCYF clinical social worker and the Project First Step program manager. LADCs provide their services for a flat hourly rate that covers assessment, direct service, and case management (no billable hours). To be consistent with the integrated service model, LADCs must also be certified counselors. Health insurance and typical fringe benefits can be built into the hourly rate. So far, LADC services in each district office approximate full-time hours.

DCYF has developed a coordinated system for supervising LADCs that involves workers, mentors, supervisors, and administrators. Regarding their clinical practice, LADCs are required to arrange for their own clinical supervision. LADCs also are included in supervision sessions by district office CPS supervisors, ideally with CPSWs who are jointly assigned to specified cases. This approach provides an opportunity for essential discussions about child safety, stability, permanency, and well-being in the context of the parent's substance abuse and recovery. LADCs provide regular reports to the Project First Step program manager, specifying the quantity and types of interventions and treatment recommendations resulting from the CPS cases referred to them. CPS supervisors and LADCs from each district office come together on a regular basis to present progress resulting from Project First Step.

LADCs participate in the child welfare core New Worker Training, which includes shadowing child welfare staff. They also participate in trainings on case planning and permanency planning. With this training, Project First Step LADCs can better facilitate clients' compliance with both their treatment plan and child welfare case plan, as well as facilitate collaboration between treatment providers and CPSWs.

Project First Step LADCs provide ongoing education at district office staff meetings for CPSWs to learn when and how to use the LADCs effectively. They also provide education on community issues. In Nashua and Manchester, they have conducted sessions on the growing heroin use, and in Nashua, the LADC has educated CPSWs on how to recognize and approach clients who may be using methamphetamine. LADCs and CPSWs also can evaluate how they handled past cases and discuss how they can improve service delivery for future cases.

Joint Accountability, Outcomes and Evaluation

To evaluate the Title IV-E Waiver Demonstration Project, HHS secured a 5-year contract with UNH. The contract allowed the university to have access to CPSWs and their files, including notes from confidential interviews. The contract covered all DCYF policies and procedures. Additionally, UNH and DCYF professionals consulted with each other to develop a mutual understanding of evidence-based evaluation and child welfare practice.

Given DCYF involvement with families often entails several short-term interventions, the evaluation of the Title IV-E Waiver Demonstration Project included a longitudinal component. UNH was able to track families longitudinally, over a 5-year period, even during the times when DCYF was not involved. The university secured families' participation by providing stipends. The research indicated that children in the enhanced group slept better, experienced less mobility, and had greater declines than children in the standard group in the following categories: anxiety and depression, withdrawn/depressed, somatic problems, attention problems, aggressive behavior, thought problems, and rule breaking.[13]

Since the random assignments and control and experiment groups were concluded in 2004, DCYF has not contracted UNH to do continued analysis. Since 2004, LADCs have been reporting data to their DCYF supervisors. LADCs are to answer the same set of questions for each client in a Microsoft Excel spreadsheet. Questions include the following:

- How quickly the LADC was involved with the client;
- When the client received an assessment;
- What services were recommended to the client;
- Had the client been served by the LADC in the past; and
- Percentage of males versus females served.

DCYF uses the data from these reports to shape the future applications of Project First Step to other regions in the State and to justify the use of PSSF and CAPTA grants to support the program. Also, the information is aiding in the design of other community-based treatment models being developed by the New Hampshire HHS.

CONTACT: Erica Gesen, Administrator
Division for Children, Youth and Families
New Hampshire Department of Health and Human Services Phone: 603-271-7298
E-mail: eungarelli@dhhs.state.

Sacramento County: Early Intervention Specialists and Specialized Treatment and Recovery Services

Background and Purpose

In 1995, Sacramento County implemented the Alcohol and Other Drug Treatment Initiative (AODTI) in response to evidence that substance abuse was a problem for a large number of families served by county agencies. The AODTI was enacted to ensure that substance abuse services would be an integral part of the health and human services system. The goal of the AODTI was to develop the ability of child welfare social workers, public health nurses, eligibility workers, and neighborhood- based services staff to provide systematic screening and intervention services to clients with substance use disorders. The AODTI planned to accomplish this goal by enhancing the workers' understanding of substance use, abuse, and dependence.

Because of the AODTI, five system-wide reforms were subsequently instituted throughout Sacramento County: (1) a comprehensive cross-system joint training program, (2) a substance abuse treatment system of care, (3) a dependency drug court, (4) Early Intervention Specialists (EISs), and (5) specialized treatment and recovery services. The comprehensive cross-system joint training program involves training all child welfare workers on substance use disorders and ways to access treatment resources. This program also involves training substance abuse treatment providers on the child welfare and dependency court systems. The substance abuse treatment system of care includes a managed wait list, expansion of group services, implementation of pre-treatment groups, and prioritization of child welfare clients for immediate access to substance abuse services (after Federally mandated priority access to clients).

The EIS workers and the Specialized Treatment and Recovery Services (STARS) workers are the two ways that Sacramento County provides substance abuse specialists in connection with the Sacramento County Dependency Drug Court (DDC). EIS workers ensure timely assessment and treatment authorization for families at the initial detention hearing. STARS workers are recovery management specialists who assist parents in entering and completing substance abuse treatment and other court requirements.

Roles and Responsibilities

A preliminary step in the court procedure involves the identification of parents who meet the DDC admission criteria at the time of the initial child detention hearing. The EIS worker reviews intake petitions from Child Protective Services (CPS) and identifies petitions alleging neglect or abuse related to parental substance use, including cases in which a child tested positive for drugs at birth. The EIS worker administers a preliminary substance abuse assessment to parents. From the results of the preliminary assessment, the EIS worker provides the county's authorization for treatment payment and makes a referral to the appropriate level of care.

The EIS workers and STARS workers employ Motivational Interviewing (MI) techniques to initially engage parents and motivate them to enter treatment. The EIS worker refers parents to the STARS program, which provides specialized recovery case management. The EIS worker develops a preliminary substance abuse recovery plan, reflecting the appropriate level of care, in consultation with the STARS worker. Each parent who is referred to STARS is matched with a recovery specialist who assists the parent in accessing substance abuse treatment services, develops a liaison role with CPS and other professionals, and provides monitoring and accountability for the parent in complying with treatment requirements. The STARS program provides immediate access to substance abuse assessment and engagement strategies, intensive management of the recovery aspect of the child welfare case plan, and routine monitoring and feedback to CPS and the court.

The primary responsibility of the STARS worker is to maintain a supportive relationship with the parent, emphasizing engagement and retention in substance abuse treatment while providing recovery monitoring for CPS and the DDC. Optimal caseloads are 18–20 clients per STARS worker. The STARS worker monitors urine testing, substance abuse treatment, and self-help group compliance and provides regular compliance reports to the court, social worker, and minor's counsel. Drug testing is administered on a random basis, and collection is observed by the STARS worker. The STARS worker provides regular compliance reports regarding drug testing, treatment participation, and self-help group attendance. Compliance reports are sent to CPS, legal counsel, and the DDC twice each month.

Through a supportive relationship based on MI strategies, the STARS worker supports the parent's adherence to the case and treatment plans and court orders. The STARS worker helps the parent integrate learned rehabilitation skills into his or her daily life. The STARS worker also acts as a liaison between the court, client, and recovery center and provides referrals to self-help meetings that are close to the parent's home and appropriate to the parent's needs. In addition, the STARS program provides aftercare services and follow-up to families to decrease the probability of relapse. Aftercare services ensue when the parent has completed formal treatment and continue for as long as CPS has an open case with the family.

Locations and Settings

CPS and Alcohol and Drug Services (ADS) jointly employ EIS workers. These workers are out-stationed at the dependency court, where they administer the preliminary substance abuse assessment at the time of the detention hearing, make a referral to an appropriate level of substance abuse treatment, and refer parents to the STARS program.

The STARS program is operated by a local, non-profit, community-based organization that provides treatment services through a contract with Sacramento County. The recovery specialist attends DDC hearings and acts as a liaison with community-based treatment to ensure linkages to treatment recovery and supports. STARS program service contacts are conducted in a variety of locations, including in the home, at substance abuse treatment agencies (residential, outpatient, and intensive outpatient), in hospitals, and at community agencies. The parent is initially required to meet with his or her STARS worker at least twice each week. Based on the parent's progress, the intensity is then lowered to one contact per week and then decreased to once every 2 weeks.

The STARS program also is located close to the court, which reduces the number of clients who may get "lost" on their way from court to the program. The program in Sacramento is located right across the street from the court house.

Underlying Values and Principles

The Juvenile Dependency Drug Court Steering Committee meets twice each year to discuss evaluation results and any changes recommended to the DDC. A Memorandum of Agreement (MOA) was signed by key court, CPS, STARS, and evaluation staff. This MOA emphasizes the collaborative nature of the DDC and allows the evaluation team access to client records to conduct evaluations and research and to ensure client protection.

Funding

Original resources used to develop and begin implementation of the system improvements involved one-time grant funds. When presented with evidence of cost-effectiveness and efficiencies by the administration, the Sacramento County Board of Supervisors has consistently acted in support of these efforts. The EIS worker position is funded through CPS. The STARS program is funded through local tobacco litigation settlement funds (30 percent), which are used to match State and Federal Title IV-B and case management funds (70 percent).

Staff Development, Training, and Supervision

EIS workers are master's level social workers with training and experience in substance abuse services and motivational enhancement therapy. CPS supervises these workers.

STARS workers must possess an alcohol and drug counselor certification and are trained in motivational enhancement therapy as well. Three supervisors within the STARS program closely monitor the STARS workers. In addition, every STARS worker meets weekly with the clinical director, who is a licensed clinical social worker.

Since 1995, all child welfare workers have been required to participate in joint training with substance abuse treatment provider staff on substance abuse, child welfare, and the courts. The training is provided by a professional trainer. This comprehensive cross-system joint training began with three levels of training: (1) 4 days of required basic information on substance abuse for all child welfare staff; (2) 4 days of required information on substance abuse screening, brief intervention, motivational enhancement, and substance abuse treatment for all child welfare workers with cases; and (3) 4 days of required group treatment skills for all substance abuse treatment provider staff. The group intervention training was voluntary for any CPS staff.

This comprehensive cross-system joint training is provided at all levels (administrators, managers, and supervisors) to clarify training goals and practice expectations. Training supervisors reinforce change in practice and quality assurance.

Recently, the training program was revised to meet the changing needs of CPS and substance abuse treatment provider staff. The 8 days of training for child welfare staff has been consolidated into 4 days of core training, and mandatory 2-day training on MI was added. The group intervention training was renamed "co-facilitation," and Sacramento County now offers voluntary 4-day training on adolescent mental health and substance abuse.

Joint Accountability, Outcomes and Evaluation

Sacramento DDC program outcomes are assessed in two primary areas: parental treatment status and child placement outcomes. Analyses are conducted to examine differences between comparison and treatment cohorts for parental treatment participation: length of stay in treatment, treatment modality (residential versus outpatient), and satisfactory completion of treatment. Analyses related to child placement outcomes are conducted including child placement type (reunification versus other permanency outcomes) at various time points after the child's initial placement in out-of-home care, time to reunification among those who reunified, and total time in out-of-home care. A separate follow-up analysis among those children who were reunified is conducted to examine rates of reentry into out-of-home care. In addition, analyses are conducted on the relationship of the parent's primary drug to both treatment completion and the child's placement.

Evaluation results are reviewed twice each year to assess the program's continued success. The most recent evaluation report includes information on six groups of parents and children, a comparison group, and five cohorts of DDC participants. Comparison participants are those who entered the dependency system before EIS and STARS implementation (January through May 2001) and met the criteria for DDC. This group received standard CPS and ADS Division services. Court-ordered participants are those who entered the dependency system from October 1, 2001, through September 30, 2007, and who received EIS and STARS services and were court-ordered to receive DDC supervision.

The DDC program produced substantial cost savings from increased 24-month reunification rates of court-ordered children relative to the comparison group. The cost-savings estimate takes into account the reunification rates, time of out-ofhome care, time to reunification, and cost per month of out-of-home care. The 24 month reunification rate for the comparison group was 27.2 percent. The 24 month reunification rate for the court-ordered group was 46.1 percent, which accounted for 962 children.

If we assumed a reunification rate of only 27.2 percent for the court-ordered group, then 394 fewer children would have reunified. By deducting the time to reunification for the court-ordered group (9.22 months) from the average length of out-of-home care for the comparison group (33.1 months), we find a 23.88 month difference. The savings due to the estimated additional 394 children who reunified through the DDC program totals $17,572,290 (394 children multiplied by 23.88 months multiplied by $1,867.66 out-of-home care costs).

CONTACT: Sharon DiPirro-Beard, Program Coordinator
Sacramento County Alcohol and Drug Services Division
Phone: 916-875-2038
E-mail: dipirro-beards@saccounty.net

Washington: Substance Abuse Services Initiative

Background and Purpose

In 2005, the Washington State Children's Administration (Children's) became increasingly aware that a relatively high percentage of its clients needed substance abuse and mental health treatment services. Children's was also aware that a relatively low percentage of its clients received those needed services. In fiscal years 2004–2005, 31 percent of dependency cases filed involved substance abuse as a contributing factor, whereas only 6 percent of the parents completed treatment.

However, 31 percent was understood to be an underestimate because it was based on information obtained during the initial investigation phase. Children's ongoing caseworkers anecdotally estimate the number of cases in which substance abuse is a factor to be 75–80 percent.

The identified issues were parents not following through on substance abuse assessment recommendations and being unable to engage sufficiently in the treatment process.

The situation provided Children's with the motivation to seek increased collaboration with the Division of Alcohol and Substance Abuse (DASA). Both Children's and DASA are part of Washington's Department of Social and Health Services (DSHS). The collaboration effort is called the Substance Abuse Services Initiative (SASI). The Chemical Dependency Professional (CDP) program, as part of the overall collaborative effort, provides substance abuse specialists.

In 2005, DSHS appealed to the Washington legislature to allocate funding to the CDP initiative. DSHS received funding through Senate Bill 5763, the Omnibus Treatment of Mental and Substance Abuse Disorders Act of 2005, for 22 full-time employees statewide. These substance abuse specialists, or CDPs, help social workers by providing case management services to parents who are in need of substance abuse services. CDPs focus on case management to enhance clients' motivation to engage in the treatment process through treatment completion.

Roles and Responsibilities

The Washington legislature and the SASI oversight committee established the roles, responsibilities, and qualifications of the CDPs. The legislation's full list of potential CDP roles is as follows, with the italicized roles being those that the SASI oversight committee recommends:

Conducting on-site chemical dependency screening and assessment, *facilitating progress reports to department social workers and staff on substance abuse issues,* in-service training of department social workers and staff on substance abuse issues, *referring clients from the department to treatment providers,* and *providing consultation on cases to department social workers.*

Washington's DSHS system has six regions and thirty nine counties that vary considerably. For example, one region has thirteen small counties, but another has just one large county. Each region also has varying characteristics in population and access to services. Some are urban and have high population density, whereas others are rural with small populations.

Because of these regional differences, the SASI oversight committee provided some local flexibility for counties to determine the exact roles and responsibilities of CDPs. Although conducting assessments can be a component of a CDP's role, SASI did not recommend assessment as a primary role for CDPs because of the identified need for case management services. Case management includes referring clients for assessment, helping clients to access services, and bridging gaps in service systems. CDPs can conduct assessments, however, in situations when the assessments cannot be conducted in a timely manner by a local treatment agency. In rural areas, where there are fewer treatment agencies, for example, a CDP might focus on conducting assessments. In urban areas, where there are comparatively more treatment agencies, CDPs are more likely to provide case management services.

Locations and Settings

Currently, Washington funds 22 full-time Children's CDP positions. In essence, the CDPs are stationed in local Children's offices, but are hired and clinically supervised by local treatment agencies. The SASI oversight committee approves job descriptions and contracts.

DASA contracts with counties to provide State-licensed treatment services. Counties subcontract with local treatment agencies to hire and clinically supervise CDPs. The county and Children's management jointly identify and hire the CDPs. The county hiring authority announces the position and conducts interviews of candidates. Children's management participates in the interviews.

CDPs are stationed in local Children's offices. The positions were distributed based on client population. Each county Children's office is responsible for establishing a workspace for its CDP. Typically, the Children's office determines the most appropriate location for the CDP.

Underlying Values and Principles

The SASI oversight committee, made up of professionals from both Children's and DASA, meets every 2 months to administer and oversee the CDP initiative. SASI was made formal in 2005 after more than a year of planning and development. The collaboration is guided by a Memorandum of Understanding (MOU), which outlines joint values and principles. The MOU is useful in motivating all agencies involved to work together despite traditionally varying principles between child welfare and substance abuse systems. On the practice level, however, philosophical differences may remain in such areas as whether the client is the parent, child, or family; whether the goal is child safety, family preservation, or parental recovery; and the appropriate timelines for meeting those goals.

Beyond these incentives to work together that are outlined in the MOU, the agencies also collectively recognize that investing in the collaboration supports clients through treatment completion. Parents who complete treatment are more likely to reunify with their families. The prospect of reunifying with children can be a strong motivator for parents to complete treatment. In addition, the legislature's funding for mutual clients is influenced by the development and success of these collaborative efforts.

Funding

Washington Senate Bill 5763, mentioned previously, provided expanded funding for substance abuse treatment of approximately $32 million for adults and $6.7 million for youth. The State legislature allocates funding authorized in Senate Bill 5763 to Children's for 22 full-time employees statewide.

Washington spends $1.144 million per year on CDPs' salaries and benefits. This total does not cover the full costs to support the program. DASA and Children's contribute additional dollars from other sources to supplement training, travel, and administrative costs. In addition, the agencies alternate funding the substance abuse program manager, who acts as a liaison between the agencies and is responsible for implementing the initiative.

Children's had 10,873 total clients (including children and youth) involved with DASA treatment services at some level in fiscal years 2004–2005. As SASI increases its ability to identify and refer clients in need of treatment, treatment capacity issues arise. Accessibility to treatment services varies from county to county. Treatment capacity is augmented by the treatment expansion funds allocated under Senate Bill 5763, as well as discretionary grants from the Federal Government, such as Access to Recovery (ATR) funds. The State of Washington ATR initiative provides vouchers for substance abuse treatment and/or recovery support services to low-income individuals who are involved with child protective services, shelters and supported housing, free and low-income medical clinics, and community detoxification programs. The target areas are Snohomish, Clark, Pierce, Yakima, King, and Spokane counties. The SASI oversight committee also identifies and seeks ways to meet funding challenges.

Staff Development, Training and Supervision

Each CDP must have completed an associate's degree, a chemical dependency certification, and 2,000 hours of clinical supervision. Currently, Washington State faces a shortage of qualified CDP professionals. DASA and the Department of Health, which handles the licensing and certification, are working to address this challenge.

Children's headquarters provides training for all new CDPs, but is still determining the best way to provide ongoing training and development. Ongoing cross-training is desired, but goals have to be negotiated between county-level needs and DASA as well as Children's statewide objectives.

The CDP reports to a designated manager in his or her county Children's office. The county office is responsible for developing workflow procedures and often does this in consultation with its CDP. Children's and county management jointly resolve employee disputes and conduct CDP evaluations.

Joint Accountability, Outcomes and Evaluation

Oversight is provided by the SASI oversight committee, made up of professionals from both Children's and DASA. Children's and DASA are continuing to refine their roles in tracking and analyzing outcomes of the CDP initiative. As part of the treatment expansion funds allocated under Senate Bill 5763, for example, DASA documents how much money this program has saved the State by comparing the cost of substance abuse treatment with the costs clients typically incur without treatment. Children's, DASA, and the counties are also working on ways to improve information sharing and track clients across systems. The SASI oversight committee is helping to design and implement simple strategies for overcoming these challenges.

The attention of State legislators also provides for a certain level of accountability. State legislators have inquired about the program's effectiveness. DASA and Children's are preparing data to demonstrate that more clients have entered and completed treatment since the program's inception. If DASA and Children's are able to demonstrate the program's success, the program may receive more funding in the future.

CONTACT: Sue Green, Family Services Manager
Department of Social and Health Services
Division of Behavioral Health and Recovery
Phone: 360-725-3732
E-mail: sue.green@dshs.wa.gov

Table 1. Commonalities Matrix of Substance Abuse Specialist Programs.

	Connecticut	Delaware	Illinois	Massachusetts	New Hampshire	Sacramento County	Washington
Background							
Year program began	Early 1990s	1996	2000	2004	1998	2001	2005
Number of specialists in program	8-9	4	20-24	6	2	25	22
Title IV-E Waiver Demonstration site		X	X		X		
Previous history of collabo-ration between systems			X	X		X	
Purpose							
Responds to Federal decree	X						
Reduces costs of out-of-home placements and/or reduces time of children in foster care		X	X		X	X	
Removes barriers and improves linkages between CWS and AOD to better serve parents		X	X	X	X	X	X

Table 1. (Continued).

	Connecticut	Delaware	Illinois	Massachusetts	New Hampshire	Sacramento County	Washington
Improves the capacity of CWS to serve parents with AOD problems	X			X			X
Improves collaboration between systems	X	X	X	X	X	X	X
Employment and Licensing							
Employed by State or county CWS agency	X			X			X
Employed by community-based AOD treatment agency		X					
Employed by contracted service provider		X				X	
Self-employed and contracted by child welfare					X		
Unionized employees	X			X			
Licensed/certified AOD counselors	X	X	X	X (preferred)	X	X	X
Licensed Clinical Social Workers	X						
Specialists' Location (place of work)							
Area, regional, county, or district CWS offices	X	X		X	X		X
Contracted service provider's office, near juvenile court			X			X	
Roles and Responsibilities							
Case management		X	X		X	X	X
Screening and/or assessment		X	X		X	X	X
Referral to treatment	X	X			X	X	X
Facilitation of access to treatment		X			X	X	X
Urine testing	X	X	X			X	
Consultation to CWS	X	X	X	X	X		X
Training to CWS	X	X	X	X	X		X
Training to court			X				
Support to parents while in treatment		X	X			X	X
Home visits	X	X	X			X	
Information sharing with CWS and/or courts		X	X			X	X
Development and implementation of substance abuse capacity-building plans for CWS				X			
MOU or other agreement formally outlines joint values and principles for the program						X	X

Table 1. (Continued).

	Connecticut	Delaware	Illinois	Massachusetts	New Hampshire	Sacramento County	Washington
MOU or other agreement outlining joint values and principles influences the implementation of the program (but was not specifically developed for the program)		X		X		X	
Underlying Values and Principles							
MOU or other agreement outlines systems' and/or other programs' roles in program implementation	X	X	X				X
Other factors influence ongoing development of joint values and principles	X	X		X	X	X	
Funding							
State funded	X	X		X			
Federal funds (i.e., CAPTA, Title IV-E, Title IV-B)			X		X		
Multiple sources (i.e., partial State funding, tobacco settlement, and agency budget reallocation)						X	X
Staff Development, Training, Supervision							
Supervised by CWS	X				X	X	X
Supervised by contracted service provider			X			X	
Receives dual supervision		X		X			
Attends regular meetings to maintain program purpose and/or foster collaborative relationships		X	X	X	X	X	X
Receives CWS New Worker Training		X		X	X		
Participates in cross- training	X	X	X	X	X	X	
Joint Accountability, Outcomes, and Evaluation							
Regularly collects data	X	X	X		X	X	
Collects standardized data			X		X	X	
Regularly analyzes and reports data			X			X	

CWS = child welfare services; AOD = alcohol and other drugs.
MOU = Memorandum of Understanding; CAPTA = Child Abuse Prevention and Treatment Act.

End Notes

[1] Lewis, M. A., Giovannoni, J. M., & Leake, B. (1997, June). Two-year placement outcomes of children removed at birth from drug-using and non drug-using mothers in Los Angeles. *Social Work Research, 21*(2), 81–90.

[2] Walker, C., Zangrillo, P., & Smith, J. M. (1991). *Parental drug abuse and African American children in foster care.* Washington, DC: National Black Child Development Institute.

[3] U.S. Department of Health and Human Services. (1999). *Blending perspectives and building common ground: A report to Congress on substance abuse and child protection.* Washington, DC: U.S. Government Printing Office.

[4] Young, N. K., Gardner, S. L., & Dennis, K. (1998). *Responding to alcohol and other drug problems in child welfare: Weaving together practice and policy.* Washington, DC: CWLA Press.

[5] U.S. Department of Health and Human Services. (1999). *Blending perspectives and building common ground: A report to Congress on substance abuse and child protection.* Washington, DC: U.S. Government Printing Office.

[6] Semidei, J., Radel, L. F., & Nolan, C. (2001). Substance abuse and child welfare: Clear linkages and promising responses. *Child Welfare, 80*(2), 109–128.

[7] Green, B. L., Rockhill, A., & Burrus, S. (2008). The role of inter-agency collaboration for substance-abusing families involved with child welfare. *Child Welfare* 87(1):29-61.

[8] Green, B. L., Rockhill, A., & Burrus, S. (2008). Ibid.

[9] Austin, M. J., & Osterling, K. L. (2006, January). *Substance abuse interventions for parents involved in the child welfare system: Evidence and implications.* Berkeley, CA: University of California at Berkeley, School of Social Welfare. Available online at: http://cssr.berkeley.edu/bassc/public/EvidenceForPractice4_ Su bstance%20Abuse_FullReport. pdf#search ='austin%20%26%20osterli ng%20 a nd%20su bsta nce%20a buse%20i nterventions

[10] Bluhm, B. (2007). *Project First Step: Approaches to co-occurrence of child maltreatment and substance abuse.* Unpublished. 1.

[11] Children's Bureau. (2007, June 5). Profiles of the Child Waiver Demonstration Project: New Hampshire – Services for caregivers with substance use disorders. Accessed August 1, 2007, from http://www.acf.HHS prog rams_fund/cwwaiver/2007/newham pshire. htm

[12] Bluhm, B. (2007). *Project First Step: Approaches to co-occurrence of child maltreatment and substance abuse.* Unpublished. 1.

[13] Bluhm, B. (2007). Ibid.

In: Parents with Substance Use Disorders and Child Protection... ISBN: 978-1-60692-400-6
Editor: Thomas P. Brouwer © 2011 Nova Science Publishers, Inc.

Chapter 5

SUBSTANCE-EXPOSED INFANTS: STATE RESPONSES TO THE PROBLEM

United States Department of Health and Human Services

ACKNOWLEDGMENTS

This document was prepared by the National Center on Substance Abuse and Child Welfare (NCSACW) under Contract No. 270-027108 for the Substance Abuse and Mental Health Services Administration (SAMHSA) and the Administration for Children and Families (ACF), both within the U.S. Department of Health and Human Services (HHS). Nancy K. Young, Ph.D., developed the document with assistance from Sid Gardner, M.P.A.; Cathleen Otero, M.S.W., M.P.A.; Kim Dennis, M.P.A.; Rosa Chang, M.S.W.; Kari Earle, M.Ed., L.A.D.C.; and Sharon Amatetti, M.P.H. Sharon Amatetti, M.P.H., served as the Government Project Officer from the Center for Substance Abuse Treatment (CSAT) and Irene Bocella, M.S.W., served as the Project Officer from Children's Bureau.

EXECUTIVE SUMMARY

In 2005–2006, the National Center on Substance Abuse and Child Welfare (NCSACW) undertook a review and analysis of States' policies regarding prenatal exposure to alcohol and other drugs, in order to help local, State, and Tribal governments:

1. Gain a better understanding of current policy and practice in place at the State level that address substance-exposed infants (SEIs); and
2. Identify opportunities for strengthening interagency efforts in this area.

This study assessed State policy from the broadest perspective: prevention, intervention, identification, and treatment of prenatal substance exposure, including immediate and ongoing services for the infant, the mother, and the family. It reviewed States' policies regarding:

- Pre-pregnancy prevention efforts;
- Screening and assessment in the prenatal period;
- Testing at birth and notification of child protective services (CPS) in cases in which infants are identified as substance-affected;
- The provision of services to SEIs and their parents after a CPS referral is made or other agencies become involved; and
- The processing of SEI-related referrals to developmental disabilities agencies.[1]

This review discovered considerable variations among the States in both policy and practice regarding SEIs. States have responded in different ways to mounting concerns over the negative effects that prenatal exposure to illicit drugs and alcohol have on developing infants. They have also responded differently to Federal legislation (the Child Abuse Prevention and Treatment Act [CAPTA] amendments of 2003) requiring that a newborn determined to be exposed prenatally to illegal drugs must be referred to CPS.

States have instituted a range of policies to address prenatal substance exposure. These policies are carried out by multiple agencies and organizations, and practice does not always conform to official policy. To gain a better understanding of what States are currently doing about the issue, this study reviewed States' policies and practices by examining legislation and policy in all States and by conducting intensive interviews with State-level staff in 10 selected States.

The report describes the findings of the study, which NCSACW conducted under its contract with the Substance Abuse and Mental Health Services Administration, Center for Substance Abuse Treatment (CSAT), and the Administration on Children, Youth and Families (ACYF)/Children's Bureau (CB). This report identifies opportunities for strengthening interagency collaboration to address the SEI problem. The findings will be of interest to policymakers and officials concerned with the issue of SEIs, and to professionals in the fields of maternal and child health, child welfare, treatment of substance use disorders, education, and community services.

FIVE-POINT INTERVENTION FRAMEWORK

Since many SEIs are not identified prenatally or at birth, an approach that addresses all stages of development for the affected child is critical. Most previous work related to SEIs has focused on pregnancy and the birth event. However, a more comprehensive view is needed that takes multiple intervention opportunities into account, beginning with pre-pregnancy and continuing throughout a child's developmental milestones.

The framework around which this report is organized asserts that there are five major timeframes when intervention in the life of the SEI can reduce the potential harm of prenatal substance exposure:

1. PRE-PREGNANCY
   This timeframe offers the opportunity to promote awareness of the effects of prenatal substance use among women of child-bearing age and their family members;
2. PRENATAL
   This intervention point encourages health care providers to screen pregnant women for substance use as part of routine prenatal care and make referrals that facilitate access to treatment and related services for women who need those services;
3. BIRTH
   Interventions during this timeframe incorporate testing newborns for substance exposure at the time of delivery;
4. NEONATAL
   Developmental assessment and the corresponding provision of services for the newborn as well as the family at this intervention point, immediately after the birth event, are the emphasis; and
5. THROUGHOUT CHILDHOOD AND ADOLESCENCE
   This timeframe calls for ongoing provision of coordinated services for both child and family.

This framework formed the basis for a review of State practices with SEIs. Within this context, States' policies and practices in developing system linkages within and among State agencies were reviewed. States need interagency collaboration to address the SEI problem. This need makes the issue of developing system linkages as important as the issue of handling each of the five intervention points, since the linkages pull the interventions in the five areas together.

METHODOLOGY

The information presented in this report draws from the in-depth review of 10 States and the broader review of State policy across the Nation. Information was gathered and analyzed from three sources: a review of Federal policies and actions; a review of existing literature and summaries of State policies; and structured interviews with key informants in 10 States. These 10 States were selected for in-depth review of their policies and practices pertaining to SEIs. This approach required contacting multiple informants in each State to gather information about SEI initiatives sponsored, operated, and funded by different State, local, and private agencies. The variations within and among States are the result of the independent roles of the States and counties; variations in attitudes in different States toward addiction, parenting, and child safety; and differences in how the set of agencies that handle SEI issues is organized.

This initial review of SEI issues based on prior surveys done by other organizations found that 39 of the 50 States and the District of Columbia had developed legislation, policies, or programs that addressed at least one of the five intervention points (pre-pregnancy interventions, prenatal interventions, identification at birth, immediate postnatal interventions, and postnatal services to children and their parents). Ten of these 39 States were selected for in-depth reviews. States were included from different regions of the Nation and of different sizes to provide a useful sample. States were also selected based on references in publications on SEI policy and practice. The States selected were California, Hawaii, Illinois, Maryland, Massachusetts, Minnesota, Rhode Island, South Carolina, Virginia, and Washington.

Three to five individuals were contacted in each of these 10 States, typically beginning with the Women's Treatment Coordinator in the drug and alcohol treatment agency. The typical informants were officials in State agencies responsible for child welfare, maternal and child health, and drug and alcohol treatment. Other contacts included staff from family or dependency courts, developmental disabilities agencies, and hospitals.

An interview guide was drafted based on the primary policy questions to be assessed. Pilot test interviews were conducted with two States, and final revisions to the interview guide were then made. Each interview lasted 30–60 minutes; follow-up calls were made as needed to verify specific points or to pursue documents referenced in the interviews. A content analysis emphasizing the five-point framework was conducted on the qualitative interview data. Additional documentation, such as State legislation, administrative guidelines, and practice protocols, was compiled from the States based on information provided in the interviews. These materials were added to the literature reviewed for each State.

During the data collection phase, information was reviewed and contacts were made with additional States, including Arkansas, Colorado, Maine, and Texas. These States had asked NCSACW for guidance on CAPTA-related issues. News reports on the current legislative proposals in these States were collected, reviewed, and summarized for inclusion in this report as additional detail.

HIGHLIGHTS

This in-depth review of State legislation and regulations, interagency agreements, and budget allocations provided the evidence of State policy. Each of the 10 States interviewed had policies in place that addressed one or more of the five intervention points, and the national research on other State policy across the Nation revealed other examples of policy focused on SEIs. These are summarized briefly below.

Pre-Pregnancy Awareness

Nineteen of the States have public education campaigns that emphasize the harm done by using alcohol, tobacco, and illicit drugs during pregnancy. Some States also have worked with institutions of higher education to disseminate this message. However, the national rates of use during the first trimester suggest that the message is not getting through to many women before they are aware of their pregnancies, especially those who are younger.

Prenatal Screening

To reduce substance exposure during the pregnancy and improve chances for a healthy birth outcome, an effective link must exist between screening and facilitating a woman's access to necessary treatment and related support services. Good model programs for prenatal screening operate in most of the 10 States, but no service delivery system in the Nation *requires* prenatal screening for substance use. Although Medicaid covers the cost of 37% of births nationally, there is no Medicaid requirement for prenatal screening for substance use. Although several States have done one-time prevalence studies, no State has current prevalence data on substance use during pregnancy. And it is difficult to assess the results of SEI policy because of the lack of data on prenatal screening and referrals for treatment.

Testing at Birth

Hospitals' policies and practices vary widely regarding the testing of newborns for evidence of substance exposure, with very few using universal screening and most conducting testing that is based on somewhat subjective criteria. Seven of the 10 States interviewed consider prenatal exposure to be evidence of child abuse or neglect, whereas three others do not. Hospitals do not usually provide CPS or other State agencies with data on the total number of infants tested at birth, results of the tests, or referrals to CPS. However, recent legislation in some States has expanded the requirement that a CPS referral be made when drug exposure is detected, based on States' effort to follow Federal policy in the CAPTA amendments. Fetal Alcohol Spectrum Disorders (FASD) have received increased attention in some States, although detection of FASD is challenging.

Immediate Postnatal Services for Newborns and Families

Responses to the CAPTA legislation requiring that substance-affected infants receive a developmental assessment under the Individuals with Disabilities Act (IDEA) are still evolving. There are few estimates of referral trends resulting from the new Federal policy. Of the 10 States studied in depth, only two have strong links between IDEA referrals and CPS agencies. Because of the lack of uniformity in child welfare-referred developmental assessments used in most States, it is difficult to assess status in immediate postnatal services and the variability in State policy and practice is itself a finding.

Services for Children and Families

Ideally, services for the infant or child and the parents are woven together in a comprehensive approach. More typically, the primary emphasis is on the child or the parents, rather than on both simultaneously. However, there are strong models of family-centered services in some States. SEIs are at higher risk of coming into contact with the child welfare system at some point, and findings regarding children in foster care indicate that most children do not actually receive the assessments and services they need. It is important to understand the intended, potential, and actual linkages between the programs that address postnatal interventions for developmental disabilities, in order to take the next step related to developing effective policy and practice in postnatal intervention.

Data Systems and Interagency Organizational Efforts

SEI issues must be handled in an intensely collaborative setting, since no single agency has the resources, the information base, or the dominant role to address the full range of needs of all substance-exposed or substance-affected newborns and their families. The lack of critically needed data that could be shared across agencies was noted as a major barrier to collaboration. There are gaps in how SEIs are tracked by State data systems through screening, assessment, and service delivery that inhibit States' ability to measure whether they are making progress on addressing the problem. The information gaps at each of these hand-off points are substantial. Such gaps weaken the ability of the systems to work together to track children and families as they move from one agency to another. State SEI policies and practices tend to develop within a complex system that includes diverse agencies within Federal and State government. States' interagency organizational efforts usually relegate SEI efforts to other interagency activities.

CONCLUSION AND KEY RECOMMENDATIONS

When the needs of substance-exposed children are addressed, it is apparent that the connections across the five points discussed in this report are as important as the actual interventions. The handoffs from one point to the next and the linkages needed to coordinate services become a comprehensive services framework, rather than a series of fragmented initiatives. The following action steps are recommended to provide the proper foundation for this framework to result in better outcomes:

- Given that Medicaid pays for 37% of births nationally and well above that level in several States, States could use Medicaid regulations and resources to their greatest advantage. They could influence hospitals and providers to adopt prenatal screening policies that embody the guidelines set forth by the American College of Obstetricians and Gynecologists (ACOG) (described in Section 3) in their Medicaid schedules and reimbursements;
- Current statewide prevalence estimates of substance-exposed births are needed to establish baseline data for each State in order to understand the level of need and define the priorities for meeting that need sufficiently;
- The necessary statutory or administrative support must be in place to authorize the appropriate interagency coordinating bodies to address SEI policy in a comprehensive and systemic manner as part of their mandates, and to establish and monitor interagency outcomes for SEI programs annually;
- States need to augment the capacity of their existing information systems to collect data on how many parents of SEIs are referred, how many enter treatment, how many complete treatment, and how many succeed in continuing their recovery. Existing data collection systems should be better linked to understand from where clients are referred and what responses are available from treatment systems. These data are crucial to understanding the costs and cost-effectiveness of programs (Yates, 1999); and

- States must creatively use multiple funding sources to support the implementation and expansion of SEI-related interventions. Comprehensive treatment is essential for SEI families, and capacity-building for this level of service requires the strategic use of multiple funding streams. As one powerful example, States can take better advantage of Medicaid to finance mental and behavioral health assessments, therapies, wraparound services, and other interventions for children who are at high risk of emotional problems because of substance abuse by one or both parents (Johnson, Knitzer, & Kaufmann, 2002). Also, prioritizing an investment of funds in prevention and early intervention services to women results in significant cost-savings opportunities to the child welfare, health care, education, and criminal justice systems.

Definitions

Assessment refers to a verbal interview by a substance-abuse treatment professional to determine the nature and extent of the mother's substance use disorder and to establish an effective plan of treatment.

Screening refers to verbal questioning designed to determine whether the mother has a substance use disorder.

Substances, in this report, refers to alcohol and illegal drugs, since these substances are emphasized in the policy guidelines reviewed.[2]

> Note: There is substantial evidence that alcohol and tobacco cause harm, and potentially more severe harm, to more children than do illegal drugs (Andres & Day, 2000; Britt, Ingersol, & Schnoll, 1999; Lambers & Clark, 1996; Levin & Slotkin, 1998; Slotkin, 1998). There is also substantial evidence that mothers who use substances during pregnancy often use more than one substance (e.g., alcohol, tobacco, and an illegal drug) (SAMHSA, 2007; Arria et al., 2006). This factor makes it difficult to distinguish the effects of a particular substance from the effects of a second substance or the combination of substances.

Substance use is the use of any drug or combination of drugs in social situations, or for social reasons (U.S. Department of Health and Human Services, 1999). Social alcohol and other drug use can lead to further and elevated use, but most social users remain in this classification.

Substance use disorder is a complex behavioral disorder characterized by preoccupation with obtaining alcohol or other drugs (AOD) and by a narrowing of the behavioral repertoire toward excessive consumption and loss of control over consumption. It is usually also accompanied by the development of tolerance and withdrawal and impairment in social and occupational functioning.

Substance abuse is characterized by the presence of consequences related to the person's alcohol and other drug use. One definition is the use of a psychoactive drug to the extent that its effects seriously interfere with health or occupational and social functioning (Center for Substance Abuse Treatment [CSAT], 1994). Abuse may or may not involve physiological dependence or tolerance. The essential feature of substance abuse is a "maladaptive pattern of substance use manifested by recurrent and significant adverse consequences related to the repeated use of substances." Neglect of children is specifically listed as a potential symptom of substance abuse (American Psychiatric Association [APA], 2000).

Substance dependence involves continued alcohol and other drug use or abuse despite significant substance-related problems. There is "a pattern of self-administration that usually results in tolerance, withdrawal, and compulsive drug-taking behavior" (APA, 2000). The American Society of Addiction Medicine includes psychological or physical dependence in its definition (CSAT, 1994). Psychological dependence centers on the user's need of a drug to reach a level of functioning or well-being. Physical dependence involves the establishment of tolerance or withdrawal upon cessation of alcohol and other drug use (CSAT, 1994).

Substance-affected infants refers to infants for whom prenatal substance exposure produces negative effects, which may or may not be detected. The effects of substance exposure depend on many factors, including the timing, frequency, and intensity of the exposure. The phrase "substance-affected infant" is used in the CAPTA legislation, but is not defined there or in Federal regulations; each State is able to use its own interpretation.

Substance-exposed infants, or SEIs, refers to infants exposed to AOD ingested by the mother in utero, whether or not this exposure is detected.

> Note: Some sources may use other terms to refer to these infants, such as substance-exposed births (SE Bs), substance-exposed newborns (SENs), drug-exposed births (DE Bs), and prenatally exposed infants (PEIs).

Testing refers to a laboratory test, such as urinalysis or meconium testing, that indicates whether alcohol or illicit drugs are present in the mother's or infant's body.

SECTION 1. FRAMING THE ISSUE

Each year, an estimated 400,000–440,000 infants (10–11% of all births) are affected by prenatal alcohol or illicit drug exposure, as described in the analysis in this section. Prenatal exposure to alcohol, tobacco, and illicit drugs has the potential to cause a wide spectrum of physical, emotional, and developmental problems for these infants. The harm caused to the child can be significant and long-lasting, especially if the exposure is not detected and the effects are not treated as soon as possible.

The current system of identifying these infants and responding to their needs is fragmented and fails to identify and serve most of these children. There are, however, Federal efforts to monitor substance use among pregnant and recently pregnant women, which enable the estimates of prenatal *exposure* to drugs and alcohol cited previously. The following studies are examples of reports that have estimated substance use by pregnant women and the number of infants exposed.

National Survey on Drug Use and Health (NSDUH). The latest Federal data available from the NSDUH report 2004–2005 annual averages of substance use by pregnant women aged 15–44. As Table 1 shows, rates of use vary by type of substance and trimester of pregnancy. For all substances, prevalence rates are highest in the first trimester. Lower rates in the second and third trimesters are encouraging and suggest that pregnant women are responding to education and other interventions to reduce prenatal substance use. However, the data also highlight a need to strengthen efforts to identify and reach women before they get pregnant, as well as in early pregnancy, when substance exposure can have significant consequences for the developing fetus. Prior studies based on this annual survey have found similar rates of substance use.[3] When these percentages are applied to the approximately 4.1 million infants born each year, the projections result in a wide range of estimated substance-exposed infants (SEIs).

As Figure 1 makes clear, substance use rates among pregnant women also vary by age groups, with both past month illicit drug and alcohol use highest among teenagers (Substance Abuse and Mental Health Services Administration [SAMHSA], 2006).

Table 1. Substance use by Pregnant Women, by Length of Gestation and Estimated Number of Infants Exposed (2004–2005 Annual Averages).

Substance Used(past month)	First Trimester	Second Trimester	Third Trimester
Any Illicit Drug	7.0% women 286,510 infants	3.2% women 130,976 infants	2.3% women 94,139 infants
Alcohol	20.6% women 843,158 infants	10.2% women 417,486 infants	6.7% women 274,231 infants
Binge Alcohol	7.5% women 306,975 infants	2.6% women 106,418 infants	1.6% women 65,488 infants
Cigarettes	23.7% women 970,041 infants	12.9% women 527,997 infants	13.7% women 560,741 infants

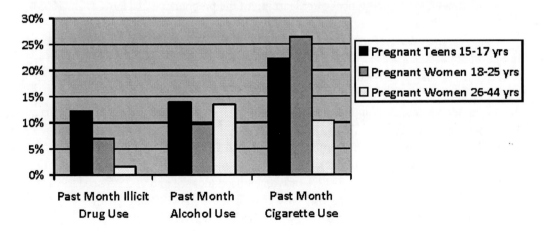

Figure 1. Substance Use by Pregnant Women, by Age Groups (2004–2005).

Table 2. Percentage of females aged 15–44 classified as needing treatment, by pregnancy status: 2005.

Needed Treatment in Prior Year for:	Pregnant	*Not* Pregnant
Alcohol or Illicit Drug Use	7.6%	10.5%
Illicit Drug Use	3.5%	3.9%
Alcohol Use	5.5%	8.4%

Source: Online Analysis of NSDUH Public Use File.

The NSDUH also provides information beyond substance use to capture the number of individuals who need alcohol or drug treatment for substance *abuse* or *dependence*. Table 2 shows the results of an analysis using the 2005 NSDUH public use file on the percentage of females classified as needing alcohol or drug treatment, by pregnancy status.

Fetal Alcohol Surveillance Network (FASSNet) and State-Based Fetal Alcohol Syndrome (FAS) Prevention Program. From 1997–2003, the Centers for Disease Control and Prevention (CDC) funded FASSNet, a statewide, population-based surveillance network to determine the prevalence of FAS within a geographically defined area. CDC studies from FASSNet showed FAS prevalence rates ranging from 0.2–1.5 cases per 1,000 live births in different areas of the United States. Other prenatal alcohol-related conditions, such as alcohol-related neuro-developmental disorders (ARND) and alcohol-related birth defects (ARBD), are believed to occur about three times as often as FAS (CDC, 2005). Although the FASSNet cooperative agreements with five States ended in 2003, the FASSNet methodology has been adapted for use by the CDC's more recently funded FAS Prevention Program, which includes cooperative agreements with seven States.[4] The CDC also monitors the prevalence of alcohol use among women of child-bearing age through the Behavioral Risk Factor Surveillance System survey.

Screening During Pregnancy. In a study of more than 7,800 pregnant wome enrolled in prenatal care clinics in five communities and screened for substance use with the *4P's Plus*©, approximately one-third (32.7%) had a positive screen. Four of the communities conducted follow-up assessments on all women with a positive screen and found that 15% of those women continued to use substances after learning of the pregnancy (Chasnoff et al., 2005).

The Pregnancy Risk Assessment Monitoring System (PRAMS). PRAMS, currently used in 32 States, collects data based on self-reported maternal behaviors and experiences that occur before, during, and shortly after pregnancy. Through cooperative agreements between the CDC and these 32 State governments, information on the use of alcohol and tobacco before and during pregnancy is compiled; questions on illegal drug use are included in the survey at the discretion of the State.[5]

In some of these States, maternal substance use is reported at levels that corroborate States' other estimates and national survey data. For instance, PRAMS indicates that during their last trimester of pregnancy 2–12% of women used alcohol and 7–25% used tobacco. Of the 10 States reviewed for this report, only two of the PRAMS States, Hawaii and South Carolina, compile data on illicit drug use, which are included in Table 3.

None of the States in which interviews were conducted for the current study had up-to-date statewide prevalence estimates of substance-exposed births (SEBs). Such estimates require regularly updated surveys or other data collection methods. Most States have a historic baseline based on a one-time survey that has not been regularly renewed or updated. Section 3 describes States' experiences with these intermittent prevalence surveys as a component of their interagency coordinating and monitoring efforts.

The need for routine data collection and monitoring remains important, given that the number of women with substance use disorders has not decreased significantly over the last few years. For example, the percentage of females aged 12 and older with illicit drug or alcohol dependence or abuse increased slightly from 6.1% in 2002 to 6.4% in 2005 (Office of Applied Studies, 2005).

When the figures in Tables 1–3 are analyzed together, the data can be summarized as follows:

- An estimated 10–11% of the 4.1 million live births (in 2005) involved prenatal exposure to alcohol or illegal drugs;
- Prenatal exposure to alcohol rises to as high as one in five pregnancies during the first trimester; and
- When tobacco data are included, the three data elements—prenatal use of alcohol, tobacco, and illegal drugs—are the basis for the statement that "more than one million" children are affected by prenatal exposure (McGourty & Chasnoff, 2003). This figure differs from the 400,000–440,000 figure because the smaller figure measures only prenatal use that can be detected at a point in time—birth—whereas the surveys that are the basis for the larger figure cover prenatal substance use during the entire period of pregnancy.[6]

Table 3. Substance use during pregnancy—available State prevalence data.

State	Estimate	Sources/Date
California	11.35% tested positive for drugs or alcohol	Statewide random screening (California Department of Alcohol and Drug Programs, 2006)
Hawaii	12.7% tested positive for drugs	Random screening/(Hawaii State Department of Health, 1996)
South Carolina	12.1% used alcohol and drugs (urine) 22.4% used alcohol and drugs (meconium only) 25.8% used alcohol and drugs (both methods)	Sample (South Carolina Department of Health and Environmental Control, 1991)
27 PRAMS States	6.8% (Utah) to 25.3% (West Virginia) smoked during last 3 months of pregnancy 2.0% (West Virginia) to 11.6% (Vermont) used alcohol in last 3 months of pregnancy	State PRAMS reports/2002; self-reported (Williams et al., 2006)

> **CHILD ABUSE PREVENTION AND TREATMENT ACT (CAPTA) REQUIREMENTS FOR STATES**
>
> In reauthorizing CAPTA legislation in 2003, Congress responded to concerns about prenatal drug exposure by making three important changes in the law. In order to maintain their CAPTA grant funding, States must assure that they have:
> - Policies and procedures (including appropriate referrals to child protection service systems and for other appropriate services) to address the needs of infants born and identified as affected by illegal substance abuse or withdrawal symptoms resulting from prennatal drug exposure, including a requirement that health care providers involved in the delivery or care of such infants notify the child protective services system of the occurrence of such condition in such infants, except that such notification shall not be construed to establish a definition under Federal law of
>   - what constitutes child abuse or require prosecution for any illegal action;
>   - A plan of safe care for the infant born and identified as being affected by illegal substance abuse or withdrawal symptoms;
>   - Procedures for the immediate screening, risk and safety assessment, and prompt investigation of such reports.
>
> CAPTA also requires States to establish procedures to refer children younger than 3 years who have substantiated cases of child abuse or neglect to early intervention services, funded under the Individuals with Disabilities Education Act (IDEA). Although the CAPTA amendments regarding SEIs state that the identification of an SEI shall not be construed as establishing actual child abuse or neglect, these infants can be included in the group of children who can be referred for developmental assessments.
>
> (National Early Childhood Technical Assistance Center, 2006; DHHS, Administration for Children and Families, 2006)

Historical Perspective

The issue of SEBs first came to public attention in the United States during the 1980s and early 1990s because of the concern about infants affected by their mother's use of crack cocaine during pregnancy. Earlier work on fetal alcohol exposure took place in the late 1960s and early 1970s.[7] National focus on the problem has re-emerged over the past few years in response to several developments:

- In 2003, Congress passed amendments to CAPTA requiring that substance-affected infants be referred to CPS (see the CAPTA sidebar);
- A growing body of research on Fetal Alcohol Spectrum Disorders (FASD) and alcohol-related neuro-developmental disorders (ARND) has included longitudinal studies documenting the long-term mental and emotional effects of prenatal exposure to alcohol. This research has led to the development of new federally funded resource centers and the formation of a congressional caucus to address the SEI problem;

- Concern has grown about the increasing number of pregnant women and children affected by maternal use of methamphetamines and about households in which children are exposed to the dangers of methamphetamine manufacture;[8] and
- Some States have enacted or proposed legislation directed at maternal substance abuse, including legislation in some States that has led to the incarceration of mothers of SEIs.

Increased interest and attention to FASD in particular has taken several different forms at the State level, and has been the focus of considerable legislative activity. This increase is partly in response to the leadership and information clearinghouse services provided by the SAMHSA FASD Center for Excellence. The Center summarized in its 2004 report on FASD State legislation that:

> Analysis of the data shows that State legislatures are responding to the societal cost of FASD by placing continually more emphasis on prevention and intervention services. State legislative actions range from calling for coordinated State FASD efforts to requiring FASD information to be given to persons applying for marriage licenses. (DHHS, SAM HSA, FASD Center, 2006)

For example, the 2004 Hawaii legislature adopted a proposal to address FASD more comprehensively and charged the Department of Health with developing a coordinated statewide effort to address the issue.[9] Similar legislation is currently pending in Maryland. Also, the 2004 Minnesota legislature transferred funds from the Commissioner of Health to a statewide organization focused solely on prevention of and intervention with FASD. Shortly thereafter, a contract was signed between the Minnesota Organization on Fetal Alcohol Syndrome and the Minnesota Department of Health to address issues of research on FASD, public education, professional education, and community grants.

The focus on prenatal substance exposure is also intensified by increasing evidence that for SEIs and children, *early intervention makes a difference*. In the early 1990s, some practitioners and researchers held that prenatal drug exposure inevitably produced lasting damage, especially when the drug was cocaine. Others held that drug-exposed children were not significantly different from other infants who faced similar socioeconomic challenges. As information has accumulated over the past decade, both positions have been supported. There is growing evidence of the harmful effects of prenatal exposure to illegal drugs, alcohol, and tobacco. At the same time, it is clear that early intervention and nurturing home environments are important mediating factors that can lead to positive outcomes for substance-exposed children (Chasnoff, 2001).

Policy Perspective

This study reviews State legislation and regulations, interagency agreements, and budget allocations as the best evidence of State policy. Although there are several national compilations of State policy information, data collection is not standardized and different definitions are applied to commonly used terms. For example, some national compilations categorize States in groups according to their reporting requirements and definitions of child abuse and neglect, but the categorization is dependent on the author's interpretation of legislative intent and implementation practices.[10] The interviews helped clarify some of these inconsistencies.

The problem of prenatal substance exposure can be viewed from a narrow perspective focused primarily on the birth event (identification of prenatally exposed newborns through toxicological testing and screening for maternal risk factors). Or, it can be viewed from a comprehensive perspective that extends beyond the birth event to include the wider issues of pre-pregnancy prevention, prenatal and postnatal intervention, and support for affected children throughout childhood and adolescence. This broader view addresses the prevention and treatment of substance use disorders among women of child-bearing age, pregnant women, and parents, as well as the ongoing effects of these disorders on the women's children and families.

The policies and practices that States adopt reflect varying values for parenting, addiction, treatment, foster care, and parents' versus children's rights. These underlying values lead some jurisdictions to prefer a prevention-focused health and social services response to the issue of SEIs. Other jurisdictions may adopt a more response-oriented approach that encompasses a wider array of issues surrounding prenatal and postnatal substance exposure and effects. The particular perspective of a given State subsequently influences which agencies are involved in carrying out a State's SEI policies. These agencies can range from a "core" representation of hospitals, maternal and child health agencies, and child welfare agencies, including a broader spectrum of substance abuse prevention and treatment, education, early intervention, mental health, and developmental services.

This study assessed State policy from the broadest perspective: prevention, intervention, identification, and treatment of prenatal substance exposure, including immediate and ongoing services for the infant, the mother, and the family. It reviewed States' policies regarding:

- Pre-pregnancy prevention efforts;
- Screening and assessment in the prenatal period;
- Testing at birth and notification of CPS in cases in which infants are identified as substance- affected;
- The provision of services to SEIs and their parents after a CPS referral is made; and
- The processing of SEI-related referrals to developmental disabilities agencies.[11]

A SNAPSHOT OF NEED: DATA FROM THE STATES INTERVIEWED

- Washington State officials and publications indicate that from 8,000–10,000 infants were exposed to drugs and alcohol in 2002, of 99,672 births statewide. They estimate that from 800–1,000 of these infants are "drug or alcohol affected," indicating a more serious impact. The estimate is based on a projection by State staff, given their review of national data, that 10–12% of all substance-exposed births (SEBs) are also substance-affected. An assessment of Medicaid claims and review of medical charts for prenatal care in Washington State from 1989–1995 documented that 6% of births involved prenatal exposure to alcohol or illicit drugs (Washington State Department of Health, 2002).

- In 1997, Maryland's General Assembly passed the Children in Need of Assistance—Drug Addiction at Birth—Parental Rights Act (DABA) in response to the heightened awareness of substance-exposed infants (SEIs). During the same year DABA was enacted, Maryland considered legislation that sought to increase screening at birth. In conjunction with the proposed legislation, State agency staff provided an estimate of 6,783 SEIs born each year (interview on February 10, 2005).
- The Illinois Department of Public Health, Division of Epidemiologic Studies, issued a report titled "Surveillance of Illinois Infants Prenatally Exposed to Controlled Substances 1991- 1999," in November 2001. The report is no longer compiled, and some respondents expressed concern that the data are incomplete because they show a 25% decrease in SEI reports from 1991–1999. According to the Department of Children and Family Services, a total of 1,172 SEBs were reported in fiscal year 2004, and 1,060 of these were substantiated (Fornoff, Egler, & Shen, 2001).
- Some States have assessed the number of cases in which a woman gives birth to more than one SEI. For example, Washington reviewed its prenatal databases during 1994–1995. The State found that 53% of women delivering drug-exposed infants had previously given birth to a drug-exposed infant. It also found that 27% of women delivering drug-affected infants had previously given birth to a drug-affected infant. First births were not included in the study (Washington State Department of Health, 2002).
- Similarly, Illinois found that the percentage of repeat SEIs, defined as a subsequent reported SEI for the same mother, increased from 14% in 1990 to 46% in 1999 but declined slightly to 42% in 2001 (Fornoff et al., 2001).
- Virginia conducted a one-time assessment in 2001, revealing that 23.2% of the women in the sample (43 cases randomly selected from 256 statewide SEB reports) had other children in foster placement because of maternal substance abuse. Also, of these women, 14% had given birth to other prenatally exposed children, with an average of 2.5 children for each mother (Virginia Department of Health, 2004).
- A final set of estimates focus on the special needs for treatment among child welfare parents. In one of the only studies of substance abuse treatment need that assessed a child welfare population, researchers in Illinois found that of women with children in the child welfare system, 46.6% needed treatment, compared with 4.2% in the general female population in Cook County (Fornoff et al., 2001).

SECTION 2. COMPREHENSIVE FRAMEWORK FOR INTERVENTION

Since many substance-exposed infants (SEIs) are not identified prenatally or at birth, an approach that addresses all stages of development for the affected child is critical. Additions to the Child Abuse Prevention and Treatment Act (CAPTA) legislation require States to establish procedures to refer children younger than 3 years with substantiated cases of child abuse or neglect to early intervention services, funded under the Individuals with Disabilities Education Act. These services constitute an additional opportunity beyond perinatal settings to identify and respond to both substance exposure in children and substance use disorders in the family.

Infants and very young children are especially vulnerable to abuse and neglect. Federal data show that in 2003 children from birth–3 years had the highest rates of victimization, at 16.4 per 1,000 children. Of the estimated 1,500 children who died as a result of child abuse or neglect, 79% were younger than 4 years. Additionally, infants and toddlers are the fastest-growing age group of children being removed from their homes as a result of abuse or neglect and placed in foster care in the United States (Goldson, 2001; Shaw & Goode, 2005). Children with disabilities are at two to three times the risk for abuse or neglect than children without disabilities (Sullivan & Knutson, 2000). The fact that substance-exposed children may have disabilities that put them at higher risk for maltreatment adds to the need for a framework that assists States and communities in organizing their policies and services across the developmental continuum.

The Policy and Practice Intervention Points for Children and Families framework (see Figure 2) defines the points when policy and practice interventions can benefit substance-exposed children and their families. It begins with the period before pregnancy, when the intervention is to increase awareness of the effects of prenatal substance use. It proceeds through the prenatal period and birth, when the interventions include the screening of pregnant women for substance use and the testing of infants for substance exposure. It ends with the long-term development of the child and the ongoing needs of the family, when multiple services are needed.

Many States have policies and/or practices addressing one or more of these five intervention points. In addition to identifying the intervention points, the framework indicates points when system linkages would allow coordination of needed interventions and services provided by multiple agencies.

The framework illustrates a number of important issues:

- The birth event is only one of several opportunities to affect outcomes for the SEI and family, and interventions are needed throughout the child's developmental stages;
- All family members need services, which is the basis for the movement toward a family- centered approach; and
- The importance of system linkages is emphasized in coordinating services across the spectrum of prevention,intervention, and treatment.

The vertical arrows indicate potential linkages between systems or agencies that provide interventions at the different developmental stages in the life of the child and family. An example of this kind of system linkage is communication between the prenatal clinics involved at intervention point 2 and the birthing hospitals involved at intervention point 3 to support the identification of newborns affected by prenatal substance exposure.

The horizontal arrows indicate potential linkages between the systems and agencies that provide interventions for either the child or the parents within the same developmental timeframe. For example, a woman may be identified at intervention point 2 as abusing substances while she is pregnant; she would need a substance abuse intervention as well as prenatal care. Communication between her prenatal care provider and substance abuse service provider would allow coordination of services to ensure appropriate care.

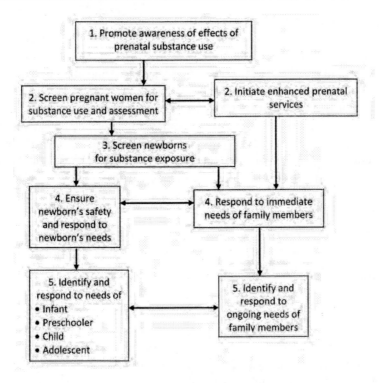

Figure 2. Policy and Practice Intervention Points for Children and Families.

Multiple Agencies and Collaborative Efforts

State SEI policies and practices develop in a complex system that includes diverse agencies within Federal and State government. These agencies have important *program* roles, but do not typically come together to develop and monitor comprehensive *policy*. As a result, this study required contacting multiple informants in each State to gather information about SEI initiatives sponsored, operated, and funded by different State, local, and private agencies. The variations within and among States are the result of the independent roles of the States and counties; variations in attitudes in different States toward addiction, parenting, and child safety; and differences in how the set of agencies that handle SEI issues is organized.

Policy innovation in the States can take place across and within a broad array of agencies. These agencies include child welfare, substance abuse treatment, family/dependency courts, child care and development, special education, maternal and child health, developmental disabilities, family support, and juvenile justice agencies. Important stakeholders in the private and nonprofit sectors include hospitals, health care management plans, and private physicians responsible for obstetric and pediatric care. However, the involvement of a large number of agencies and stakeholders has the potential to inhibit innovation, unless resources and communications are sufficient to enable effective interagency efforts and monitoring of their effectiveness.

To fully address SEI issues, they must be handled in an intensely collaborative setting, since no single agency has the resources, the information base, or the lead role to address the full range of needs of all substance-exposed or substance-affected newborns and their families. If concern for these children is to continue past birth, the number of families who may need services increases to several million; these are the families of preschoolers who were prenatally exposed, many of whom may also be affected by continuing substance use disorders in their families. These increases in the scope and complexity of States' interagency networking are important aspects of the context for State SEI policy and its implementation.

For these reasons, this study reviewed States' policies and practices in developing system linkages within and among State agencies. States need interagency collaboration to address the SEI problem. This need makes the issue of developing system linkages as important as the issue of handling each of the five intervention points, since the linkages pull the interventions in the five areas together.

SECTION 3. INTERVENTION POINTS

Pre-Pregnancy

Policies and practices that address the substance-exposed infant (SEI) problem by preventing substance abuse *before* a woman becomes pregnant tend to focus on three areas:

1. Health warnings;
2. Provision of educational materials; and
3. Public education and awareness media campaigns.

The relevance of these strategies has increased because of the prevalence data on drug and alcohol use, in particular binge drinking, by both pregnant women and women of child-bearing age.

Health Warnings

Studies show that warning signs raise awareness and may reduce alcohol consumption among light to moderate drinkers (Fenaughty & MacKinnon, 1993). Warning signs are most effective if they are part of a larger, comprehensive strategy to provide information and link women to needed treatment services.

In 1981, the U.S. Surgeon General issued a public health advisory warning that alcohol use during pregnancy could cause birth defects. This advisory suggested that pregnant women limit the amount of alcohol they drink. In 2005, in the light of new information on Fetal Alcohol Syndrome and Fetal Alcohol Spectrum Disorders (FAS/FASD), the Surgeon General updated and reissued the advisory on alcohol use during pregnancy—this time stating that "no amount of alcohol consumption can be considered safe during pregnancy" (DHHS, 2005).

In addition to the Surgeon General's efforts, the Federal government has enacted legislation to help inform and educate the general public about the health hazards that may result from the use or abuse of alcoholic beverages. The Alcoholic Beverage Labeling Act of 1988 mandates health-warning labels on all alcohol containers that must include warnings against drinking during pregnancy because of the risk of birth defects. Although an important step, the legislation prohibits States from mandating any additional or alternative warnings on alcohol containers.

Aside from beverage warning labels, no Federal statutes require alcohol retailers or health care providers to post warnings against drinking during pregnancy. Still, many States have taken the initiative to mandate warning signs that further caution women and the larger public about the risks of prenatal alcohol and drug use.

Provision of Educational Materials

Several States also have enacted legislation requiring educational information (e.g., a brochure or pamphlet) about the effects of substance use during pregnancy. This information is to be provided to women in select venues at opportune times, such as physicians' offices where women go for medical services or the county clerk's office where couples go to request a marriage license (DHHS, SAM HSA, n.d.).

Policy at the Federal level also promotes the distribution of education materials. The Drug-Free Schools and Communities Act Amendments of 1989 require universities and educational institutions receiving Federal funding to establish substance abuse prevention programs for their employees and students. The act mandates that institutions annually distribute to each student and employee written materials that include a description of the various health risks associated with the use of illicit drugs and abuse of alcohol. These risks include the dangers of drinking during pregnancy.

Public Education and Awareness Media Campaigns

Public education media campaigns are a third strategy to address pre- pregnancy prevention. These campaigns target three audiences:

- Women of child-bearing age and their partners, family, and friends;
- Health and social service providers who serve women; and
- The general public.

Minnesota is an example of one State whose public awareness campaigns have spanned all these audiences. (See "Findings" in this section for more details.)

The Federal government is often a key promoter and funding source for such public education campaigns (see sidebar). State and local agencies and private non-profits also contribute significant resources to these prevention efforts.

HOW THE FEDERAL GOVERNMENT SUPPORTS LOCAL OUTREACH

The National Institute on Alcohol Abuse and Alcoholism (NIAAA) recently completed a 2-year multimedia public awareness campaign, "Play it Smart. Alcohol and Pregnancy Don't Mix."

The research-based campaign targeted African-American women aged 21–29, their friends, and family living in Washington, DC. NIAAA conducted the campaign with oversight from the National Organization on Fetal Alcohol Syndrome (NOFAS) and supplementary funding from the National Center on Minority Health and Health Disparities. The multimedia campaign included:

- Print materials (posters, magnets, and bookmarks);
- Broadcast materials (television and radio public service announcements, information booths, magazines, newspapers, and mass transit advertising);
- Community events with neighboring churches, hospitals, and government agencies;
- Metrorail placards and advertising in select movie theaters; and
- Help line telephone services.

(NIAAA, 2004)

The existence of State policy (i.e., legislation, statutes, and regulations) that actually mandates these types of public education campaigns is minimal. Still, States such as California and Maryland have stepped up prevention efforts by enacting legislation that helps facilitate the development and implementation of such large-scale public education campaigns.

Sample State Initiatives

POLICIES AND PRACTICES BRIDGING INTERVENTION POINTS 1 AND 2—KENTUCKY'S EARLY CHILDHOOD INITIATIVE

In 2001, with State Tobacco Settlement funds, Kentucky developed a comprehensive Early Childhood Initiative that placed the issue of substance use during pregnancy at the forefront. This initiative included a statewide Healthy Babies Campaign to increase public awareness and education about Fetal Alcohol Syndrome, the impact of substance abuse on pregnancy and childrearing, and the importance of smoking cessation.

The campaign distributed 800,000 marketing pieces in the first 6 months, established a toll-free number and Website to access information and resources, provided all new parents with written materials and a videotape emphasizing the significance of a child's first few years for growth and development, and ran a series of Healthy Baby television and radio spots. Early focus group results showed a general awareness of the importance of not using drugs and engaging in other healthy behaviors while pregnant.

The Early Childhood Initiative also established the KIDS NOW Substance Abuse and Pregnancy Initiative to provide alcohol, drug, and tobacco screening, as well as prevention education and treatment services to all pregnant women in the State. KIDS NOW provides services to all pregnant women identified and referred by health care and other social service providers. KIDS NOW has evolved since its inception in 2001 (KIDS NOW, n.d.).

Year 1 began with the Kentucky Medical Association encouraging physicians to screen and refer pregnant women. Screening and referrals began in year 2, as practitioners were trained on how to use the 4P's screening tool. With screening underway, the next couple of years focused on establishing strong linkages with community agencies and health departments to facilitate the screening, assessment, and treatment entry process (Kentucky's Early Childhood Initiative, 2006).

On average, about 3,000 women are screened each year; the percentage of women who are referred to and enter treatment has ranged from 33–57% (Kentucky's Early Childhood Initiative, 2006).

Table 4. Summary of State policy initiatives on pre-pregnancy intervention.

	Health Warnings	Educational Materials	Media Campaigns
Alaska	X		
Arizona	X		
California	X	X	X
Delaware	X		
Georgia	X		
Hawaii		X	
Illinois	X		
Kentucky	X	X	X
Maryland		X	
Massachusetts	X		
Minnesota	X	X	X
Missouri	X	X	
Nebraska	X		
Nevada	X		
New Hampshire	X		
New Jersey	X		
New Mexico	X		
New York	X		
North Carolina	X		
Oregon	X		
South Dakota	X		
Tennessee	X		
Washington	X		
West Virginia	X		
Washington, DC	X		

(States in italics were part of the in-depth review sample.)

Pregnancy and the Prenatal Period

The second opportunity to intervene and engage women at risk of delivering an SEI is during pregnancy, when screening by health care providers can result in early identification, referral for comprehensive assessment, and a timely connection to appropriate substance abuse treatment services. These interventions should occur as early in the pregnancy as possible, to minimize risk of exposure for the developing infant.

This part of the intervention framework emphasizes the incorporation of brief (non-laboratory) screening methods into standard prenatal care practice. Such methods detect potential substance use during pregnancy and provide follow-up referrals to treatment and other supportive services for pregnant women who are identified as needing those services.

Screening

Screening methods can include self-report, interviews, or clinical observation. Prenatal care guidelines issued by the American College of Obstetricians and Gynecologists (ACOG) Committee on Obstetric Practice clearly state that "all pregnant women should be questioned at their first prenatal visit about past and present use of alcohol, nicotine, and other drugs" (American Academy of Pediatrics & ACOG, 2002). In 2004, ACOG's Committee on Ethics issued a statement asserting that "physicians have an ethical obligation to learn and use techniques for universal screening questions. . . ." In the same document, ACOG concluded that "physicians have been slow to implement universal [prenatal] screening . . ." (ACOG, 2004).

One barrier to implementing standardized prenatal screening identified by those interviewed in this study is the lack of a widely accepted screening tool. Yet several screening tools that take 10 minutes or less to administer have been validated for pregnant women. These include the T-ACE, the TWEAK, and the *4P's Plus* © (see sidebar)

THE 4P'S PLUS©—AN EVIDENCE-BASED SCREENING TOOL

The 4P's Plus© is a quick, five-question screen designed to identify pregnant women who need an in-depth assessment or follow-up monitoring for risk of alcohol, drug, and tobacco use. The tool is administered during a woman's prenatal care visit; it asks:

- Did either of your parents ever have a problem with alcohol or drugs?
- Does your partner have a problem with alcohol or drugs?
- Have you ever drunk beer, wine, or liquor?
- In the month before you knew you were pregnant, how many cigarettes did you smoke?
- In the month before you knew you were pregnant, how many beers/how much wine/how much liquor did you drink?

A recent study evaluated the 4P's Plus© and found that it was effective in identifying severe, moderate, or mild alcohol and drug use by pregnant women, thereby increasing opportunities for early intervention. Because of the brevity of the tool, it is practical to implement in clinical practice. And because of its early identification and intervention capabilities—which can prevent or reduce the major financial, physical, psychological, and socioeconomic costs associated with a substance- exposed infant—this tool is potentially very cost- effective.

(Chasnoff et al., 2005)

Most States that have prenatal screening programs track the total number of women participating in the program and the total number of drug-free babies delivered at the end of the program. However, these data are not compared with the State's total number of births or its baseline estimate of SEIs. The focus is on the number of identified women served, rather than on the total number of pregnant women who need services.

Complete data on prenatal screening programs would enable these States to better assess the effectiveness of the prevention program or to expand its scope. Such data on how these programs relate to the larger context of all births and all pregnant and parenting women who need substance use treatment would also help States in those efforts. In addition, measuring only drug-free births, while significant, does not address longer-term recovery outcomes.

Some States have done one-time effectiveness studies of prenatal prevention efforts, but without the resources set aside to update the evaluation on an ongoing basis.

Given that Medicaid pays for 37% of births nationally, and well above that level in several States, Medicaid can provide substantial impetus for States to adopt prenatal screening policies that embody the ACOG guidelines in their Medicaid schedules and reimbursements. For example, in Washington, Medicaid covered 43% of births in 2002, and in South Carolina, it covered 47% (Williams et al., 2006; South Carolina Department of Health and Environmental Control, 1991). However, few States have leveraged their Medicaid resources and regulations to make such screening part of all prenatal care.

Follow-Up Referrals for Treatment and Supportive Services

To reduce substance exposure during the pregnancy and improve chances for a healthy birth outcome, there must be an effective link between screening and facilitating a woman's access to necessary treatment and related support services. Too often, there is a gap at this critical juncture. This gap is, in part, due to a perceived lack of appropriate treatment options for pregnant women held by those outside the substance abuse treatment system who are not familiar with its resources. For cases in which primary care providers have some knowledge of treatment options available in their community, they may not have sufficient information regarding how to access that information. Additionally, primary care providers are often reluctant to broach the delicate topic of a potential substance use disorder with their patients, for fear of driving substance-using women away from seeking prenatal care.

To counteract this last concern, some States have implemented policy to remove or reduce punitive policies regarding prenatal substance use in order to facilitate access to treatment for pregnant women. Washington, for instance, promotes "information only" referrals of pregnant women who might be using substances to local prenatal support programs; these types of referrals are not recorded as formal child protective services (CPS) cases. Hawaii passed legislation in 2004 that provides immunity from criminal prosecution for drug offenses for pregnant women seeking prenatal treatment.

To some extent the perceived lack of treatment resources is accurate. National data clearly indicate a significant treatment gap for pregnant women: in 2005, only 6% of the pregnant women aged 15–44 who were classified as needing treatment for alcohol or illicit drug use actually received treatment.[12] Further, although 86% of substance abuse treatment facilities *accept* women, the number with a *specific program* for pregnant and postpartum women is only 17% (Office of Applied Studies [OAS], 2006. Online Analysis of National Survey of Substance Abuse Treatment Services [N-SSATS] Profile: United States 2005).

The Federal Treatment Episode Data Set (TEDS) is a key tool that States can use to obtain a picture of SEI issues at both the national and State levels. In addition to tracking trends on the percentage of women who are pregnant at treatment admission, TEDS data on pregnant women can also be analyzed for drug of choice, number of substances used, prior treatment admissions,[13] primary source of referral, and other useful information.[14] As Table 5 shows, 6 of the 10 States interviewed for this report had admission rates for pregnant women above the national average—as a percentage of all female admissions (OAS, SAMHSA, 2005).

Part of making an effective link to treatment is ensuring that the treatment provided is appropriate for pregnant women and comprehensive enough to meet a pregnant woman's unique needs. Colorado's Prenatal Plus program augments routine medical prenatal care with additional needed services (see sidebar on the following page).

At the Federal and State levels, policies and practices are in place to help increase treatment access for pregnant women. The Federal Substance Abuse Prevention and Treatment Block Grant (SAPTBG) requires that States set aside a certain percentage of their block grant funds (equal to or greater than a State's fiscal year 1994 expenditures) for services designed for pregnant women and women with dependent children. It also mandates that such women receive priority access to treatment and be provided with treatment services within 48 hours of request.[15]

Table 5. Percentage of Female and Pregnant Female Treatment Admissions among the 10 Study States, 2005.

State	Percentage of Female Admissions	Pregnant Admissions— As Percentage of All Admissions (male and female)	Pregnant Admissions— As Percentage of All Female Admissions
National Average	32.0	1.3	3.9
California	35.5	2.0	5.7
Hawaii	35.5	1.1	3.0
Illinois	32.6	1.3	4.1
Maryland	33.2	1.8	5.4
Massachusetts*	28.5	Not Available	Not Available
Minnesota	32.1	1.2	4.0
Rhode Island	32.0	1.1	3.5
South Carolina	30.2	1.5	5.2
Virginia	32.4	1.5	4.3
Washington	37.5	1.3	3.4

*Massachusetts reports these data differently from all other States and is thus not comparable.
Source: Online Analysis of TEDS, OAS, SAMHSA, 2006.

Table 6. Summary of State Policy Initiatives on Pregnancy and Prenatal Prevention.

	Prenatal Screening Encouraged	Universal Screening Policy	Brief Intervention	Referral for Treatment and/or Supportive Services
California (select counties)	X		X	X
Colorado				X
Kentucky	X			X
Massachusetts	X		X	
Minnesota				X
Virginia		X		X
Washington		X	X	X

(States in italics were part of the in-depth review sample.)

COLORADO'S PRENATAL PLUS PROGRAM

In 1996, Colorado implemented Prenatal Plus to improve the health of high-risk Medicaid-eligible women to help assure healthy birth outcomes. The program seeks to decrease the prevalence of low birth weight infants, improve the nutritional and psychosocial health of the target population, and help women develop and maintain healthy lifestyles— in particular, stopping alcohol, drug, or tobacco use—both during and after pregnancy. Clients are referred by a health or human service practitioner or are self-referred.

Services provided by a multidisciplinary team are designed to complement regular medical prenatal care and include risk assessments, care coordination, mental health services, and nutrition counseling. Women receive services throughout their pregnancy and for up to 60 days after delivery. The "model care" package that results in the best outcomes is a minimum of eight office visits and two home visits.

Prenatal Plus is funded using a combination of Medicaid, Federal Maternal and Child Health (MCH) Block Grant dollars, and local funds. The Department of Health Care Policy and Financing and the Department of Public Health and Environment, Women's Health Unit, manage the program collaboratively.

(Colorado Department of Public Health and Environment, Women's Health Unit, Prenatal Plus, n.d.; Colorado Department of Public Health and Environment, 2006)

The Federal government monitors these requirements via States' SAPTBG applications, which must certify this policy is in effect. State substance abuse agencies are well aware of the SAPTBG requirements and monitor county and provider compliance primarily through contract compliance audits and provider program plans. Some States, such as Virginia, have procedures in place in which the mandated regional perinatal councils are advised to call State agency headquarters to seek priority treatment within the 48-hour limit for pregnant women.

State child welfare agencies may not be as familiar with SAPTBG requirements and typically do not monitor referrals of pregnant women for treatment, since they do not routinely screen for substance abuse. In fact, none of the child welfare representatives in the 10 States interviewed could provide a count of women enrolled in treatment under the 48-hour provision.

Approximately 21 States have specific substance abuse treatment standards or protocols for women and/or pregnant women. Most of these standards include a common set of regulations that reflect SAPTBG requirements. Pregnant women must receive priority admission and must be admitted within 48 hours, or must be provided with interim services if admission is not possible. Emphasis is placed on ensuring that pregnant women receive prenatal care and education on the effects of substance use during pregnancy. California provides a more comprehensive list of interim services. Colorado's standards specify that pregnant women may not be discharged from treatment solely for failure to maintain abstinence and that every effort shall be made to retain pregnant women for the duration of their pregnancies (Dennis, 2005).

Sample State Initiatives

All 10 States interviewed for this study indicated that they had policies requiring or encouraging prenatal screening to identify a woman's substance use and prevent a substance-exposed birth (SEB). However, formal policies on universal screening for the general population are rarely implemented universally, as intended. Table 6 summarizes the policy initiatives that States have launched related to pregnancy and prenatal intervention. See the narrative in the Appendix for further detail.

WASHINGTON STATE'S MODEL: PRENATAL SCREENING AND LINKAGES TO SERVICES

In 1998, Washington passed legislation directing the Department of Health to develop screening criteria for identifying pregnant and nursing women at risk of having a substance-exposed baby. With input from an Advisory Workgroup and key informant surveys, guidelines for screening pregnant women were developed and widely disseminated to health care providers. The guidelines are organized using a framework of Ask, Advise, Assess, Assist, and Arrange, emphasizing the importance of linking this critical prenatal stage to other early intervention opportunities and treatment services for pregnant women. The guidelines highlight the benefits of universal screening and strongly urge health care providers to conduct screening on all pregnant women. Providers are advised to use interview-based or self-administered screening tools (examples are provided); the limitations and weaknesses of urine toxicology screens are outlined. The guidelines also stress the need for open, ongoing relationships between patients and providers; provider training on how and when to screen; and a team approach involving the primary provider, clinic nurse, social worker, public health nurse, substance abuse treatment providers, and the patient (Washington State Department of Health, 2002).

Washington also has established the following two noteworthy programs that provide early intervention and other services to pregnant women.

Safe Babies, Safe Moms (Cawthon, 2004; Cawthon & Westra, 2003). In 1999, in accordance with legislative mandate, Washington developed a comprehensive program for mothers with substance use disorders and their young children through age 3. The overall purpose of the project is to improve early identification of pregnant women who are using substances and to increase access to and coordination of health care, substance abuse treatment, and family-oriented intervention services for mothers and their children. Key service components include: targeted intensive case management, residential and outpatient substance abuse treatment, parenting education, housing support services, and child developmental assessments and referrals. Each woman receives an individualized care plan. The project is an interagency collaborative effort, and referrals come from multiple systems, including substance abuse treatment, hospitals, criminal justice (e.g., drug courts and law enforcement), child welfare, and welfare, as well as friends and family. Three pilot sites served 445 women and their children from January 2000 through June 2003. Program evaluation findings demonstrate positive outcomes that include: decreased low birth weight rates, decreased rates of child protective services referrals, decreased criminal justice involvement, and decreased parenting stress levels.

Parent-Child Assistance Program (PCAP).[16] In 1991, with multiyear funding from the Center for Substance Abuse Prevention (CSAP), Washington developed and implemented the Parent-Child Assistance Program (originally known as the Seattle Birth to 3 Program) to measure the effectiveness of intensive, long-term paraprofessional advocacy with high-risk pregnant women who abuse alcohol or drugs and are disconnected from community service providers. PCAP's goals are to help mothers establish healthy lifestyles, assure children are in safe and stable environments, and prevent future substance-exposed births. Rather than provide direct treatment services, PCAP paraprofessional advocate case managers link families with community services, coordinate services between multiple providers and systems, and help mothers follow through with recommendations of substance abuse treatment providers.

When Federal funding ended in 1996, the State legislature appropriated funding to maintain and expand the initiative to include sites in Tacoma, Spokane, and Yakima. PCAP has the capacity to serve 360 families statewide. Participating mothers are identified through community referrals and a postnatal screening process conducted at two hospitals in Seattle and Tacoma. Women are enrolled during pregnancy and receive services for 3 years. Since its inception, PCAP has served more than 650 women and their families. This program also has demonstrated positive short- and long-term outcomes in areas such as substance abuse treatment completion, sustained recovery, and prevention of substance use during subsequent pregnancies.

Time of Birth

This intervention point, time of birth, presents perhaps the most complex set of issues on the ramifications of State policy for both parents and children. One complex issue is that the need to identify infants prenatally exposed is perceived by some to conflict directly with privacy rights. Another is that methods of detection at birth are limited to very recent use. This section will summarize those complexities in an effort to provide some guidance for jurisdictions that are grappling with the need to establish well-informed policy.

To date, none of the States have mandated universal testing of newborns for illegal drugs, and testing of newborns is a controversial issue in all States.[i] This is partially illustrated in an Illinois eport covering 1991–1999, in which officials expressed concern that a decline in reported SEIs may indicate reduced testing rather than reduced incidence.[17] To understand the context for this intervention point, it is necessary to consider that an estimated *90–95% of babies born prenatally exposed to alcohol or illegal drugs do not have that exposure detected at birth and simply go home with their birth parents.*[ii]

---

[i] Although screening (i.e., an interview or protocol for review of a case) is not the same as drug testing, the terms are used interchangeably by most States. We distinguish them only when drug testing is specifically intended to be the focus.

[ii] Many hospitals may not test or may have inconsistent policies on testing, as noted in the Abandoned Infants Assistance report, and in fact, most births are not tested in most hospitals. Furthermore, tests detect only very recent use, within the last 24–72 hours, so use during the critical first trimester and beyond would not be detected by a test at birth. The total number of documented SEI reports on the prevalence of substance exposure estimates ranges from 2–10% of the estimates. CPS reports on 0–1 year olds and on removals of children in the first year of life, for all reasons, state that these children are a very small percentage of the more than 4 million births each year. This estimated percentage is based on an analysis of the several States and localities that have reported a specific number of detected drug-exposed births, compared with total births in those sites. More detailed analysis of this percentage will be available once reports of drug-affected births mandated by the Child Abuse Prevention and Treatment Act (CAPTA) are aggregated at State and Federal levels in future years.

Most States lack clear, standardized procedures for newborn testing. Nearly all States test infants for other health conditions like human immunodeficiency virus (HIV)[18] and phenylketonuria (PKU),[19] which, in reality, impact far fewer children than prenatal exposure to alcohol and illicit drugs. Yet States do not consider SEI screening to be in the same category as these procedures.[20]

A number of factors influence the approach that States have taken to address the issue of testing for substance exposure at birth. And policy has often been formed within a debate between advocates for expanded testing and those who argue that mandated testing may deter women from seeking prenatal treatment. As noted, no State has a universal testing policy in place (Ondersma, Simpson, Malcoe, & O'Steen, 1999). On the one hand, there is the argument that universal testing of all neonates would ensure fairness and maximize the chances that an exposed infant will receive any needed services at the earliest possible time. But there are those who cite the numbers of false positives that may result, the costs of universal or widened testing, and the possibility of violating civil liberties and privacy.

They also cite the lack of certainty that testing will in fact lead to treatment and supportive services for infants or their mothers, as opposed to consequences that may include child removal from the home and prosecution of the mother. As the treatment improvement protocol (TIP) issued by the Center for Substance Abuse Treatment (CSAT) explains:

> State and local laws that require maternal alcohol and other drug use and fetal drug exposure to be reported to authorities have a significant impact on women and their children. . . . Knowing that such a report is in the offing, some women may forgo their prenatal care or the follow-up services they need. The closer communities move toward measures that *detain* pregnant, substance-using women, the more punitive, detrimental, and potentially dangerous it becomes for these women and their children. (Center for Substance Abuse Treatment, 2003; TIP 2. Emphasis added.)

Further complicating the issue is the fact that State policies vary widely in:

- How child abuse and neglect are defined in prenatal substance exposure;
- What the parameters of testing at birth for substance exposure are;
- What the appropriate follow-up is in response to a positive test (e.g., filing an abuse/neglect report or making a referral to CPS); and
- Which types of substances are covered by policy.

Defining Prenatal Substance Exposure as Child Abuse or Neglect

The Alan Guttmacher Institute indicates that as of 2005, 16 States consider substance abuse[21] during pregnancy to be a form of child abuse, up from 12 States in 2000 (Dailard & Nash, 2000). (The actual definitions used by States rarely distinguish between substance abuse and substance use, equating the two in most cases.) Seven of the 10 States interviewed in this study have formulated policy that defines prenatal substance exposure, however it is detected, as evidence of or the legal equivalent to child abuse or neglect (Illinois, Maryland, Massachusetts, Minnesota, Rhode Island, South Carolina, and Virginia) (Dailard & Nash, 2000). Minnesota, South Dakota, and Wisconsin consider the use of illicit substances during pregnancy as grounds for civil commitment that may include forced admission to treatment.

Only three of the States interviewed do not consider prenatal exposure alone to be evidence of child abuse or neglect (California, Hawaii, and Washington State).

In the 5-year period from 2000–2005, the Guttmacher Institute's analysis indicates that the number of States that require health care professionals to report suspected prenatal drug abuse to CPS (in contrast with those that define exposure and abuse or neglect) has increased from 7 to 10 (Alan Guttmacher Institute, 2005). Additionally, four States (Iowa, Minnesota, North Dakota, and Virginia) require that health care agencies test women and/or infants for prenatal drug exposure if they suspect substance use.

Beyond policies and statutes, States and localities demonstrate varying practices in documenting prenatal substance exposure as substantiating child abuse or neglect, and in filing subsequent petitions[iii] for court intervention and child removal. A national study of 200 counties responding to a 1999 survey found that:

- 21% of counties reported that they never file dependency petitions on behalf of substance- exposed newborns;
- 47% of the responding counties note that they file petitions in at least 41% of such cases; and
- 25% of the counties file in 75% of the cases. (Ondersma et al., 1999)

A landmark decision by the South Carolina State Supreme Court in 1997 (*Whitner v. State of South Carolina*) held that if the health or welfare of a viable fetus has been or may be adversely affected by the abuse of an illegal drug, then this action is defined as "child abuse" for which the mother could be imprisoned for up to 10 years. Only illegal drugs (cocaine, heroin, LSD, amphetamines, marijuana, and their derivatives) are included under the South Carolina law. The U.S. Supreme Court refused to review this case, and South Carolina remains the only State that has successfully prosecuted a woman for the transmission of controlled substances to her child in utero. (It is believed that no more than 10 women have been sentenced under this law for infant exposure to illegal substances, and none in recent years. The prosecution referred to occurred in 2001.)

In Texas, a controversy continues over the interpretation of Senate Bill 319, a bill addressing the definition of child abuse, passed by the legislature and signed by the Governor in 2003. Despite a ruling by the Attorney General that under Texas law a "physician is not obligated to report a pregnant patient's use of a controlled substance as child abuse," a local district attorney prosecuted eighteen women after their doctors shared their confidential information. In response, more than 70 child welfare and public health organizations sent a letter protesting this interpretation of the new law (Drug Policy Alliance, 2005). The controversy is unresolved, but the rapid mobilization of a wide array of organizations in response to policy changes underscores the volatility of these issues.

[iii] Filing a petition does not necessarily result in a substantiated report of abuse or neglect, nor does it mean that a child is subsequently removed from his or her parents. The petition simply triggers a hearing at which the judge must decide on the further status of the child and whether additional action is needed.

Defining the Parameters for Testing at Birth

It should be emphasized that CAPTA does not require testing at birth; it requires that "health care providers involved in the delivery or care of such infants (i.e., those "born and identified as affected by illegal substance abuse or withdrawal symptoms resulting from prenatal drug exposure") notify the child protective services system of the occurrence of such condition in such infants . . ." and ensure "the development of a plan of safe care for the infant born and identified as being affected by illegal substance abuse or withdrawal symptoms . . ." as well as "procedures for the immediate screening, risk and safety assessment, and prompt investigation of such reports."

The interviews conducted for this paper did not reveal any reports that either CAPTA changes or other State policies in this area deterred women from seeking prenatal care. However, it is a concern frequently vocalized by women's advocates and others concerned with family preservation. Barth has written in favor of a policy that moves toward wider testing, but also points out that testing, and subsequent reporting, provides no guarantee for connecting a woman to adequate treatment services (Barth, 2001).

He notes that ". . . most women who received child welfare services received little more than a referral to possible services or no more than six months of in-home services in concert with their children in their own home" (Barth, 2001). Barth recommends a differential referral system, in which reports of positive tests to CPS would trigger services, rather than punitive action. He emphasizes that it is critical for services to be in place for this system to be effective.

In addition to the concern that testing at birth may negatively impact the likelihood of whether a woman with a potential substance use disorder will obtain prenatal care, there is a commonly held perception that neonatal testing is more likely to be focused on poor minority women than on their higher-paid, white counterparts. Indeed, past studies have documented this bias (Chasnoff, Landress, & Barrett, 1990; Ondersma, Malcoe, & Simpson, 2001). However, several interviewees for this report also expressed this concern, but the only evidence suggested by several of the State interviewees was that data on SEIs were more readily available from hospitals with higher percentages of Medicaid births.

Legal interpretations of consent requirements, and the requirements of the Health Insurance Portability and Accountability Act of 1996 (HIPAA), are perceived by some States to further complicate decisions about testing at birth. Washington State addressed this issue in its State HIPAA guidelines (2002):

> No uniform policy or State law exists regarding consent for newborn drug testing. This is a complex issue and care providers may wish to seek legal consultation regarding regional practice standards. . . , the intent of the testing may determine the type of consent. Women with admitted histories of drug use, or women and infants exhibiting signs of drug exposure, can be tested under the general consent because results of the test influence medical care and follow up. However, if the total or partial intent of the testing is to bring legal action against the woman, a consent containing specific language defining possible consequences is advisable. . . . If a patient refuses testing, this should be documented and testing not performed . . . Many hospitals do not seek parental consent for newborn testing, citing its use as a medical diagnostic tool. (Washington State Department of Health, 2002)

In 2002, Zellman and her colleagues obtained responses from 506 hospitals across the Nation and found that only one-third of the 166 responding hospitals had prenatal substance exposure protocols. Of those with protocols, only 56% included any instructions for reporting SEBs to external agencies such as CPS, and only 41% included any discussion of consent issues, all of which varied widely. The study also noted a lack of communication between physicians and staff regarding these issues, and a further lack of communication between obstetricians and pediatricians. The Zellman study concluded that the hospitals' protocols were "insufficiently precise, and most fail to address one or more key components of appropriate detection and medical management of prenatal substance exposure . . . the authors of the protocols did little to encourage their use, increase their credibility or facilitate modifications and improvements to them" (Jacobson, Zellman, & Fair, 2003).

Further evidence of the variance in hospital policy is apparent in the study of eight large urban areas, performed by the National Abandoned Infants Assistance (AIA) Resource Center, which is summarized as follows:

> . . . this study revealed that, regardless of state policy, hospital staffs report virtually all newborns that test positive for an illicit drug and, with varying degrees of expedience, child welfare agencies investigate almost all such reports. Whereas most hospitals have a protocol to determine who to test for substances, these protocols are used inconsistently with resulting bias in who gets tested. Moreover, some hospitals do not even test delivering women or newborns for alcohol, and child welfare agencies are inconsistent in their response to reports of prenatal alcohol exposure. Thus, it is likely that not all substance exposed newborns are being identified or offered services.
>
> Additionally, according to the nursing and social work staff in participating hospitals, very little data is collected on the numbers of mothers and newborns that are tested for substances or the outcomes of the tests. Further, hospital staff generally do not track or follow up on referrals that they make to drug treatment services, and many limit their involvement in this area to providing women with a list of treatment providers. (Drescher- Burke & Price, 2005)

This evidence supports the report of interviewees. They repeatedly suggested that policy does not always translate into practice and that there can be tremendous disparity between what is written down and what actually occurs.

What Happens Next? Reports versus Referrals

Some State officials make a distinction between reports and referrals, pointing out that a report may be defined as a formal case being opened by the CPS agency, whereas a referral may mean only that a call was placed to the CPS agency. In other States, the definitions are reversed, with reports being calls from another agency and referrals being calls formally logged in by the CPS agency.

Whatever the language used, the issue of reporting requirements overlaps with the issue of whether prenatal exposure is legally viewed as abuse and/or neglect, since exposure must be reported if it is defined as abuse or neglect. In either case, the distinction between a mandate to test and a mandate to report test results remains critical, and States have considerable discretion in reporting. For example, one State agency official interviewed indicated that in some cases, the parent would not be reported to CPS, even after obtaining a positive toxicology result, when the parent accepted a voluntary referral to services. This particular interpretation of policy is premised on the value that enrolling the parent in treatment is more beneficial than filing a CPS report. The result of a report filing might be to deter future treatment admission.

Even in States with specific screening and referral policies, it is not clear how widely these procedures are actually used. In most States, there are no available counts of such referrals from hospitals. In those States in which hospitals report SEBs to child welfare agencies, whether or not the reports are mandated, no State indicated that the State child welfare agency had received hospital data. Also, no State indicated that its child welfare agency had compiled summaries from such data on the total number of screenings at birth, results of the screenings, or the number of referrals to the CPS agency as a percentage of screenings. Furthermore, no child welfare agency cited the use of Medicaid oversight as a resource, despite the high percentage of births covered by Medicaid.

In some cases, State legislation exists that answers the question posed by CAPTA: what happens *after* the telephone call to CPS? In one State, for instance, a detailed protocol specifies that after a positive toxicology report, a response team consisting of the attending physician, a worker from the CPS agency, a hospital social worker, law enforcement, and drug treatment personnel must meet to track the family's progress. However, a respondent from the State said that it was unclear about whether the prescribed teams actually convene on any regular basis. The perception was that this decision is typically at the discretion of the CPS agency.

For this particular State, neither the information on the State's annual totals of positive toxicology reports to CPS nor the meeting of teams in response to reports was available through the CPS agency. Therefore, it was understandably difficult for that agency to discern when and whether the protocol should be put into action.

Defining "Substances"

The attempt to define what is meant by "substance," or to distinguish between licit and illicit substances, can create further confusion for those trying to carry out the letter of the law in an effort to establish practice that will achieve the law's actual intent. This quandary is alluded to in Virginia's 2002 summary of SEI reports from its regional agencies, which notes that:

> Drug exposed infants are more likely to be identified at birth than alcohol exposed infants. Unless a woman is intoxicated at delivery, it is extremely unlikely her alcohol use will be identified. Although Virginia's legislation requires physicians to report Fetal Alcohol Syndrome (FAS) when identified at delivery, both FAS and alcohol related birth effects are extremely difficult to detect in a newborn and typically aren't identified until the child is significantly older.[22]

As with the other complexities surrounding this third intervention point, States vary significantly in specifying what kind of substance use is considered child abuse or neglect when detected at birth. For example:

- Minnesota's definition refers to "*a controlled substance*";
- Massachusetts refers to "*an addictive drug*" (which interviewees from Massachusetts said, in practice, includes alcohol, and the State's screening criteria explicitly refer to

FAS). Massachusetts policy also explicitly mentions methadone and screens out reports of methadone use if the mother is in an approved program (interview on September 14, 2005);
- State policy in both South Carolina and Illinois refers to "a controlled substance," but also includes "a medical diagnosis of fetal alcohol syndrome";
- Virginia refers to "non-prescription, controlled substances or signs of fetal alcohol syndrome";
- Maryland's definition is the most restrictive of the States interviewed in this study, referring only to "cocaine, heroin or a derivative thereof." Methamphetamine was added in 2007. In Maryland, a proposal to include alcohol as one of the substances to be screened for in the 1997 legislation Children in Need of Assistance—Drug Addicted Babies, was rejected in a legislative committee (Reese & Burry, 2004);
- Washington refers to "controlled substances," but also calls for identifying "pregnant or lactating women addicted to drugs or alcohol"; and
- California, which does not define fetal exposure as child abuse or neglect, refers in its latest legislation on this subject (1991) to "a positive toxicology screen," "maternal substance abuse," and "a substance-exposed infant," without defining any of these terms (California Department of Alcohol and Drug Programs, 2006). (Note: The 1992 California prevalence study found that a higher percentage of women tested positive for alcohol than for illegal drugs, consistent with national findings from the National Survey on Drug Use and Health [Vega et al., 1993].) In some California counties, methadone use is treated as addiction and is reported as use of a drug; however, there is no statewide policy regarding this.

Sample of State Initiatives

Table 7 summarizes the policy initiatives that States have established related to intervention at the time of birth. See the narrative in the Appendix for further detail.

Postnatal Services for Infants, Children, and Parents

The final two points in the intervention framework occur in the postnatal period immediately after birth, as well as throughout the SEI's childhood. These intervention points emphasize the delivery of services for the infant, parents, and other family members. Ideally, services for the infant or child and the parents are woven together in a comprehensive approach, although it is more commonly the case that the primary emphasis is on the child or the parents, rather than on both simultaneously.

Extensive literature exists on the need for developmental assessments to determine the degree to which prenatal drug exposure affects infants and toddlers, and on the importance of postnatal follow-up services (Lester, Boukydis, & Twomey, 2000; Mayes, Bornstein, Chawarska, & Granger, 1995; National AIA Resource Center, 2003). SEIs are at higher risk of coming into contact with the child welfare system at some point, and findings regarding children in foster care indicate that most children do not actually receive the assessments and services they need (Halfon, Mendonca, & Berkowitz, 1995). In fact, Lester's analysis of State policies beginning in 2003 notes that only two States (California and Wisconsin) require postnatal assessment of a newborn who is referred to CPS because of a positive toxicology result (Lester, 2000).

For resources, three distinct programs authorized by Federal legislation address postnatal interventions for developmental disabilities. These include:

- CAPTA provisions of the Keeping Children and Families Safe Act (Administration for Children and Families [ACF]);
- Part C of the Individuals with Disabilities Education Act (IDEA) (which is specific to Early Intervention Programs for Infants and Toddlers with Disabilities in the Department of Education); and
- Head Start provisions that provide services for young children, including children who may be substance-exposed (ACF).

It is important to understand the intended, potential, and actual linkages between these three programs, in order to take the next step related to developing effective policy and practice in postnatal intervention.

Table 7. Summary of State policy initiatives on intervention at the time of birth (2007).

	Maternal and/or Newborn Drug Testing Policy	Hospital and/or State Protocols to Handle Newborn Exposure	Prenatal Exposure Defined as Abuse/Neglect	Reporting Requirements	Screening and Referral Policies
California		X			
Colorado			X		X
Illinois			X		X
Iowa				X	
Louisiana			X	X	
Maine		X			
Maryland					X
Massachusetts	X		X		
Minnesota			X	X	
Missouri	X			X	
Nevada				X	
North Dakota				X	
Rhode Island			X		
South Carolina			X		
Virginia		X	X	X	X
Washington			X		X

(States in italics were part of the in-depth review sample.)

Services for Children: Linkages between CAPTA, IDEA, and Head Start

CAPTA provisions (see text box on page 14) require notification of CPS when an infant is identified as affected by illegal substance abuse or withdrawal symptoms. CAPTA also refers to the intent to "identify infants at risk of child abuse and neglect so appropriate services can be delivered to the infant and mother to provide for the safety of the child." This section of the legislation requires State child welfare agencies to have procedures in place for the referral of children 0–2 years (where abuse or neglect is already substantiated) to early intervention services under Part C of IDEA (Section 114, P.L. 108-36).

Similarly, IDEA 2004 mandates that States have policies and procedures in place that require the referral of a child younger than age 3 for early intervention services who:

(a) is involved in a substantiated case of child abuse or neglect; or
(b) is identified as affected by illegal substance abuse, or withdrawal symptoms resulting from prenatal drug exposure.

This IDEA requirement was written to be consistent with CAPTA, but in separate, linked legislation to apply specifically to the IDEA agencies that handle developmental disabilities. The American Bar Association summarized the importance of the IDEA section of the CAPTA amendments in the following statement:

> Possibly no other new change to CAPTA can have a greater impact than this mandatory Part C referral provision, if it is effectively implemented for maltreated children with the help of attorneys, judges, and other advocates. For this to have the most meaningful effect on accessing the $400 million-plus Federal program to help these children, CPS personnel, foster parents, family services providers, and legal/judicial system personnel will need to be trained on this new requirement, the Part C law and its regulations, and strategies for accessing applicable evaluation and treatment services. (Davidson, 2004)

The State policy on referrals is required to be included in CAPTA plans on the child welfare side and in States' IDEA plans on the disabilities side. In an attempt to maximize access to intervention services, IDEA identifies FAS as a condition of risk that can create eligibility for 0–2 year olds through "presumptive eligibility."[23] Five States add prenatal exposure through parental substance abuse as an environmental risk factor that should result in a referral for developmental screening.[24]

There are important challenges to developing stronger linkages between CPS and developmental disabilities agencies. An assessment of one model project, the Massachusetts Early Childhood Linkage Initiative, highlighted the challenges in standardizing the referral of young children from child protection agencies to Part C systems:

> In addition to the increased numbers of children that Part C will assess and serve if referrals from child protection are regularized, the types of Part C services required may change. Specifically, it seems likely that children involved with child protection will have social- emotional and behavioral issues more frequently than other children served by Part C . . . Part C may also need to enhance its ability to address parental issues that affect children's mental health, such as parental substance abuse, domestic violence, and parental mental health problems, especially maternal depression. (Robinson & Rosenberg, 2004)

Starting with this review, none of the States interviewed had compiled information on total referrals to IDEA agencies from hospitals detecting SEIs at birth. These States also had not compiled information on the number of substantiated allegations of abuse or neglect based on subsequent CPS identification of prenatal exposure (although Arizona officials estimated that a 20% increase in referrals to Part C agencies took place in the first 9 months of implementation of the new requirement[25]). States involved in federally funded pilot projects that addressed the needs of children with developmental delays in child welfare cases have a growing body of information that provides further support and justification for the new requirement. For example, in the first year of the Massachusetts project that began in 2002 before the CAPTA/IDEA amendments, 67% of the referred child welfare cases that involved children younger than 3 years old were demonstrated to be eligible for early intervention services for children with developmental problems (Massachusetts Early Intervention Project, 2005).

Based on this review of State policies, linkage appears to be minimal at the State level between the SEI efforts and Part C programs, except in Rhode Island and Massachusetts. A few States reported that the CAPTA legislation has prompted them to assess how well their referrals to early intervention programs are working. Minnesota's Department of Education, for example, is preparing an interagency agreement regarding Part C referrals made by child protection workers. And Maryland staff indicated that they have recently reviewed referral linkages because of the new IDEA-CAPTA changes. However, in most States reviewed, no interagency effort had yet taken place between the Part C agency and the child welfare agency to estimate the number of increased referrals that might result, or to plan different procedures for handling those referrals that actually occur.

Finally, at the Federal level, language has been added over the past 5 years to Head Start legislation that gives greater emphasis to coordination with child welfare agencies, training in services related to child abuse and neglect, and eligibility that makes more children in the child welfare systems eligible for Head Start. The extent to which child welfare agencies use these provisions for preschool-aged children who were prenatally or postnatally exposed is unknown, but few program descriptions refer to such eligibility.

Hawaii's Healthy Start Program

In response to significant increases in substantiated child abuse and neglect cases in the mid-1970s to the mid-1980s, Hawaii's State legislature authorized the Healthy Start Program (HSP). The program screens all statewide births for an array of at-risk factors that are typically associated with child abuse and neglect. Examples of these factors include a history of substance abuse, poverty, marital status, employment, and housing. If a family meets eligibility criteria, HSP provides home visiting in which trained paraprofessionals enter the family's home to assist parents in adjusting to the daily stressors of childrearing. Initially, the home visitors' goal is to establish rapport and trust with the parents to facilitate their role in increasing positive family functioning and child development. As a result, home visitors assume multiple roles as mentors, advocates, educators, and role models.

Hawaii's HSP has added substance abuse counseling as a parent support service in recent years, and is able to follow up on about 80% of the most at-risk births. (One-fifth of all births are defined as high-risk, using a protocol of several items.) Hawaii is also under a mandate for special education funding that created a consent decree requiring students with disabilities to receive services, including early intervention services, as part of a system of care. And HSP now provides strengthened developmental assessment for newborns as part of the State's compliance with the consent decree requirement for a system of care.

(Duggan et al., 1999)

Services for Parents

The parents of an SEI often are unable to provide a safe and nurturing environment for their children. Parents' failure to address their problems could eventually lead to their children being taken into custody and placed out of home. In order to work toward family preservation and reunification, responding to the parents' needs is a critical segment of SEI policy and practice.

Although most substance-affected births are not detected at birth, the opportunities for intervention continue as parents come into contact with numerous other agencies and organizations: home visiting programs for high-risk families, developmental screening programs of the type just described, child welfare agencies investigating reports of alleged abuse and neglect, preschool providers, hospitals, and others. Referrals to treatment agencies result from some of these contacts, and some parents seek treatment voluntarily, recognizing that they would be better parents if they were in recovery.

For those parents who arrive at substance abuse treatment because of a referral under the CAPTA requirement to report drug-affected infants to CPS or another child welfare contact, there are policy issues. The issues surround the type and quantity of treatment that is available, the quality of that treatment, and the likely outcomes of treatment for the substance-exposed child.

Type and Quantity of Treatment Available

According to the 2005 National Survey of Substance Abuse Treatment Services (N-SSATS), most substance abuse treatment facilities *accept* women (86%), yet only 33% of treatment facilities reported they had a women-specific program, and 14% had a program for pregnant and/or postpartum women. (The Federal definition of "pregnant and parenting" means that these policies, in effect, cover some women for continuing treatment after the birth of a drug- exposed child.) Unfortunately, just 4% of programs provide residential beds for clients' children (OAS, 2006).

In 2005, treatment admissions of pregnant women represented only 1.3% of total public treatment admissions and 3.9% of all female admissions, equaling 24,000 women. Yet an analysis of the 2005 NSDUH public use file indicated that more than 182,000 pregnant women aged 15–44 needed treatment for either alcohol or illicit drug abuse or dependence. Moreover, as described in Section 1, of the 4.1 million live births in 2005, an estimated 8–11% (328,000– 451,000) involved prenatal exposure to alcohol and illegal drugs.

As previously discussed, the federally required TEDS information system captures information on the pregnancy status of most females admitted to publicly funded treatment. But the admission of *parenting* women to treatment is not documented, nor is their referral status from child welfare caseloads. In Federal data collected as part of the Treatment Outcomes and Performance Pilot Study, Enhancement II (TOPPS-II), approximately 60% of the admissions had minor children. Still, neither the child welfare system nor the treatment system knows the number of mothers referred to treatment, nor does either system know the number of mothers admitted to treatment programs with children who may have been prenatally exposed to a substance.

Some programs serving parents of drug-exposed infants originated under the federally funded demonstration programs awarded by SAMHSA/CSAT in the mid-1990s to residential programs that served pregnant and postpartum women and children. Several of these programs have since become some of the best-known models of comprehensive treatment available, and extensive literature is available on their lessons learned (Chen, Burgdorf, & Herrell, 2001; Treatment Improvement Exchange, n.d.).

FAMILY DRUG TREATMENT COURTS

A further model of postnatal parent-targeted services is the network of family/dependency court- sponsored drug treatment courts. The main goals of Family Treatment Drug Courts are to protect infants and children whose safety and welfare may be negatively impacted by substance-abusing parents, to support and reinforce the family unit, to increase parental capacity to meet the physical and developmental needs of their infants, and to accelerate permanency for infants and children under the State's care.

In October 2001, the Specialized Treatment and Recovery Services (STARS) program was created in Sacramento County, California, to assist parents in the child welfare system with substance abuse disorders. An integral part of the Sacramento County Drug Dependency Court (DDC), STARS also focuses on engaging fathers in intensive treatment and case management. Through identifying the obstacles in seeking drug treatment and by offering many support services, STARS is committed to increasing reunification rates for parents and their children.

Initially, parents undergo a thorough intake process in which they are assessed for substance abuse during their Detention Hearing. Immediately thereafter, alcohol and drug treatment services are available, and parents are assigned to a Recovery Specialist. Three main strategies of the STARS program are motivational interviewing, role modeling, and accountability. Motivational interviewing techniques integrate four key components that include showing empathy, supporting self-efficacy, rolling with resistance, and developing discrepancy between thoughts, aspirations and personal behaviors that interfere with reaching their goals. Recovery Specialists play a critical role in helping parents to achieve program goals through their unyielding support, non-judgmental attitude, continuous belief, and ability to relate through their own experience in recovery. Since the program's inception through 2006, 1,738 parents have participated in the DDC.

At 12-month follow-up:
If the parent graduated, 58.9% of the children were reunified;
If the parent received a 90-day certificate, 42% of the children were reunified;
If the parent did not meet either landmark, only 15.6% of the children were reunified.

At 18-month follow-up:
If the parent graduated, 72.9% of the children were reunified;
If the parent received a 90-day certificate, 52.3% of the children were reunified;

If the parent did not meet either landmark, only 18.7% of the children were reunified.

At 24-month follow-up:
If the parent graduated, 70.9% of the children were reunified;
If the parent received a 90-day certificate, 49.9% of the children were reunified;
If the parent did not meet either landmark, only 17.9% of the children were reunified.
(The dip in reunification rates from 18–24 months is due to the re-entries seen with the DDC cohorts.)
(Sacramento County Department of Health and Human Services, 2006; Boles & Young, 2007)

The capacity of these programs, however, is small relative to the need for them, given estimates of SEI prevalence. In fact, where programs do exist, the small scale of some programs leads staff outside the treatment funding world to assume that few or no slots are available to parents of SEIs. However, for those States reporting information on treatment wait times to TEDS, the picture seems much more promising. In 2005, 60.8% of the treatment admissions involved no wait, and another 23% were admitted to treatment within one week. Even more surprisingly, there were no substantial differences in wait times among men, non-pregnant women, and pregnant women.[26]

In order to maximize use of the available treatment services, it is vital for communities and referral sources to understand what services and resources are available. This point is underscored by a recent analysis of the treatment slots available in one large county, compared with the needs of the child welfare system. This analysis demonstrated that a shift of less than 1% of the total treatment system resources would enable the child welfare agency to meet its Federal reunification targets by serving approximately 100 more clients (California Department of Alcohol and Drug Programs, 2006).

A study in California in the mid-1990s revealed that half of hospital nurse-managers believed that substance abuse treatment resources were not available for women giving birth in their communities. This assumption is often held by health care practitioners and other community service providers, and is invariably based on a lack of awareness among child welfare, health, and other staff about the treatment system, its funding streams, the turnover in treatment slots, and how to access services. Not surprisingly, the picture improves in some settings where this information is available.

Sample of State Initiatives
Table 8 summarizes the policy initiatives that States have established related to postnatal services for infants, children, and parents. See the narrative in the Appendix for further detail.

SECTION 4. BARRIERS TO ADDRESS: THE NEED FOR SYSTEM LINKAGES

When the needs of substance-exposed children are addressed, it is apparent that the connections across the five points discussed in this report are as important as the actual interventions. The handoffs from one point to the next and the linkages needed to coordinate services become a comprehensive services framework, rather than a series of fragmented initiatives.

The States interviewed for this report employed various coordination strategies, including the establishment of interagency entities, some of which focus on substance-exposed infant (SEI) issues directly and some of which address those issues within a broader context (e.g., perinatal services, maternal and child health, developmental disabilities, and child welfare reform). State staff readily acknowledge that there are unique collaborative challenges associated with addressing any issue that requires the involvement and support of multiple public agencies and private groups. The lack of critically needed data that could be shared across agencies was noted as a major barrier to collaboration.

Information gaps undeniably hamper the capacity of States to implement SEI policy in a coordinated fashion. Baseline data on any aspect of the issue are rare. For example, none of the States interviewed had current statewide prevalence estimates of substance-exposed births, other than the data provided to those States that participate in Federal Pregnancy Risk Assessment Monitoring System (PRAMS) data collection. (PRAMS focuses only on alcohol, with two exceptions.) Some States do have historic SEI baseline data, but these data are based on a point-in-time survey that has not been regularly renewed or updated. In general, States' experiences with these intermittent prevalence surveys have not been frequent enough to support the use of these data as a baseline to monitor progress or seek expanded support.

Table 8. Summary of State Policy Initiatives on Postnatal Services.

	Postnatal Assessment	Referral Protocols	Care Coordination Policies	Initiatives to Improve Linkages to Services
California	X			
Colorado				X
Illinois				X
Iowa			X	
Maryland		X	X	X
Massachusetts				X
Minnesota				X
Missouri		X		
Ohio		X	X	X
Rhode Island				X
Wisconsin	X	X	X	

(States in italics were part of the in-depth review sample.)

SEI initiatives seeking to work across agency boundaries have been bogged down by funding dilemmas, including a dearth of innovative funding strategies that might support putting good policy into practice. Even the potential leveraging of Medicaid resources has not been widely exercised, despite the logical connection to that resource based on the substantial number of birth-related costs paid for by Medicaid.

Interagency Coordinating Bodies

Each State reviewed had one or more interagency entities that were charged with addressing one or more facets of the SEI issue. In some cases, such as Hawaii's interagency council, the entity is mandated by State legislation, whereas in other States, the coordinating body was created by administrative action. The four sets of generic interagency bodies that exist in most of these States included:

1. An interagency body reviewing the State's Program Improvement Plan (PIP) under the Child and Family Services Review (CFSR) requirements, with a focus on child welfare outcomes;
2. An interagency group of treatment providers who meet regularly on a statewide basis, or a policy and planning group who focuses on the State's treatment policies, primarily addressing access to treatment;
3. An interagency coordinating group, such as the Early Start coalition, is focused on early intervention programs for developmentally disabled children and/or children affected by early mental health issues; and
4. An interagency group defined by perinatal outcomes and primarily oriented to maternal and child health agencies.

Regardless of whether they originated legislatively or administratively, these entities tend to be housed in a single agency. They also tend to have SEI issues as a focal point under a broader mission, such as child welfare reform, or at the intersection of child welfare and substance abuse. Because SEI issues are related to, but not the primary focus of, the work of these coordinating bodies, the SEI issue typically goes unmentioned and unprioritized in the larger agency strategic plans. None of the 10 States included SEI issues as part of their CFSR PIPs. Furthermore, none of these groups that address SEI policy as part of their mandates had developed interagency outcomes for SEI programs that are monitored annually by an interagency group, based on a strategic plan for SEI issues, or guided by an inventory of all State programs that affect SEI outcomes.

The Issue of Reporting Gaps and Data Systems

The extent of interagency organizational capacity in the States is entwined with the issues related to reporting requirements and implementation monitoring. Most States lack the systems to provide regular reports summarizing and analyzing their own data collection efforts. From initial hospital reporting of SEI births, to child protective services (CPS) recording referrals from hospitals, to the drug and alcohol treatment system capturing referral sources and the presence of prenatally exposed children, and on to the early childhood and developmental disabilities systems recording developmental assessments of SEIs—the information gaps at each of these hand-off points are substantial. Such gaps weaken the ability of the systems to work together to track children and families as they move from agency to agency.

Most States do not break out SEI referrals by CPS as part of the overall intake to publicly funded treatment. (Washington and Hawaii are exceptions.) None of the States sampled track total referrals of SEI parents into treatment or the outcomes achieved by those parents in treatment. States monitor their own pilot projects, especially the results of their prenatal programs, but only for the clients enrolled in these programs. No State has an information system that can track the full range of SEI-involved or prenatally targeted parents into and out of the entire treatment system.

Data on how many SEI parents are referred, how many enter treatment, how many complete treatment, and how many succeed in continuing their recovery are needed. These data are crucial to understanding the costs and cost-effectiveness of programs (Yates, 1999). Only the strongest programs can map these "drop-off points" where clients fail to enroll or drop out of treatment or recovery; no States require that such data be collected by their treatment grantees serving SEI parents. Thus, the data on treatment for pregnant and parenting mothers are restricted to those who make it into treatment, not the presumably larger group who need treatment or the group who enter but do not sustain their enrollment.

The client information data systems are limited because some data elements are required, whereas others are optional or ignored. In the Federal and most State child welfare information systems, recording use of alcohol or illegal substances by parents is not a required data element. Another data gap exists in the Medicaid information system, which does not require any data on substance exposure or prenatal screening results. In the current Federal information system for treatment (as well as in the proposed data elements for new treatment outcome monitoring reflected in the National Outcomes Measurement System—NOMS), information on child abuse or even the presence of children related to the parent in treatment is also not required. In both cases, some States and counties have believed this information is so critical that they have added new data fields that include these items.

Data issues in the States include the efforts they have made to monitor the prevalence of pregnant women and births impacted by alcohol and drug use. Although several States have carried out studies to determine prevalence estimates, none do so on a regular basis. Federal surveys, as discussed earlier, can provide some support for State-level estimates, but States that have done their own detailed surveys have produced more targeted information.

These data issues and information gaps make up a major part of the organizational challenge for States seeking to give SEI issues greater visibility and priority. Such issues and gaps are a challenge because what cannot be counted—or simply is not counted at present—cannot be assessed for its ultimate effectiveness and impact.

Funding

Funding is a constant constraint, but some States have begun to more creatively use multiple funding sources to support the implementation and expansion of SEI-related interventions. At the Federal level, several different funding streams exist that can be leveraged to provide services for both women and their children. These include, but are not limited to (Dennis, Young, & Gardner, in press):

- Substance Abuse Prevention and Treatment Block Grant (SAPTBG);

- Temporary Assistance to Needy Families;
- Medicaid and the Early and Periodic Screening, Diagnosis, and Treatment Program (Medicaid's child health benefit package);
- Maternal and Child Health Services Block Grant (Title V);
- Child Abuse and Neglect State Grants;
- Community-Based Child Abuse Prevention Program;
- Title IV-B—Foster Care and Title IV-E—Adoption Assistance;
- Child Welfare Services—State Grants, Title IV-B, Subpart 1;
- Promoting Safe and Stable Families, Title IV-B, Subpart 2;
- Chafee Foster Care Independence Program;
- Child Care and Development Fund and the Child Care and Developmental Block Grant;
- Individuals with Disabilities Education Act Grant Programs (Part B, Section 619—Special Education Preschool Grants and Part C—Special Education Grants for Infants and Families with Disabilities);
- Developmental Disabilities Basic Support and Advocacy Grants;
- Community Mental Health Services Block Grant; and
- Social Services Block Grant.

The National Governors Association (NGA) has documented efforts by a number of States to expand Medicaid coverage for pregnant women, including substance abuse treatment (NGA Center for Best Practices, 2004). States also can take better advantage of Medicaid to finance mental and behavioral health assessments, therapies, wraparound services, and other interventions for children who are at high risk of emotional problems because of substance abuse by one or both parents (Johnson, Knitzer, & Kaufmann, 2002).

Several of the States interviewed described using Medicaid coverage in concert with Federal SAPTBG funding to cover residential and outpatient services for mothers who have delivered SEIs, as well as for women referred from prenatal clinics. However, because SAPTBG sources represent only about 40% of the documented funding available for publicly funded treatment (and an even smaller percentage of funding for child welfare clients, given use of child welfare funding for some of these slots), a wider approach is needed than reliance on the SAPTBG as the primary target.

In addition to Federal funding, there are also resources at State and local levels, primarily in the form of State General Revenue Funds and private funding. A substantial research base documents the effectiveness of treatment programs for pregnant and parenting women in enhancing the well-being of the mother (e.g., reduced substance use and improved functioning), as well as that of the infant or child (e.g., positive birth outcomes and increased parent-child attachment). Increasingly, States are beginning to comprehend the need to upgrade their treatment programs to incorporate the lessons and findings of these evaluations.

A Washington State-based study of its prenatal programs summarized the components of a comprehensive program:

> . . . characteristics of a comprehensive program that would most likely yield positive outcomes include family-focused services, a continuum of services from pregnancy through early childhood, coordinated services, individually tailored chemical dependency treatment,

and parenting skills training and family relationship enhancement (McGee, Rinaldi, & Peterman, 2002).

Innovation continues in weaving together multiple funding sources, but each State (and, in many cases, each program) tackles these tasks on its own, without the cross-cutting authority to move funding across different streams of categorical finance. Waiver authority in child welfare programs has enabled some innovation, but has not yet affected SEI policy beyond Illinois (DHHS, 2005b; *Synthesis of Findings*).

The various agencies whose support is needed for comprehensive SEI funding may be more likely to team up on this issue when they consider that in addition to the physical, social, and emotional impacts of drug-exposed births, there are also substantial financial costs. Estimates of total lifetime costs of caring for a medically complex SEI range from $750,000–$1.4 million (Kalotra, 2002). Investing funds in prevention and early intervention services to women provides significant cost-savings opportunities to the child welfare, health care, education, and criminal justice systems.

Sample State Initiatives

Table 9 summarizes the policy initiatives that States have launched related to improving system linkages. See the narrative in the Appendix for further detail.

Table 9. Summary of State Policy Initiatives on Improving System Linkages.

	Multiagency Funding Streams	Interagency Efforts	Reporting Gaps and Data Systems
California	X	X	X
Hawaii		X	X
Illinois	X	X	X
Missouri		X	
Rhode Island	X		
South Carolina			X
Virginia		X	X
Washington		X	X

(States in italics were part of the in-depth review sample.)

SECTION 5. SUMMARY AND OPTIONS FOR POLICY CHANGES

As this review of State policy and practice has shown, State policy regarding substance-exposed infants (SEIs) is varied and evolving. The State and local models of SEI policy and practice that have been discussed are evidence of how far some States have progressed in developing responses to the SEI issue. At all five levels of intervention identified as the framework of SEI policy, States have innovated and broadened their responses to the SEI problem. They have:

- Worked in the pre-pregnancy arena of public awareness;
- Developed prenatal screening efforts;
- Addressed problems that can be identified at birth; and
- Developed specific services that address the needs of both infants and their parents in the postnatal environment.

States have also developed innovative financing approaches, and have worked in collaborative efforts with the wide array of public and private agencies whose cooperation and resources are essential to addressing the SEI problem.

At the same time, it is clear that States have not yet developed comprehensive policy that addresses the entire spectrum of the framework with strategies that have yielded positive results at each intervention point. To move toward comprehensive policy, State agencies and their respective interagency bodies are challenged with building on the achievements of specific programs, as they seek to widen the scale of efforts to solve the SEI problem. And it should be underscored again that the policy spotlight on that problem is brighter as a result of the passage of the Child Abuse Prevention and Treatment Act (CAPTA) amendments of 2003, as well as the continuing Substance Abuse and Mental Health Services Administration (SAMHSA) mandate for timely services for pregnant and parenting women.

With basic information lacking in so many areas of SEI policy, stronger information systems are fundamental to ensuring accountability for results. The foundations of current policy in each of these separate levels of policy can provide a base for expanded resources and improved results across all five levels.

Intervention Point 1. Pre-Pregnancy

Although several States have developed public education campaigns focused on pre-pregnancy messages to women of child-bearing age, a critical minority of pregnant women, especially younger women, do not appear to be influenced by the messages, based on recent data on substance use. The messages may not be widespread enough or penetrating the audience well enough to effect changes in first trimester substance use by this group of women.

The expanded messages in recent years regarding the effects of fetal alcohol exposure have resulted in overall decreases in the use of alcohol in second and third trimesters, which is encouraging. But the reported use levels of alcohol, tobacco, and illicit drugs in the first trimester and by the youngest pregnant women are both cause for concern and an ideal area for intensified prevention efforts. Ongoing efforts at both State and Federal levels to improve the targeting and effectiveness of the pre-pregnancy messages are a continuing priority within the broad array of SEI policies. In particular, Federal and university assessment of message effectiveness may help to refine the targeting and content of pre-pregnancy information campaigns.

Intervention Point 2. Prenatal Screening

Those States that have made the greatest investments over the longest periods, most notably Washington, have demonstrated that near-universal screening has been achieved and that universal prenatal screening is an achievable goal. Yet a wide range of physician behavior remains with regard to screening. No States require universal prenatal screening for substance use, and few States have screening policy that supports private physicians' efforts beyond pilot project scale. Priority status in entering treatment is given to pregnant women, in accord with Federal requirements, but referrals to treatment from prenatal screening and progress in treatment are not monitored on a statewide basis, and the total number of pregnant women entering treatment from referrals based on screening efforts is a very small percentage of total admissions. States could review their prenatal screening activities because of the very thorough efforts already under way in States such as Washington.

Intervention Point 3. Testing At Birth

States have varying policies concerning whether prenatal exposure to drugs is viewed as child abuse and neglect, which leads to wide variations in practices in hospitals and child protective services (CPS) agencies. Hospitals' policies and practices vary widely; some test and refer more extensively than others. But very few hospitals are able to annually track their total testing relative to total births, the results of their testing, or their referrals based on positive results. And no States had data systems able to capture treatment outcomes for women referred from prenatal screening, except for small groups of women in discrete projects.

Recent legislation in some States has expanded requirements for referrals when drug exposure is detected. At the time of the survey undertaken for this report in 2005–2006, this requirement appeared to be in response to concerns about increases in methamphetamine use in some States. Since that time, some increases in referrals may be due to Federal CAPTA requirements. Issues with Fetal Alcohol Spectrum Disorders have received increasing attention in some States, notably in Hawaii and Minnesota, in the form of recent State legislation and a national spotlight resulting from congressional interest. However, some State staff see the detection of Fetal Alcohol Syndrome as a problem, as noted previously in discussing Virginia's 2002 report on SEIs. It pointed out that drug exposure is easier to detect than alcohol exposure.

Intervention Points 4 and 5. Postnatal Services for Infants, Children, and Parents

Since most drug exposure is not detected prenatally or at birth, postnatal services for both parents and children are important, regardless of how clients come to the attention of the several systems in which these services may be provided.

Opportunities for Advancing Policy: State Self- Assessments

At all five intervention levels, the policy question that States must address is whether the current array of services available to children and families—screening, admissions to treatment, family support for parents, and screening and services for children—is an appropriate response to the potential effects of drug exposure. Each State needs to weigh the adequacy of its response to both parents and children, from the percentages of pregnant women entering treatment to the very low percentages of children entering the caseloads of agencies that respond to developmental disabilities.

There is no "right level" of services; each State needs to assess needs and responses to the problems of these parents and children, along with competing needs and resources. But the overall level of these services is low. This finding suggests that most States may not assess the very high potential for later financial and human costs in sufficient depth. Such an assessment might ensure an adequate response to the problems that led to the passage of the CAPTA amendments in the first place—as well as the Federal treatment priority for pregnant and parenting women.

It would not be appropriate to assess current policy against an ideal standard or a level of service that met all need. But it is fair, and necessary, to assess current programs against current policy. The two clearest expressions of that policy are contained in the CAPTA amendments and the SAM HSA priority for treatment for pregnant and parenting women. Neither of those policies specifies a required level of services or admissions, but both set a standard that encourages States to annually review how these overlapping groups of parents and children are faring in treatment agencies and child-serving systems. States could undertake such a review by using the five-level framework to inventory current efforts at all five levels, by comparing their efforts with similar States, and by determining appropriate outcomes that would enable measuring progress against the State's own baselines. Although no States were found that are currently undertaking these tasks in a comprehensive manner, the progress made in several of these States provides a strong foundation for linking the initiatives under way at each level of the framework.

States have shown in each of the five levels that substantial progress can be made in responding to these policy and programmatic challenges. Getting started with a broad review of where the State is at all levels could involve at least four steps:

- Conducting an inventory of current statewide and community efforts that address each of the levels, with the inventory ideally including data on funding streams, level of funding, number of clients, and current results as measured by the agency or program;
- Comparing the State's outcomes and resources to those of similar States;
- Collecting data on current levels of need, demand, and treatment capacity relevant to the population affected by the CAPTA and SAMHSA mandates:
  - Need assessment should include a compilation of all available data on prevalence of SEIs;
  - Demand assessment should include a review of the effectiveness of special efforts to engage pregnant and parenting women in the treatment population;

- Capacity assessment should include State versions of National Survey of Substance Abuse Treatment Services (N-SSATS) data on facilities' capacity to respond to the needs of children as well as to those of their parents. These data would compare admissions to treatment against the current capacity of the system to provide treatment services that build on the principles of family-centered treatment; and
- Considering supporting interagency councils with broad membership and the authorization to collect data across systems. These councils could develop strategic plans for SEI policy that include annual review of progress in meeting goals developed on an interagency basis. Interagency councils would help States and communities that are trying to link multiple funding sources for SEI programs to review and spotlight the models of those sites that have done the best job in achieving multifunded projects (Dennis, Young, & Gardner, in press).

CONCLUSION

Existing policies, strategies, and activities that compose the national response to the problem of prenatal substance exposure are considerably stronger than they were in the late 1980s and early 1990s when the cocaine epidemic was at its peak. But if these tools are still used in fragmented ways in small-scale programs, States and communities may be missing the opportunity to increase the impact of policy on the SEI problem. The nature of the SEI problem requires close ties across the boundaries of public and private systems serving children and their families. To measure the effectiveness of those ties, it is necessary to have robust information systems and a willingness to use those systems to support accountability in achieving interagency missions. The SEI problem also requires greater attention to the gaps between policy as it is stated and policy as it is actually carried out at State and local levels.

The States reviewed in this report have shown that SEI policy can be made effective, and that it can be taken to scale. Now it must also be shown that policy can be coherent, connecting previously separate activities in a continuum of better-linked programs serving children and parents affected by substance use disorders as they move through developmental milestones at the several possible points of intervention. From better-linked programs can come more effective policy and better outcomes for those children and families, and that is the task that lies ahead.

APPENDIX: SAMPLE STATE INITIATIVES

I. Pre-Pregnancy

- As of January 1, 2005, 22 States had enacted policies requiring mandatory warning signs about alcohol use during pregnancy at the point of sale (e.g., bars, restaurants, and other licensed establishments that sell alcohol). Two of these States also require physicians and/or other health care providers to post such warnings, and three States require that warnings be posted in languages in addition to English.[1]

- *Missouri* has enacted two laws. One requires that warning signs about the harmful effects of alcohol use during pregnancy be displayed at retail establishments selling alcohol. The other mandates physicians to advise their patients (verbally and by providing written materials) about the effects of prenatal use of tobacco, alcohol, and controlled substances (DHHS, SAM HSA, n.d.).
- In compliance with the Drug-Free Schools and Communities Act, the University of Massachusetts Alcohol and Drug Policy addresses the hazards of parental substance use by providing this warning message to all students: "Mothers who drink alcohol during pregnancy may give birth to infants with fetal alcohol syndrome. These infants have irreversible physical abnormalities and mental retardation. In addition, research indicates that children of alcoholic parents are at greater risk than others of becoming alcoholics (University of Massachusetts, 2002).
- Since 1995, the Minnesota Department of Health (MDH) has developed and disseminated several public awareness campaigns to reduce the risks associated with drinking during pregnancy (MDH, n.d.). The overall goal is to educate all Minnesotans that "There is no known safe level, time, or type of alcohol to use during pregnancy" (interview on March 21, 2005).
- Statewide campaigns in Minnesota in 1995 and 1998 distributed information to the general public through radio and television ads, print materials, and poster placement in restaurants and bars and on buses. Post-campaign survey findings found that Minnesotans' understanding of the adverse effects from prenatal alcohol exposure improved (interview on March 21, 2005).
- In 2003, MDH launched a Fetal Alcohol Syndrome (FAS) prevention media campaign specifically designed for populations of color. The campaign focused on urban and rural African-American, Latino, and American Indian women of child-bearing age, as well as their partners, family, and friends, and health and social service providers. In addition to broadcast ads, print materials, and posters, the campaign included pocket cards with tips and resources, tip sheets to encourage providers to ask about alcohol use and refer women to assessment and treatment services, a mailing of campaign materials to 4,000 providers, a toll-free telephone line for the public and providers, and a Website portal page (interview on March 21, 2005).
- California has both statewide and local/regional efforts under way to educate women and the general public about the risks of substance use during pregnancy. At the State level, California established a Mass Media Communications Account for public education on subjects that include the prevention of tobacco, alcohol, and drug use by pregnant women (California Health and Safety Code Section 130100-130155, 2007). This large-scale media effort is funded by 6% of the California Children and Families Trust Fund. The Trust Fund includes all revenue—an estimated $700 million annually—generated by Proposition 10, a publicly supported cigarette and tobacco tax to provide early intervention services to children ages 0–5. See http://www.ccfc.ca.gov/press/prop.asp
- At the local/regional level, the University of California, Los Angeles (UCLA) is one of three sites receiving funding from the Federal Centers for Disease Control and Prevention (CDC) to refine and test pre-pregnancy substance abuse prevention

messages. (The other two sites are St. Louis University and the University of Iowa.) UCLA is evaluating a social marketing campaign using a "narrowcasting approach"—i.e., directed to a highly specific segment of the public—that warns women about the dangers of drinking alcohol during pregnancy. The purpose of the project is to change norms and perceptions of women who are light or moderate drinkers both before and during pregnancy. Print materials have been developed and disseminated, saturating specific neighborhoods in two Southern California communities over a 12-month period; a third community serves as a comparison group (CDC, n.d.)

- Four of the 10 States were surveyed through interviews (California, 2004 and 2005; Hawaii, September 19, 2005; Maryland, February 10, 2005; and Minnesota, March 21, 2005). These States said that they currently had pre-pregnancy public education efforts under way. These various public education efforts are occurring at both statewide and local/regional levels; and States may include public awareness as one component of a broader maternal and child health strategy, such as Kentucky's Early Childhood Initiative. Others focus on a single facet of substance abuse, such as Maryland's FAS efforts.

II. Pregnancy and the Prenatal Period

- *Virginia* passed legislation more than 10 years ago that requires all licensed prenatal care providers to screen all pregnant women for substance use. The State subsequently developed a perinatal substance use guide for health care providers (Virginia Department of Health, 2003). However, a 2004 survey of perinatal providers in Virginia indicated that only 35% screen for substance use (Virginia Department of Health & Department of Mental Health, Mental Retardation and Substance Abuse Services, 2004; *Perinatal Practice Survey Regarding HIV and Substance Use in Childbearing Age Women*).
- Other States, including *Washington*, encourage and explicitly highlight the benefits of universal screening in their guidelines for health care providers (Washington State Department of Health, 2002), but are still seeking to expand the impact of these policies.
- *Kentucky* uses a hybrid *4P's Plus*© that includes questions about intimate partner violence, and their obstetrical/gynecological staff are extensively trained to ensure that they are qualified to make referrals and develop a safety plan when needed (Kentucky Medical Association, n.d.).
- *Massachusetts's* Alcohol Screening Assessment in Pregnancy program (Kennedy, Finkelstein, Hutchins, & Mahoney, 2004) also uses a modified *4P's Plus*©. A positive response to any of the interview questions triggers a brief intervention developed as the modification of a model created by the National Institute on Alcohol Abuse and Alcoholism. Currently, however, overall data on the total number of pregnant women screened and on the number of positive results are not compiled (interview on September 14, 2005).

- Of the 10 States surveyed, *Washington* provides the fullest implementation of statewide prenatal screening. In addition to developing and issuing prenatal screening guidelines (as required by State legislation), Washington also operates two broadly based intervention programs for women and children affected by substance use disorders (interview on January 18, 2005).
- At the local level, some cities and counties have invested resources in prenatal screening programs. A number of California counties have adopted the Screening, Assessment, Referral, and Treatment (SART) mode, using Proposition 10 tobacco tax funding dedicated to early childhood programs. SART, developed by Children's Research Triangle in Chicago, is a comprehensive prenatal screening approach that involves:
  1. Raising public awareness about the consequences of substance use during pregnancy;
  2. Creating a multidisciplinary team;
  3. Developing an action plan;
  4. Building public support; and
  5. Motivating and assisting health care providers in screening pregnant women for substance use.

  Follow-up takes place at two levels: (1) when mothers are initially referred to treatment services; and (2) in the "Pediatric SART" program, which is a second set of linked interventions that focus on continuing screening and developmental services to children affected by parental substance abuse (McGourty & Chasnoff, 2003).
- To further expand treatment capacity for pregnant and parenting women, *California* has allocated State General Funds in amounts well above the required Federal Substance Abuse Prevention and Treatment Block Grant (SAPTBG) women's set-aside for pregnant and parenting women. Further, California has allocated additional amounts of Temporary Assistance for Needy Families (TAN F) funding for women with substance use disorders involved in the TANF system. In accord with the Federal SAPTBG requirements, pregnant women who are not able to enter treatment within 48 hours must be provided interim services (Center for Substance Abuse Treatment, 2007).

  In California's Perinatal Services Network Guidelines (California Department of Alcohol and Drug Programs, 2004), interim services are defined as:
  1. Human immunodeficiency virus and tuberculosis education and counseling and referrals for testing;
  2. Referrals for prenatal care;
  3. Education on the effects of alcohol and drug use on the fetus; and
  4. Referrals based on individual assessments that may include, but are not limited to, self- help recovery groups; pre-recovery and treatment support groups; housing, food, and legal aid support; case management; children's services; medical services; and TANF/Medi-Cal services.
- In *Minnesota*, the Circle of Women Project, modeled after Seattle's Fetal Alcohol Syndrome- Birth to 3 Project, provides intensive in-home visitation and advocacy services for women who are engaging in heavy alcohol and/or drug use during

pregnancy and have no involvement with other community services. The Circle of Women Project provides services for the pregnant women and their children for 3 years. The Minnesota Department of Human Services funds two sites for the Circle of Women Project, one serving women in Minneapolis and one serving women of the Leech Lake Reservation in Cass County (interview on March 21, 2005).

III. Time of Birth

- In *Massachusetts*, testing policy is stated as follows: "Neonates will be administered toxicology screens upon delivery, with the permission of the mother, if: 1) maternal alcohol or other drug use has been revealed to obstetrical staff during prenatal visits and noted on the obstetric 'problem list'; or, 2) maternal behavior raises concern amongst prenatal staff (many missed appointments, late prenatal care, etc.); or, 3) pre-term delivery or early abruption" (interview on September 14, 2005).
- In *Washington*, new legislation resulted from a child death related to substance abuse. Under this legislation, women testing positive for drugs would be assessed for other risk factors, such as single parent status, no prenatal visits in first trimester, and so on, and referred to early intervention programs, with higher-risk cases opened for child protective services (CPS) investigation (interview on January 18, 2005). Legislation has passed in Colorado that addresses similar issues (Washington State Fetal Alcohol Syndrome Interagency Work Group [FASIAWG], 2007).
- In *Colorado*, new legislation allows a newborn's testing positive for controlled substances to be considered evidence of child neglect (Child Welfare Information Gateway, 2007). The original draft of the bill would have allowed for termination of parental rights if an infant tested positive for controlled substances. Prior practice would have required the case to enter and proceed through the child welfare system's regular investigation and assessment processes (Colorado Department of Public Health and Environment, 2006).
- In *Arkansas*, statewide associations of physicians supported a bill redefining neglect. The bill requires babies born exposed to illegal drugs or with health problems resulting from the mother's use of an illegal drug during pregnancy to be reported to the State for child neglect (Thompson, 2005). A test of the mother's or child's bodily fluids or bodily substances may be used as evidence to establish neglect. The bill was intended to protect doctors who report babies affected by prenatal exposure from liability for violating patient confidentiality. New Arkansas legislation also requires the child welfare agency to develop and maintain statewide statistics of the incidents of neglect reported or investigated and to make annual reports of those incidents.
- *Louisiana*'s legislature in 2005 expanded the definition of child neglect to include prenatal substance abuse. Health care providers are required to report to the State when a newborn is affected by prenatal drug use (Child Welfare Information Gateway, 2007a).
- *Nevada* enacted a measure in 2005 that will amend the State's child abuse statutes. The measure will require health professionals and anyone who reasonably believes an infant has been harmed to report to the State when an infant shows signs of

withdrawal or indications of prenatal substance abuse. The measure also will establish that prenatal substance abuse *may* be a reason to remove the infant from the parent (Child Welfare Information Gateway, 2007a).
- At least two States (*California and Virginia*) have required the development of prenatal substance exposure protocols in hospitals. In California, Senate Bill (SB) 2669 was enacted in 1990, requiring the "health and welfare agency to develop needs assessment protocol for pregnant and postpartum substance abusing women and a review of referral systems." Virginia's House Bill 813, enacted in 1992, requires the "State secretary of health to develop treatment protocols and prenatal care providers to adopt screening protocols for substance abusing pregnant women; requires providers to inform patients about the effects of drug use on the fetus and to refer pregnant substance abusers to appropriate care." But in neither State has this provision led to systematic patterns of reporting or hospital practice, as indicated by studies in both States (Albert, Klein, Noble, Zahand, & Holtby, 2000; Zellman, Fair, Houbé, & Wong, 2002; Virginia State interviews). Virginia is currently assessing the effectiveness of these provisions. The State is also reviewing information systems intended to capture data on how widely these systems are implemented.
- An assessment of *California's* SB 2669 legislation that encouraged hospitals to develop screening protocols with a detailed description of an ideal health assessment process concluded that the legislation was not enforced, and as a result, hospitals' practices varied widely (Albert et al., 2000). Further interviews suggested that policy varied from doctor to doctor and from one nurse or hospital social worker to another (Simmes, 2004). A 2002 assessment of perinatal programs in 31 of California's 58 counties concluded that protocols are routinely implemented in only one-third of the hospitals in these counties (Aved, 2002, p. 30).
- *Illinois* legislation requires a CPS referral to local prenatal care providers, the development of a case management plan, a requirement that treatment be provided to any pregnant woman referred through this network, and monitoring by the prenatal provider of the woman's progress in treatment (Child Welfare Information Gateway, 2007b).
- In *Maine*, new legislation in 2004 developed in response to Child Abuse and Prevention Treatment Act (CAPTA) requires the State to act to protect newborns identified as affected by illegal substance abuse or suffering from withdrawal symptoms resulting from prenatal drug exposure, *whether or not the prenatal exposure was to legal or illegal drugs,* and regardless of whether or not the infant is abused or neglected. The State agency is required to receive reports, investigate, determine whether the infant is affected, determine whether the infant is abused or neglected, and develop a plan for safe care (Child Welfare Information Gateway, 2007a, 2007b).

IV. Postnatal Services for Infants, Children, and Parents

- *Maryland* is addressing the requirements of the CAPTA legislation through statewide policies and procedures implemented by its local departments of social services

(LDSSs). Hospital social workers refer drug-exposed newborns considered to be at high risk for abuse and neglect to the local department's Child Protective Services screening unit, and the referral is accompanied by the Drug-Exposed Newborn Reporting Form. The reporting form provides a uniform and consistent format to document risk and safety factors as identified by hospital staff. All Maryland hospitals have been provided with the Drug-Exposed Newborn Risk Matrix to assist hospital staff in making comprehensive assessments of the risk and protective factors in a family. However, staff report that there still is considerable variation among physicians and hospitals regarding whom to screen and when to screen.

Each local department identified a Drug-Exposed Newborn Care Plan Coordinator within child welfare to form a team of experienced staff to work with these families. This team collaborates with staff from partnering agencies and meets on a regular basis to update the status of referrals and to coordinate services for the newborns, the mothers, and families. The group also identifies resources, barriers to care, and gaps in services.

- The Heller School for Social Policy and Management developed the *Massachusetts Early Childhood Linkage Initiative*. By establishing a strong relationship between the Department of Social Services, which focuses on family investigations of child abuse and neglect, and the Department of Public Health, which ensures developmental evaluations for children, MECLI aims to enhance and expand early intervention services for at-risk children (Heller School for Social Policy and Management, n.d.). Under the program, the child welfare system refers all children younger than 3 with a recently opened case to receive support services through early intervention systems designated under Part C of the Individuals with Disabilities Education Act (IDEA) (ZERO TO THREE Policy Center, 2004). MECLI program goals include expanding service integration, increasing State capacity to offer early intervention services, and advocating for policy change.
- *Colorado* has done a more detailed assessment of likely caseload increases than most States. The data compiled indicated that in a sample of children in the child welfare caseload in one county, 12.2% were presumptively eligible for Part C services under IDEA, but only 16.9% of those children were actually enrolled (113 of 668 eligible). Of the entire State child welfare population, only 4.8% were enrolled in Part C; through extensive Child Find efforts, this percentage was raised to 7.9% (Robinson & Rosenberg, 2004).
- *Wisconsin* has also developed a detailed procedure for a plan of safe care for drug-exposed infants. CPS will accept reports of an infant identified at birth as having controlled substances or controlled substance analogs in his or her system and will assess the safety of the infant. CPS will develop a plan of care that reduces risk to the child and supports a safe environment, either an agency-managed safety plan or a referral to appropriate preventive community services. Or CPS will determine that the family has in place a plan of safe care for the infant. After a referral is accepted for assessment, information on family functioning, parenting practices, home environment, and individual child and parent functioning is used to assess and document safety in the Wisconsin version of the federally mandated child welfare client tracking system (Wisconsin Department of Health and Family Services, 2004).

- Blank Children's Hospital (Child Abuse Program) in *Des Moines, Iowa,* emphasizes the importance of implementing a postnatal plan of care for substance-exposed infants (SEIs) (Shah, 2000). The plan focuses on providing developmentally sensitive and age-appropriate interventions for these infants. It also emphasizes early recognition of potential developmental challenges and obtaining specialized care to facilitate improved health outcomes. The care plan is delineated into three categories based on the infant's age.

  During 0–6 months, the care plan stresses providing appropriate sensory stimulation for neuromotor development; creating opportunities for bonding and attachment through physical, visual, and verbal interaction; and responding appropriately to potential stress and anxiety. From 6 months–2 years, substance-exposed children typically enter a dormant phase in which they are symptom-free. Children 3 years and older have a greater risk of having school-related problems such as being able to stay on task, maintain focus, and manage emotions. Successful implementation of this developmental care plan requires careful collaboration of parents, health care professionals, early childhood educators, and community support.
- *California* has invested in residential treatment programs for pregnant and parenting women with its own general funds, a major portion of its TANF services funding, and a new tobacco tax dedicated to 0–5 early childhood programs. Yet, waiting lists for residential care for women with their infants remain significant. A 2002 survey indicated that in the 31 counties responding, the average waiting time for treatment for 81% of pregnant and parenting clients was "less than 1 month" to 3–6 months; only 19% of clients with children living with them had immediate access to treatment (i.e., no wait time). For those who entered treatment without their children, only 31% had no wait time (Aved, 2002).
- In Illinois, the Department of Children and Family Services (DCFS) and the Department of Alcoholism and Substance Abuse developed the Project SAFE model in response to the problem of substance-abusing mothers showing a substantiated history of child abuse and neglect (Lighthouse Institute, n.d.). Project SAFE is linked with a sister program that provides enhanced services, including case management and early intervention under the heading of the Family Intervention Substance Abuse Treatment (FIRST) program. FIRST allocates funds for both enhanced services and Project SAFE and is specifically designed for children identified as SEI.

  In 1986, Project SAFE was initially piloted in four diverse communities. Currently, nineteen programs operate throughout the State, and have served approximately 5,700 women. Recent trends concerning the children in the program indicate a rise in the number of referrals for drug-exposed infants and children and identification of emotional and/or behavioral disabilities. In order to address the negative effects of substance-abusing women and their children, Project SAFE provides a wide range of support services including intensive outreach and advocacy, comprehensive case management, residential and outpatient substance abuse treatment involving a clinical services component, onsite and offsite day care, in-depth parent training developed by DCFS, linkage with critical support groups, and aftercare programs. Program findings showed that outreach workers serve as a key program ingredient that motivates substance-abusing women to enroll in treatment because of their ability to engage, support, and connect with the women (Lighthouse Institute, n.d.).

Project SAFE promotes positive, healthy family functioning by offering direct treatment services for chemical dependency in addition to addressing the multiple barriers that impede the fragile recovery process.
- Since 2001, Rhode Island's Vulnerable Infants Program (VIP) has provided services to drug- exposed infants, serving 150 babies and their parents annually. As summarized by Dr. Barry Lester of Brown University:

> A special Family Treatment Drug Court designed specifically for the families of drug-exposed infants has been established for VIP clients based on the "treatment with teeth" concept. The program allows mothers the opportunity to get the appropriate treatment to be reunited with their infants and to provide the kinds of ancillary services including mental health, to make reunification effective and facilitate the development of the mother-infant attachment relationship. In this voluntary program, the VIP treatment plan is court ordered and sanctions are used for noncompliance, the ultimate sanction, of course, being loss of custody of the infant. (Lester, 2000)

> With VIP, mothers get more comprehensive services including drug treatment, mental health treatment, and parent training. The mothers have shown a significant reduction in mental health symptoms. Fathers participate, and services are also provided for other children in the family. A VIP liaison with the State Early Intervention Program ensures that these drug-exposed infants receive early intervention services. Permanency within 1 year has been achieved for 62% of the children in keeping with the Adoption and Safe Families Act guidelines (Lester & Jeremiah, 2003).

> Procedure in this hospital, one of the largest birthing hospitals in Rhode Island, relies significantly on the professional judgment of care providers. Reporting is described as "mandated" if a positive toxicological screen exists and the judgment of the professional is that a report is necessary; interviewees agreed that different professionals could interpret this discretion differently. If the mother reported having used substances at any point during her pregnancy, but no toxicological test was done, then reporting is left to the judgment of the professional.

- At the local level, in *St. Louis, Missouri,* the Linkages program was developed by the Missouri Division of Family Services and Catholic Community Services to offer support to mothers of drug-exposed infants (Loman & Sherburne, 2000). Funded by Prevent Child Abuse Missouri (the Missouri Chapter of the National Committee to Prevent Child Abuse), the program provides home visitation from birth–2 years for mothers and their infants. Home visitors are paraprofessionals who identify needs and provide referrals for housing, food, transportation, financial assistance, and enrollment in substance abuse treatment programs. Services are also provided by the Department of Family Services (DFS) on an ongoing basis.

Mothers participating in the Linkages program reside in St. Louis and are identified as high- risk candidates by a statewide infant reporting system. The referral process begins when hospitals screen for risk levels by testing the newborns for the presence of drugs and alcohol in their system. Hospitals will report all instances of prenatal substance exposure to the Missouri Child Abuse and Neglect Reporting Unit. The reports are subsequently sent to DFS, which is responsible for follow-up on these high-risk mothers and infants. The DFS worker interviews mothers to assess the situation and determine whether court involvement, child removal, or additional services are necessary. Since the program accepts only cases in which the infant remains in the home with the mother, DFS refers cases that meet this eligibility criterion.

- In 1997, the Sobriety Treatment and Recovery Teams (START) program was developed and implemented as a response to the dramatic increase of referrals resulting from substance- abusing parents in *Cuyahoga County, Ohio*. In fact, 75% of all child welfare intakes involved drug abuse as a contributing factor (Kinney, 2001). The program views addiction as a disease rather than a lifestyle choice involving potential relapse and varied levels of support services to abstain from drugs. The initial focus of START revolves around treating the parents' addiction upon thorough assessment. After the intake is complete, drug treatment is accessible within 72 hours. The program adheres to a team decision-making process, ensuring regular communication with the parents and other support services. An important program goal is to assist parents in overcoming their substance abuse addiction through a collaboration of partners, which include health care providers, drug treatment centers, housing assistance, family, friends, and the surrounding community.

START accepts women, 150 per treatment group, who gave birth to babies at one of five hospitals located in Cuyahoga County, Ohio (Kinney, 2001). To be eligible, the women must have had a positive drug screen. For staffing, START comprises 10 teams who are managed by two supervisors. An advocate and child welfare social worker is assigned to each team, overseeing a caseload of fifteen families. Since most advocates have been in recovery for a minimum of 2 years, they are able to empathize with the obstacles and hardships associated with achieving abstinence. Advocates and social workers also make referrals to the drug treatment centers, physically escorting the mothers to their first three appointments. This approach directly links the mother and provider, helping to facilitate a positive relationship. Beyond escorting the mothers, START teams continue to follow up and consult with the treatment providers on a regular basis to monitor progress.

- Under the jurisdiction of Judge Leonard Edwards, former President of the U.S. National Council of Juvenile and Family Court Judges, *Santa Clara County, California,* established one of the first Family Treatment Drug Courts in 1998 (National Abandoned Infants Assistance [AIA] Resource Center, 2005). As a result of Judge Edwards' request, the *Celebrating Families!* Program (CFP) commenced in 2002 to help recovering families acquire the basic knowledge and skills for effective parenting while offering support services to their children. Funded by a grant from the Substance Abuse and Mental Health Services Administration, CFP's main goal is to "foster the development of whole, fulfilled, addiction-free individuals by increasing resiliency factors and decreasing risk factors in participants' lives" (National AIA Resource Center, 2005). Overall curriculum objectives include breaking the cycle of addiction and decreasing participants' use of alcohol and other drugs through educating families about chemical dependency and healthy life skills.

CFP's unique curriculum is based on current research regarding brain chemistry, risk and resiliency factors, asset development, life skills education, and community service. The model consists of 15 weekly, 90-minute sessions, followed by a structured family activity. Examples of session topics include goal setting, feelings-defenses, anger management, chemical dependency as a disease, and healthy boundaries. The curriculum incorporates interactive and experiential learning that is individually tailored for substance-abusing parents and their children. Evaluation results from a study conducted on the Drug Court and CFP's effectiveness revealed a decrease in the length of time children are in the Child Welfare System (CWS) to 6–12 months, compared with 13–18 months in Drug Court without participating in the program. Family reunification rates for Drug Court and CFP were 72%, compared with 37% in CWS without CFP services (Quittan, 2004). This program is currently offered at three test sites in California. Other community-based sites in New Jersey, New York, and Idaho are replicating the program model.

V. Improving System Linkages

Multiagency funding streams

The States that have been most active in SEI policy have been able to tap multiple funding sources. For example:

- *Illinois* uses Federal SAPTBG funding, Title IV-E Child Welfare funding, Medicaid, Maternal and Child Health (Title V) funding for outreach, and general funds for its SEI programs. Other interviewees from the 10 States indicated that some of these sources had been used, as well as TANF funding for screening pregnant women in the TANF program and for residential treatment for eligible women, Part C Early Intervention funding, funding from CDC for fetal alcohol screening and treatment, and adult and dependency drug court funding for the portion of drug court populations that include parents of SEIs (interview on September 14, 2005).
- *California* uses funding from its statewide Proposition 10 tobacco tax funds for county-level prenatal screening in seven counties. See http://www.ccfc.ca.gov/press/prop.asp
- In *Rhode Island*, skillful negotiation, and a leadership position taken by the insurance industry, appears to have succeeded in allowing private insurance coverage of many of the women in the *Project LINK* program (interview on March 10, 2005).

Interagency efforts

- *Virginia*, which has an especially decentralized service delivery system, has statewide interagency efforts in place as well as links with local Community Service Boards (CSBs) that address treatment issues and local child welfare services. Some of these local entities have worked together to serve hospital-referred postpartum substance-using women and their infants. In 1998, legislation required that annual reports be made of SEI totals; the final report was submitted in 2002. In 2002, the CSBs were awarded funds to support education and collaboration efforts with local hospitals, community medical providers, and child welfare offices regarding perinatal substance use and the SEI legislation. At the statewide level, in response to its 2001 study of a sample of cases, Virginia State agencies formed an interagency work group to assess implementation of this legislation, including the Departments of Health, Social Services, and Mental Health, Mental Retardation and Substance Abuse Services (interview on March 23, 2005).

- *Hawaii's* 22-member statewide interdepartmental council began in 1991 and addresses perinatal issues through five different programs, including Baby S.A.F.E. (Substance Abuse Free Environment). This council works closely with the Healthy Mothers, Healthy Babies program, which operates and provides oversight for several perinatal initiatives, including the Baby S.A.F.E. program (interview on September 19, 2005).
- An *Illinois* law established the Committee on Women's Alcohol and Substance Abuse Treatment of the Illinois Advisory Council on Alcoholism and Other Drug Dependency in 1997. This committee addresses women's treatment and provides for child care for women in treatment (interview on September 14, 2005).
- *California* has a county-based system of perinatal councils that began in 1991. As with many of the perinatally oriented bodies, they address a wide range of issues, including SEI topics (interview in 2004 and 2005).
- In 1995, *Washington* passed legislation requiring the formation of a Fetal Alcohol Syndrome Interagency Work Group (FASIAWG). The legislation charged the Department of Social and Health Services, the Office of Superintendent of Public Instruction, the Department of Health, and the Department of Corrections to devise an agreement as a way of coordinating the many programs that target children born exposed to alcohol and women at risk of giving birth to children exposed to alcohol (Washington State FASIAWG, 2007). FASIAWG also included representatives from several agency and advocacy groups that play an integral part in the planning, expansion, administration, and review process. FASIAWG members recommend further exploration and implementation in three general areas: (1) providing services for children and adults with Fetal Alcohol Syndrome Disorders (FASD) by institutionalizing a "no wrong door" approach; (2) providing FASD education and training to professionals and to parents of children with FASD; and (3) supporting public agencies, professional and educational organizations, and family-run advocacy groups that will enable them to provide effective services and programs (Washington State FASIAWG, 2007). Washington also has a senior-level steering committee on substance abuse and child welfare. And interviewees believed that discussions about possible consolidation of prenatal programs and the new urgency given to links between substance abuse and child welfare were leading to consideration of expanding SEI efforts to a broader scale. (This new urgency is as a result of recent court orders and Child and Family Services Review follow- up.)
- For more than 15 years, *Kansas City, Missouri,* has worked through a Metropolitan Task Force on Drug Exposed Infants to address the numerous issues resulting from SEIs. Key topics of concern focus on lack of followthrough within the medical community, varying interpretations of child protection laws, the role of the community in the family's case management, and the State's function regarding supervision and custody (Missouri Metropolitan Task Force on Drug Exposed Infants, 2003; *Fact Sheet*). Physicians and health care providers, social workers and

child protection personnel, early childhood educators and professionals, court staff, and substance abuse treatment providers joined efforts to address obstacles preventing mothers from receiving treatment and ensuring that the necessary safeguards are in place for SEIs. In 1990, eight prosecutors representing city, county, State, and Federal levels signed an agreement to refrain from indicting substance-abusing pregnant women if they agreed to participate in drug treatment. SB 190 was signed into law in June 1991, requiring health care providers to educate and counsel all pregnant women about the effects of substance use during pregnancy. It also identifies pregnant women as a priority in receiving drug treatment. In 1992, SB 90 was enacted designating the Missouri Department of Health as the local Disciplinary Team. Recently, the Task Force has helped to coordinate family drug court activities with treatment efforts (Missouri Metropolitan Task Force on Drug Exposed Infants, 2003; *Fact Sheet*).

Reporting gaps and data systems

- In *Washington*, the treatment system attaches a code to cases referred by CPS, so there is a record of those referrals coming *into* treatment. However, there is no total of prenatal or hospital screenings, the results of those screenings, or referrals to treatment made *from* the CPS side, so that the gaps between referrals and enrollment could be assessed over time (Washington State FASIAWG, 2007).
- In *Virginia*, a statewide total of 278 referrals during 2000–2001 was cited in a 2002 report, but no annual totals of substance-exposed births (SEBs) are currently collected (interview on March 23, 2005).
- *California* reports the total number of women treated in the statewide perinatal programs, but not the number of referrals received by treatment agencies from hospitals or CPS agencies (interviews in 2004 and 2005).
- *Illinois,* as cited previously, reported 1,060 substantiated SEBs in 2003–2004 (interview on September 14, 2005).
- *Washington* is a good example of a State that does do follow-up on both parent recovery and child outcomes with mothers and babies in the Safe Babies, Safe Moms program until the children are 3 years old (interview on January 18, 2005; Washington State FASIAWG, 2007).
- In response to the growing public concern on the issue of cocaine-exposed infants in the early 1990s, *California* conducted a statewide perinatal prevalence study of alcohol and drug use. In 1992, the Department of Alcohol and Drug Program's Office of Perinatal Substance Abuse funded this study in an attempt to develop better estimates of SEBs, focusing on maternal substance use documented at the time of delivery. Anonymous urine samples were obtained at the time of birth from 29,494 pregnant women throughout 202 maternity hospitals in California. Significant findings were that 69,000 (11.35%) infants were born to mothers who had consumed alcohol and/or drugs and that 41,000 (6.72%) infants were born to mothers abusing alcohol within hours or a few days before delivery. On the basis of self-report, 53,000 (8.82%) infants were born to mothers who used tobacco preceding delivery (Vega, Kolody, Hwang, & Noble, 1993).

These numbers are viewed as conservative since they specifically measured alcohol and drug use at time of delivery that would indicate substance use in a range of 24–72 hours prior to birth. Thus, this study (and any study focused on testing at birth) fails to capture statistics on women who used substances throughout the duration of their pregnancy, but not just prior to birth. It also does not capture use during the first trimester before pregnancy is verified. Although this study provides critical population estimates of substance use at an isolated point in time, it does not provide comprehensive data measuring the extent of SEIs.

- Negotiations in *Monterey County, California,* between the county public health staff and local hospitals recently reached an agreement to update the statewide perinatal prevalence study of alcohol and drug use for the county's three birthing hospitals. Replication of this survey is currently under way, using the county's Proposition 10 (tobacco tax) funding and based on extensive negotiations with the birthing hospitals around privacy and Health Insurance Portability and Accountability Act of 1996 issues. A second California county is committed to replicating the Monterey survey in 2006, based on a 2005 report on SEI issues in that county (interviews in 2004 and 2005).

- In 1996, *Hawaii's* Alcohol Drug Abuse Division conducted a blind screening across Maui, Kauai, Hawaii, and Honolulu counties in order to accurately assess the prevalence of substance use and treatment needs for women of child-bearing age. Data measuring substance use were extrapolated through an anonymous questionnaire and coded urine samples from pregnant women. Study findings showed that 12.7% of the women tested positive for illicit drugs (testing was only for major illicit drugs). Given the sample of pregnant women, 3.5% of those tested met *Diagnostic and Statistical Manual of Mental Disorders,* third edition, revised, diagnostic criteria for alcohol dependency, and 3.9% met criteria for marijuana dependence (Hawaii Department of Health, 1996). Utilizing both urine toxicologies and questionnaires enabled data to be collected on recent use as well as frequency, prior treatment history, and other critical information.

- In 1991, *South Carolina's* State Council on Maternal, Infant and Child Health authorized a substance abuse prevalence study among pregnant women. Results indicated that 12.1% of delivering women used alcohol or drugs based on urine testing which detects more recent use and 22.4% used alcohol or drugs based on meconium testing, which detects more longterm use. The rate based on both testing methods combined was 25.8%. The study measured substance use toward the latter stage of pregnancy, thus potentially omitting data on early and middle stages. In contrast with these numbers, which would result in a range of 14,000 SEBs if the 1991 levels remain accurate, South Carolina indicated that there were 207 reports of drug-impaired infants in 2000 and 163 reports of drug-impaired infants in 2004. Contacts in the State suggested that there may be a problem with under-reporting, due to the increasing numbers of pregnant women giving birth with midwives (South Carolina Department of Health and Environmental Control, 1991).

REFERENCES

[1] Abel, E. L. & Kruger, M. (2002). Physician attitudes concerning legal coercion of pregnant alcohol and drug abusers. *American Journal of Obstetrics and Gynecology, 186(4)*, 768–772.

[2] Alan Guttmacher Institute. (2005, December 1). State policies in brief: Substance abuse during pregnancy. Washington, DC: Author.

[3] Alan Guttmacher Institute. (2007, September 1). State policies in brief: Substance abuse during pregnancy. Washington, DC. Retrieved November 30, 2007, from http://www.guttmacher.org/statecenter/spibs/spib_SADP.pdf.

[4] Albert, V., Klein, D., Noble, A., Zahand, E. & Holtby, S. (2000, February). Identifying substance abusing delivering women: Consequences for child maltreatment reports. *Child Abuse and Neglect, 24(2)*, 173–183.

[5] Alcohol Policy Information System. (2005). Information on alcohol and pregnancy and mandatory warning signs. Retrieved November 9, 2005, from http://alcoholpolicy.niaaa.nih.gov.

[6] American Academy of Pediatrics, Fetus Committee on the Newborn, & American College of Obstetricians and Gynecologists, Committee on Obstetric Practice. (2002). Guidelines for perinatal care (5th ed.). Elk Grove Village, IL, and Washington, DC: Authors.

[7] American College of Obstetricians and Gynecologists. (2000, February). Alcohol and pregnancy. Washington, DC: Author.

[8] American College of Obstetricians and Gynecologists, Committee on Ethics. (2004, May). At-risk drinking and illicit drug use: Ethical issues in obstetric and gynecologic practice. ACOG Committee Opinion No. 294. American College of Obstetricians and Gynecologists. *Obstetrical Gynecology, 103,* 1021–1031.

[9] American Psychiatric Association. (2000). *Diagnostic and statistical manual of mental disorders* (4th ed.). Washington, DC: Author.

[10] Andres, R. L. & Day, M. C. (2000). Perinatal complications associated with maternal tobacco use. *Seminars in Neonatology, 5(3)*, 231–241.

[11] Arria, A. M., Derauf, C., LaGasse, L. L., Grant, P., Shah, R. & Smith, L., et al. (2006). Methamphetamine and other substance use during pregnancy: Preliminary estimates from the Infant Development, Environment, and Lifestyle (IDEAL) study. *Maternal and Child Health Journal, 15,* 1–10.

[12] Aved, B. (2002, July). Working in partnership: Needs and opportunities for improving perinatal substance abuse services in California. Prepared for the California Conference of Local Directors of Maternal, Child, and Adolescent Health.

[13] Barth, R. P. (2001). Research outcomes of prenatal substance exposure and the need to review policies and procedures regarding child abuse reporting. *Child Welfare, 80(2)*,275–296.

[14] Bearer, C. (2001). Markers to detect drinking during pregnancy. *Alcohol Research and Health, 25(3)*, 210–218.

[15] Bertrand, J., Floyd, R. & Weber, M. K. (2005, October 28). Guidelines for identifying and referring persons with fetal alcohol syndrome. Morbidity and Mortality Weekly

Report, 54(RR11), 1–10. Retrieved November 13, 2005, from http://www.cdc.gov/mmwr/preview/mmwrhtml/rr5411a1.htm.

[16] Boles, S. & Young, N. K. (2007, March). Sacramento County Drug Dependency Court: The first four years. Irvine, CA: Children and Family Futures.

[17] Britt, G. C., Ingersoll, K. S. & Schnoll, S. H. (1999). Developmental consequences of early exposure to alcohol and drugs. In P. J. Ott, R. E. Tarter, & R. T. Ammerman (Eds.), Sourcebook on substance abuse: Etiology, epidemiology, assessment, and treatment (pp. 75–97). Needham Heights, MA: Allyn & Bacon.

[18] California Department of Alcohol and Drug Programs. (2004). Perinatal Services Network guidelines 2004 for non- drug Medi-Cal perinatal programs. Retrieved September 27, 2005, from http://www.adp.cahwnet.gov/Perinatal/pdf/Guidelines_04.pdf.

[19] California Department of Alcohol and Drug Programs. (2006, November). Fact sheet: Substance-exposed infants (Senate Bill 2669). Sacramento, CA: Program Services Division, Office of Perinatal Substance Abuse. Retrieved December 8, 2006, from http://www.adp.cahwnet.gov/FactSheets/SB_2669.pdf.

[20] California Health and Safety Code Section 130100-130155. (2007, July). Retrieved September 14, 2007, from http://caselaw.lp.findlaw.com/cacodes/hsc/130100-130155.html.

[21] Cawthon, L. (2004, January). First steps database Safe Babies, Safe Moms fact sheet. Olympia, WA: Research and Data Analysis, Department of Social and Health Services. Retrieved August 26, 2005, from http://www1dshs.wa.gov/pdf/ms/rda/research/4/36/f.pdf.

[22] Cawthon, L. & Westra, K. (2003). *Safe Babies, Safe Moms program evaluation. Olympia, WA: Research and Data Analysis, Department of Social and Health Services*. Retrieved August 26, 2005, from http://www1.dshs.wa.gov/rda/research/4/36/default.shtm.

[23] Center for Substance Abuse Treatment. (1994). *Intensive outpatient treatment for alcohol and other drug abuse.* Treatment improvement protocol series 8. (DHHS Publication No. (SMA) 94-2077). Rockville, MD: U.S. Department of Health and Human Services.

[24] Center for Substance Abuse Treatment. (2003). *Legal and ethical guidelines for the care of pregnant, substance- using women* (chap. 3). In Pregnant, substance-using women treatment improvement protocol (TIP), series 2. Retrieved August 28, 2005, from http://ncadi.samhsa.gov/govpubs/bkd107/2f.aspx.

[25] Center for Substance Abuse Treatment. (2007). *Substance Abuse Prevention and Treatment Block Grant (SAPT) and women's set-aside.* Treatment Improvement Exchange. Retrieved October 9, 2007, from http://womenandchildren.treatment.

[26] Centers for Disease Control and Prevention. (n.d.). *Increasing public awareness of the risks of alcohol use during pregnancy through targeted media campaigns.* Atlanta, GA: National Center on Birth Defects and Developmental Disabilities. Retrieved November 1, 2007, from http://www.cdc.gov/ncbddd/fas/pubawarenss.htm.

[27] Centers for Disease Control and Prevention. (2004, July*). Fetal alcohol syndrome: Guidelines for referral and diagnosis.* Atlanta, GA: National Center on Birth Defects and Developmental Disabilities. Retrieved November 13, 2005, from http://www.cdc.gov/ncbddd/fas/documents/FAS.

[28] Centers for Disease Control and Prevention. (2005). *Fetal alcohol spectrum disorders. Atlanta, GA: National Center on Birth Defects and Developmental Disabilities.* Retrieved September 28, 2005, from http://www.cdc.gov/ncbddd/factsheets/FAS.

[29] Centers for Disease Control and Prevention. (2006, May 2). *State-based FAS prevention programs.* Atlanta, GA: National Center on Birth Defects and Developmental Disabilities. Retrieved July 27, 2006, from http://www.cdc.gov/ncbddd/fas/whatsnew.htm.

[30] Chasnoff, I. J. (2001). *The nature of nurture: Biology, environment, and the drug-exposed child.* Chicago: National Training Institute Publishing.

[31] Chasnoff, I. J., Landress, H. J. & Barrett, M. E. (1990). The prevalence of illicit-drug or alcohol use during pregnancy and discrepancies in mandatory reporting in Pinellas County, Florida. *New England Journal of Medicine, 322,* 1202–1206.

[32] Chasnoff, I. J., McGourty, R. F., Bailey, G. W., Hutchins, E., Lightfoot, S. O. & Pawson, L. L., et al. (2005). The 4P's Plus© screen for substance use in pregnancy: Clinical application and outcomes. *Journal of Perinatology, 25(6),* 368–374. Chicago: National Training Institute Publishing.

[33] Chavkin, W., Breitbart, V., Elman, D. & Wise, P. H. (1998). National survey of the states: Policies and practices regarding drug-using pregnant women. *American Journal of Public Health, 88,* 117–119.

[34] Chen, X., Burgdorf, K. & Herrell, J. (2001). Predicting outcomes of residential substance abuse treatment for pregnant and parenting women. *Drug and Alcohol Dependence, 63(1),* s20.

[35] Child Welfare Information Gateway. (2006, August). *Parental drug use as child abuse: Summary of state laws.* State statutes series 2006. Washington, DC: Author. Retrieved August 2, 2007, from http://www.childwelfare.gov/systemwide/laws.

[36] Child Welfare Information Gateway. (2007a, April). *Definitions of child abuse and neglect: Summary of state laws.* State statutes series. Retrieved August 2, 2007, from http://www.childwelfare.gov/systemwide/laws.

[37] Child Welfare Information Gateway. (2007b, September). State statutes. Retrieved October 2, 2007, from http://www.childwelfare.gov/systemwide/laws.

[38] Christian, S. (2004, September). Substance-exposed newborns: New federal law raises some old issues. Washington, DC: National Conference of State Legislatures. Retrieved February 18, 2005, from http://www.ncsl.org/print/cyf/newborns.pdf.

[39] Colorado Department of Public Health and Environment, Women's Health Unit. (n.d.). Prenatal Plus Program. Retrieved September 28, 2005, from http://www.cdphe.state.

[40] Colorado Department of Public Health and Environment. (2006). Prenatal Plus Program Annual Report 2006. Denver, CO. Retrieved December 13, 2007, from http://www.cdphe.state.

[41] Dailard, C. & Nash, E. (2000, December). Laws pertaining to pregnant women who use drugs [Table]. *The Guttmacher Report on Public Policy, 3(6).* Retrieved December 13, 2007, from http://www.guttmacher.org/tables/gr030603t.html.

[42] Dailard, C. & Nash, E. (2000, December). State responses to substance abuse among pregnant women. *The Guttmacher Report on Public Policy, 3(6).* Retrieved December 13, 2007, from http://www.guttmacher.org/pubs/tgr/03/6/gr030603.html.

[43] Davidson, H. (2004). *Significant new changes to the Federal Child Abuse Prevention and Treatment Act: Practical implications for child and family advocates.* Washington, DC: American Bar Association, Center on Children and the Law.

[44] Dennis, K. (2005). Women's substance abuse treatment standards: Key themes from state standards. Prepared for State Women's Treatment Coordinators 2005 Annual Meeting, June 3, 2005. Irvine, CA: Children and Family Futures.

[45] Dennis, K., Young, N. & Gardner, S. (in press). *Funding family-centered treatment for women with substance use disorders,* (Vol. 2). Irvine, CA: Children and Family Futures.

[46] DiFranza, J. R. & Lew, R. A. (1995). Effect of maternal cigarette smoking on pregnancy complications and sudden death syndrome. *Journal of Family Practice, 40(4)*, 385–394.

[47] Drescher-Burke, K. & Price, A. (2005). Identifying, reporting, and responding to substance-exposed newborns: An exploratory study of policies and practices. Berkeley, CA: National Abandoned Infants Assistance Resource Center.

[48] Drug Policy Alliance. (2005). Over 70 child welfare and public health organizations, experts, and advocates condemn the prosecution of pregnant women in Texas. Retrieved August 26, 2005, from http://www.drugpolicy.org/news/pressroom/pressrelease/pr030105.cfm.

[49] Duggan, A. K., McFarlane, E. C., Windham, A. M., Rohde, C. A., Salkever, D. S. & Fuddy, L., et al. (1999, Spring/Summer). Evaluation of Hawaii's Healthy Start Program. *The Future of Children, 9(1)*, 66–90.

[50] Ebrahim, S. H. & Gfroerer, J. (2003, February). Pregnancy-related substance use in the United States during 1996–1998. *Obstetrics and Gynecology, 101(2)*, 374–379.

[51] Fenaughty, A. M. & MacKinnon, D. P. (1993). Immediate effects of the Arizona alcohol warning poster. *Journal of Public Policy & Marketing, 12(1)*, 69–77.

[52] Fornoff, J. E., Egler, T. & Shen, T. (2001, November). Surveillance of Illinois infants prenatally exposed to controlled substances 1991-1999. Epidemiological report series 01:4. Springfield, IL: Illinois Department of Public Health.

[53] Goldson, E. (2001). Maltreatment among children with disabilities. *Infants and Young Children, 13(4)*, 44–54.

[54] Halfon, N., Mendonca, A. & Berkowitz, G. (1995). Health status of children in foster care: The experience of the Center for the Vulnerable Child. *Archives of Pediatrics and Adolescent Medicine, 149*, 386–392.

[55] Hawaii State Department of Health. (1996). 1996 blind study of substance abuse and need for treatment among women of childbearing age in Hawaii. Hawaii Department of Health. Retrieved February 10, 2005, from http://www.hawaii.gov/health.

[56] Heller School for Social Policy and Management (n.d.). The Heller school takes lead on early intervention for victims of child abuse [Press release]. Retrieved August 28, 2005, from http://www.heller.brandeis.edu/welcome/news_press_releases.asp? PressRelease Number=20.

[57] Jacobson, P. D., Zellman, G. L. & Fair, C. C. (2003, September). Reciprocal obligations: *Managing policy responses to prenatal substance exposure, Milbank Quarterly, 81(3)*, 475–497.

[58] Jones, K. L. & Smith, D. W. (1973, November 3). Recognition of the fetal alcohol syndrome in early infancy. *Lancet, 2(7836),* 999–101. Retrieved November 13, 2005, from Medline.

[59] Johnson, K., Knitzer, J. & Kaufmann, R. (2002, August). Making dollars follow sense: Financing early childhood mental health services to promote healthy social and emotional development in young children (Policy Paper No. 4, Promoting the emotional well-being of children and families). New York: National Center for Children in Poverty. Retrieved February 27, 2005, from http://www.nccp.org/ publications/pdf/ text_483.pdf.

[60] Kalotra, C. J. (2002, March). *Estimated costs related to the birth of a drug and/or alcohol exposed baby.* Washington, DC: Office of Justice Programs Drug Court Clearinghouse and Technical Assistance Project. Retrieved August 15, 2005, from http://www.indianaperinatal.org/files/Calendar%20files/SPAB%20Meeting%20Files/Estimated%20costs.pdf.

[61] Kennedy, C., Finkelstein, N., Hutchins, E. & Mahoney, J. (2004, September). Improving screening for alcohol use during pregnancy: The Massachusetts ASAP Program. *Maternal and Child Health Journal, 8,* 3.

[62] Kentucky's Early Childhood Initiative. (2006, June). Kentucky's early childhood initiative summary. Retrieved December 11, 2007, from http://www.kde.state 3CA8E9CBE24F/0/InitiativeSu m ma rywbu 1 lets91106.pdf.

[63] Kentucky Medical Association. (n.d.). KMA model health care protocol on abuse, neglect & exploitation: Child, spouse/partner, adult & elder. Retrieved December 11, 2007, from http://www.kyma.org/Committees/Protocol/Screening_Identification.php.

[64] KIDS NOW. (n.d.). Kentucky's early childhood initiative summary. Retrieved December 11, 2007, from http://www.healthychildcare.org/pdf/KIDSnow.pdf.

[65] Kinney, J. (2001). *Cuyahoga START Executive Summary: A child welfare model for drug-affected families.* Baltimore: Annie E. Casey Foundation.

[66] Lambers, D. S. & Clark, K. E. (1996). The maternal and fetal physiologic effects of nicotine. *Seminars in Perinatology, 20(2),*115–126.

[67] Lester, B. (2000). Vulnerable Infants Program of Rhode Island. Program funded by the Robert Wood Johnson Local Initiative Funding Partners Program and the Abandoned Infants Assistance Project 2000.

[68] Lester, B., Boukydis, C. & Twomey, J. (2000). Maternal substance abuse and child outcome. In C. H. Zeanah (Ed.), *Handbook of infant mental health (2nd ed., pp. 161–175). New York:* Guilford Press.

[69] Lester, B. & Jeremiah, J. S., Jr. (2003, April 4). Our choice: V.I.P. or R.I.P. George Street Journal. Retrieved August 28, 2005, from http://www.brown.edu/Administration/ George_Street_Journal/vol27/27GSJ23e.html.

[70] Levin, E. D. & Slotkin, T. A. (1998). Developmental neurotoxicity of nicotine. In W. Slikker & L. W. Chang (Eds.), *Handbook of developmental neurotoxicology (pp. 587–615).* San Diego, CA: Academic Press.

[71] Lighthouse Institute. (n.d.). Project Safe overview. Retrieved August 15, 2005, from http://www.chestnut.org/LI/projectsafe/overview.html.

[72] Little, B. B., Snell, L. M., Rosenfeld, C. R., Gilstrap, L. C. & Gant, N. F. (1990). Failure to recognize fetal alcohol syndrome in newborn infants. *American Journal of Diseases of Children, 144,* 1142–1146.

[73] Loman, L. A. & Sherburne, D. (2000, April). Intensive home visitation for mothers of drug-exposed infants: An evaluation of the St. Louis Linkages Program. St. Louis, MO: Institute of Applied Research. Retrieved February 18, 2005, from http://iarstl.org/papers/Linkages.pdf.

[74] March of Dimes. (2007). Quick references and fact sheets: PKU (phenylketonuria). Retrieved August 15, 2007, from http://www.marchofdimes.com/professionals.

[75] Maryland Department of Health and Mental Hygiene. (2005, Early Winter). Perinatal Network [Electronic newsletter].

[76] Massachusetts Early Intervention Project. (2005). Retrieved February 6, 2006, from http://eip.uoregon.edu/conferences/DEC/2005/MASSACHUSETTS%20EI%20PROJECT.pdf.

[77] Mayes, L. C., Bornstein, M. H., Chawarska, K. & Granger, R. H. (1995). Information processing and developmental assessments in three month olds exposed prenatally to cocaine. *Pediatrics, 95(4)*, 539–545.

[78] McGee, S., Rinaldi, L. & Peterman, D. (2002, December). Drug-affected infants in Washington State: Services for pregnant, postpartum, and parenting women. Olympia, WA: Washington State Institute for Public Policy. Retrieved October 2, 2005, from http://www.wsipp.wa.gov/rptfiles/DrugAffInfants.pdf.

[79] McGourty, R. F. & Chasnoff, I. J. (2003). Power beyond measure: A community-based approach to developing integrated systems of care for substance abusing women and their children. Chicago: National Training Institute Publishing.

[80] Minnesota Department of Health. (n.d.). Alcohol Exposed Pregnancy Prevention Project (Fetal Alcohol Syndrome prevention). Retrieved October 28, 2005, from http://www.health.

[81] Minnesota Statute 626.5562 (2007). Toxicology tests required. Subd. 2., Newborns. Retrieved August 15, 2007, from http://ros.leg.mn/bin/getpub.php? pubtype=STAT_CHAP_SEC&year=current&section=626.5562.

[82] Missouri Metropolitan Task Force on Drug Exposed Infants. (2003, September 15). Fact sheet. Retrieved November 9, 2005, from http://aia.berkeley.edu/media.

[83] Mountain Plains Regional Resource Center. (n.d.). Retrieved November 15, 2007, from http://www.rrfcnetwork.org/mprrc.

[84] National Abandoned Infants Assistance Resource Center. (2003, Spring). Juggling the multiple facets of case management with relative caregiver families. *Source, 12(1)*, 1–32.

[85] National Abandoned Infants Assistance Resource Center. (2005, Spring). Celebrating families: An innovative approach for working with substance abusing families. *The Source, 14(1)*, 6–10. Retrieved October 2, 2005, from http://aia.berkeley.edu/media

[86] National Early Childhood Technical Assistance Center. (2006). *Referral requirements under CAPTA and IDEA*. Retrieved September 19, 2006, from http://www.nectac.org/topics/earlyid/capta.asp.

[87] National Governors Association, Center for Best Practices. (2004). *Healthy babies: Efforts to improve birth outcomes and reduce high risk births*. Washington, DC: Author. Retrieved February 10, 2005, from http://www.nga.org/cda/files/406BIRTHS.Pdf.

[88] National Institute of Allergy and Infectious Diseases. (2004, July). HIV infection in infants and children. Retrieved October 18, 2005, from http://www.niaid.nih.gov/factsheets/hivchildren.htm.

[89] National Institute on Alcohol Abuse and Alcoholism. (2004, May 27). NIAAA Director's Report on Institute Activities to the National Advisory Council on Alcohol Abuse and Alcoholism. Retrieved September 28, 2005, from http://www.niaaa.nih.gov/AboutNIAAA/AdvisoryCouncil/DirectorsReports/Council5-04.htm.

[90] National Newborn Screening and Genetics Resource Center. (2007, October 17). National newborn screening status report. Austin, TX: Author. Retrieved December 5, 2007, from http://genesus.uthscsa.edu/nbsdisorders.pdf.

[91] Office of Applied Studies. (2005). *Results from the 2004 National Survey on Drug Use and Health: National findings* (DHHS Publication No. SMA 05-4062, NSDUH Series H-28). Rockville, MD: Substance Abuse and Mental Health Services Administration.

[92] Office of Applied Studies. (2006). National Survey of Substance Abuse Treatment Services (N-SSATS) profile: United States 2005. Rockville, MD: Substance Abuse and Mental Health Services Administration. Retrieved February 27, 2007, from http://wwwdasis.samhsa.gov/webt/state.

[93] Office of Applied Studies, Substance Abuse and Mental Health Services Administration (2005). Online analysis of Treatment Episode Data Set (TEDS) 2005 [Computer File], conducted February 27, 2007. Ann Arbor, MI: Inter- university Consortium for Political and Social Research [Distributor]. Retrieved November 12, 2007, from http://www.icpsr.umich.edu/SAMHDA/das.html.

[94] Ondersma, S. J., Malcoe, L. H. & Simpson, S. M. (2001). Child protective services' response to prenatal drug exposure: Results from a nationwide survey. *Child Abuse and Neglect, 25(5),* 657–668.

[95] Ondersma, S. J., Simpson, S., Malcoe, L. H. & O'Steen, M. (1999, June). Prenatal drug exposure: A nationwide survey of child welfare policy and practice. Paper presented at the American Professional Society on the Abuse of Children, San Antonio, TX. Cited in S. Ondersma, S. Simpson, E. Brestan, & M. Ward, Prenatal drug exposure and social policy: The search for an appropriate response. *Child Maltreatment, 5(2),* May 2000, 93–108.

[96] Quittan, G. (2004, April). An evaluation of the impact of the Celebrating Families Program and family drug treatment court (FTDC) on parents receiving family reunification services. San Jose, CA: San Jose State University, College of Social Work. Retrieved October 28, 2005, from http://www.prevention partnership.us/pdf/recent_evaluation2.pdf.

[97] Reese, A. & Burry, C. L. (2004). Evaluating Maryland's response to drug-exposed babies: SB 512, children in need of assistance: Drug-addicted babies. *Psychology, Public Policy, and Law, 10,* 3, 349–369.

[98] Robinson, C. C. & Rosenberg, S. A. (2004). Child welfare referrals to Part C. *Journal of Early Intervention, 26(4),* 284–291.

[99] Sacramento County Department of Health and Human Services. (2006). Dependency Drug Court/STARS facts and information. Available at http://www.sacdhhs.com/article.asp?content=1016.

[100] Shackelford, J. (2006, July). State and jurisdictional eligibility definitions for infants and toddlers with disabilities under IDEA. NECTAC Notes, 21, 1–16. Retrieved September 19, 2006, from http://www.nectac.org/~pdfs/pubs/nnotes21.pdf.

[101] Shah, R. Z. (2000). Second chance kids: Providing development focused care for drug-exposed infants. Retrieved October 18, 2005, from http://www.addictionrecov.org/paradigm/P_PR_SP00/cont_shah.htm.

[102] Shaw, E. & Goode, S. (2005, December). The impact of abuse, neglect and foster care placement on infants, toddlers and young children: Selected resources. Chapel Hill, NC: NECTAC Clearinghouse on Early Intervention and Early Childhood Special Education. Retrieved July 27, 2006, from http://www.nectac.org/~pdfs/pubs/abuseneglect.pdf.

[103] Simmes, D. (2004). Findings of an assessment of substance-exposed births in San Diego County. A report for Children and Family Futures, Irvine, CA.

[104] Slotkin, T. A. (1998). Fetal nicotine or cocaine exposure: Which one is worse? *Journal of Pharmacology and Experimental Therapeutics, 285(3)*, 931–945.

[105] South Carolina Department of Health and Environmental Control. (1991). South Carolina Pregnancy Risk Assessment Monitoring System. Retrieved November 9, 2005, from http://www.scdhec.gov/co/phsis/biostatistics/index.asp?page=prams.

[106] Substance Abuse and Mental Health Services Administration. (2006). Results from the National Survey on Drug Use and Health, 2005. Detailed tables on pregnancy. Rockville, MD: Substance Abuse and Mental Health Services Administration, Office of Applied Studies. Retrieved February 2, 2006, from http://www.oas.samhsa.gov/nsduh/2k5nsduh/tabs/Sect7peTabs68to75.pdf.

[107] Substance Abuse and Mental Health Services Administration. (2007). Substance abuse and mental health statistics. Retrieved February 27, 2007, from http://www.oas.samhsa.gov/.

[108] Sullivan, P. M. & Knutson, J. F. (2000). Maltreatment and disabilities: A population-based epidemiological study. *Child Abuse and Neglect, 24(10)*, 1257–1273.

[109] Thompson, D. (2005, February 15). Bill to report addicted birth mothers clears committee. Arkansas News Bureau. Retrieved October 18, 2005, from http://www.arkansasnews.com/archive/2005/02/15/News/317327.html.

[110] Treatment Improvement Exchange. (n.d.). RWC/PPW cross-site evaluation [Fact sheet]. Retrieved October 27, 2005, from http://womenandchildren.treatment

[111] University of Massachusetts. (2002, May 1). Alcohol and drug policy. Retrieved November 13, 2005, from http://media.

[112] University of Washington. (2006, August 28). *The Parent-Child Assistance Program (PCAP) [Brochure]*. Retrieved September 19, 2006, from http://depts.washington.edu/fadu/PCAP_Brochure_8_28_06.pdf.

[113] U.S. Department of Health and Human Services. (1999, April). *Blending perspectives and building common ground: A report to Congress on substance abuse and child protection*. Retrieved November 9, 2005, from http://aspe.hhs.gov/HSP/subabuse99/subabuse.htm.

[114] U.S. Department of Health and Human Services. (2005, February 21). U.S. Surgeon General releases advisory on alcohol use in pregnancy [Press release]. Retrieved November 13, 2005, from http://www.hhs.gov/surgeongeneral/pressreleases/sg02222005.html.

[115] U.S. Department of Health and Human Services, Administration for Children and Families. (2006). Child Abuse Prevention and Treatment Act as amended by the Keeping Children and Families Safe Act of 2003. Retrieved September 19, 2006, from http://www.acf.hhs.gov/programs/cb/laws.

[116] U.S. Department of Health and Human Services, Administration on Children, Youth and Families. (2005a). Child maltreatment 2003. Washington, DC: U.S. Government Printing Office.

[117] U.S. Department of Health and Human Services, Administration on Children, Youth and Families. (2005b). Synthesis of findings: Substance abuse child welfare waiver demonstrations. Washington, DC: U.S. Government Printing Office.

[118] U.S. Department of Health and Human Services, Substance Abuse and Mental Health Services Administration, Fetal Alcohol Spectrum Disorders Center for Excellence. (n.d.). State laws related to posting of alcohol warnings at point of sale. Washington, DC. Retrieved November 9, 2005, from http://fascenter.samhsa.gov/resource/signageLaws.cfm.

[119] U.S. Department of Health and Human Services, Substance Abuse and Mental Health Services Administration, Fetal Alcohol Spectrum Disorders Center for Excellence. (2006, April). Legislation by state: 2005-2006 legislative sessions. Washington, DC. Retrieved November 12, 2007, from http://www.fasdcenter.samhsa.gov/documents/FASDLegislationByState_April2006.pdf.

[120] Vega, W. A., Kolody, B., Hwang, J. & Noble, A. (1993, September 16). Prevalence and magnitude of perinatal substance exposures in California. *New England Journal of Medicine, 329(12)*, 850–854.

[121] Vega, W. A., Kolody, B., Noble, A., Hwang, J., Porter, P. & Bole, A., et al. (1993). *Profile of alcohol and drug use during pregnancy in California*. 1992: Perinatal substance exposure study general report. Sacramento, CA: Department of Alcohol and Drug Programs, Office of Perinatal Substance Abuse.

[122] Virginia Department of Health. (2003). *Perinatal substance use: A guide for hospitals and health care providers: Virginia legal requirements and health care practice implications*. Richmond, VA. Retrieved October 27, 2005, from http://www.dss.virginia.gov/files/division/dfs/cps/publications/perinatal.

[123] Virginia Department of Health & Department of Mental Health, Mental Retardation and Substance Abuse Services. (2004). *Perinatal practice survey regarding HIV and substance use in childbearing age women*. Richmond, VA: Authors.

[124] Washington State Department of Health. (2002). Substance abuse during pregnancy: Guidelines for screening (pp. 16–50). Olympia, WA: Author.

[125] Washington State Fetal Alcohol Syndrome Interagency Work Group. (2007, July). Final report to the Governor's Council on Substance Abuse. Retrieved August 15, 2007, from http://depts.washington.edu/fasdwa/PDFs/FASIAWG%20Report%20July%202007%20FINAL.pdf.

[126] Williams, L., Morrow, B., Shulman, H., Stephens, R., D'Angelo, D. & Fowler, C. I. (2006). PRAMS 2002 surveillance report. *Atlanta, GA: Centers for Disease Control and Prevention, National Center for Chronic Disease Prevention and Health Promotion*, Division of Reproductive Health Centers for Disease Control and Prevention. Retrieved August 2, 2007, from http://www.cdc.gov/prams/2002PRAMSSurvReport/PDF/2k2PRAMS.pdf.

[127] Wisconsin Department of Health and Family Services. (2004, June 25). Addendum to the child protective service investigation standards: Assessing the safety of drug-affected infants. Retrieved December 8, 2004, from http://dhfs.wisconsin.gov/dcfs_info/num_memos/2004/2004-12_attach.pdf.

[128] Yates, B. T. (1999). Measuring and improving cost, cost-effectiveness, and cost-benefit for substance abuse treatment programs: A manual. Bethesda, MD: National Institute on Drug Abuse, Division of Clinical and Services Research.

[129] Zellman, G., Fair, C., Houbé, J. & Wong, M. (2002, September). A Search for guidance: Examining prenatal substance exposure protocols. *Maternal and Child Health Journal, 6(3)*, 205–212.

[130] ZERO TO THREE Policy Center. (2004, July). Infants, toddlers and child welfare fact sheet. Retrieved August 28, 2005, from http://www.zerotothree.org/site/DocServer/childwelfarestate.pdf?docID=682.

End Notes

[1] The Child Abuse and Prevention Treatment Act (CAPTA) language requires State policies and procedures for hospitals that assure CPS is notified of all children born affected by illegal substance abuse or withdrawal symptoms resulting from prenatal drug exposure; requires CPS to develop a plan of safe care for every such drug- exposed infant referred to it; and mandates CPS to make a Part C referral (to special education agencies handling developmental disabilities) in all cases involving substantiated victims of child maltreatment younger than 3 years (DHHS, ACYF, 2005a).

[2] Although the CAPTA legislation is silent on fetal alcohol effects, the work of the Interagency Coordinating Committee on Fetal Alcohol Syndrome, Federal Websites on fetal alcohol problems, Federal funding for fetal alcohol-related initiatives, and congressional language regarding resources for fetal alcohol problems make clear that both the executive and legislative branches of the Federal government recognize the issues of alcohol as they relate to SEIs. Congressional initiatives, including the leadership of Congressman Jim Ramstad of Minnesota, a cofounder of the Congressional Caucus on Fetal Alcohol Spectrum Disorders, have added earmarked Federal funding for a variety of fetal alcohol-related projects. In addition, Congress in 2002 requested the Centers for Disease Control and Prevention to update and refine diagnostic criteria for fetal alcohol syndrome (Bertrand, Floyd, & Weber, 2005; see http://www.cdc.gov/mmwr/preview/mmwrhtml/rr5411a1.htm).

[3] In a 2003 study, Ebrahim and Gfroerer estimated that in 1998 there were 202,000 pregnancies exposed to illicit drugs; 1,203,000 pregnancies exposed to cigarettes; and 823,000 pregnancies exposed to alcohol. The study used data from the 2000 National Household Survey on Drug Abuse.

[4] The five States participating in FASSNet were Alaska, Arizona, Colorado, New York, and Wisconsin. The seven States currently participating in the FAS Prevention Program are Colorado, Michigan, Minnesota, Missouri, Oregon, South Dakota, and Wisconsin. See http://www.cdc.gov/ncbddd/fas/whatsnew.htm

[5] Among the set of ten States in this sample, seven—Hawaii, Illinois, Maryland, Minnesota, Rhode Island, South Carolina, and Washington—are included in PRAMS. For the U.S. map on page 3 of this document that highlights several States, including the seven, see http://www.cdc.gov/prams/2002PRAMSSurvReport/PDF/2k2PRAMS.pdf.

[6] A significant number of incidents of prenatal exposure to alcohol or illegal drugs take place in pregnancies that do not lead to a live birth (which totals 37% of all pregnancies). It should not be assumed, however, that the ratio of prenatal exposure in births is the same as that in pregnancies, given the harmful prenatal effects that lead to a disproportionate number of terminations of pregnancies and unintended pregnancies resulting from use of illegal and legal drugs (ACOG, 2000; DiFranza & Lew, 1995).

[7] Jones, K. L., & Smith, D. W. (1973, November 3). Recognition of the fetal alcohol syndrome in early infancy. Lancet, 2(7836), 999–101. Retrieved November 13, 2005, from Medline.

[8] There has been an overall increase in the methamphetamine/amphetamine treatment admission rate in the United States, from 10 admissions per 100,000 to 57 admissions per 100,000 population aged 12 or older from 1992–2003 (Office of Applied Studies [OAS], 2005).

[9] The bill called for (1) public awareness aimed at the general public, including awareness targeted at high-risk populations, as well as public education on how to prevent FASD; (2) professional education to teach professionals about FASD so that they can recognize and identify FASD for referrals to diagnose, treat, and intervene, and teaching professionals to diagnose and screen and intervene using effective techniques; (3)

screening high-risk populations, including both women of child-bearing age and children already affected; (4) diagnosing high-risk populations, including children already affected and women at risk; (5) surveillance and data, including collecting and analyzing prevalence and incidence statistics to help define and describe the problem; and (6) intervening with high-risk populations, including treating women of child-bearing age to reduce and eliminate the risk of an alcohol- exposed pregnancy and preventing secondary conditions in children already affected by FASD.

[10] The sources, which have been very helpful to NCSACW in developing this report, include:

S. Christian. (September 2004). Substance-Exposed Newborns: New federal law raises some old issues. See http://www.ncsl.org/print/cyf/newborns.pdf

Alan Guttmacher Institute. (September 1, 2007). State policies in brief: Substance abuse during pregnancy. See http://www.guttmacher.org/statecenter/spibs/spib_SADP.pdf

Child Welfare Information Gateway. (2006). Parental drug use as child abuse: Summary of state laws. State statutes series 2006. See http://www.childwelfare.gov/systemwide/laws

Alcohol Policy Information System, National Institute on Alcohol Abuse and Alcoholism. Its Website, http://www.alcoholpolicy.niaaa.nih.gov/, includes mapping capacity and tables with detailed legislative citations indicating which States have adopted different reporting policies on pregnancy and alcohol use.

A prime example of the differences in interpretation is the issue of whether any States require prenatal testing or testing at birth. One widely cited source indicates that four States (Iowa, Minnesota, North Dakota, and Virginia) require health care professionals "to test some or all pregnant women or newborns for prenatal drug exposure" (Alan Guttmacher Institute, 2005). Another source says "no State requires systematic detection policies such as toxicology screens for all pregnant women" (Jacobson, Zellman, & Fair, 2003.) And a third source says that "A national survey of State policy directors (Chavkin, Breitbart, Elman, & Wise, 1998) regarding perinatal substance abuse revealed that 12% of respondents' States in 1995 had mandatory drug testing policies for pregnant women (up from 2% in 1992), and 7% indicated that their State also required testing of all neonates (up from 0% in 1992)" (Ondersma, Malcoe, & Simpson, 2001). Even allowing for the different periods covered by these three reviews, the disparity is too wide to permit confidence in using any of these without further investigation. What appears to be the problem is that some of these sources define testing to be required if prenatal use is suspected—which is far from a universal screening policy, since it is still triggered by a professional's judgment. Minnesota's language is illustrative: "A physician shall administer a toxicology test to each newborn infant under the physician's care to determine whether there is evidence of prenatal exposure to a controlled substance, if the physician has reason to believe based on a medical assessment of the mother or the infant that the mother has used a controlled substance for a non-medical purpose prior to birth. If the test is positive, the physician shall report the result as neglect" Minn. Stat.626.5562 Section 6 (2007).

[11] The CAPTA language requires State policies and procedures for hospitals that assure CPS is notified of all children born affected by illegal substance abuse or withdrawal symptoms resulting from prenatal drug exposure; requires CPS to develop a plan of safe care for every such drug-exposed infant referred to it; and mandates CPS to make a Part C referral (to special education agencies handling developmental disabilities) in all cases involving substantiated victims of child maltreatment younger than 3 years.

[12] This figure was derived from an analysis of the 2005 NSDUH public use file. The number of pregnant women aged 15–44 classified as needing treatment is 182,013, and the number who received treatment is 10,944. 10,944 divided by 182,013 equals 0.0601 or 6%. The number of those receiving treatment may be very low, so weighted estimates may be less than reliable. Treatment admission data are from the Treatment Episode Data Set (TEDS), whereas data on the numbers needing treatment are from NSDUH. TEDS shows 18,759 pregnant women aged 15–44 admitted to publicly funded treatment in 2003 (excludes missing data), whereas NSDUH reports an estimated 211,678 pregnant women aged 15–44 classified as needing treatment for alcohol or illicit drug use in that same year, and 17,804 who received treatment (8.4%).

[13] When it comes to prior treatment admissions, nationally, more than half of pregnant women (56.3%), non-pregnant women (57.9%), and men (56.6%) admitted to treatment in 2003 had been previously admitted for treatment. Of the States interviewed and captured in TEDS, the percentages of prior treatment admissions for pregnant women ranged from a low of 46.8% in Illinois to a high of 93.8% in Rhode Island. For non-pregnant women, it ranged from a low of 44.8% in Virginia to a high of 99.8% in Rhode Island (the percentages for men were similar). Of the 10 study States, Massachusetts, South Carolina, and Washington did not have data in TEDS in 2003 on the number of prior treatment admissions for pregnant women; South Carolina and Washington also did not have these data for non-pregnant women.

[14] States may collect additional or more detailed information beyond the minimum data set required by the Federal government. Treatment providers, child welfare agencies, policymakers, and others should contact the appropriate State agencies in each of these fields to find out what data are available.

[15] For further information on the Federal Substance Abuse Prevention and Treatment Block Grant, see http://womenandchildren.treatment.

[16] The Parent-Child Assistance Program is part of the Fetal Alcohol and Drug Unit at the University of Washington. For a brochure, see http://depts.washington.edu/fadu/PCAP_Brochure_8_28_06.pdf.

[17] In Illinois, for example, the 2004–2005 reports and "indicated" (i.e., substantiated) reports of SEIs declined consistent with a 12-year decline in reports, from a high in 1993–1994 of 3,342 indicated SEI reports to 897 in 2004–2005. In California, there was a decline in 0–1-year-old substantiated reports (which is a weak surrogate for SEI reports) in 2004, consistent with an overall decline in reports statewide for all ages.

[18] The United States has a relatively small percentage of the world's children living with human immunodeficiency virus/acquired immunodeficiency syndrome (HIV/AIDS). From the beginning of the epidemic through the end of 2002, 9,300 American children younger than age 13 had been reported to the Centers for Disease Control and Prevention (CDC) as living with HIV/AIDS. Most HIV-infected children acquire the virus from their mothers before or during birth or through breast feeding. Only 92 new cases of pediatric AIDS were reported in 2002. All children born to infected mothers have antibodies to HIV, made by the mother's immune system, that cross the placenta to the baby's bloodstream before birth and persist for up to 18 months. Because these maternal antibodies reflect the mother's but not the infant's infection status, the test for HIV infection is not useful in newborns or young infants (National Institute of Allergy and Infectious Diseases, 2004).

[19] Phenylketonuria (PKU) is an inherited disorder of body chemistry that, if untreated, causes mental retardation. Through routine newborn screening, almost all affected newborns are now diagnosed and treated early, allowing them to grow up with normal intelligence. About 1 baby in 25,000 is born with PKU in the United States, according to the March of Dimes (March of Dimes, 2007). For more information on newborn screening, see National Newborn Screening and Genetics Resource Center (2007) and http://genes for the National Newborn Screening Status Report.

[20] In a survey in Michigan, 77% of responding physicians "agreed that screening for acquired immunodeficiency syndrome during pregnancy should be mandatory. Almost as high a percentage (61% to 75% depending on subspecialty) was also in favor of mandatory screening for alcohol abuse; agreement for screening for illicit drugs was much lower (43% to 55% depending on subspecialty). Despite their consensus (61%) that fear of prosecution would deter pregnant abusers from seeking prenatal care, most were in agreement that existing laws regarding child abuse and neglect need to be redefined to include alcohol (54%) and drug abuse (61%) during pregnancy; 52% were in favor of enacting a statute that includes drug or alcohol use during pregnancy as 'child abuse' for purposes of removing that child from maternal custody. Physicians were highly in favor of compulsory treatment for illicit drug use and alcohol abuse for women already in the criminal justice system (82%-83%) and opposed to criminal prosecution for either alcohol abuse (18%-31% depending on subspecialty) or illicit drug use (23%-34%) during pregnancy." The conclusion drawn was that "other than criminal prosecution, physicians are not opposed to involvement of the legal justice system in preventing alcohol and drug abuse during pregnancy" (Abel & Kruger, 2002).

[21] Testing positive for controlled substances is assumed to be substance abuse in most of the legislation. Illinois refers to a "pregnant person who is addicted" as defined by other State legislation, which makes a distinction between use and addiction. Maryland refers to a child "born exposed" without any distinction about amounts; other States refer to "trace amounts" of drugs in the infant's blood or urine.

[22] "Substance Exposed Infants Identified and Served Under §63.2-1509B and §32.1-127." Department of Mental Health, Mental Retardation and Substance Abuse Services, Richmond, VA. Cynthia Bearer cites one study in which researchers missed the diagnosis of FAS in 100% of newborns who were diagnosed later in childhood (Bearer, C., 2001, citing Little, Snell, Rosenfeld, Gilstrap, & Gant, 1990).

[23] "A particularly appealing aspect of the Part C portion of IDEA is that FAS is considered a "presumptive eligibility" diagnosis. Presumptive diagnoses allow children "at risk" of later developmental delay to be served without meeting particular eligibility criteria. That is, children who are at risk for later developmental problems can receive services, even if they test in the normal range or do not meet other eligibility criteria. This is very important for children with FAS because only about 25% score in the significantly developmentally delayed range" (CDC, 2004).

[24] "Children at environmental risk include those whose caregiving circumstances and current family situation place them at greater risk for delay than the general population. As with biological/medical risk, states are not required, but may choose to include children at environmental risk under the optional eligibility category of at risk. Examples of environmental risk factors that states have listed include parental substance abuse, family social disorganization, poverty, parental developmental disability, parental age, parental educational attainment, and child abuse or neglect" (Shackelford, 2006). Hawaii, Massachusetts, New Hampshire, New Mexico, and West Virginia were the only States using the environmental at-risk designation starting in July 2006 (see http://www.nectac.org/%7Epdfs/pubs/nnotes21.pdf).

[25] The Arizona estimate was made in a teleconference with the Mountain Plains Regional Resource Center, funded by the Federal Office of Special Education Programs. For information about the Center, see http://www.rrfcnetwork.org/mprrc

[26] Only 25 States reported information on wait times to TEDS (OAS, SAMHSA, 2005). This analysis included only those 18 States whose data on wait times were at least 75% complete: Arkansas, Arizona, Florida, Georgia, Hawaii, Iowa, Kansas, Louisiana, Maine, Maryland, Michigan, Mississippi, Montana, Nebraska, New Hampshire, South Carolina, Texas, and Utah.

CHAPTER SOURCES

The following chapters have been previously published:

Chapter 1 – This is an edited, reformatted and augmented version of United States Department of Health and Human Services, Administration for Children and Families, Administration on Children, Youth and Families, Children's Bureau, Office on Child Abuse and Neglect publication, dated 2009.

Chapter 2 – This is an edited, reformatted and augmented version of United States Department of Health and Human Services, Administration for Children and Families, Administration on Children, Youth and Families, Children's Bureau, Child Welfare Information Gateway publication, dated January 2009.

Chapter 3 – This is an edited, reformatted and augmented version of United States Department of Health and Human Services, Substances Abuse and Mental Health Services Administration, Publication No. 10-4556.

Chapter 4 – This is an edited, reformatted and augmented version of United States Department of Health and Human Services, Substances Abuse and Mental Health Services Administration for Children and Families, Publication No. 10-4557.

Chapter 5 – This is an edited, reformatted and augmented version of United States Department of Health and Human Services, Substances Abuse and Mental Health Services Administration for Children and Families, Publication No. 09-4369.

INDEX

A

academic performance, 29, 55
access, 6, 35, 50, 59, 69, 74, 75, 111, 112, 128, 129, 155, 161, 182, 185, 188, 189, 190, 191, 192, 193, 195, 198, 201, 207, 211, 212, 215, 216, 217, 218, 221, 225, 231, 233, 252, 255, 256, 259, 270, 276, 277, 295
accessibility, 99, 213
accountability, 65, 67, 142, 162, 184, 187, 188, 217, 224, 274, 282, 286
accounting, 112, 127
acetone, 32
ACF, 115, 117, 118, 121, 137, 181, 229, 268, 269
acid, 99, 101
acquired immunodeficiency syndrome, 315, 316
adaptation, 130
Addiction, 2, 12, 13, 14, 59, 75, 85, 103, 104, 115, 117, 119, 122, 124, 125, 133, 134, 193, 203, 237, 245
Adjudicatory Hearings, 75
Administration for Children and Families, 58, 69, 115, 137, 140, 181, 229, 242, 268, 312
administrative support, 235
administrators, 39, 49, 62, 189, 206, 214, 219
adolescents, 12, 29, 101, 118
Adoption and Safe Families Act, 6, 46, 56, 75, 127, 138, 198, 296
adulthood, 119
adults, 17, 20, 27, 28, 39, 62, 101, 103, 104, 145, 222, 300
adverse effects, 287
advocacy, 68, 79, 90, 91, 120, 132, 260, 290, 295, 300
African-American, 90, 251, 287
age, 12, 22, 23, 47, 52, 82, 104, 120, 231, 238, 240, 244, 247, 250, 251, 259, 270, 282, 287, 294, 302, 307, 313, 314, 315, 316

agency collaboration, 227
aggression, 20, 100
aggressive behavior, 33, 215
AIDS, 18, 50, 315
Alaska, 94, 253, 314
Alcohol abuse, 18
alcohol consumption, 87, 97, 250
alcohol dependence, 103, 241
alcohol problems, 30, 131, 314
alcohol use, 9, 12, 24, 25, 39, 103, 105, 125, 146, 147, 148, 151, 166, 238, 240, 250, 267, 286, 287, 305, 308, 312, 314, 316
Alcohol Use Disorders Identification Test, 103, 105
alcoholics, 116, 287
alcoholism, 104, 106, 119, 131
Alcoholism, 76, 87, 104, 106, 110, 116, 118, 131, 200, 251, 289, 295, 299, 310, 314
alertness, 100
alters, 27
ambivalence, 52, 58
American Psychiatric Association, 9, 115, 121, 180, 237, 303
ammonia, 32
amphetamines, 100, 146, 151, 175, 263
anger, 37, 43, 45, 53, 57, 298
annual review, 285
antibody, 149
anticonvulsant, 99
antigen, 149
anti-social attitudes, 103
anxiety, 9, 16, 18, 19, 28, 29, 57, 98, 99, 100, 215, 294
AOD, 76, 224, 225, 227, 237
APA, 237
appetite, 31
appointments, 57, 154, 157, 163, 199, 202, 290, 297
arrest, 34, 40
arrests, 8, 9, 98, 117, 125
assault, 18, 84, 99, 116

assessment, 6, 7, 17, 36, 37, 38, 39, 40, 42, 53, 54, 67, 72, 76, 78, 82, 109, 121, 130, 138, 139, 140, 143, 144, 157, 158, 159, 160, 180, 183, 185, 189, 191, 196, 197, 202, 203, 206, 210, 211, 212, 214, 215, 216, 217, 218, 220, 221, 225, 230, 231, 234, 235, 242, 245, 246, 253, 254, 264, 268, 271, 272, 283, 284, 285, 287, 291, 292, 293, 294, 297, 304, 311, 315
asset development, 298
attachment, 24, 27, 118, 125, 280, 294, 296
audit, 110
audits, 258
authorities, 29, 80, 262
authority, 68, 81, 222, 281
avoidance, 141
awareness, 17, 28, 77, 212, 231, 245, 247, 249, 250, 252, 275, 314

B

barbiturates, 44, 99, 146, 151
barriers, 17, 37, 42, 48, 52, 59, 71, 123, 135, 165, 166, 199, 212, 224, 293, 295
base, 75, 119, 144, 177, 183, 235, 249, 280, 282
basic needs, 5, 16, 28, 51, 81, 125
beer, 30, 32, 254
behavioral change, 57
behavioral problems, 26, 44, 54
behaviors, 8, 14, 22, 25, 28, 29, 43, 45, 46, 47, 48, 53, 57, 76, 77, 78, 83, 103, 156, 240, 252, 274
benefits, 9, 30, 31, 37, 194, 201, 203, 223, 259, 289
benzodiazepine, 162
beverages, 250
bias, 264, 265
binge drinking, 12, 127, 250
birth weight, 23, 25, 26, 100, 125, 126, 258, 260
births, 23, 233, 235, 238, 240, 241, 245, 246, 255, 260, 261, 264, 266, 272, 273, 276, 278, 279, 281, 283, 301, 309, 311, 314
blends, 35
blood vessels, 99
bloodstream, 151, 315
bonding, 25, 27, 294
boredom, 37, 57
brain chemistry, 298
brain functions, 15
breast feeding, 315
breathing, 31
budget allocation, 233, 244
burnout, 62, 70

C

Cabinet, 3
caffeine, 99
caliber, 130
calibration, 177
campaigns, 91, 233, 249, 251, 252, 282, 283, 287, 305
cancer, 18, 98
candidates, 109, 208, 214, 222, 296
capacity building, 206, 207
capsule, 101, 102
CAPTA, 74, 77, 80, 130, 213, 215, 226, 227, 230, 232, 234, 237, 242, 243, 246, 261, 264, 266, 268, 270, 271, 273, 282, 284, 285, 292, 293, 309, 313, 315
caregivers, 27, 28, 29, 59, 114, 133, 212, 228
caregiving, 28, 29, 138, 316
CASA, 76, 79
Case Closure, 76
Case Plan, 51, 53, 76
Caseworker Competency, 76
catalyst, 161
categorization, 244
CDC, 115, 120, 240, 288, 298, 315, 316
cell phones, 35
central nervous system, 24, 100
Central Registry, 76
certificate, 70, 274, 275
certification, 144, 153, 176, 179, 194, 198, 199, 203, 218, 223
challenges, 6, 17, 19, 23, 43, 49, 50, 61, 62, 63, 65, 70, 159, 184, 191, 196, 223, 224, 244, 271, 276, 285, 294
character traits, 46
chemical reactions, 149
chemical structures, 150
chemicals, 32, 33, 81
Chicago, 91, 119, 201, 289, 305, 309
chicken, 20
Child Abuse Prevention and Treatment Act, 22, 71, 77, 90, 117, 140, 156, 213, 227, 230, 242, 246, 261, 282, 306, 312
child development, 28, 79, 260, 272
child maltreatment, ix, x, 2, 4, 5, 6, 7, 17, 19, 22, 33, 35, 42, 51, 56, 68, 70, 73, 74, 75, 76, 77, 79, 80, 83, 84, 85, 88, 92, 109, 110, 116, 124, 125, 128, 135, 138, 142, 159, 182, 228, 303, 313, 315
child protection, 1, 6, 12, 22, 78, 80, 81, 84, 115, 135, 159, 183, 192, 211, 227, 242, 271, 300, 312
child protective services, 1, 4, 7, 22, 30, 42, 53, 61, 64, 76, 90, 93, 101, 106, 119, 124, 157, 192, 223, 230, 242, 256, 260, 264, 278, 283, 291
Child Protective Services, 42, 53, 61, 77, 90, 139, 155, 162, 179, 211, 216, 293
Child welfare professionals, x, 137

Index

child welfare system, ix, x, 1, 5, 6, 22, 26, 27, 32, 42, 46, 48, 51, 58, 59, 65, 67, 123, 127, 129, 130, 140, 159, 182, 188, 189, 193, 209, 228, 234, 246, 268, 272, 273, 274, 275, 291, 293
childhood, 21, 22, 25, 27, 30, 65, 114, 118, 119, 133, 244, 268, 278, 280, 289, 294, 300, 307, 308, 316
childrearing, 52, 118, 120, 252, 272
chloroform, 100
chromatography, 150
Chronic Disease, 13, 313
cigarette smoking, 306
cities, 193, 289
citizens, 66, 80
City, 2, 85, 300
civil law, 79
civil liberties, 261
classification, 9, 237
cleaning, 100
clients, 31, 45, 49, 52, 56, 61, 63, 73, 84, 108, 142, 152, 167, 168, 169, 174, 193, 196, 197, 200, 201, 202, 203, 204, 205, 206, 207, 210, 211, 213, 214, 216, 217, 218, 220, 221, 222, 223, 224, 236, 273, 275, 278, 280, 284, 285, 295
clinical assessment, 201, 202
clinical psychology, 194
closure, 78
clothing, 16, 33, 51, 81
clusters, 193
coaches, 59, 188, 201, 202, 203, 204
cocaine, 11, 20, 23, 25, 26, 44, 45, 97, 100, 102, 118, 127, 146, 151, 164, 243, 244, 263, 267, 286, 301, 309, 311
cocaine abuse, 23
coercion, 303
coffee, 20, 35
cognition, 28
Cognitive Behavioral Therapy, 77
cognitive deficit, 26
cognitive deficits, 26
cognitive-behavioral therapy, 46
collaboration, 64, 65, 66, 67, 68, 69, 70, 71, 80, 90, 128, 182, 183, 184, 185, 186, 189, 190, 191, 200, 204, 205, 206, 207, 214, 220, 222, 225, 230, 231, 235, 249, 276, 294, 297, 299
collective bargaining, 194
color, iv, 32, 145, 149, 163, 166, 169, 287
coma, 116
commercial, 99, 101, 102, 145
communication, 37, 41, 43, 57, 66, 74, 78, 80, 182, 183, 185, 188, 189, 190, 202, 207, 247, 265, 297
communication skills, 43
communities, 5, 21, 66, 86, 109, 110, 117, 119, 121, 132, 133, 240, 247, 262, 275, 285, 286, 288, 295

community, ix, 25, 35, 46, 51, 52, 54, 66, 78, 79, 81, 86, 90, 92, 109, 110, 114, 129, 130, 140, 151, 152, 186, 188, 189, 190, 191, 197, 202, 204, 206, 207, 211, 212, 214, 215, 218, 223, 225, 231, 244, 252, 256, 260, 275, 285, 288, 290, 294, 297, 298, 299, 300, 309
community service, 211, 231, 260, 275, 290, 294, 298
community support, 294
compensation, 213
compilation, 285
complement, 38, 258
complexity, 249
compliance, 39, 112, 129, 145, 148, 155, 159, 162, 174, 214, 217, 258, 272, 287
complications, 13, 303, 306
compounds, 21, 102, 150
compulsion, 15, 79
compulsive behavior, 57
computer, 62, 64, 197, 203, 204
computer systems, 64
Concurrent Planning, 77
conference, 90, 198, 208
confidentiality, 44, 64, 68, 69, 70, 71, 73, 74, 109, 121, 139, 177, 212, 213, 291
Confidentiality Laws, 71
configuration, 67
conflict, 65, 80, 156, 260
confrontation, 58
consensus, 316
consent, 72, 73, 110, 111, 114, 192, 194, 264, 265, 272
consolidation, 300
consulting, 193
consumers, 87
consumption, 8, 76, 79, 84, 237
containers, 33, 99, 165, 176, 250
contamination, 145, 147, 148
content analysis, 232
control group, 204, 211
controversial, 261
controversies, 116
cooperation, 69, 88, 155, 282
cooperative agreements, 240
coordination, 24, 33, 80, 99, 109, 127, 159, 160, 182, 183, 247, 248, 258, 259, 272, 276
correlation, 17
cost effectiveness, 152
cost saving, 196, 201, 204, 220
cough, 21, 103
coughing, 33
counsel, 153, 156, 175, 217, 300

counseling, 48, 50, 51, 62, 91, 194, 198, 203, 214, 258, 272, 290
covering, 160, 192, 261
CPS, 4, 6, 7, 12, 16, 19, 20, 21, 22, 23, 26, 30, 31, 32, 33, 34, 35, 36, 38, 39, 40, 42, 43, 45, 46, 49, 51, 52, 53, 54, 55, 56, 57, 58, 59, 61, 62, 63, 64, 65, 66, 67, 68, 69, 70, 71, 72, 73, 75, 76, 77, 78, 79, 80, 81, 83, 84, 85, 93, 94, 162, 164, 165, 166, 211, 212, 214, 216, 217, 218, 219, 230, 234, 243, 245, 256, 261, 262, 264, 265, 266, 268, 270, 271, 273, 278, 283, 291, 292, 294, 301, 313, 315
CPS case information, 72
Craving, 77
credentials, 64, 194
Crime, 20, 119, 134
criminal activity, 16, 43, 48
criminal behavior, 35, 66
criminal investigations, 72, 73
criminal justice system, 29, 57, 66, 127, 236, 281, 316
cues, 15, 27
Cultural Competence, 77
cure, 59
curricula, 89
curriculum, 298

D

danger, 83, 103, 126
data collection, 71, 152, 187, 191, 203, 204, 232, 235, 240, 244, 276, 278
data set, 315
database, 76, 85, 131, 132, 204, 304
deaths, 12
decision-making process, 297
decomposition, 150
decontamination, 33
defects, 24, 26, 87, 125, 126, 240, 250
defensiveness, 103, 105
deficiencies, 24
deficit, 24
delinquency, 27
demonstrations, 183, 312
denial, 13, 33, 37, 53, 142, 156
Denial, 13, 38, 77
Denial and Concealment, 13
Department of Agriculture, 115
Department of Education, 268, 271
Department of Health and Human Services, vii, ix, 1, 2, 11, 58, 74, 108, 112, 113, 114, 115, 116, 117, 118, 119, 120, 121, 122, 123, 131, 135, 137, 172, 178, 179, 181, 195, 210, 215, 227, 229, 237, 275, 304, 310, 311, 312

Department of Justice, 117, 122, 131, 134, 144, 150, 180
Department of Transportation, 146, 153, 176, 179
deposits, 165
depressants, 98
depression, 9, 17, 28, 30, 97, 98, 100, 119, 215, 271
depth, 24, 232, 233, 234, 253, 254, 257, 269, 277, 281, 284, 295
depth perception, 24
derivatives, 263
designers, 186, 211
despair, 99
destruction, 113
detachment, 25
detainees, 117
detectable, 39
detection, 145, 146, 147, 148, 151, 156, 177, 234, 260, 265, 284, 315
detention, 216, 218
detoxification, 44, 49, 223
Detoxification, 44, 77
developing brain, 118
developmental care, 294
developmental disorder, 26, 126, 243
developmental milestones, 231, 286
DHS, 200, 203
diabetes, 13
Diagnostic and Statistical Manual of Mental Disorders, 9, 97, 180, 203, 302
diagnostic criteria, 302, 314
Differential Response, 77
dignity, 44
directives, 68
directors, 194, 315
disability, 87, 88, 132, 316
disclosure, 38, 70, 71, 74, 110, 111, 112, 154
discomfort, 37, 43, 44
discrimination, 48
diseases, 13, 18, 76
disorder, x, 1, 2, 5, 17, 18, 19, 24, 34, 47, 59, 61, 64, 76, 86, 87, 93, 99, 103, 110, 114, 116, 124, 125, 137, 138, 155, 161, 180, 182, 196, 236, 237, 256, 264
disposition, 78, 84, 85, 138, 178
Dispositional Hearings, 78
distress, 8, 84, 97, 98
distribution, 250
District of Columbia, 23, 94, 232
dizziness, 33
doctors, 10, 97, 100, 263, 291
dogs, 35
domestic violence, 2, 5, 17, 18, 33, 35, 59, 62, 65, 80, 116, 120, 122, 190, 199, 201, 202, 206, 271

dopamine, 100
draft, 291
drawing, 9, 16
drug abusers, 303
drug addict, 4, 15, 116, 117
drug addiction, 4, 15, 116
drug dependence, 36
drug offense, 20, 256
drug screenings, 192
drug testing, 39, 138, 139, 141, 142, 143, 144, 145, 146, 149, 150, 151, 152, 153, 154, 155, 156, 157, 158, 159, 160, 161, 162, 163, 165, 167, 170, 174, 175, 176, 177, 178, 179, 180, 205, 217, 261, 264, 315
drug treatment, 5, 119, 120, 175, 239, 265, 266, 274, 296, 297, 300, 310
Dual Track, 78
due process, 210

E

economic problem, 19
education, 62, 65, 76, 88, 132, 214, 231, 236, 238, 244, 245, 249, 250, 251, 252, 258, 259, 281, 288, 290, 298, 299, 300, 314
educational attainment, 316
educational institutions, 250
educational materials, 249
educators, 80, 272, 294, 300
eligibility criteria, 272, 316
emergency, 80, 110
emotional disorder, 17
emotional distress, 44
emotional problems, 22, 27, 58, 236, 280
emotional well-being, 22, 307
empathy, 27, 274
empirical studies, 182
employees, 185, 203, 221, 222, 225, 251
employers, 39, 176, 179
employment, 19, 43, 48, 50, 57, 62, 76, 198, 272
encouragement, 51, 157
energy, 19, 28, 213
enforcement, 80
England, 81
enhanced service, 7, 109, 211, 212, 295
enrollment, 163, 279, 296, 301
environment, 15, 22, 30, 44, 147, 162, 180, 190, 272, 282, 294, 305
enzyme, 149
epidemic, 133, 286, 315
epidemiologic studies, 115
epidemiology, 304
equipment, 32, 35, 152, 153, 162, 164, 208
equity, 66

ethics, 39, 203
ethnicity, 14
euphoria, 98
evacuation, 33
evidence, 18, 24, 39, 47, 84, 85, 97, 140, 142, 155, 159, 162, 176, 215, 216, 218, 233, 234, 236, 244, 262, 264, 265, 282, 291, 315
evidence-based program, 47
examinations, 30
expenditures, 256
expertise, 1, 58, 70, 105, 153, 188, 189, 192, 194, 195, 196, 204, 205, 206, 210
exploitation, 22, 80, 84, 92, 308
extreme poverty, 19

F

fairness, 261
false positive, 152, 261
Family Assessment, 53, 54, 78, 120
family behavior, 78
family environment, 72, 133
family functioning, 54, 55, 125, 272, 294, 295
Family Group Conferencing, 78
family interactions, 54
family life, 19
family members, 28, 32, 33, 34, 37, 38, 39, 40, 52, 54, 59, 61, 68, 70, 72, 78, 79, 183, 201, 231, 247, 268
family planning, 74
family support, 138, 202, 212, 249, 284
family therapy, 51, 118
Family Unity Model, 78
family violence, 116
FAS, 24, 25, 132, 240, 250, 267, 270, 287, 288, 305, 314, 316
FDA, 147, 149
fear, 18, 26, 50, 52, 57, 71, 99, 141, 256, 316
Federal Adoption and Safe Families Act, x, 181
Federal funds, 22, 80, 226
Federal Government, 223, 251
federal law, 306, 314
feelings, 9, 24, 29, 43, 57, 98, 99, 100, 298
fetal alcohol syndrome, 87, 118, 125, 267, 287, 304, 307, 308, 314
fetal development, 23, 24
fetal growth, 118, 133
fetus, 24, 25, 26, 238, 263, 290, 292
fights, 98
filters, 32
financial, 19, 48, 158, 162, 176, 255, 281, 284, 296
financial support, 162
first responders, 31, 33
flashbacks, 19, 99

flexibility, 77, 147, 188, 221
fluid, 100, 101, 144, 145, 147
fluorescence, 149
food, 9, 16, 48, 51, 81, 290, 296
formation, 243, 299
foundations, 282
fringe benefits, 214
Full Disclosure, 79
funding, 50, 64, 68, 129, 156, 184, 187, 191, 196, 198, 205, 206, 208, 211, 213, 221, 222, 223, 224, 226, 236, 242, 250, 251, 260, 272, 275, 276, 277, 279, 280, 281, 285, 288, 289, 290, 294, 298, 302, 314
funds, 59, 68, 91, 127, 129, 130, 162, 185, 186, 194, 198, 208, 210, 211, 213, 218, 222, 223, 224, 236, 243, 252, 256, 258, 281, 290, 294, 295, 298, 299

G

gambling, 57
General Accounting Office, 128, 135
general knowledge, 66
genes, 14, 310, 316
genetic factors, 14
genetic predisposition, 14
genitals, 83
Georgia, 253, 316
glue, 100, 102
goal setting, 298
governments, x, 229, 240
GPS, 35
grants, 129, 191, 208, 213, 215, 223, 244
group therapy, 46
growth, 26, 141, 252
guardian, 79, 114
Guardian ad Litem, 79
guidance, ix, 4, 23, 35, 48, 103, 121, 137, 139, 156, 159, 176, 193, 206, 232, 261, 313
guidelines, 56, 64, 66, 74, 81, 88, 115, 119, 144, 145, 146, 151, 153, 166, 176, 179, 232, 235, 236, 254, 255, 259, 264, 289, 296, 304
guilt, 18, 57

H

Habituation, 79
hair, 100, 138, 144, 145, 148
hallucinations, 31
harmful effects, 82, 84, 244, 286
Hawaii, 94, 232, 240, 241, 243, 253, 256, 257, 262, 272, 277, 278, 281, 284, 288, 299, 302, 307, 314, 316
hazardous materials, 32
hazards, 8, 21, 84, 250, 287

healing, 47
Health and Human Services, 115, 116, 120, 121
health care, 23, 38, 43, 65, 75, 80, 105, 163, 171, 194, 208, 231, 236, 242, 249, 250, 252, 254, 259, 262, 264, 275, 281, 286, 288, 289, 294, 297, 300, 308, 312, 314
health care professionals, 262, 294, 314
health condition, 261
health information, 75, 87, 158
health insurance, 158, 198
Health Insurance Portability and Accountability Act, 74, 111, 114, 158, 264, 302
health problems, 17, 271, 291
health risks, 98, 251
health services, 131
heart disease, 13
heart rate, 99
heavy drinking, 127
helium, 100
hepatitis, 18, 76
heroin, 11, 16, 18, 26, 48, 100, 118, 127, 152, 197, 211, 214, 263, 267
HHS, ix, 123, 124, 125, 126, 128, 137, 150, 153, 174, 176, 178, 179, 180, 181, 210, 211, 213, 214, 215, 228, 229
higher education, 233
high-risk populations, 314
HIPAA, 74, 75, 111, 112, 113, 121, 158, 264
hiring, 39, 62, 189, 192, 194, 203, 222
history, 30, 40, 50, 72, 109, 119, 151, 154, 161, 180, 189, 200, 204, 224, 272, 295, 302
HIV/AIDS, 62, 76, 120, 315
Home Visitation Programs, 79
homelessness, 19, 29, 30, 117, 119
Homelessness, 19, 117
homes, ix, 19, 28, 32, 35, 63, 76, 135, 211, 247
homework, 29
homicide, 13, 18
honesty, 162
host, 129, 190
House, 292
housing, 17, 39, 48, 57, 59, 62, 65, 129, 190, 202, 223, 259, 272, 290, 296, 297
human, 2, 8, 69, 71, 89, 208, 216, 258, 261, 284, 315
human behavior, 8
human immunodeficiency virus, 261, 315
human subjects, 71
hybrid, 289
hydroxyl, 99
hygiene, 141
hypersensitivity, 26
hypertension, 13

I

ideal, 283, 284, 292
identification, 38, 128, 154, 195, 216, 230, 232, 242, 244, 245, 248, 254, 255, 259, 271, 295
identity, 25
illegal drug use, 177, 240
illicit drug use, 11, 49, 88, 118, 127, 177, 240, 256, 303, 315, 316
illicit substances, 20, 262, 267
images, 55
immune system, 315
immunity, 256
Immunity, 79
immunodeficiency, 290
improvements, 13, 218, 265
impulses, 81
in utero, 237, 263
inattention, 81
incarceration, 125, 243
incidence, 109, 261, 314
income, 19, 32, 65, 223
income support, 65
independence, 24
Independence, 280
independent living, 139
individuals, 5, 8, 9, 11, 12, 13, 14, 15, 16, 17, 18, 19, 20, 31, 32, 38, 40, 42, 43, 44, 46, 48, 49, 52, 56, 58, 59, 62, 65, 66, 69, 71, 73, 80, 82, 87, 100, 103, 104, 109, 144, 160, 175, 192, 223, 232, 239, 297
Individuals with Disabilities Education Act, 242, 246, 268, 280, 293
industry, 299
infancy, 307, 314
infant mortality, 125
infants, 23, 125, 140, 156, 200, 230, 234, 237, 238, 239, 242, 243, 244, 245, 246, 247, 258, 260, 261, 263, 264, 265, 267, 268, 270, 273, 274, 276, 282, 287, 294, 295, 296, 299, 301, 302, 304, 307, 308, 309, 311, 313, 316
infection, 48, 309, 316
information exchange, 71
information sharing, 64, 74, 190, 202, 224
ingest, 99
inherited disorder, 316
inhibition, 100
Initial Assessment or Investigation, 79
inmates, 20, 117
insanity, 14, 99
insecurity, 19
insomnia, 99, 100
institutions, 81, 233, 251

Intake, 79
integration, 185, 205, 213, 293
integrity, 150, 178
intelligence, 316
interagency relationships, 69, 207
intercourse, 83
interpersonal skills, 25
Interview Protocol, 79
intoxication, 17, 97, 98, 116
investment, 109, 152, 191, 236
investments, 186, 283
Involuntary Commitment, 80
iodine, 32
Iowa, 95, 262, 269, 277, 288, 294, 314, 316
irritability, 21

J

job skills, 62
jurisdiction, 81, 83, 143, 158, 159, 182, 297
justification, 271
Juvenile and Family Courts, 80
juvenile delinquency, 80
juvenile justice, 249

K

Keeping Children and Families Safe Act, 22, 23, 77, 80, 268, 312
kinship, 212, 213
Kinship Care, 80

L

labeling, 27
laboratory tests, 162
lack of confidence, 28
languages, 106, 286
Lapses and Relapses, 13
law enforcement, 21, 32, 35, 56, 80, 83, 92, 260, 266
laws, 63, 69, 70, 71, 73, 74, 75, 79, 118, 121, 189, 212, 213, 262, 286, 300, 306, 312, 314, 316
laws and regulations, 63, 70
lawyers, 174
lead, 8, 19, 28, 63, 99, 126, 149, 156, 208, 237, 244, 249, 261, 272, 307, 314
leadership, 189, 205, 206, 208, 243, 299, 314
learning, 26, 69, 77, 125, 133, 194, 213, 240, 298
learning disabilities, 26, 125
legal issues, 75, 139
legislation, x, 23, 62, 140, 182, 221, 230, 232, 233, 234, 237, 242, 243, 244, 245, 246, 250, 252, 256, 259, 266, 267, 268, 270, 271, 272, 277, 284, 288, 289, 291, 292, 293, 299, 313, 316
legislative proposals, 233

lens, 115
Liaison, 80, 90
lifestyle changes, 43
lifetime, 20, 104, 281
light, 40, 250, 288
liquids, 32
litigation, 218
livestock, 35
living environment, 35
local community, 188
local government, 130
loneliness, 57
Louisiana, 269, 291, 316
love, 81
LSD, 101, 151, 263
lysergic acid diethylamide, 151

M

magazines, 251
magnets, 251
magnitude, 312
majority, x, 9, 181, 210
Maltreated children, ix, 123, 126
maltreatment, ix, 4, 6, 17, 30, 51, 53, 54, 59, 68, 71, 76, 78, 79, 82, 83, 84, 85, 93, 114, 115, 117, 119, 124, 125, 133, 134, 143, 155, 159, 201, 208, 212, 247, 312
man, 20
management, 1, 2, 13, 46, 48, 59, 61, 62, 64, 70, 109, 154, 161, 163, 170, 182, 183, 191, 192, 194, 196, 197, 201, 203, 206, 208, 209, 212, 214, 216, 217, 218, 221, 222, 223, 225, 249, 259, 265, 274, 290, 292, 295, 298, 300, 309
Mandated Reporter, 80
manufacturing, 31, 88, 125
mapping, 314
marijuana, 11, 25, 27, 33, 98, 118, 145, 146, 147, 151, 263, 302
Marijuana, 11, 18, 98, 101, 121, 127, 173, 175
marital status, 272
marketing, 2, 86, 252, 288
marriage, 243, 250
Maryland, 2, 3, 4, 92, 183, 195, 232, 243, 245, 252, 253, 257, 262, 267, 269, 271, 277, 288, 293, 309, 310, 314, 316, 317
mass, 150, 251
mass spectrometry, 150
MAST, 104
materials, 21, 89, 93, 101, 103, 131, 176, 232, 250, 251, 252, 287, 288
matrix, 144, 145, 146, 152, 177, 188, 209
matter, iv, 19, 23
measurement, 83, 177, 179

meconium, 138, 144, 146, 238, 241, 302
media, 62, 68, 86, 118, 249, 251, 287, 288, 305, 309, 311
Medicaid, 196, 233, 235, 236, 245, 255, 257, 258, 264, 266, 277, 279, 280, 298
medical, 4, 21, 29, 34, 43, 44, 48, 50, 56, 76, 77, 81, 84, 99, 110, 154, 171, 177, 223, 245, 250, 256, 258, 265, 267, 290, 299, 300, 315, 316
medical care, 48, 50, 81, 265
medical reason, 177
medication, 8, 10, 44, 152, 154, 163, 170
medicine, 99, 101
melting, 101
membership, 88, 89, 285
Memorandum of Understanding, 80, 108, 197, 208, 222, 227
memory, 13, 15, 20, 99, 100
memory loss, 20, 100
memory processes, 15
mental disorder, 9, 20, 62, 115, 121, 303
mental health, 17, 35, 50, 51, 52, 59, 62, 65, 80, 117, 121, 132, 190, 193, 194, 199, 201, 202, 206, 209, 214, 219, 220, 245, 258, 271, 277, 296, 307, 308, 311
mental health professionals, 80, 193
mental illness, 5, 17, 19, 33, 62, 78, 88, 125, 133
Mental Illness, 17
mental impairment, 25
mental retardation, 287, 316
mentor, 49
mentoring, 128, 129
messages, 29, 175, 282, 283, 288
metabolism, 39, 146
metabolites, 138, 144, 145, 147, 149, 150, 176, 177, 178, 179
methodology, 150, 160, 177, 240
Mexico, 95, 253, 316
Michigan Alcoholism Screening Test, 104, 106
Microsoft, 215
military, 19, 76
Minneapolis, 290
minors, 81
miscarriage, 25, 125
mission, 68, 130, 131, 186, 278
Missouri, 85, 95, 253, 269, 277, 281, 286, 296, 300, 309, 314
misuse, 152, 154, 160, 177
models, 46, 47, 48, 59, 118, 126, 182, 215, 234, 272, 274, 282, 286
modifications, 15, 158, 265
molecules, 15
Montana, 95, 317
mood swings, 57

morbidity, 114, 133
morphine, 100
motivation, 55, 103, 121, 142, 199, 200, 220, 221
motor skills, 15
Multidisciplinary Team, 81
multimedia, 251
multiple factors, 14

N

narcotic, 100, 102, 170
National Center for Missing and Exploited Children, 92
National Center on Substance Abuse and Child Welfare, x, 69, 129, 131, 134, 137, 140, 141, 181, 229
National Indian Child Welfare Association, 90
National Institutes of Health, 47, 87, 115, 131
National Research Council, 118
National Survey, 11, 21, 49, 115, 133, 238, 256, 268, 273, 285, 310, 311
natural disaster, 18, 19
natural disasters, 18, 19
nausea, 9, 16
NCSACW, x, 131, 137, 140, 159, 181, 229, 230, 232, 314
negative consequences, 8, 9, 29
negative effects, 5, 82, 230, 237, 295
negative outcomes, 126
negotiating, 51, 152, 195
neonates, 261, 315
nerve, 81
nervous system, 18
networking, 91, 249
neuromotor, 294
neurons, 118
neurotoxicity, 308
neurotransmitter, 81
neurotransmitters, 81
Neurotransmitters, 81
neutral, 196, 204
New England, 118, 305, 312
nicotine, 254, 308, 311
nightmares, 19
nitrous oxide, 99
nurses, 174, 216
nursing, 194, 208, 259, 265
nutrition, 23, 125, 258

O

OAS, 114, 117, 120, 256, 257, 273, 314, 316
obstacles, 71, 274, 297, 300
offenders, 20, 91

officials, 21, 59, 67, 68, 69, 230, 232, 245, 261, 266, 271
Oklahoma, 96
opiates, 100, 146, 151, 152, 164
opioids, 100, 151
opportunities, 49, 54, 62, 68, 126, 135, 162, 198, 230, 231, 236, 247, 255, 259, 273, 281, 294, 303
optic nerve, 24
organ, 25
organism, 78
organs, 13, 24
outreach, 193, 201, 202, 295, 298
overlap, ix, 6, 61, 62
oversight, 197, 205, 214, 221, 222, 223, 251, 266, 299
ownership, 191
oxygen, 99

P

pain, 9, 11, 18, 23, 33, 100, 102, 151, 152, 171
pain management, 151
paranoia, 17, 31, 33, 99
Parens Patriae Doctrine, 81
parental consent, 265
parental treatment, 219
parenting, 19, 40, 51, 52, 54, 79, 123, 125, 127, 128, 139, 202, 232, 244, 248, 255, 259, 273, 278, 280, 281, 282, 284, 285, 290, 294, 297, 305, 309
parole, 39, 45, 63, 66
participants, 45, 46, 47, 65, 66, 67, 68, 104, 188, 204, 219, 298
pathology, 14
pathways, 108, 115, 135
Patient Placement Criteria, 81
PCP, 102, 146, 151, 164, 173, 175
peer group, 25
perinatal, 195, 246, 258, 276, 278, 288, 292, 299, 301, 302, 303, 304, 312, 313, 315
permission, 74, 103, 104, 290
permit, 74, 112, 315
personal communication, 174
personal qualities, 76
personality, 99
phencyclidine, 99, 146, 151, 164
phenylketonuria, 261, 308
Philadelphia, 116, 195
phosphorous, 32
Physical Abuse, 82
physical health, 14, 17, 19, 54, 55
physicians, 174, 249, 250, 252, 254, 265, 267, 283, 286, 287, 291, 293, 316
placenta, 24, 315
pleasure, 100

polarization, 149
police, 35, 66, 73, 80, 84, 93
policy initiative, 253, 259, 268, 269, 276, 281
policy issues, 89, 139, 273
policy makers, 131
policy responses, 307
policymakers, 89, 138, 139, 175, 230, 315
politics, 208
population, 4, 11, 12, 20, 21, 38, 49, 82, 99, 117, 127, 161, 192, 193, 213, 221, 222, 240, 246, 259, 285, 294, 301, 311, 314, 316
population density, 221
porosity, 145
positive behaviors, 46
positive reinforcement, 143, 157, 161
positive relationship, 47, 297
posttraumatic stress, 116
post-traumatic stress disorder, 19, 47
poverty, 5, 17, 19, 62, 116, 272, 316
Poverty, 19, 307
prejudice, 23
premature death, 13
preparation, iv, 177
preschool, 118, 272, 273
preschoolers, 249
preservation, 120, 186, 193, 213, 222, 264, 272
preservative, 164
prevention, 47, 66, 79, 82, 85, 88, 90, 91, 93, 104, 120, 128, 130, 131, 132, 156, 158, 203, 230, 236, 243, 244, 245, 247, 250, 251, 252, 255, 260, 281, 283, 287, 288, 305, 309
primary caregivers, 27, 51
Primary Prevention, 82
principles, 47, 49, 58, 61, 64, 184, 186, 187, 190, 198, 208, 222, 226, 285
prisons, 20
probability, 141, 217
probation officers, 39
problem behavior, 13, 55
problem behaviors, 13
problem solving, 100
problem-solving, 48
producers, 126
professional development, 7, 69
professionals, x, 20, 26, 39, 56, 68, 70, 80, 81, 86, 87, 89, 92, 110, 137, 139, 141, 155, 180, 186, 187, 188, 191, 194, 202, 208, 210, 215, 217, 222, 223, 230, 291, 296, 300, 308, 314
profit, 218
prognosis, 199, 200
program administration, 208
program outcomes, 219
programming, 68

progress reports, 221
Progressive Nature, 13
project, 59, 121, 132, 195, 196, 197, 200, 201, 204, 207, 210, 211, 212, 213, 259, 271, 283, 288
promoter, 251
propane, 100
protection, 79, 81, 83, 116, 122, 158, 192, 218, 271, 300
protective factors, 293
Protective Factors, 82
psychiatric diagnosis, 78
psychiatric disorders, 28
psychiatry, 133
psychoactive drug, 237
psychological development, 118
psychological distress, 19, 144
Psychological Maltreatment, 82
psychological problems, 9
psychologist, 180, 193
Psychophysical with drawal, 16
psychotherapy, 77
PTSD, 19, 116
public assistance, 49
public awareness, 86, 91, 92, 132, 251, 252, 282, 287, 288, 289, 305, 314
public concern, 301
public education, 233, 244, 251, 252, 282, 287, 288, 314
public health, 5, 23, 66, 115, 208, 216, 250, 259, 263, 302, 306
Public Health Service Act, 74
public policy, 1, 39, 86, 88
public safety, 66
public service, 251
public support, 289
publishing, 91
Puerto Rico, 96
punishment, 82
purity, 99, 178

Q

qualifications, 153, 160, 198, 221
quality assurance, 219
quality control, 153, 178
quality improvement, 191, 207
quality of life, 87
quality of service, 77
quantization, 176
questioning, 236
questionnaire, 106, 302

R

radio, 251, 252, 287
random assignment, 189, 215
rape, 84
reaction time, 98
reactivity, 150
reality, 261
reasoning, 16, 100
recognition, 8, 13, 55, 97, 294
recommendations, iv, 205, 214, 220, 260
Recovery, 42, 43, 49, 56, 58, 82, 140, 154, 159, 161, 163, 164, 166, 167, 168, 169, 170, 171, 172, 173, 187, 200, 201, 202, 203, 208, 210, 216, 223, 224, 274, 297
recovery plan, 217
recovery process, x, 57, 128, 162, 182, 203, 204, 295
recreational, 97
reform, 77, 121
reforms, 161, 216
Registry, 47, 76, 119, 132, 198
regulations, 71, 72, 73, 111, 113, 114, 146, 233, 235, 237, 244, 252, 255, 258, 270
rehabilitation, 48, 52, 217
Rehabilitation Act, 110
reinforcement, 49
Relapse, 55, 82
relapses, 13, 157
relational model, 47
relatives, 80
relevance, 250
reliability, 37, 164
relief, 19
remorse, 25, 26, 27
reporters, 74, 79, 80
requirements, x, 26, 39, 49, 63, 64, 70, 71, 79, 90, 112, 127, 141, 143, 144, 154, 162, 164, 166, 176, 182, 198, 210, 216, 217, 244, 258, 264, 266, 277, 278, 283, 284, 290, 293, 309, 312
researchers, 5, 23, 244, 246, 316
resistance, 14, 274
resolution, 118
resources, 5, 21, 47, 53, 70, 82, 85, 101, 108, 119, 124, 131, 132, 133, 184, 186, 188, 189, 190, 191, 192, 200, 206, 213, 216, 218, 235, 249, 251, 252, 255, 256, 268, 275, 277, 280, 282, 284, 285, 287, 289, 293, 311, 314
respiration, 100
respiratory problems, 18
response, 20, 27, 54, 56, 65, 77, 78, 83, 118, 121, 177, 216, 243, 244, 245, 262, 263, 265, 266, 272, 284, 286, 289, 292, 295, 297, 299, 301, 310
Response Time, 83

restaurants, 286, 287
restrictions, 112
retail, 287
retardation, 26
retention rate, 200
revenue, 288
rewards, 46
rights, iv, x, 46, 79, 81, 128, 138, 156, 182, 244, 260, 291
risk assessment, 138, 144, 160, 258
risk factors, 23, 48, 78, 82, 114, 244, 272, 291, 298, 316
risks, 9, 21, 44, 51, 55, 58, 155, 250, 251, 287, 305
Role maladaptation, 16
routines, 28
rubber, 32, 100
rules, 25, 28, 68, 69, 70, 74
rural areas, 221

S

sadness, 26, 37
saliva, 138, 144, 145, 147, 149
sanctions, 296
savings, 211, 220, 236, 281
scarce resources, 28, 186
scent, 30
school, 8, 26, 28, 29, 77, 80, 92, 98, 100, 179, 294, 307
school achievement, 28
school performance, 29
schooling, 81
science, 39, 115, 118, 132
scope, 40, 59, 62, 68, 127, 155, 249, 255
scripts, 149
Secondary Prevention, 83
security, 32, 75
sedative, 99
sedatives, 11, 44
self-control, 24
self-efficacy, 274
self-employed, 214
self-esteem, 30, 119
self-reports, 141, 161
self-sufficiency, 49, 186
seminars, 197
Senate, 120, 221, 222, 223, 224, 263, 292, 304
sensation, 16, 18, 31
sensitivity, 44, 176
sentencing, 66
Service Agreement, 83
service organizations, 73, 113
service provider, 40, 42, 63, 65, 83, 89, 131, 158, 185, 187, 225, 227, 248, 251, 252, 287

Service Provision, 83
sex, 50, 150
Sexual Abuse, 83
sexual assaults, 19
sexual behavior, 50, 83
sexually transmitted diseases, 76
shame, 68
shape, 139, 215
shelter, 51
shortage, 194, 223
shortness of breath, 33
short-term memory, 16
showing, 177, 274, 295
siblings, 29, 54
signals, 81
signs, 31, 35, 59, 82, 141, 160, 161, 165, 166, 250, 265, 267, 286, 291, 303
skills training, 281
skin, 16, 21, 31, 33, 102, 145, 147
smoking, 97, 252
smoking cessation, 252
social adjustment, 26
social cognition, 28
social environment, 14, 54
social impairment, 84
social interactions, 28
social policy, 310
social problems, 5, 8, 13, 14, 27, 84
social relations, 144
social relationships, 144
Social Security, 120
social services, 52, 67, 77, 244, 293
social situations, 237
social skills, 25, 28, 55
social support, 23
social welfare, 67
social workers, 80, 174, 192, 194, 216, 218, 221, 293, 297, 300
socialization, 126
societal cost, 243
society, 88, 133
solution, 33, 70, 77, 149, 177, 178
South Dakota, 253, 262, 314
special education, 81, 249, 272, 313, 315
specialists, 59, 161, 162, 163, 164, 165, 166, 182, 183, 184, 185, 188, 189, 190, 191, 192, 193, 194, 195, 216, 221, 224
specifications, 196
speech, 24, 31
spending, 19, 210
Spring, 307, 309
stability, 128, 154, 187, 191, 214
staff development, 184, 187

staff members, 144, 175, 190
staffing, 139, 159, 205, 206, 297
stakeholders, 183, 190, 249
state, 82, 84, 119, 133, 195, 200, 209, 215, 242, 254, 261, 265, 305, 306, 308, 310, 312, 314
state laws, 305, 306, 314
statistics, 10, 11, 91, 291, 301, 311, 314
statutes, 23, 71, 73, 80, 146, 250, 252, 263, 291, 305, 306, 314
sterile, 176
steroids, 102, 151
stigma, 14, 23, 27, 29, 37, 49, 50, 69, 118
stimulant, 100
stimulus, 77
storage, 148, 151, 177, 178
street drugs, 30
stress, 5, 15, 19, 23, 37, 70, 116, 125, 259, 260, 294
stressors, 116, 272
stroke, 99
structure, 14, 37, 66, 75, 78, 126, 145, 149, 184, 187, 200
subpoena, 73
substance addiction, 14
substance use disorders, iv, ix, x, 4, 7, 21, 30, 53, 85, 86, 88, 110, 123, 124, 125, 126, 127, 130, 131, 135, 139, 140, 141, 142, 143, 154, 159, 160, 161, 181, 182, 183, 185, 189, 194, 195, 196, 200, 208, 210, 216, 228, 231, 241, 244, 247, 249, 259, 286, 289, 290, 306
substitutes, 48
substitution, 147
substitutions, 176
success rate, 204
SUD screening information, 72
SUDs, ix, 4, 5, 6, 7, 12, 13, 14, 16, 17, 18, 19, 21, 23, 27, 28, 29, 30, 31, 32, 33, 34, 35, 37, 38, 40, 42, 43, 45, 46, 47, 48, 49, 50, 52, 53, 54, 55, 56, 57, 58, 61, 62, 63, 65, 66, 67, 68, 69, 70, 71, 74, 75, 76
suicide, 13, 18
supervision, ix, 5, 27, 28, 35, 54, 70, 81, 125, 137, 178, 184, 187, 198, 199, 203, 209, 214, 219, 223, 227, 300
supervisor, 35, 40, 73, 155, 156, 166, 198, 199, 202
supervisors, 68, 189, 190, 197, 203, 204, 210, 212, 214, 215, 218, 219, 297
support services, 48, 50, 59, 65, 84, 183, 223, 233, 255, 260, 274, 293, 295, 297
Supreme Court, 263
surveillance, 120, 240, 313, 314
survivors, 91
suspensions, 98
sustainability, 189, 191

sweat, 49, 138, 144, 145, 147
Switzerland, 105
symptoms, 8, 9, 16, 17, 19, 21, 28, 47, 75, 76, 82, 85, 97, 98, 141, 160, 161, 242, 264, 270, 292, 296, 313, 315
synapse, 81
syndrome, 97, 305, 306

T

target, 47, 190, 191, 223, 251, 258, 280, 299
target population, 190, 191, 258
taxes, 198
teachers, 28
team members, 189, 190
teams, 81, 129, 187, 188, 202, 207, 266, 297
technical assistance, 1, 86, 89, 90, 93, 195
technical support, 209
techniques, 34, 38, 64, 69, 79, 157, 217, 254, 274, 314
technologies, 149
technology, 35, 39, 149, 150
teens, 116, 121, 139
teeth, 31, 295
telephone numbers, 93, 94
telephones, 213
television ads, 287
temperature, 150, 164, 165, 166, 176
Tertiary Prevention, 84
test procedure, 166, 176
testing program, 144, 150, 151, 152, 155
textbook, 115
theft, 171
therapeutic community, 46
therapeutic relationship, 44
therapist, 45, 48, 49, 71
therapy, 48, 57, 218
thoughts, 14, 99, 274
threats, 155
time commitment, 105
time frame, 56, 145
tissue, 84
Title I, 59, 80, 121, 183, 185, 187, 192, 195, 196, 198, 201, 210, 211, 212, 213, 215, 218, 224, 226, 279, 280, 298
tobacco, 98, 218, 226, 233, 236, 238, 240, 241, 244, 252, 254, 258, 283, 287, 289, 294, 298, 301, 302, 303
toddlers, 247, 268, 311, 313
toxicology, 162, 259, 266, 267, 268, 290, 315
trade, 50, 171
trafficking, 88
training, 1, 7, 35, 51, 62, 64, 66, 68, 69, 70, 86, 88, 89, 90, 103, 105, 106, 109, 127, 129, 131, 141, 143, 152, 153, 159, 160, 161, 182, 183, 184, 185, 187, 188, 189, 192, 194, 195, 198, 199, 201, 203, 204, 205, 206, 209, 212, 213, 214, 216, 218, 219, 221, 223, 227, 259, 272, 295, 296, 300
training programs, 62, 69
tranquilizers, 11
transformation, 15
transmission, 263
transport, 151, 202
transportation, 50, 51, 52, 57, 65, 200, 213, 296
trauma, 17, 18, 30, 47, 116, 120, 189
traumatic events, 13, 29
triggers, 55, 263, 289
Trust Fund, 288
tuberculosis, 76, 290
turnover, 276
twins, 14

U

U.S. Department of Labor, 120
ulcer, 97
uniform, 264, 293
United States, ix, 4, 11, 12, 20, 77, 117, 240, 243, 247, 256, 307, 310, 314, 315, 316
Universal Prevention, 85
universities, 1, 250
urban areas, 221, 265
urinalysis, 46, 49, 198, 202, 238
urine, 138, 144, 145, 147, 148, 149, 150, 151, 162, 164, 165, 166, 170, 172, 173, 176, 197, 217, 241, 259, 301, 302, 316

V

vacuum, 16
variations, 230, 232, 248, 283
venue, 206
victimization, 30, 116, 118, 247
victims, 4, 18, 29, 30, 91, 134, 307, 313, 315
videotape, 252
violence, 8, 18, 20, 23, 29, 33, 47, 65, 88, 100, 116, 118, 124, 133, 289
violent behavior, 99
violent crime, 18
vision, 49
vitamin K, 101
volatility, 263
vomiting, 16, 21, 33
vouchers, 223
vulnerability, 14, 82

W

waiver, 59, 121, 134, 183, 195, 196, 201, 204, 210, 312
walking, 15
water, 33, 101, 102, 150
weakness, 14
welfare reform, 1, 120, 276, 278
welfare system, ix, x, 1, 5, 6, 22, 26, 27, 32, 42, 46, 48, 51, 58, 59, 65, 67, 123, 127, 129, 130, 140, 159, 182, 188, 189, 193, 209, 228, 234, 246, 268, 272, 273, 274, 275, 291, 293
well-being, ix, x, 6, 29, 31, 46, 55, 63, 75, 79, 90, 99, 128, 130, 132, 137, 162, 208, 211, 214, 237, 280
White House, 131
windows, 32, 35
Wisconsin, 106, 262, 268, 277, 294, 313, 314
withdrawal, 180, 237, 242, 264, 270, 291, 292, 313, 315
workers, ix, 52, 59, 69, 119, 127, 129, 134, 137, 138, 141, 155, 156, 157, 158, 161, 162, 183, 184, 185, 186, 192, 193, 194, 195, 196, 200, 201, 202, 203, 204, 205, 206, 208, 214, 216, 217, 218, 219, 221, 271, 295
workflow, 223
workforce, 129
workplace, 144, 150, 174, 176, 178, 179
World Health Organization, 105, 115, 116
worry, 70

Y

yield, 38, 152, 280